Mortgage-Backed Securities Including REMICs and Other Investment Vehicles

Dear Bruce,

Best Regards,

Robert Kuhn

THE LITTLE, BROWN TAX PRACTICE SERIES

Mortgage-Backed Securities Including REMICs and Other Investment Vehicles

1995 Edition

Thomas A. Humphreys
Brown & Wood
New York, New York

Robert M. Kreitman
Brown & Wood
New York, New York

This volume is current through June 1995.

Little, Brown and Company
Boston New York Toronto London

Library of Congress Catalog No. 95-77098
ISBN 0-316-381535

ICP

Published simultaneously in Canada
by Little, Brown & Company (Canada) Limited

Printed in the United States of America

This book is dedicated to
Joanna, Elizabeth, and Thomas,
Jack, Claire, Riki,
Rena, Cheryl, Benjamin, and Elana.

Summary of Contents

Contents

1

Mortgage Pass-Throughs   1

2

Collateralized Mortgage Obligations   37

3

Real Estate Mortgage Investment Conduits   47

Contents

4

Taxable Mortgage Pools 117

5

Original Issue Discount   127

About the Authors

Thomas A. Humphreys, Esq., is a tax partner in the New York City office of the law firm of Brown & Wood. Mr. Humphreys received an AB from the University of California, Los Angeles in 1974, a JD from the University of California, Hastings College of Law in 1977, and an LL.M. in Taxation from New York University in 1979. He has been Chairman of the American Bar Association's Section of Taxation Committee on Regulated Investment Companies (1985-1987) and Co-chairman of the New York State Bar Association's Section on Taxation Committee on Financial Instruments (1988) and the Committee on Pass-Through Entities. He is currently Co-chairman of the New York State Bar Association's Section of Taxation Committee on Financial Instruments and a member of the NYSBA's Tax Section Executive Committee. Mr. Humphreys is also an adjunct professor of law at New York University where he teaches a course entitled "Taxation of Financial Instruments" in the LL.M. program.

Robert M. Kreitman, Esq., is a tax partner in the New York City office of the law firm of Brown & Wood. Mr. Kreitman received a BA from Yeshiva University in 1982, a JD from the Georgetown University Law Center in 1985, and an LL.M. in Taxation from New York University in 1988. Mr. Kreitman is a member of the New York and New Jersey Bars. Mr. Kreitman has delivered numerous lectures dealing with the tax issues relating to mortgage-backed securities, including REMICs and TMPs.

Acknowledgments

The authors wish to express their appreciation for the work of Gregory Raykher, Esq., Brown & Wood, New York, New York, without whose tireless efforts this volume could not have been published. The authors also wish to thank their secretaries, Claudette Clark and JoAnn Bennett, for their transcription of the manuscript.

Introduction

§1 PLANNING OPPORTUNITIES AND PITFALLS

This volume discusses the federal income tax treatment of mortgage-backed securities (MBS) transactions. Its primary focus is to provide practitioners with an organized framework to decide which structure is best suited to a particular MBS transaction. In this regard, it discusses the real estate mortage investment conduit (REMIC) in detail. It also discusses non-REMIC mortgage securitization transactions, which, as it will be seen, still have many applications even after the REMIC legislation.[1] Finally, it discusses several collateral issues including original issue discount, market discount and premium, and the taxable mortgage pool rules, which make REMIC the primary means to structure multiple-class MBS.

This volume is organized around three basic MBS transactions:

(1) mortgage-backed pass-through certificates issued by so-called grantor trusts;
(2) collateralized mortgage obligations (CMOs) issued by corporations or trusts where no REMIC election is made; and
(3) mortgage-backed pass-throughs (including multiple-class pass-throughs) and CMOs structured under the REMIC rules.

This volume also discusses nontax considerations that are important to the practitioner in structuring MBS transactions. These include accounting and regulatory considerations that in many cases will play a significant role in determining which MBS structure is used.

The federal income tax treatment of MBS, as the reader will soon observe, is derived from an odd amalgamation of federal statutes, Treasury regulations, published and private IRS rulings, and common law, with a good dose of "practice in the profession" added in. This volume is designed to help the practitioner cope with the standard MBS transactions as well as some more unique structures that arise from time to time. Even though its focus is the taxation of MBS, the principles discussed herein (with some notable exceptions, including REMIC), can be applied equally well to the tax treatment of nonmortgage asset securitization. Thus, this volume is designed as a reference work for those transactions as well.

---

§1 [1]P.L. 99-514, 99th Cong., 2d Sess. (1986) (hereinafter referred to as the 1986 Act).

§2 THE ROLE OF FEDERAL INCOME TAXATION IN THE SECONDARY MORTGAGE MARKET

The development of the secondary mortgage market has been one of the most significant trends in U.S. capital markets in the last 15 years. In 1978, approximately $1.2 billion in MBS were sold in public and private offerings. By 1993, that number had grown to $420 billion.

One key factor in this growth has been the favorable federal income tax treatment of MBS transactions. This treatment has resulted from a combination of both public and private sector initiatives including: (1) the initial IRS published rulings that treated mortgage-backed pass-through transactions as nontaxable "grantor" trusts for federal income tax purposes, (2) the ability of tax lawyers to create leveraged corporations to issue MBS in multiple-class format (thereby overcoming restrictions on multiple-class trusts), (3) the development in 1985 of the "owner" trust to issue multiple-class MBS, (4) the enactment of the REMIC legislation in the Tax Reform Act of 1986,[1] and (5) the promulgation of REMIC regulations in 1992 clarifying important REMIC issues.[2]

§3 ECONOMIC TRENDS BEHIND GROWTH OF THE SECONDARY MORTGAGE MARKET

To understand the reasons for the generally favorable federal income tax treatment of MBS transactions, some understanding of the economic trends that underlie the secondary mortgage market is helpful. Moreover, these economic trends will determine the long-term health and viability of this market.

The growth of the secondary mortgage market was the result of the rapid increase in interest rates in the late 1970s and early 1980s. U.S. savings and loan associations experienced a profit squeeze during this period as a result of two primary factors: (1) the practice of originating and holding fixed rate long-term mortgage loans rather than either selling such loans immediately after origination or originating floating rate loans (for example, in the United Kingdom, almost all mortgage loans are floating rate nonamortizing loans), and (2) the predominance of short-term funding through deposits (which, after 1981, were not subject to interest rate limits) and other debt instruments whose cost increased as interest rates increased.[1]

§2 [1]Id.
[2]See §§103 and 104.

§3 [1]Based on statistics compiled by the Federal Home Loan Bank Board, in 1976 thrift institutions insured by the Federal Savings and Loan Insurance Corporation (FSLIC) were earning an average rate of 8 percent and paying an average rate of 6.38 percent. By the latter half of 1981, the average rate of interest earned was 10.07 percent, but the average rate of interest paid was 11.53 percent. See Edson & Jacobs, Secondary Mortgage Market Guide, §4.01[3] at 4-4 (1987).

Introduction

One response to this problem was for thrift institutions to sell their mortgage loans immediately after origination, in effect changing the business strategy to one of earning income on loan origination and servicing fees as opposed to interest income. If a thrift institution could sell long-term mortgage loans shortly after origination, it could reduce its risk and simultaneously acquire funds to originate new mortgage loans paying market interest rates.

There were significant problems, however, with selling such mortgage loans. Thus, so-called whole-loan mortgage sales were, and are, cumbersome and inefficient. Additionally, the market for such loans was essentially limited to buyers familiar with mortgage loans, such as other thrifts. Thrift institutions therefore needed to dispose of their long-term fixed-rate mortgage loans in a way that would attract nontraditional investors with large amounts of capital. Securitizing mortgage loans and selling them in the secondary market provided thrift institutions with access to capital markets made up of institutional investors that had little experience investing in mortgage loans but were experienced in purchasing investments similar to corporate bonds and Treasury securities.[2] An expanded secondary market for mortgage loans also would allow mortgage bankers, as well as thrift institutions, an inexpensive interest rate hedge: As mortgage loans are originated, the ability to immediately resell them in a secondary mortgage market allowed mortgage originators to limit their exposure to rising interest rates.[3]

§4 GOVERNMENT SPONSORED MORTGAGE-LOAN SECURITIZATION TRANSACTIONS

The exponential growth of the United States' MBS market could not have occurred without the participation of government and quasi-government mortgage guarantors including: (1) the Government National Mortgage Association; (2) the Federal Home Loan Mortgage Corporation; and (3) the Federal National Mortgage Association. These agencies provided a standardized credit quality for MBS transactions, and a basic understanding of their single-class MBS programs is important in understanding the underpinnings of the MBS market. These programs also marked the initial stage of the development of the federal income tax treatment of MBS.[1]

---

[2]The effectiveness of the secondary market in absorbing mortgage loans for thrift institutions during the years of rapid rises in interest rates is illustrated by these statistics: in 1981 the Federal National Mortgage Association (Fannie Mae) started its mortgage-backed securities (MBS) program and issued a total of $717 million of MBS; in 1982, Fannie Mae issued $13.97 billion of MBS; in 1988, Fannie Mae issued $54.88 billion of MBS; and, in 1992, Fannie Mae issued $194.04 billion of MBS. Fannie Mae Investor/Analyst Report, First Quarter 1993.

[3]Edson & Jacobs, *supra* note 1, at 4-5. For a thorough analysis of the evolution of the secondary market for mortgage loans, see Edson & Jacobs, *supra* note 1.

§4 [1]See §§103 and 104.

§4.1 Government National Mortgage Association Mortgage-Backed Pass-Through Certificates

The Government National Mortgage Association (GNMA or Ginnie Mae) introduced large scale mortgage loan securitization in 1970 with the establishment of its MBS program.[2] The predominant type of security issued under this program is the modified pass-through certificate,[3] which represents the beneficial ownership of an undivided portion of the principal and interest from mortgage loans in a pool (Ginnie Mae certificates). Ginnie Mae certificates are guaranteed by Ginnie Mae as to the timely payment of principal and interest on the mortgage loans in the pool. Because Ginnie Mae is a U.S. government corporation,[4] the Ginnie Mae guarantee carries the full faith and credit of the U.S. government, thereby eliminating any credit risk to the holders of Ginnie Mae certificates. In 1984, approximately $28 billion of Ginnie Mae certificates were issued. In 1991, however, approximately $62.8 billion of Ginnie Mae certificates were issued.[5] This dramatic increase illustrates the effectiveness of the Ginnie Mae certificate program in creating access for thrift institutions to a secondary market for mortgage loans.

§4.2 Federal Home Loan Mortgage Corporation Mortgage Participation Certificates

The first mortgage pass-through certificate backed by conventional mortgage loans (that is, mortgage loans not guaranteed or insured by government agencies or instrumentalities) was the Federal Home Loan Mortgage Corporation (FHLMC or Freddie Mac)[6] Mortgage Participation Certificate (PC) introduced in 1971. The owner of a PC owns an undivided interest in a pool of first-lien conventional

---

[2]Under this program, mortgage lenders apply to Ginnie Mae for approval to issue Ginnie Mae securities. The mortgage lender then originates or purchases mortgage loans guaranteed by the Veterans Administration (VA) and the Farmers Home Administration (FmHA), or insured by the Federal Housing Administration (FHA), and pools mortgage loans having similar payment terms. The lender then transfers the mortgage documentation to a custodian holding on behalf of Ginnie Mae and Ginnie Mae receives a schedule of the mortgages in the pool, a servicing agreement from the lender, and certain other documentation for review. Ginnie Mae then authorizes securities to be issued in book-entry form. The lender pays Ginnie Mae a monthly guarantee fee.

[3]The holder of a modified pass-through certificate is guaranteed the timely payment of principal and interest regardless of whether it is collected by the servicer. The holder of a straight pass-through certificate is guaranteed the timely payment of principal and interest to the extent collected by the servicer.

[4]Ginnie Mae was created by Congress under the Housing and Urban Development Act of 1968.

[5]Ginnie Mae Investment Facts, U.S. Department of Housing and Urban Development (July 1992).

[6]Freddie Mac was created by Congress in 1970 pursuant to the Emergency Home Finance Act to develop a secondary market for conventional residential loans. Freddie Mac's common stock is owned by the Federal Home Loan Banks.

residential mortgage loans.[7] Freddie Mac guarantees timely payment of interest and ultimate collection of principal on the mortgage loans underlying its PCs. Unlike Ginnie Mae certificates, Freddie Mac's guarantee of its PCs is not backed by the full faith and credit of the United States. Between 1988 and the end of 1992, Freddie Mac had sold over $458 billion of PCs.[8]

§4.3 Federal National Mortgage Association MBS

Freddie Mac was followed by the Federal National Mortgage Association (Fannie Mae),[9] which introduced its MBS program in 1981. Under this program, lenders originate mortgage loans and sell them to Fannie Mae, which pools the mortgage loans and issues mortgage-backed pass-through securities. Fannie Mae guarantees timely payment of principal and interest on its mortgage-backed pass-through securities. This guarantee is not backed by the full faith and credit of the U.S. government, but the Secretary of the Treasury is authorized in its discretion to loan Fannie Mae up to $2.25 billion.[10] As of March 31, 1993, Fannie Mae had $457 billion of MBS outstanding.[11]

§4.4 Federal Agricultural Mortgage Corporation

The latest entrant in the mortgage securitization market is the Federal Agricultural Mortgage Corporation (Farmer Mac). Farmer Mac was established in 1988[12] to aid the development of a secondary market for agricultural and residential mortgage loans in rural areas by providing guarantees for the timely payment of principal and interest on securities representing interests in, or obligations backed

---

[7]Freddie Mac offers its PCs through its cash or guarantor programs. Under its cash program, Freddie Mac purchases mortgage loans from lenders on a daily basis and aggregates them into large pools represented by PCs. The PCs are then offered at a daily auction through securities dealers including the Security Sales and Trading Group of Freddie Mac. Freddie Mac's guarantor program (introduced in 1981) allows lenders holding conventional and FHA/VA mortgage loans to swap their loans for PCs. See the Information Statement dated April 9, 1993, for the Federal Home Loan Mortgage Corporation.

[8]Id.

[9]Fannie Mae was incorporated in 1938 pursuant to Title III of the National Housing Act and is now a publicly owned, federally chartered corporation.

[10]12 U.S.C. §1719(c).

[11]Fannie Mae Investor/Analyst Report, First Quarter 1993. The growth in popularity of Ginnie Mae, Freddie Mac, and Fannie Mae mortgage pass-through certificates provided the foundation for the evolution of private mortgage pass-through certificates issued by trusts and usually backed by some type of private credit support. See offering circular for Mortgage-Backed Certificates, Series A, $8\,3/8$ percent pass-through rate, Bank of American National Trust and Savings Assoc., dated September 22, 1977.

[12]Farmer Mac is a federally chartered instrumentality of the United States, established by the Farm Credit Act of 1971, as amended by the Agricultural Credit Act of 1987. See 12 U.S.C. §§2279aa-1.

by, pools of qualified loans meeting Farmer Mac's standards (pool securities).[13] This guarantee will not be backed by the full faith and credit of the U.S. government, but Farmer Mac is authorized to borrow up to $1.5 billion from the Secretary of the Treasury to fulfill its obligations under any guarantee.[14] Farmer Mac launched its MBS program in 1992 with the creation of over $1 billion in REMIC securities.[15]

§5 MULTIPLE-CLASS MBS

The rapid growth of the secondary market for mortgage loans facilitated by the popularity of government-guaranteed mortgage pass-through certificates created an incentive for lenders desiring to dispose of mortgage loans to develop new types of securities to meet the specific needs and funding requirements of potential investors. One such requirement was call protection. Investors such as pension funds that can determine the amount of payouts they will make to beneficiaries many years in advance need to purchase investments that provide for payments to match those liabilities. A mortgage pass-through certificate could carry a guarantee of the payment of principal and interest on the underlying mortgage loans, but it could not protect a purchaser against the prepayment of the underlying mortgage loans.[1] The response to this limitation was the creation of the "collateralized mortgage obligation."[2] CMOs are debt obligations collateralized by a pool of mortgage loans and usually issued in several classes[3] (tranches) with varying maturities.[4] By reallocating the cash flows from the pool of mortgage loans to pay

[13]A secondary market for agricultural mortgage loans is intended to provide farmers with access to fixed-rate long-term mortgages, a kind of credit that has not been available in today's adjustable-rate farm mortgage market.

[14]12 U.S.C. §§2279aa-13.

[15]Farmer Mac's business can be distinguished from the primary business of Fannie Mae and Freddie Mac since it does not acquire inventory or otherwise deal in agricultural mortgages. Farmer Mac is similar to Ginnie Mae in that it guarantees securities backed by mortgage loans. It is functionally distinguishable, however, in two important respects. First, Ginnie Mae guarantees pools of mortgage loans that are already insured by the FHA or the VA. There is no requirement of prior insurance of mortgage loans in Farmer Mac pools. Second, unlike Ginnie Mae, Farmer Mac requires a minimum of 10 percent credit enhancement through the creation of reserves or subordinated interests.

§5 [1]See discussion below of the shortcomings of mortgage-backed pass-through trusts at §104.

[2]Freddie Mac issued the first CMO in 1983. It consisted of three classes with an aggregate principal amount of $1 billion. See the Offering Circular dated June 7, 1983 for the Federal Home Loan Mortgage Corporation Collateralized Mortgage Obligations, Series 1983-A. In 1986, the year before the REMIC statute took effect, approximately $44.8 billion of CMOs were issued. Mortgage-Backed Securities Letter, Vol.II No.1 (Jan. 5, 1987).

[3]Generally trusts issuing mortgage pass-through certificates are prevented by Treasury regulations from issuing multiple classes. See discussion at §105.

[4]A hybrid between a pass-through certificate and a CMO is the "pay-through" bond. The typical pay-through bond is a single class debt instrument secured by a pool of mortgages. Principal and interest on the mortgages are passed directly through to the investors. In comparison, "mortgage-backed" bonds are also debt obligations of the issuer collateralized by a pool of mortgage loans, but the principal and interest are not necessarily passed through to the bondholders and payments on the bonds may be made from other funds of the issuer.

down the principal balances of the classes in the order of their stated maturity (a so-called "fast-pay, slow-pay" structure), the sponsor can reduce the impact of mortgage loan prepayments. In addition, because CMOs are debt instruments rather than pass-through certificates,[5] the sponsor has the freedom to construct the payment terms of the CMOs in whatever way will achieve its marketing goals.

§6   REAL ESTATE MORTGAGE INVESTMENT CONDUIT

By 1986, Congress saw the benefits of a vast secondary market for mortgage loans but also understood the complexities and uncertainty that federal income tax laws added to the structuring of MBS transactions.[1] In response, as part of the 1986 Act, Congress created the REMIC.[2] Congress intended that the REMIC, with certain exceptions, would not be subject to an entity-level tax and, after a transition period, would be the exclusive vehicle for issuing multiple-class MBS.

The IRS issued proposed REMIC regulations in 1991. The regulations were finalized in late 1992. They were extremely helpful in clarifying many different tax issues in REMIC transactions and have helped make REMIC the vehicle of choice for mortgage securitizations.

§7   CREATING A TRANSPARENT ENTITY

The critical tax issue in choosing an MBS vehicle is to ensure that the vehicle does not pay a corporate-level tax. As discussed in the following paragraphs, there are several ways this can be accomplished. So long as no corporate level tax is imposed, a mortgage securitization will be superior to an outright sale of the mortgage loans (i.e., a so-called whole loan sale).[1] If, however, a corporate-level tax is imposed on the income from the mortgages, this tax will reduce the cash flow from the mortgages by an amount equal to the federal (and possibly state or local) income tax rate. This, in turn, will make any mortgage securitization transaction far worse than a whole loan sale. Accordingly, the mortgage securitization transaction can only be accomplished with a "transparent" mortgage securitization vehicle.

---

[5]See discussion in text of restrictions on structuring a trust issuing mortgage pass-through certificates at §104.

§6   [1]See Staff of the Joint Comm. on Tax'n General Explanation of the Tax Reform Act of 1986 at 411-412.

[2]The REMIC provisions are in Code §§860A through 860G of the Internal Revenue Code of 1986 (see Appendix B).

§7   [1]See §3, *supra.*

§7.1 Transparency Under the Grantor Trust Rules

The first and most basic way to achieve tax transparency is through the combination of the rules applicable to fixed investment trusts under Reg. §301.7701-4(c)(2) and the rules applicable to "grantor" trusts under Code §§671 through 679. As discussed below, creating a trust in which the trustee has no power to vary the investment of the certificate holders and issuing a single class of certificates (with important exceptions for senior-subordinated classes and coupon-stripping transactions) will ensure that the entity is classified as a trust rather than as an association taxable as a corporation or a partnership for federal income tax purposes. The grantor trust rules, as expanded by IRS rulings, have been interpreted to permit the beneficiaries of such a trust to be treated as the direct owners of the trust's assets. As such, there is no second level of taxation and the desired tax transparency is accomplished.

§7.2 Tax Transparency Through the Code §163 Interest Deduction

A second way to achieve tax transparency is to offset income from mortgages held by the mortgage securitization vehicle by interest deductions on debt that the vehicle issues. In this context, the only limits on the interest deduction are the limits on leverage imposed by debt-equity concerns (i.e., whether the mortgage-backed debt instruments are actually equity in the issuer) and by pledge versus sale concerns (i.e., whether the issuer in substance has sold the mortgages to the debt owners). As discussed below, issuers commonly borrow a significant percentage of the value of the mortgage collateral, thereby achieving substantial tax transparency because interest on the borrowing substantially offsets income from the mortgages.

§7.3 Tax Transparency Through the Partnership Rules

The next form of tax transparency is achieved through the partnership tax rules under subchapter K. It is unusual, however, for the mortgage securitization vehicle to be formed as a state law partnership. Instead, the standard transaction uses a trust which, if not classified as such, would be treated as a tax partnership for federal income tax purposes under Reg. §301.7701. Such "owner" trusts are typically used in conjunction with an issuance of mortgage-backed debt described in the preceding paragraph. The use of the partnership rules plus the Code §163 interest deduction achieves total tax transparency for such a vehicle.

§7.4 Tax Transparency Through the REMIC Rules

The next way to achieve tax transparency is through the REMIC rules. By meeting the requirements for REMIC status, the Code confers tax transparency on the REMIC entity, whether it is formed as a corporation, trust, or partnership or simply as a segregated pool of assets. As will be seen, REMIC was Congress's answer to tax uncertainty caused by other mortgage-securitization vehicles. While it has been used in an overwhelming number of mortgage-securitization transactions since its enactment, as discussed below there are still cases in which the other MBS vehicles can and should be used.

§7.5   Other Transparent Vehicles

The grantor trust, interest deductions, partnership and REMIC rules are not the only ways to achieve tax transparency for mortgage-securitization transactions. For example, in special situations the real estate investment trust (REIT), regulated investment company (RIC),[2] or subchapter S rules can be used to achieve such transparency. While these vehicles are outside the scope of this volume, they should not be completely ignored in deciding upon a mortgage-securitization vehicle.

[2]See Hillman, Regulated Investment Companies (The Little, Brown Tax Practice Series 1995).

Mortgage-Backed Securities Including REMICs and Other Investment Vehicles

1

Mortgage Pass-Throughs

---

§101   REASONS TO USE A MORTGAGE PASS-THROUGH

The primary reason a private issuer will still use a mortgage pass-through structured as a grantor trust under the Code even after the real estate mortgage investment conduit (REMIC) legislation is its simplicity. Thus, some mortgage originators have been selling mortgage loans for several years using single class or senior-subordinated non-REMIC pass-throughs. They have established documentation and procedures that would have to be changed if a REMIC election were made for the transaction. For example, in a REMIC, a residual interest is necessary.[1] Even though a noneconomic residual is possible, creating such an interest still may require reworking the documents. Additionally, there are different reporting requirements for a REMIC, including the Form 1066Q, a quarterly report for residual holders, and the Form 1066, the REMIC's annual informational federal income tax return. In the case of a mortgage pass-through, the trustee must file an annual Form 1041 and send Form K-1s to investors.[2] These may seem like small items, but in a mortgage sale program under which hundreds of thousands of mortgages are sold each year, they can make a large difference to the selling institution.

§102   THE TYPICAL TRANSACTION

Mortgage pass-through securities were the first and most basic mortgage-backed security (MBS).[1] In a typical transaction, the sponsor conveys the mortgage loans to a trustee or custodian (for convenience, this arrangement is hereafter referred to as a trust) pursuant to a pooling and servicing agreement.[2] The sponsor may

---

§101   [1]See §306.

[2]See Appendix D for a copy of IRS Form 1041.

§102   [1]As noted above, the Ginnie Mae MBS program created the first large-scale mortgage pass-through security program in 1970 by guaranteeing the payment of principal and interest to holders of pass-through certificates backed by FHA, VA, and FmHA mortgage loans. See Introduction, §4 note 2, and accompanying text.

[2]Cf. Fannie Mae MBS which represent interests in pools of mortgage loans held for the benefit of certificate holders by Fannie Mae as trustee pursuant to the terms of a trust indenture, as amended, and supplemented for a related issue of MBS by an Issue Supplement.

be the mortgage originator,[3] a conduit,[4] or a government agency such as Freddie Mac or Fannie Mae.[5] Alternatively, the sponsor transfers the mortgage loans to the trust pursuant to a loan sale agreement, and a third-party services the loans. In exchange for the mortgages, the sponsor receives pass-through certificates issued by the trust that represent undivided interests in the pool of mortgage loans. The sponsor may retain the pass-through certificates or sell them in a public or private transaction.[6]

In general, each pool will contain mortgage loans with similar payment terms,[7] although the principal amounts and interest rates of the mortgage loans may vary.

After the transfer, mortgages in the trust are serviced by a mortgage "servicer," generally either the sponsor or a third party. Mortgage servicing involves (1) collecting principal and interest on the mortgages, (2) collecting other charges (e.g., assumption and prepayment fees), (3) keeping track of the principal balance of the mortgages, (4) working out problem loans, including defaulted loans, and (5) other incidental functions. The "mortgage pool" servicer may be compensated in a variety of ways. For example, if the mortgage loans in a pool provide for interest payable at different fixed rates, the servicer may be entitled to the percentage of each interest payment on each mortgage loan in the pool that would allow the pass-through certificates issued by the trust holding that pool to pay a single fixed rate of interest.[8] Alternatively, the servicer may be entitled to a fixed percent-

---

[3]Mortgage originators include S&L institutions, commercial banks, mortgage companies, mutual savings banks, and credit unions. Mortgage originators converting their mortgage loans into pass-through certificates may (1) have the pass-through certificates guaranteed by Ginnie Mae (if the mortgage loans are FHA, VA, or FmHA loans), (2) issue the pass-through certificates as Freddie Mac PCs (under the Freddie Mac Guarantor program) or sell the mortgage loans to Freddie Mac which, in turn, will issue PCs backed by the mortgage loans, (3) sell the mortgage loans to Fannie Mae which will issue MBS backed by the mortgage loans, or (4) issue the pass-through certificates in the mortgage originator's own name with private credit support.

[4]A conduit generally is an organization such as a mortgage insurance company or an investment bank that buys whole mortgage loans or participations and packages them for resale to investors.

[5]Under the Freddie Mac Cash Program, Freddie Mac purchases newly originated and seasoned fixed- and adjustable-rate mortgage loans primarily for resale as PCs. See note 7 at §4. Under Fannie Mae's MBS program, Fannie Mae will purchase mortgage loans from originators in exchange for MBS, or it will issue MBS backed by mortgage loans from its own portfolio.

[6]See text *infra* at §107.1.3 for the prerequisites to finding a sale of mortgage loans for federal income tax purposes. The financial accounting treatment of a sale of mortgage pass-through certificates is governed by the Statement of Financial Accounting Standards No. 77, Reporting by Transferors for Transfers of Receivables with Recourse, December 1983 (FASB 77). In general, FASB 77 requires the following three conditions to be met before a transfer of receivables with recourse will be recognized as a sale: (1) the transferor must surrender control of the future economic benefits embodied in the receivables; (2) the transferor's obligations under the recourse provisions can be reasonably estimated; and (3) the transferee cannot require the transferor to repurchase the receivables except pursuant to the recourse provisions. FASB 77, ¶5.

[7]For example, a pool of mortgage loans represented by Fannie Mae MBS contains promissory notes secured by first mortgages or deeds of trust on one- to four-family residential properties or multifamily projects of five or more dwelling units. Each pool contains either fixed-rate level payment mortgage loans, fixed-rate growing equity mortgage loans that provide for annual increased payments applied to principal, fixed-rate graduated payment mortgage loans that provide for deferred interest, conventional variable-rate mortgage loans, other adjustable rate mortgage loans, or fixed-rate mortgage loans secured by multifamily projects providing for irregular payment features.

[8]See text *infra* at §107.2.2 for a discussion of the potential application of the stripped bond rules to stripped interest or "retained yield" servicing fees.

age of the interest payments on each mortgage loan in the pool so that the pass-through certificates will pay a weighted average interest rate that will change as disproportionate payments (including prepayments) of principal are made on mortgage loans bearing different fixed interest rates.

§103 ACHIEVING TAX TRANSPARENCY THROUGH THE GRANTOR TRUST RULES

In order to avoid a federal income tax liability at the entity level, the pass-through trust must be classified as a trust for federal income tax purposes rather than as an association taxable as a corporation.[1] If the trust is classified as an association taxable as a corporation, the trust's net income will be taxed at the appropriate Code §11 corporate rates, and distributions to certificate holders will be treated as nondeductible dividends.[2] Simply stated, if the trust is treated as an association, the income from the mortgage loans will be taxed twice: once at the trust level and again on distribution to the certificate holders. On the other hand, because a pass-through certificate reserves for its holder a pro rata ownership interest in the income and corpus of the trust, if the trust is classified as a trust for federal income tax purposes, the trust will be considered a "grantor" trust subject to the rules of Code §§671 through 679.[3] As such, each pass-through certificate holder will be considered under the provisions of Code §671 as an owner of a pro rata portion of the income and corpus of the trust.[4]

Consequently, the certificate holders, rather than the trust, will include the income of the trust in gross income and will be entitled to any deductions attributable to the mortgage loans held by the trust.[5]

---

§103 [1] An example of the legal opinion regarding the classification for federal income tax purposes of a typical pass-through trust is as follows:

> Counsel to the Depositor has advised the Depositor that, in its opinion, the Mortgage Pool and the arrangement to be administered by the Servicer under which the Trustee will hold, and the Servicer will be obligated to service, the Mortgage Loans and pursuant to which Certificates will be issued to Certificate holders, will not be classified as an association taxable as a corporation, but, rather will be classified as a grantor trust under subpart E, Part I of Subchapter J of the Internal Revenue Code of 1986, as amended.

See also the sample opinions at Appendix C.

[2] See Reg. §301.7701-2(a).

[3] See Rev. Rul. 61-175, 1961-2 C.B. 128 (creation of an investment trust by several grantor banks caused each grantor bank to be considered as an owner of a pro rata portion of the trust under Code §671).

[4] Id.

[5] Id.; Reg. §1.671-3(a). See discussion in text *infra* at §107.2, regarding the federal income taxation of certificate holders. The IRS has issued a number of revenue rulings classifying pools of mortgage loans as grantor trusts for federal income tax purposes. See, e.g., Rev. Rul. 84-10, 1984-1 C.B. 155 (pool of residential mortgage loans represented by Fannie Mae MBS treated as a grantor trust for federal

§104   BASIC FEDERAL INCOME TAX PRINCIPLES APPLICABLE TO ALL PASS-THROUGH TRUSTS

The basic rules governing pass-through trusts are contained in Reg. §301.7701-4. These regulations are part of the entity classification regulations promulgated by the Treasury Department to distinguish trusts, partnerships, and corporations from each other for federal income tax purposes.[1]

These basic rules set forth two essential requirements for a trust to be classified as a fixed investment trust, rather than as an association taxable as a corporation or a partnership: (1) there must be no power to vary the investment of the certificate holders in order to take advantage of market fluctuations, and (2) the trust cannot have multiple classes of ownership unless the trust is formed to facilitate direct investment in the trust assets and the existence of such classes is merely incidental to such purpose. The first requirement is one rooted in case law more than 50 years old; the second requirement is a result of some attempts in the mid-1980s to expand the use of the pass-through trust. If the trust fails either of these requirements, it will be classified as an association taxable as a corporation or a partnership according to principles found in the entity classification regulations.

§104.1   *The Prohibition Against Any Power to Vary the Investment of Certificate Holders*

The classification of an entity as a trust for federal income tax purposes generally is limited to arrangements created to conserve and protect property for the beneficiaries who do not create the trust or acquire its interests but instead merely accept its benefits.[2] "Investment" trusts, however, have been recognized by the courts and the IRS as trusts for federal income tax purposes, even though the beneficiaries may create the trust and voluntarily acquire its interests.[3] Under the

income tax purposes); Rev. Rul. 77-349, 1977-2 C.B. 20 (pool of residential mortgage loans backed by a mortgage guaranty insurance policy issued by a private mortgage insurer and represented by private pass-through certificates); Rev. Rul. 71-399, 1971-2 C.B. 433 (pool of mortgage participation certificates represented by Freddie Mac PCs), *amplified by* Rev. Rul. 81-203, 1981-2 C.B. 137, Rev. Rul. 80-96, 1980-1 C.B. 317, Rev. Rul. 74-300, 1974-1 C.B. 169, Rev. Rul. 74-221, 1974-1 C.B. 365, and Rev. Rul. 72-376, 1972-2 C.B. 647; Rev. Rul. 70-545, 1970-2 C.B. 7 (pool of FHA, VA, and FmHA mortgage loans represented by Ginnie Mae "fully-modified pass-through" certificates), *clarified by* Rev. Rul. 84-10, 1984-1 C.B. 155, and *modified by* Rev. Rul. 74-169, 1974-1 C.B. 147; Rev. Rul. 70-544, 1970-2 C.B. 6 (pool of FHA, VA, and FmHA mortgage loans represented by "straight pass-through" certificates guaranteed by Ginnie Mae), *clarified by* Rev. Rul. 84-10, and *modified by* Rev. Rul. 74-300, 1974-1 C.B. 169, and Rev. Rul. 74-169, 1974-1 C.B. 147.

§104   [1]Reg. §§301.7701-1 through 301.7701-4. See also Stand. Fed. Tax Rep. (CCH) ¶43,882.01, et seq.
[2]See T.D. 8080, 1986-1 C.B. 371; Reg. §301.7701-4(a).
[3]Id. See also Commissioner v. Chase National Bank, 122 F.2d 504, 41-2 U.S.T.C. ¶9643 (2d Cir. 1941). The Treasury regulations do not define "investment" trust. Instead, they define in general terms "ordinary" trusts (arrangements created by will or inter vivos declaration for the conservation of property for the beneficiaries and governed by the rules applied in chancery or probate courts) and "business" trusts (trusts created by the beneficiaries to carry on a profit-making business) and imply that investment trusts are not to be considered ordinary trusts or business trusts.

entity classification regulations, whether an investment trust (such as a grantor trust issuing pass-through certificates) will be classified as a trust for federal income tax purposes, rather than as an association taxable as a corporation, depends in part on whether there is a power under the governing instruments to vary the investment of the certificate holders.[4] In other words, if the trustee or some other person has the power (even if it is contingent) under the governing instruments to change the investment of the certificate holders, the arrangement becomes a "business."[5]

There is no precise definition of what constitutes a power to vary the investment of the certificate holders within the meaning of Reg. §301.7701-4(c). The IRS has addressed different aspects of the issue in a number of revenue rulings. The general definition embodied in these rulings is that the power to vary the investment of the certificate holders is "one whereby the trustee, or some other person,[6] has some kind of managerial power over the trusteed funds that enables him to take advantage of variations in the market to improve the investment of all the [certificate holders]."[7]

§104.1.1 Power to Make Temporary Investments

In Rev. Rul. 75-192, the IRS ruled that the trustee of a fixed investment trust could temporarily invest cash distributions from the trust's assets pending distribution on quarterly distribution dates to the trust's certificate holders. The trustee was limited to the reinvestment of such cash distributions in obligations that matured prior to the next certificate distribution date and that were held until maturity.[8]

---

[4]Reg. §301.7701-4(c)(1). Under Reg. §301.7701-2(a), characteristics common to trusts and corporations are centralization of management, continuity of life, free transferability of interests, and limited liability. Consequently, in determining whether a trust will be classified as such for federal income tax purposes, these characteristics are to be ignored and association classification will result if there are associates and an objective to carry on a business and divide the gains therefrom. The investors in an investment trust may be considered associates; therefore, classification of an investment trust as an association will turn on whether there is an objective to carry on a business.

[5]Commissioner v. North American Bond Trust, 122 F.2d 545, 546, 41-2 U.S.T.C. ¶9644 (2d Cir. 1941), *cert. denied*, 314 U.S. 701 (1941). In *North American Bond Trust*, the "depositor," acting under the authority of the trustee, had the power at any time prior to the termination of the trust agreement to sell certificates of beneficial interest in a trust holding bonds. With each investment of new money by new certificate holders, the depositor could purchase new bonds. As a result, the depositor could take advantage of market fluctuations to benefit all certificate holders. The court considered this arrangement to be a "business," i.e., "a method of profiting by the rise and fall of securities." Id.

[6]This person may be the servicer or the sponsor. Although most of the relevant revenue rulings assume that the trustee is administering the pool of obligations, the holdings of these rulings presumably are applicable to any other person acting under the authorization of the trust documents (e.g., the servicer). See, e.g., Rev. Rul. 75-192, 1975-1 C.B. 384. Thus, the restriction on varying the investment cannot be circumvented by giving the servicer or sponsor rather than the trustee a power to vary the trust's investment.

[7]Rev. Rul. 75-192, *supra* note 6.

[8]Id. Importantly, this restriction does not prevent reinvestment during the temporary period. For example, suppose that the trustee received $100 on April 25, which was to be paid to investors on June 30. The trustee could invest in one-day repurchase agreements on each day up to June 30. These would comply with the requirement of the ruling that the obligations matured before the next

The investment limitation in Rev. Rul. 75-192 applies not only to monthly principal and interest payments but to the proceeds from the sale or redemption of obligations held by a trust as well.[9] As a result, reinvested principal and interest payments and reinvested proceeds from the sale or other disposition of obligations, as well as any reinvestment income thereon, must be distributed to certificate holders by the next distribution date.[10]

The holding in Rev. Rul. 75-192 should be broad enough to permit a trust to reinvest monthly cash flows in a guaranteed investment contract (GIC) until the quarterly distribution date. A GIC is a contract, usually entered into with an insurance company, that permits the holder of the GIC to invest all cash flows from the mortgages in the GIC and to receive a guaranteed rate of return. For example, the trust might issue pass-through certificates with a 9 percent pass-through rate payable quarterly. In order to guarantee that the certificate holder's return would not decrease when substantial prepayments occur, the trust could purchase a GIC that guaranteed 9 percent interest. If substantial prepayments occurred (presumably because of falling interest rates), the certificate holder would be assured, because of the quarterly payment feature, that the yield would not decrease. So long as all cash invested in the GIC is distributed at quarter's end, the arrangement would appear to be within the reinvestment boundaries set by Rev. Rul. 75-192. In addition, the GIC arrangement gives the trustee even less discretion than if such trustee were permitted to invest cash flows temporarily in a wide range of short-term money market instruments, a power typically allowed to trustees of mortgage pass-through trusts.

---

distribution date and were held until maturity. According to the IRS, the result of these restrictions is that the person reinvesting the funds on behalf of the certificate holders is limited to a fixed return "similar to that earned on a bank account" and, consequently, such person cannot "profit from market fluctuations." Id. at 385. In Rev. Rul. 75-192, the trustee made quarterly distributions to certificate holders out of the accumulated monthly payments from a pool of FHA and VA mortgage loans, as well as the reinvestment earnings thereon. Similarly, most, if not all, single-class grantor trusts holding mortgage loans make monthly or quarterly distributions to certificate holders. The question of whether the limited discretion to reinvest mortgage loan payments allowed by Rev. Rul. 75-192 would be permissible for a grantor trust making semiannual or annual distributions to certificate holders from a pool of monthly-pay obligations has not been addressed in any published ruling. Cf. Priv. Ltr. Rul. 8311007 (Sept. 9, 1982); Cf. Rev. Rul. 73-460, 1973-2 C.B. 424 (private fixed investment trust holding municipal bonds making semiannual distributions to certificate holders held to be grantor trust for federal income tax purposes. Presumably, the underlying bonds had semiannual coupons that matured during each month of the year; cash from a coupon could therefore be held up to five months). See also James M. Peaslee and David Z. Nirenberg, Federal Income Taxation of Mortgage-Backed Securities (Probus Publishing Co., 1994), at 41.

[9]See Rev. Rul. 78-149, 1978-1 C.B. 448 (power to reinvest proceeds of redeemed municipal obligations in other municipal obligations with same credit rating and final maturity held power to vary the investment of certificate holders); Cf. Rev. Rul. 73-460, *supra* note 8 (power of trustee to accept new obligations in exchange for obligations held by trust pursuant to offer from issuers to refinance existing obligations to prevent default on such obligations held not to be a power that would allow trustee to take advantage of variations in the market).

[10]Rev. Rul. 75-192, *supra* note 6. The limitations on reinvestment imposed by these revenue rulings may restrict the establishment of a reserve fund in a mortgage pass-through trust for any reason other than permitted temporary reinvestment of mortgage loan payments and, possibly, payment of taxes, other governmental charges, and expenses. See Rev. Rul. 73-460, *supra* note 8.

§104.1.2   Other Limited Powers

Although obligations held by a trust generally may not be disposed of to allow the trustee to purchase new obligations, the IRS has allowed the trustee to (1) freely dispose of trust assets and distribute the proceeds;[11] (2) use the proceeds from the sale of pass-through certificates to acquire mortgage loans not identified at the time of sale;[12] (3) acquire substantially similar obligations when there is a failure to deliver obligations pursuant to a contract acquired by the trust on formation that requires bonds to be delivered on a "when, as, and if issued" basis;[13] (4) to permit a sponsor to substitute new mortgage loans for defective mortgage loans (that is, mortgage loans that do not meet certain representations and warranties when transferred to the trust) within a limited period of time;[14] and (5) expand the size of the trust for a limited period of time after the initial issuance of certificates to meet increased market demands by investors.[15]

§104.1.3   Power to Modify the Terms of a Mortgage Loan

If a mortgage loan provides that its terms may be changed under certain circumstances by the mortgagee or its successor (for example, the trustee), and

---

[11]Rev. Rul 78-149, *supra* note 9.

[12]Rev. Rul. 75-192, *supra* note 6.

[13]Rev. Rul. 86-92, 1986-2 C.B. 214.

[14]Rev. Rul. 71-399, *supra* §103 note 5 (defective mortgage loans backing participation certificates held in a pool represented by Freddie Mac PCs may, within a two-year period beginning on date of purchase of participation certificates, be either repurchased by seller or replaced with similar mortgages). Under the facts of Rev. Rul. 71-399, the replacement mortgage loans had to be in substantially similar amounts to the defective mortgage loans they replaced and "of a quality acceptable to FHLMC." By comparison, most pooling and servicing agreements require replacement mortgage loans to have principal balances approximately equal to the principal balances of the defective loans they replace; any difference is corrected with a cash payment. In addition, replacement mortgage loans usually are required to meet the same representations and warranties as the defective loans they replace.

Pooling and servicing agreements usually require the seller to repurchase a defective mortgage loan upon a breach of a representation or a warranty at any time throughout the life of the mortgage loan. In contrast, substitution of defective loans usually is allowed for a period of 90 to 120 days. Cf. Rev. Rul. 70-544, *supra* §103 note 5 (120 days); Rev. Rul. 70-545, *supra* §103 note 5 (120 days); Rev. Rul. 84-10, *supra* §103 note 5 (120 days). The IRS has provided little guidance for determining which representations or warranties with respect to a mortgage loan, when violated, cause the mortgage loan to be considered "defective." A typical pooling and servicing agreement will provide for representations and warranties as to terms and conditions of the mortgage loans. A breach of such a warranty would cause the loan to be considered defective. In contrast, warranties that are, in effect, guarantees (e.g., a warranty that the mortgagor will always pay his or her mortgage loan) are unusual. Therefore, if a pooling and servicing agreement provides for such warranties, there is a risk that, when the warranty is breached, the mortgage may not be considered "defective" within the meaning of the published rulings cited above. Whether this would lead to a conclusion that there is a power to vary the trust's investment is unclear.

[15]Rev. Rul. 80-96, *supra* §103 note 5 (ultimate size of a pool of mortgage loans backing Freddie Mac PCs adjusted to meet increased or decreased market demands; adjustments made no later than date of first remittance check to holders of PCs). See also Priv. Ltr. Rul. 8918026 (May 9, 1989) (depositor's power to expand size of trust during four-month start-up period will not allow depositor to take advantage of market fluctuations in value of securities for the benefit of unit holders because added securities must be as close to identical to existing securities as is practicable).

the exercise by the trustee of its power to make such a change would be considered a power to vary the investment of the certificate holders, the pooling and servicing agreement should preclude the trustee from exercising such power or require the trustee to dispose of the mortgage loan. In some instances, however, simply stating how the trustee is to exercise its power may be appropriate. For example, if a mortgage loan has a legally enforceable due-on-sale clause, requiring the trustee to enforce it should not be considered as causing the trustee to exercise a power to vary the investment of the certificate holders. Enforcing a due-on-sale clause is effectively disposing of the mortgage loan, which the trustee is free to do at any time.[16] Requiring the trustee to enforce a due-on-sale clause is therefore tantamount to requiring the trustee to dispose of the mortgage loan upon the sale of the underlying property by the mortgagor. Similarly, if the terms of a mortgage loan allow the trustee to foreclose on a defaulting mortgagor, the pooling and servicing agreement should require the trustee to sell the property securing the defaulted mortgage loan and, if possible, seek a deficiency judgment. Any powers vested in the trustee to maximize the recovery on a foreclosure should not be considered powers to vary the investment of the certificate holders if they facilitate the disposition of the property securing the mortgage loan.[17]

§104.2   The Prohibition Against Multiple Class Trusts

The second essential requirement for classification as a fixed investment trust is that, with certain limited exceptions, the trust cannot have multiple classes of ownership interests. This requirement was prompted by the attempt to develop in 1983 and 1984 so-called "fast-pay, slow-pay" pass-through trusts. In a typical fast-pay, slow-pay pass-through trust, the trust would issue four classes of pass-through certificates representing interests in a pool of single class pass-through securities, such as Ginnie Mae certificates. All of the payments (including pre-payments) from the Ginnie Mae certificates would be distributed first to the Class A certificates (excluding an amount of such payments necessary to pay stated interest on the Class B and C certificates) until they were retired. The Class B certificates would then receive all of the payments from the Ginnie Mae certificates (excluding an amount of such payments necessary to pay stated interest on the Class C certificates) until they were retired and then the Class C certificates would receive all of the payments. Finally, upon the retirement of the Class C certificates, the Class D certificates would receive all of the remaining payments from the Ginnie Mae certificates. One of the benefits of this fast-pay, slow-pay structure was a limited amount of call protection for the Class B, C, and D certificate holders: even though principal was paid on the mortgages underlying the Ginnie Mae certificates, the B, C, and D classes would not receive principal distributions (and, in the case of the Class D certificates, payments of accrued interest) until principal

---

[16]See Rev. Rul. 78-149, *supra* note 9.

[17]For example, the trustee may maintain the property during foreclosure proceedings to increase the liquidation proceeds. If the trustee holds the property for speculation however, the trustee may be considered as having substituted one investment (the mortgage loan) for another investment (the property) to take advantage of market value fluctuations and may therefore be considered as having exercised a power to vary the investment.

on the prior classes had been paid. In other words, the B, C, and D certificates had a limited protection from prepayments on the mortgage loans underlying the Ginnie Mae certificates.[18]

The trustee in a fast-pay, slow-pay trust did not have any power to vary the investment of the certificate holders. Consequently, the arrangement was a valid trust under the entity classification regulations relating to the definition of a "trust" for federal income tax purposes[19] as they existed before April 29, 1984.[20] The IRS objected to this structure, however, believing that it departed from the "traditional" fixed investment trust in that the interests of the beneficiaries were "not undivided, but diverse."[21] The IRS viewed a fast-pay, slow-pay trust as providing the beneficiaries with "economic and legal interests that could not be acquired through direct investment in the trust assets."[22] As a result, shortly after the first public offering on February 28, 1984, of a fast-pay, slow-pay trust by the Sears Mortgage Securities Corporation, the IRS issued proposed amendments to Reg. §301.7701-4(c) to deny trust status to any investment trust with multiple classes of ownership. The regulations were modified accordingly and finalized on March 21, 1986.[23] As finally adopted, the regulations provide that an investment trust with multiple classes of beneficial ownership that does not allow the trustee any power to vary the investment of the certificate holders will be classified as a trust for federal income tax purposes only "if the trust is formed to facilitate direct investment in the assets of the trust and the existence of multiple classes of ownership interests is incidental to that purpose."[24] Two types of transactions that fall within this exception are discussed in the next two sections.

§105 STRUCTURING A TRUST ISSUING A SENIOR CLASS AND A SUBORDINATED CLASS OF PASS-THROUGH CERTIFICATES

The standard for determining whether a trust arrangement facilitates direct investment in the assets of the trust seems to be the extent to which the interests of the

---

[18]The combination of the triple-A credit rating available for pass-through certificates guaranteed by agencies such as Ginnie Mae, Fannie Mae and Freddie Mac, and the limited call protection created by using a fast-pay, slow-pay structure became so desirable to institutional investors that the multiple-class fast-pay, slow-pay structure became the basic structure for offering collateralized mortgage obligations. See discussion at §§201 and 202.

[19]See T.D. 6503, 1960-2 C.B. 409.

[20]See LR-68-84 (Notice of Proposed Rulemaking), 1984-1 C.B. 777; T.D. 8080, 1986-1 C.B. 371.

[21]T.D. 8080, 1986-1 C.B. 371.

[22]Id. The IRS has never clearly explained the abuse potential in a fast-pay, slow-pay trust. The reasons set forth in T.D. 8080 imply that the IRS was concerned that the rules governing the taxation of trust income were not sophisticated enough to facilitate potentially complex allocations of income from commercial investments. Id.

[23]T.D. 8080, *supra* note 21. These regulations are commonly referred to as the "Sears Regulations."

[24]Reg. §301.7701-4(c)(1). The IRS announced in Rev. Proc. 83-52, 1983-2 C.B. 569, *superseded by* Rev. Proc. 89-3, 1989-1 C.B. 761, that it would not rule on the classification for federal income tax purposes of an investment trust with multiple classes of beneficial ownership. In T.D. 8080, *supra* note 21,

certificate holders in a multiple-class trust could be reproduced without the use of the trust.[1] One example provided by the regulations involves the creation of a trust that holds a pool of mortgage loans in which the beneficial interests are represented by a senior class and a subordinated class of pass-through certificates.[2] The interests in the mortgage loans represented by both classes of certificates are identical.[3] In the event of default on the mortgage loans, however, the subordinated certificate holders will subordinate their right to receive principal and interest on the mortgage loans to the right of the senior certificate holders. The sponsor of the trust sells the senior certificates and retains the subordinated certificates. The example states that, although the trust has multiple classes of ownership interests, the interests of the certificate holders are "substantially equivalent" to undivided interests in the mortgage loans, "coupled with a limited recourse guarantee" running from the sponsor to the senior certificate holders. As a result, the multiple-class structure is incidental to facilitating a direct investment in the mortgage loans. Accordingly, such an arrangement will be classified as a fixed investment trust rather than as an association taxable as a corporation or partnership.

§105.1   *Transferring the Subordinated Certificates*

Example (2) of Reg. §301.7701-4(c)(2) states that the sponsor retains the subordinated certificate, although retention of the subordinated certificate by the sponsor is not specifically required by example (2). The Treasury decision issued with the regulations, however, implies that retention of the subordinated certificate is required when it states that the creation of a senior class and a subordinated class of interests in a trust holding mortgage loans facilitates the direct investment in the mortgage loans "where the subordinated interest is retained as a security device by the originator of the mortgages, and is in lieu of a direct guarantee to investors."[4] Possibly because of this language in the Treasury decision, sponsors of senior-subordinated trusts were concerned that example (2) of Reg. §301.7701-

---

however, the IRS stated that further guidance as to the application of Reg. §301.7701-4(c) would be provided through the administrative ruling process. To date, there has been only one private letter ruling explaining the multiple-class prohibition or the exceptions thereto. See §105.1.

   §105   [1] T.D. 8080, *supra* §104 note 21.

   [2] Reg. §301.7701-4(c)(2) example (2). A second example provided by the regulations discusses the classification of an investment trust holding stripped bonds. Id. example (4); see §106.

   [3] In one example, the senior certificate holders are entitled to receive 90 percent of the interest and principal from the mortgage loans and the subordinated certificate holders are entitled to receive 10 percent of the interest and principal payments. In addition, both classes of certificate holders receive prepayments on the mortgage loans proportionately, rather than under a fast-pay, slow-pay structure. Id. example (2).

   The undivided portion of the mortgage loans owned by each class of a senior-subordinated trust depends almost entirely on the amount of subordination a rating agency will require to give the senior class the desired credit rating. Application of example (2) should not depend on the level of subordination.

   [4] T.D. 8080, *supra* §104 note 21, at 7.

4(c)(2) prohibits the direct transfer of the subordinated certificate to an unrelated third party.[5]

These concerns were confirmed in Priv. Ltr. Rul. 8929030,[6] in which the IRS ruled that transfer of the subordinated interest in a senior-subordinated trust formed to hold motor vehicle installment sale contracts would cause the trust to fail as a fixed investment trust. The ruling states that a transaction in which the subordinated interest is retained is

> viewed as one in which [the sponsor] pledged its interest in the pooled mortgages to guarantee timely pass-through payments on the [senior] certificates. On the other hand, sale of the subordinated interest does not facilitate investment in the pool by a single class of investors, but rather offers to investors two classes of interests to satisfy diverse (or varied) investment objectives. This arrangement is not similar to one in which the creator of a mortgage pool guarantees timely pass-through payments to investors.

In the period from 1986 to 1991, the IRS was successful in scaring off practitioners who questioned the implied restrictions on transferring the subordinated interest in a senior-subordinated grantor trust. Then, however, the IRS was ensnared by its own trap. The S&L debacle in the late 1980s led to creation of the Resolution Trust Corporation (RTC). RTC ended up owning a substantial amount of subordinated interests in senior-subordinated trusts, along with other mortgage and asset-backed securities. Moreover, the RTC's primary objective was to timely and efficiently dispose of all of its assets. Because of the IRS position, the RTC-run thrifts could not transfer the subordinated interests in these trusts. The IRS decided to beat a hasty retreat, first ruling privately, then publicly, that there was no restriction on transferring the subordinated interests.

Rev. Rul. 92-31[7] considers the same basic facts as Priv. Ltr. Rul. 8929030 — a trust formed to hold automobile installment sale contracts. The ruling holds that the analysis in example (2) of Reg. §301.7701-4(c)(2) is still applicable even when the subordinated certificates are transferred. Therefore, the ruling holds that the "sponsor's sale of the subordinated certificates to investors does not affect the classification of the investment trust as a trust for federal income tax purposes."

---

[5]Cf. H.R. No. 841, 99th Cong., 2d Sess. II-228, n.7 (1986) (hereafter referred to as the 1986 Conf. Rep.) and identical language in the Staff of the Joint Comm. on Tax'n, General Explanation of the Tax Reform Act of 1986 (hereinafter referred to as the 1986 Blue Book) at 415, n.70. The language in T.D. 8080 may be interpreted to imply that the senior-subordinated trust exception to the general prohibition against multiple-class trusts was intended to assist mortgage originators (such as S&L institutions) in selling their mortgage loans in the secondary market. As a practical matter, a sponsor (such as an investment banking firm) holding a pool of mortgage loans originated by another person and intending to sell the mortgage loans in the secondary market would not want to retain a subordinated interest in the mortgage loans. Consequently, most senior-subordinated trusts are sponsored by the originator of the mortgage loans. There is no similar limitation if the senior-subordinated trust is formed as a REMIC.

[6]April 21, 1989.

[7]1992-1 C.B. 434.

§105.2   Structural Considerations in Creating a Senior-Subordinated Pass-Through Trust

The simplest subordination feature requires the trustee to distribute to the subordinated certificate holders payments otherwise distributable on any distribution date to the subordinated certificate holders in the event of default or delinquencies on the mortgage loans (the "basic subordination feature").[8] This type of subordination provides little real credit support because it works only on a month-by-month basis. That is, the cash flow on subordinated interest in one period is not available to pay losses in later periods. Instead, sponsors have increased the credit support of the basic subordination feature by creating a reserve fund.

§105.2.1   Creating a Reserve Fund

If a reserve fund is used, the pooling and servicing agreement generally will require all distributions allocable to the subordinate certificate holders on any distribution date and not distributed to the senior certificate holders pursuant to the basic subordination feature to be paid into a reserve fund until the reserve fund reaches a specified level (the "required amount"). Thereafter, the subordinated certificate holder's percentage interest in the mortgage pool cash flows (other than those paid to the senior certificate holders pursuant to the basic subordination feature) will be paid to the subordinated certificate holders. If late payments or defaults on mortgage loans create a shortfall in the amount of required distributions to the senior certificate holders on any distribution date that cannot be eliminated by the basic subordination feature, distributions will be made to the senior certificate holders out of the reserve fund. To the extent the reserve fund is insufficient to cover required distributions to the senior certificate holders on any distribution date, the shortfall will be considered a required distribution on the next distribution date and will be paid out of amounts otherwise payable to the subordinate certificate holders. If the amount of the reserve fund, after distributions are made to the senior certificate holders on any distribution date, is less than the required amount, distributions of principal otherwise distributable to the subordinated certificate holders on such distribution date will be deposited into the reserve fund to the extent of the shortfall. If the amount of the reserve fund exceeds the required amount after distributions are made to the senior certificate holders, the excess will be distributed pro rata to the subordinated certificate holders.[9]

---

[8]For example, the rights of the subordinated certificate holders to receive distributions with respect to the mortgage loans may be subordinate to the rights of the senior certificate holders to the extent of a fixed percentage (i.e., the initial percentage interest of the subordinated certificate holders in the pool of mortgage loans) (the "subordinated amount") of the aggregate outstanding principal balance of the mortgage loans as of the date the mortgage loans are transferred to the trust. The undivided interest of the subordinated certificate holders in the pool of mortgage loans does not change as long as the subordinated certificates are outstanding.

[9]Id. The amount required to be in a reserve fund on any distribution date usually is determined by the rating agency.

The presence of a reserve fund in a senior-subordinated trust should not jeopardize the classification of the trust for federal income tax purposes.[10] In order to give "clean" opinions, however, counsel have usually required the reserve fund to be held outside the trust. Typically, to achieve this result, the sponsor will establish a separate account with the trustee for the reserve fund. The trustee will have a perfected security interest granted by the sponsor (as the subordinated certificate holder) in favor of the senior certificate holders in the reserve fund assets other than reinvestment income.[11] At all times, the subordinated certificate holders will be considered the beneficial owners of the reserve fund.[12]

§105.2.2   Inability to Use Shifting Interest Structure in a Grantor Trust

A "shifting interest" structure requires the trustee to distribute all prepayments of principal to the senior certificate holders for a stated period of time in addition to the required distributions to the senior certificate holders. The preferential right of the senior certificate holders to receive distributions of principal prepayments will have the effect of accelerating the amortization of the senior certificates while

---

[10] In Gen. Couns. Mem. 38,311 (Mar. 18, 1980), the IRS questioned whether the presence of a reserve fund in a senior-subordinated trust would "destroy the fixed investment character of the trust." The IRS concluded that it would not but stated that the trustee could reinvest the money in the reserve fund only in a manner consistent with Rev. Rul. 75-192 (see §104 note 10, *supra*). Although Gen. Couns. Mem. 39,040 (Sept. 27, 1983), revoked Gen. Couns. Mem. 38,311, thereby again raising the issue of the classification for federal income tax purposes of a senior-subordinated trust with a reserve fund, it is believed that Gen. Couns. Mem. 38,311 was revoked because of the multiple-class nature of the trust described in Gen. Couns. Mem. 38,311 and not because of the reserve fund feature.

[11] Any reinvestment income is typically distributed to the subordinated certificate holders on each distribution date.

[12] The reserve fund itself will be classified as a trust for federal income tax purposes unless some person has a power to vary the investment of the beneficial owners of the reserve fund or unless the reserve fund is structured with multiple classes of beneficial ownership in violation of Reg. §301.7701-4(c)(2). If the reserve fund violates these requirements it could be treated as an association taxable as a corporation for federal income tax purposes. Even so, as long as a corporate sponsor owns all the beneficial interests in the reserve fund, and is subject to the filing of a consolidated return, it should be treated as a member of the sponsor's affiliated group, and the income from the trust should be subject to tax only at the consolidated group level. After the issuance of Rev. Rul. 92-32, 1992-1 C.B. 434, permitting transfers of subordinated interests in senior-subordinated grantor trusts, the most vexing question to arise was how to treat the reserve fund. If a thrift has a subordinated interest it wants to sell, and the subordinated interest has an associated outside reserve fund, the easiest transaction would be simply to sell the subordinated interest to the public. Each holder in the subordinated interest, however, would also have an interest in the reserve fund. Arguably, there is a power to vary the reserve fund's investment because the reserve fund's corpus is invested and reinvested. Therefore, practitioners have been concerned that the reserve fund might be classified as an association or a partnership for federal income tax purposes. This concern has led sponsors to structure this, and similar transactions, as private placements in which interests in the subordinated interest are not freely transferable. Additionally, the sponsor will try to find one other factor to enable it to conclude that the reserve fund is treated as a partnership for federal income tax purposes. See Reg. §301.7701-2.

increasing the respective interest of the subordinate certificate holders in the trust fund.[13]

The preferential right of the senior certificate holders to receive prepayments of principal would probably cause the trust to be considered to have fast-pay, slow-pay classes in violation of Reg. §301.7701-4(c)(2).[14] Consequently, use of the shifting interest structure is limited to REMICs.[15]

§106   STRUCTURING A TRUST ISSUING STRIPPED CERTIFICATES

A bond issued at any time with interest coupons when there is a separation in ownership between the bond and any coupon that has not yet become payable is a "stripped bond."[1] A "stripped coupon" is any coupon relating to a stripped bond,[2] and a "coupon" is any right to receive interest on a bond, regardless of whether such right is evidenced by a coupon.[3] These definitions are broad enough to cause the rules of Code §1286 to apply to any non-pro rata separation[4] of principal or interest payments from the remaining payments of a bond.[5] For example, if the holder of a bond paying principal and interest semiannually for three years sells one semiannual interest payment, the holder will have sold a stripped coupon and retained a stripped bond and as many stripped coupons as there are remaining interest payments. Similarly, if the holder sells a 10 percent interest in one coupon, the same characterization will result. In contrast, if the holder sells one principal payment on the bond, the holder may be considered to have sold a stripped bond and retained as many stripped bonds and stripped coupons as there are remaining payments of principal and interest on the bond.

There are many reasons why a holder of a bond may prefer to strip the bond and sell the stripped components rather than the whole bond. A bank holding a pool of mortgage loans bearing interest at the rate of 10 percent may wish to sell

---

[13]The reduction of the interest of the senior certificate holders in the trust fund results from the reduction of the percentage of all scheduled payments of principal on the mortgage loans to which the senior certificate holders are entitled. Generally, this percentage is determined by dividing the unpaid principal balance of the senior certificates as of the distribution date by the aggregate principal balance of all mortgage loans outstanding as of a specified date (usually the last distribution date) prior to the distribution date.

[14]Reg. §301.7701-4(c)(1) and (c)(2) example (1). See discussion at §104.2.

[15]See discussion in text *infra* at §305.1.6.

§106   [1]Code §1286(e)(2).

[2]Code §1286(e)(3).

[3]Code §1286(e)(5).

[4]If a participation in a bond were sold evidencing a right to 50 percent of all of the principal and interest payments, there is no separation in ownership between the bond (or a principal payment on the bond) and a corresponding payment of interest. As a result, the rules of Code §1286 should not apply.

[5]For purposes of the stripped bond rules of Code §1286, a "bond" is defined as any bond, debenture, note, or certificate or other evidence of indebtedness. Code §1286(e)(1).

such loans at a time when the interest rate on newly originated fixed-rate mortgage loans is 7 percent. Rather than selling the mortgage loans at a premium, the bank may sell the mortgage loans at par by stripping a portion of each interest payment. Alternatively, the bank may determine that the mortgage loans are more efficiently priced by stripping all of the interest payments and selling them separately from the principal payments. The purchaser of the interest payments (the "interest-only" or "IO" piece) is buying a hedge against rising market interest rates. That is, if the interest rates on newly originated fixed-rate mortgage loans increase, the mortgage loans in the pool will prepay more slowly than the prepayment rate used in determining the purchase price of the IO piece. As a result, the IO piece will remain outstanding longer, thereby increasing its yield to the purchaser. By comparison, the principal payments (the "principal-only" or "PO" piece) are being sold at a discount from the aggregate amount of such payments and the purchaser is therefore buying a hedge against declining interest rates. As interest rates on newly originated fixed-rate mortgage loans decrease, the mortgage loans in the pool will prepay at a faster rate than the prepayment rate used in determining the purchase price of the PO piece. If the PO piece prepays at a rate faster than that assumed at the time of sale, its yield to the purchaser will increase.[6]

If mortgage loans in a pool have a variety of stated interest rates, the sponsor may strip the interest payments on the mortgage loans before transferring them to the trustee so that pass-through certificates representing the beneficial ownership of the mortgage loans pay interest to their holders at a single fixed rate rather than at a weighted average pass-through rate of all the interest rates on the mortgage loans in the pool. A stripped portion of all the interest payments on the mortgage loans in a pool that exceeds a reasonable fee for servicing such loans is often referred to as a "retained yield" and its creation will cause the mortgage loans in the pool to be recharacterized as stripped bonds and stripped coupons.[7]

§106.1   The Coupon-Stripping Exception in Reg. §301.7701-4(c)(2)

The classification of an investment trust issuing multiple classes of certificates that represent stripped bonds and stripped coupons as a trust for federal income

---

[6]Principal and interest strips from mortgage loans may be sold in any combination depending on market demand. See e.g., the Prospectus Supplement dated October 23, 1986, for the Fannie Mae Stripped Mortgage Backed Securities, SMBS Series F,G,H, and I — Fixed Rate GPM Residential Mortgage Loans (four classes of pass-through certificates entitling holders to 50 percent of the principal payments on the underlying mortgage loans and 36 percent of the interest payments; four classes of pass-through certificates entitling holders to 50 percent of the principal payments on the underlying mortgage loans and 64 percent of the interest payments). This Fannie Mae SMBS issuance was the first public offering of stripped mortgage loans.

[7]See §107.2.2 for a discussion of the tax consequences of holding stripped bonds and stripped coupons.

tax purposes is specifically permitted by Reg. §301.7701-4(c)(2).[8] The facts of example (4) of the Sears Regulations involve an investment trust issuing pass-through certificates, each of which represents the right to receive a particular payment from a specified bond held by the trust.[9] Because the interest of each certificate holder is different, the trust has multiple classes of ownership. The example states, however, that the multiple classes provide each certificate holder with a direct ownership interest in a stripped bond or a stripped coupon and, therefore, the multiple classes of trust interests "merely facilitate direct investment in the assets held by the trust."[10]

Structuring an investment trust holding stripped bonds and coupons to comply with the Sears Regulations appears simple at first blush, although even the simplest transaction may raise questions. For example, suppose a bank holds a pool of mortgage loans that pay interest at a rate equal to the three-month London Interbank Offered Rate (LIBOR) plus 300 basis points. Each of the mortgage loans is subject to a maximum interest rate (cap) of 15 percent. The bank, as seller and servicer, transfers the mortgage loans to a trustee pursuant to a pooling and servicing agreement and retains the right to receive all the interest payments on the mortgage loans in excess of the payments representing three-month LIBOR. Until three-month LIBOR rises above 12 percent, the bank will receive 300 basis points of each interest payment on the mortgage loans. Once three-month LIBOR reaches 12 percent, however, the interest rate on the mortgage loans will be at the cap of 15 percent and, to the extent three-month LIBOR exceeds 12 percent, the amount of interest the bank will receive with respect to its retained yield will decrease so that the certificate holders may continue to receive interest at three-month LIBOR. The bank's retained yield is effectively subordinated to the certificate holders' right to receive interest at three-month LIBOR to the extent three-month LIBOR exceeds 12 percent. Although there is no supporting authority on point, the bank's retained yield (which gets "squeezed" as the loan interest rate approaches its cap) should be viewed either as a coupon strip (i.e., an ownership interest in an interest coupon) or a class of ownership interest that facilitates a direct investment in the trust's assets (i.e., by giving investors greater protection against rising interest rates).[11] Because of the lack of authority, many practitioners either try to avoid such a "squeezed" interest or try to ensure that, if such an interest is retained by the servicer, it represents reasonable compensation for

---

[8] Reg. §301.7701-4(c)(2) example (4).

[9] This example was crafted to distinguish stripping transactions involving U.S. Treasury bonds such as the Merrill Lynch Treasury Investment Growth Receipts (TIGRs) from the fast-pay, slow-pay mortgage trust.

[10] This rationale has prompted counsel to allow a trust to issue a senior class and a subordinated class of pass-through certificates representing interests in a pool of stripped mortgage loans thereby combining example (4) with example (2) of Reg. §301.7701-4(c)(2).

[11] Reg. §301.7701-4(c)(2) examples (2) and (4). The same issue arises if the bank owns an interest in the trust representing such stripped interest, or if it receives the interest income from the mortgage loans corresponding to the stripped interest as an excess servicing fee.

services rendered rather than an ownership interest in the mortgage loans (or the trust).[12]

Alternatively, suppose the bank retains the right to receive 300 basis points of interest on the outstanding principal balance of each mortgage loan in all events. Regardless of whether three-month LIBOR equals 0 or 15 percent, the bank will receive 300 basis points of interest on the mortgage loans.[13] As a result, the bank's retained yield is not subordinated to the certificate holders in any way. For the same reason, the bank is not bearing the risk that three-month LIBOR will exceed 12 percent. As a result, the bank should clearly be considered as having retained a stripped interest that represents identifiable payments on the mortgage loans in accordance with example (4) of Reg. §301.7701-4(c)(2).

§107   TAX CONSEQUENCES TO THE PARTIES IN A GRANTOR TRUST TRANSACTION

§107.1   *Seller*

For federal income tax purposes, the transfer of mortgage loans to a trustee pursuant to a pooling and servicing agreement in exchange for pass-through certificates evidencing beneficial ownership of the mortgage loans is not a recognition event for the transferor (hereinafter referred to as the "sponsor"). Instead, assuming the transfer of the pass-through certificates will represent the transfer of enough benefits and burdens of ownership of the mortgage loans to qualify the transfer as a sale or other taxable disposition of the mortgage loans for federal income tax purposes, the sponsor will have a recognition event under Code §1001 when it sells the pass-through certificates.[1] In such a sale, the sponsor will generally recognize ordinary income or loss[2] with respect to each mortgage loan in the pool

---

[12]See explanation of servicing fee arrangements at §102. The IRS might argue that the existence of the bank's retained interest is contingent on three-month LIBOR not exceeding 12 percent and, therefore, the bank's retained interest does not represent ownership of a "particular payment" with respect to the mortgage loans in the trust as required by example (4) of the regulations. In comparison, the existence of the bank's retained interest as well as its yield are also contingent on the prepayment of the mortgage loans, a contingency implicitly contemplated by the regulations. Thus, the type of payment contingencies with respect to a certificate that will prevent that certificate from representing the right to receive an identifiable payment on assets in a trust in violation of example (4) of the regulations is unclear.

[13]That is, because the mortgage loans pay three-month LIBOR plus 300 basis points, the minimum rate at which interest is payable on the mortgage loans is 3 percent.

§107   [1]See Rev. Rul. 84-10, *supra* §103 note 5; Rev. Rul. 77-349, *supra* §103 note 5; Rev. Rul. 71-399, *supra* §103 note 5; Rev. Rul. 70-545, *supra* §103 note 5; Rev. Rul. 70-544, *supra* §103 note 5.

[2]The sponsor of a trust issuing pass-through certificates usually either originates the mortgage loans or buys and sells mortgage loans in the ordinary course of its trade or business or is a bank. Consequently, the pass-through certificates represent ownership of noncapital assets. See Code §§1221 and 582(c)(1). If the mortgage loans were considered capital assets in the hands of the sponsor, however, the sponsor may be required to treat any gain recognized as ordinary income to the extent of accrued market discount. Code §1276(a)(1); see discussion of market discount at §107.2.4.

equal to the difference between an allocable portion[3] of the proceeds of the sale of the pass-through certificates and the sponsor's adjusted basis in each mortgage loan.[4]

EXAMPLE

Assume that a sponsor owns two 30-year mortgage loans, A and B. Loan A has an adjusted tax basis of $100,000 and a 10 percent coupon. Loan B has an adjusted tax basis of $100,000 and a 12 percent coupon. Current market interest rates are 11 percent and loan A is worth $97,500 while loan B is worth $102,500. The sponsor contributes loan A and loan B to a trust and receives in return one class of pass-through certificates bearing interest at a weighted average pass-through rate of 11.5 percent. The sponsor then sells the pass-through certificates for $200,000 cash. On the sale of the pass-through certificates the sponsor is treated as having a $2,500 loss on the sale of loan A and a $2,500 gain on the sale of loan B.

---

§107.1.1   Taxation of Sponsor Holding Stripped Obligations and Allocation of Adjusted Basis

If the sponsor transfers the mortgage loans to the trustee and retains a portion of the principal or interest payments (or both), thereby causing the assets held by the trustee to be characterized as stripped bonds and stripped coupons, the rules of Code §1286 will apply to the sponsor.[5] As a result, the sponsor may be required to include in gross income all accrued but not previously included market discount[6] and interest on all of the mortgage loans. The sponsor's adjusted basis in each mortgage loan would be increased by the amount so included and would be allocated both to the stripped interest retained by the sponsor and the stripped

---

[3]The proceeds from the sale of the pass-through certificates will be allocated among all of the mortgage loans based on their relative fair market values. If the loans in the pool have different coupons, different amounts of gain or loss may be recognized on each loan. Rev. Rul. 71-399, *supra* §103 note 5. If the sponsor sells less than all of the pass-through certificates, the same allocation of the proceeds will be made to each of the mortgage loans held by the trustee and, to determine the sponsor's gain or loss realized from the sale, the sponsor's adjusted basis in the mortgage loans will be allocated to the certificates retained by the sponsor and those sold based on their relative fair market values. Cf. Code §1286(b).

[4]See authorities cited in note 1, *supra*.

[5]The same rules would apply regardless of whether the sponsor retains an ownership interest in the mortgage loans or is considered as retaining an ownership interest in the mortgage loans through an excess servicing fee.

[6]This rule was codified by the Tax Reform Act of 1986, Pub. L. No. 99-514 (hereinafter referred to as the 1986 Act), in Code §1286(b) and is applicable to debt instruments acquired after October 22, 1986.

interests sold (as represented by the pass-through certificates) based on their relative fair market values.[7]

§107.1.2 Allocation of Sponsor's Adjusted Basis to Subordinated Certificate

No specific authority describes how a sponsor allocates adjusted basis to the senior and subordinated interests in a senior-subordinated grantor trust,[8] but general tax principles dictate that basis is allocated according to the respective fair market value of the senior and subordinated interests at the time the senior interest is sold.[9] Although Reg. §301.7701-4(c)(2) analogizes a senior-subordinated grantor trust to a single class trust with a limited recourse guarantee running from the subordinated interest holder to the senior interest holder, no direct authority exists for treating part of the sale price of the subordinated interest as a guarantee fee.

§107.1.3 Transferring the Benefits and Burdens of Ownership: Sale of the Mortgage Loans versus Borrowing Against the Mortgage Loans

Whether a transfer of property is to be treated as a sale for federal income tax purposes depends on whether substantial incidents of ownership have been transferred with the property.[10] If money or property is received for the transfer of property and the transferor does not relinquish substantial incidents of ownership, the transferor may be considered to have pledged the property as security for a loan.[11] For example, if a sponsor transfers mortgage loans to a trustee in exchange for pass-through certificates but retains substantial incidents of ownership of the mortgage loans, the pass-through certificates may be considered as representing indebtedness of the transferor secured by the mortgage loans held by the trustee rather than undivided ownership interests in the mortgage loans.

Neither the courts nor the IRS has delineated a clear test for determining when a transfer is a sale rather than a borrowing for federal income tax purposes. Instead, authorities examine a number of incidents of ownership that vary in importance without articulating a hard and fast rule. In the context of a sale of

---

[7]For the federal income tax consequences to the sponsor of the retention of a stripped interest, see discussion at §107.2.2 regarding the federal income tax consequences to certificate holders of the ownership of stripped obligations.

[8]For a discussion of the federal income taxation of a subordinated certificate holder, see §107.2.

[9]This result is indicated in several private letter rulings that permit the sponsor to allocate basis, taking into account the coupon rate on the subordinated piece as well as the risks of default. Priv. Ltr. Rul. 8618065 (Feb. 7, 1986).

[10]See United Surgical Steel Co. v. Commissioner, 54 T.C. 1215 (1970), *acq.*, 1971-2 C.B. 3; Town & Country Food Co. v. Commissioner, 51 T.C. 1049 (1969), *acq.*, 1969-49 C.B. 5; Gen. Couns. Mem. 34,602 (Sept. 9, 1971); Gen Couns. Mem. 39,584 (Dec. 3, 1986).

[11]Id.

·an installment obligation, the IRS has stated that the two most important incidents of ownership supporting the conclusion that a sale has occurred are the ability of the purchaser to dispose of the obligation and the shifting to the purchaser of the potential for profit or risk of loss from the fluctuations in value of the obligation as a result of the changes in interest rates.[12]

Each time a grantor trust issuing pass-through certificates is structured, counsel may be faced with new features that leave some of the benefits and burdens of ownership of the mortgage loans with the sponsor. The IRS has adopted sale treatment on the transfer of pass-through certificates when the following features have been present: (1) the retention of an optional call by the sponsor with respect to the certificates when the outstanding principal balance of the mortgage loans is 10 percent or less of the initial mortgage loan pool principal balance (a "clean-up" call);[13] (2) the retention by the sponsor of prepayment penalties, late payment charges, and assumption fees with respect to the mortgage loans as part of the sponsor's servicing fee;[14] (3) responsibility of the sponsor to pay (out of its servicing fee) the trustee's fees and mortgage insurance premiums;[15] (4) right of the sponsor to guarantee the payment of principal and interest on the mortgage loans;[16] and (5) right of the sponsor to make advances to the certificate holders in the event of late payments or defaults by the mortgagors.[17]

Another issue, not addressed in any published ruling, involves liquidity contracts in pools holding convertible loans. A "convertible loan" is a loan with a floating interest rate that is convertible at the holder's option into a fixed-rate loan. When such loans are put in a mortgage trust, the sponsor will typically also contribute a liquidity contract to the trust. Pursuant to the liquidity contract, the

---

[12]Gen. Couns. Mem. 34,602, *supra* note 10. Similarly, if a transferor sells an installment obligation and guarantees the transferee against loss, the purported sale will be treated as such for federal income tax purposes if the purchaser may benefit from any increase in value of the obligation, the purchaser has the unfettered ability to dispose of the obligation, and the purchase price of the obligation is fixed when the transfer occurs. Id.

[13]Rev. Rul. 84-10, *supra* §103 note 5 (Fannie Mae, as trustee of a pool of mortgage loans, may call the MBS representing ownership of such pool when outstanding principal balance of mortgage loans is 10 percent or less of original principal balance); Rev. Rul. 80-96, *supra* §103 note 5 (Freddie Mac allowed to call PCs when principal balance of mortgage loans represented by such PCs is 10 percent or less of original principal balance). Although these rulings do not specifically require the call to be exercisable when 10 percent or less of the outstanding principal balance of the mortgage loans remains unpaid, they imply that any call right held by the sponsor should not be exercisable before the outstanding principal balance of the mortgage loans has decreased to a level at which the costs of servicing the loans and paying the expenses of the trust are equal to or greater than the fees being generated.

Generally, for financial accounting purposes, a clean-up call to prevent servicing costs from becoming unreasonable, by itself, does not prevent a transfer of receivables from being considered a sale. See FASB 77, n.4, *supra* §102 note 6.

[14]Rev. Rul. 77-349, *supra* §103 note 5.

[15]Id.

[16]Rev. Rul. 84-10, *supra* §103 note 5 (Fannie Mae guarantees timely payment of principal and interest on its MBS); Rev. Rul. 70-545, *supra* §103 note 5 (Ginnie Mae guarantees timely payment of principal and interest on its fully modified pass-through certificates).

[17]Rev. Rul. 84-10, *supra* §103 note 5 (originator of a pool of mortgage loans represented by Fannie Mae MBS acting as servicer must remit scheduled monthly payments of principal and interest to Fannie Mae whether or not collected).

sponsor is required to repurchase from the trust any loan converted by the holder into a fixed-rate loan. The reason for such a contract is that the certificate holders do not want fixed-rate loans in the pool. The issue is whether the trust owns the mortgages or a debt instrument issued by the sponsor.

Although the matter is not entirely clear, certificate holders (rather than the sponsor) should be considered for federal income tax purposes as owning the convertible loans despite the presence of the liquidity contract. This is because the sponsor has no control over whether the mortgagor will exercise the conversion option. Exercise of the conversion option depends primarily on market conditions, that is, the difference between fixed and floating mortgage interest rates at any given time. In addition to the lack of sponsor control over the conversion, the certificate holders continue to bear the entire risk of loss on the mortgages as well as the economic benefit of a rise in interest rates. Accordingly, most counsel will opine that the certificate holders own the mortgage loans despite the presence of a liquidity contract.

If, because of a retention of significant benefits and burdens of ownership of the mortgage loans, the seller is considered to continue to own such loans, the chief impact is on certificate holders who, for certain federal income tax purposes, receive beneficial treatment if a certain amount of their assets are real estate mortgages such as REITs and thrifts. If the seller owns the mortgages, the pass-through certificate is not considered a qualifying asset for such purchasers.[18] Accordingly, care should be taken to ensure that a purported sale will be treated as such for federal income tax purposes.

Counsel structuring a grantor trust issuing pass-through certificates may also want to avoid seller guarantees of yield or certificate amortization, as well as credit support features that go beyond simply advancing funds in the event of late payments or defaults by the mortgagors. The presence of one or more of these features may cause the pass-through certificates to be considered as debt of the sponsor for federal income tax purposes. In addition, if the sponsor is also the servicer, the servicing functions of the sponsor should be similar to those considered typical according to industry standards.

§107.2 Certificate Holders

The owner of a pass-through certificate representing an undivided ownership interest in a pool of mortgage loans held by the trustee of a grantor trust will be considered for federal income tax purposes as the owner of an undivided interest in the corpus and income of the entire trust.[19] As a result, a certificate holder using the cash method of accounting will include in gross income its pro rata share of interest, prepayment penalties, assumption fees, late payment charges,

---

[18]See §109. The other primary impact is that the seller will not recognize gain or loss on the transaction.

[19]See e.g., Rev. Rul. 84-10, *supra* §103 note 3; Rev. Rul. 77-349, *supra* §103 note 5; Rev. Rul. 61-175, *supra* §103 note 3. See also Reg. §1.671-3(a)(1).

and any other items of income when they are collected by the servicer.[20] A certificate holder using the accrual method of accounting will include in gross income its pro rata share of all items of income as they become due.[21] If the certificate represents the subordinated interest in a senior-subordinated grantor trust, the certificate holder would disregard the subordination feature and include the items of income of the trust in gross income pursuant to such certificate holder's method of accounting. To the extent any amounts are paid to the senior certificate holders as a result of the basic subordination feature or from a reserve fund, the subordinated certificate holder should be able to claim a bad debt deduction under Code §166.[22]

Expenses of the trust (such as reasonable servicing fees) deductible under Code §162 or §212 will be taken into account by the certificate holders to the extent allowable[23] in accordance with each certificate holder's method of accounting.[24]

The price paid for a certificate by a holder will be allocated to such holder's undivided interest in each mortgage loan in the pool based on each mortgage loan's relative fair market value.[25] As a result, a certificate holder may be considered to have purchased its undivided interest in each mortgage loan at a market discount or at a premium.[26] In addition, if mortgage loans were considered issued at an original issue discount, certificate holders may have to include a pro rata portion of such discount in gross income.[27]

§107.2.1 Original Issue Discount

The rules of the Code requiring current accrual of original issue discount (Code §§1271 through 1273 and 1275) are applicable to mortgage loans made to individuals on or after March 2, 1984.[28] These rules define original issue discount (OID) as the excess of the "stated redemption price at maturity" of a debt instrument over its "issue price."[29] In the case of a self-amortizing installment obligation,[30] such as a mortgage loan, final Treasury regulations issued under the original

---

[20]Rev. Rul. 77-349, *supra* §103 note 5. See also Rev. Rul. 84-10, *supra* §103 note 5; Rev. Rul. 71-399, *supra* §103 note 5; Rev. Rul. 70-545, *supra* §103 note 5.

[21]Rev. Rul. 77-349, *supra* §103 note 5; Rev. Rul. 71-399, *supra* §103 note 5.

[22]See Reg. §1.166-9. See also Gen. Couns. Mem. 38,311, *supra* §105 note 10.

[23]Certificate holders that are individuals may be limited by Code §67 which allows a deduction for "miscellaneous" itemized deductions only to the extent they exceed 2 percent of adjusted gross income. "Miscellaneous" itemized deductions include Code §212 expenses, i.e., expenses for the production of income paid by an individual.

[24]See authorities cited in §103 note 5, *supra*.

[25]The IRS's published rulings clearly imply that no amount is allocated to a guarantee of the mortgage loans or certificates or to mortgage pool insurance. Cf. authorities cited in §103 note 5, *supra*.

[26]See authorities cited in note 3, *supra*, and discussion at §107.2.4.

[27]Id.

[28]Code §1272(a)(2)(D).

[29]Code §1273(a)(1).

[30]A "self-amortizing installment obligation" is defined generally as an obligation that calls for equal payments of principal and qualified stated interest that are unconditionally payable at least annually during the entire term of the debt instrument with no significant additional payment required at maturity. Reg. §1.1273-1(e)(2).

discount provisions of the Code (the "Final OID Regulations")[31] define "stated redemption price at maturity" as the sum of all payments made under the debt instrument other than "qualified stated interest" payments.[32] A "qualified stated interest" payment generally is defined as a payment equal to the product of the outstanding principal balance of a debt instrument and either (1) a single fixed rate of interest, (2) one or more qualified floating rates, (3) a single objective rate, (4) a single fixed rate and one or more qualified floating rates, or (5) a single fixed rate and a qualified inverse floating rate,[33] which is actually and unconditionally payable at least annually throughout the entire term of the debt instrument.[34]

Mortgage loans may be considered as issued with OID if the mortgage originator charges points or similar charges or if some or all of the interest payable on the mortgage loan does not meet the definition of qualified stated interest.[35] Although points paid by the mortgagor that are considered reasonable by the standards of local mortgage lenders will be considered prepaid interest that is deductible when paid by a cash method taxpayer under Code §461(g)(2), such points will reduce the issue price of the mortgage loan and possibly create OID.[36] This OID will not be subject to current inclusion under Code §1272(a)(1) if it is considered de minimis.[37]

Often, the interest payments on a mortgage loan will not meet the definition of qualified stated interest (QSI) payment. For example, if a variable rate mortgage loan provides for an initial below-market interest rate (a "teaser" rate or an "interest holiday") for a fixed period of time, and the resulting foregone interest exceeds a de minimis amount, then stated interest on the mortgage loan may be treated entirely as OID rather than QSI.

Generally, the holder of a debt instrument issued with OID must include in gross income the sum of the daily portion of OID for each day during the taxable

---

[31]The final OID regulations were published in the Federal Register on February 2, 1994, and generally are applicable to debt instruments issued on or after April 4, 1994. The final OID regulations may be relied on with respect to all debt instruments issued on or after December 22, 1992. Alternatively, the proposed OID regulations, published in the Federal Register on December 22, 1992, may be relied upon with respect to all debt instruments issued on or after December 22, 1992, and before April 4, 1994. The 1992 proposed regulations superseded an earlier set of regulations proposed in April 1986 that would have applied to debt instruments issued after July 1, 1982.

[32]Reg. §1.1273-1(b).

[33]Reg. §§1.1273-1(c) and 1.1275-5.

[34]Reg. §1.1273-1(c).

[35]If mortgage loans in a pool are considered to be stripped bonds and stripped coupons, each of such stripped obligations will be considered a zero coupon bond under Code §1286(a), and therefore, the OID rules would apply to the mortgage loans.

[36]Reg. §1.1273-2(g)(2).

[37]OID will be considered de minimis if it is less than one-quarter of 1 percent of the debt instrument's stated redemption price at maturity multiplied by the number of complete years to maturity. Code §1273(a)(3). For installment obligations, the OID will be considered de minimis if it is less than one-quarter of 1 percent of the stated redemption price at maturity multiplied by the weighted average maturity of the debt instrument. Reg. §1.1273-1(d)(3). The weighted average maturity of an installment obligation is defined as the sum of the number of full years until each payment multiplied by a fraction equal to the amount of payment divided by the stated redemption price at maturity. Reg. §1.1273-1(e)(3). Alternatively, if the installment obligation calls for payments of principal no more rapidly than a self-amortizing installment obligation, OID will be considered de minimis if it is less than one-sixth of 1 percent of the stated redemption price at maturity multiplied by the number of full years from the issue date to final maturity. Reg. §1.1273-1(d)(3).

year that the holder held such debt instrument.[38] The daily portions of OID are determined by allocating to each day during any accrual period[39] its ratable portion of the amount of OID allocable to that accrual period. In general, the amount of OID allocable to any accrual period is the product of the adjusted issue price[40] of the debt instrument at the beginning of that accrual period and the yield to maturity of the debt instrument,[41] reduced (but not below zero) by payments of qualified stated interest allocable to that accrual period.[42] Because this general rule does not take into account the acceleration of payments on a debt instrument as a result of unscheduled prepayments, Congress, in the 1986 Act, enacted Code §1272(a)(6), which determines the accrual of OID on a debt instrument on which payments may be accelerated as a result of prepayments on other obligations securing such debt instrument.[43] Literally, this rule does not apply to mortgage loans held by the trustee of a grantor trust because the prepayments of mortgage loans do not depend on the prepayments of other obligations securing the loans. It does apply, however, to qualified mortgages held by a REMIC.[44] Assuming that Code §1272(a)(6) does not apply to mortgage loans, the prepayment of mortgage loans will not be taken into account in determining the accrual of OID on such mortgage loans. As a result, prepayments will generate gain. Although the gain may be considered ordinary income,[45] it will not be considered accelerated OID.[46]

---

[38]Code §1272(a)(1).

[39]In the case of mortgage loans that pay or accrue interest based on monthly payment dates, the accrual period is one month. See Reg. §1.1272-1(b)(1)(ii).

[40]The adjusted issue price of any debt instrument at the beginning of the first accrual period is its issue price. The issue price of a mortgage loan generally is the price paid by the first buyer, i.e., the amount advanced by the lender. Reg. §1.1273-2(a). The adjusted issue price of an installment obligation (such as a mortgage loan) at the beginning of a subsequent accrual period is the adjusted issue price at the beginning of the immediately preceding accrual period, plus the amount of OID allocable to that accrual period and reduced by any payments made on the obligation during the immediately preceding accrual period other than payments of qualified stated interest. Reg. §1.1275-1(b).

[41]Generally, the yield to maturity of a debt instrument is the interest rate that, when used to determine the present value of all payments to be made on the debt instrument, would produce the issue price of the debt instrument. Reg. §1.1272-(b)(1)(i).

[42]Reg. §1.1272-1(b)(3).

[43]Code §1272(a)(6)(C). Under Code §1272(a)(6)(A), the daily portion of OID will be determined by allocating to each day in the accrual period such day's ratable portion of the excess of the sum of (1) the present value of all remaining payments (regardless of how denominated) under the debt instrument as of the close of the accrual period and (2) the payments made during the accrual period of amounts included in the stated redemption price at maturity, over the adjusted issue price of the debt instrument at the beginning of the accrual period. To determine the present value of all future payments as of the close of the accrual period, the original yield to maturity is used and is calculated assuming that the obligations securing the debt instrument will prepay at a certain rate (the "prepayment assumption"). Code §1272(a)(6)(B). The legislative history of Code §1272(a)(6) indicates that the prepayment assumption will be that used in pricing the debt instrument. See generally the 1986 Blue Book, *supra* §105 note 5, at 426. The application of Code §1272(a)(6) is discussed in Chapter 6.

[44]Code §1272(a)(6)(C)(i). The rule also specifically applies to regular interest in a REMIC. Id.

[45]Code §1271(a)(1) treats amounts received on retirement of a debt instrument as amounts received in an exchange, and therefore any gain generated on the prepayment of an obligation to which it applies would be considered capital gain. Code §1271(a)(1) does not apply to any obligation issued by a natural person (such as a residential mortgage loan). Code §1271(b)(1).

[46]Under Code §1272(a)(6), prepayments generally would accelerate the inclusion of OID. See discussions at §§502 and 503 regarding the application of Code §1272(a)(6) and the effect of prepayments on the accrual of OID.

If a certificate holder is considered to have purchased an undivided interest in a mortgage loan issued with OID at a price that is less than the remaining stated redemption price at maturity but greater than the "revised issue price" (i.e., the sum of the issue price of the mortgage loan and the total OID previously included in the gross income of all prior holders of such undivided interest reduced by payments prior to the purchase of amounts included in the stated redemption price at maturity), the certificate holder will be considered as having purchased such undivided interest at an acquisition premium.[47] This premium may be used to proportionately offset the accrual of OID.[48]

§107.2.2   Stripped Mortgage Loans

Code §1286(a) provides that a stripped bond or stripped coupon is treated by the purchaser as a bond originally issued on the purchase date and having OID equal to the excess of the stated redemption price at maturity in the case of a stripped bond or, in the case of a stripped coupon, the amount payable on the due date of the coupon over the portion of the purchase price allocable to the stripped bond or the stripped coupon.

Stripped bonds and stripped coupons may result from either (1) the formal separation of principal and interest payments or (2) a deemed separation of such payments. A deemed separation will result, for example, when mortgage loans are sold to a trust owned by third-party investors in which the mortgage originator continues to service the mortgages for a fee deemed to exceed (for federal income tax purposes) reasonable compensation for services.[49] If the compensation is unreasonable, the excess is treated as a stripped coupon and the mortgages (and interest thereon) are treated as a stripped bond. For example, assume a Bank sells $100 million of 10 percent mortgage loans with a tax basis of $100 million to a Trust. Assume further that the Trust issues Class A certificates with a 6 percent coupon rate of interest for a price of $100 million. Finally, assume that the Bank continues to service the mortgage loan portfolio for the Trust. For performing these services, the Bank will receive a monthly servicing fee equal to the product of 400 basis points and one-twelfth of the principal balance of each mortgage loan at the beginning of each monthly accrual period. If a fee of only 25 basis points represents reasonable compensation for the Bank's services, the additional 375 basis points per loan that the Bank receives will be treated as a stripped coupon. Recharacterizing the Bank's fee as a stripped coupon causes the Class A certificates to be treated as a stripped bond.

Recharacterizing the Bank's fee as a stripped coupon has three principal tax effects. First, the Bank will be required to allocate its $100 million tax basis in the

---

[47]See Code §1272(a)(7) and Reg. §1.1272-2(b)(3).

[48]Reg. §1.1272-2(a).

[49]In Rev. Rul. 91-46, 1991-2 C.B. 358, the IRS held that a seller/servicer's right to a servicing fee will be treated as compensation for services only to the extent it represents reasonable compensation for services. Any excess, according to the ruling, will be treated as a stripped coupon subject to the rules under Code §1286. This ruling revokes Rev. Rul. 66-314, 1966-2 C.B. 296, in which the IRS held that retained servicing was compensation for services and should not be treated as additional sales proceeds from the sale of the mortgage loans.

mortgage loans[50] between the stripped bond it has sold and its retained interest in the stripped coupon (i.e., its right to receive 375 basis points on each mortgage loan). This allocation is based on the relative fair market values of the stripped bond and stripped coupon on the date such bond and coupon were created. If the fair market value ratio between the stripped bond and stripped coupon is 98 to 2, the Bank's basis allocable to the stripped bond would be $^{98}/_{100}$ × $100 million or $98 million. Thus, the Bank would be forced to recognize a $2 million gain on the sale of the stripped bond (i.e., the $100 million sales proceeds from the Class A certificates less the Bank's $98 million tax basis allocable to such interest). The Bank will also be required to include OID on the stripped coupon by assuming that the issue price of the stripped coupon is equal to the Bank's allocable tax basis in such stripped coupon (i.e., $2 million) and that the stated redemption price at maturity of such coupon is the total amount of payments the Bank anticipates receiving on the coupon based on the relevant prepayment assumption.[51] Although the matter is not entirely clear, aggregating the "fee payments" and treating them as one stripped coupon (i.e., as one debt instrument) for purposes of calculating yield and OID should be reasonable. Prior to the release of final regulations issued under Code §1286 (the "Section 1286 Regulations"), holders of the stripped bond would also account for their stripped bond under OID rules similar to those described above with respect to the stripped coupon.

The Section 1286 Regulations apply the de minimis rule of Code §1273(a)(3) to a stripped bond.[52] To determine whether the stripped bond has OID, the aggregation approach such as that applicable under Code §1275 should also be appropriate. Accordingly, the stripped bond would be treated as a single debt instrument issued on the date it is purchased. The preamble to the Section 1286 Regulations appears to assume that interest payments on a stripped bond may be treated as qualified stated interest payments with respect to the stripped bond. Therefore, interest payments on the stripped bond would be (1) includible as interest income by a holder of such stripped bond (i.e., a Class A certificate holder) based on such holder's method of tax accounting and (2) excluded from the stated redemption price at maturity of such stripped bond for purposes of determining the amount of any OID with respect to such bond. If the discount on the stripped bond is more than the de minimis amount and the rules discussed below with respect to certain mortgage loans do not apply, the stripped bond will be consid-

[50]Under Code §1286(b)(1) the Bank's tax basis in the mortgage loans for purposes of allocating basis under the stripping provisions must include accrued interest and market discount on the mortgages prior to their sale.

[51]If the Bank's compensation is reasonable, the proceeds derived by the Bank from the sale of the Class A certificates would be offset by the Bank's entire tax basis in the mortgage loans. Rev. Proc. 91-50, 1991-2 C.B. 778, allows a seller/servicer to treat certain maximum amounts of servicing as "reasonable" servicing and therefore not subject to the coupon stripping rules. For one- to four-family residential mortgages, these amounts are (1) 25 basis points for conventional fixed-rate mortgages, (2) 44 basis points for mortgages less than one year old that are insured by the FHA, VA, or FmHA, and (3) 37.5 basis points for any other one- to four-family residential mortgages. If the Bank's fee were only 25 basis points, and therefore "reasonable," the Bank would not recognize any gain from the sale of its mortgage loans. Instead, the Bank would include the full amount of the servicing fee each year as ordinary fee income.

[52]Reg. §1.1286-1.

ered to have been issued with OID (equal to the amount of the actual discount on the bond).

The Section 1286 Regulations also provide that certain stripped bonds representing interests in real estate mortgages will be treated under the market discount provisions of Code §1278. The market discount rules will apply if either (1) the amount of OID with respect to the stripped bond is treated as zero under the de minimis rules, or (2) no more than 100 basis points (including any amount of servicing in excess of reasonable servicing) is stripped off the mortgage loans. Accordingly, a stripped bond representing an interest in real estate mortgages may be treated as having no OID even when such a stripped bond has been issued at a true discount, if no more than 100 basis points are stripped off of a mortgage loan (determined on a mortgage-loan-by-mortgage-loan basis). The reason for this rule is administrative simplicity. Prior to the adoption of this rule, practitioners were concerned that, under the coupon stripping rules, retention of an unreasonable servicing fee by a mortgage pool sponsor would result in investors in the mortgage pool holding stripped bonds. This, in turn, would put those investors on an economic accrual method of income inclusion with respect to the mortgage loans. While basically a timing issue, reporting under this method would be complicated, particularly if each mortgage held by the mortgage pool were treated as a stripped bond. The IRS safe harbor avoids these problems, with little harm to the government.

§107.2.3   Super-Premium Certificate

If a pass-through certificate represents the right to receive a disproportionately large amount of interest such that the remaining amount of principal to be received is substantially less than the purchase price of the certificate (a super-premium certificate),[53] and if prepayments on the mortgage loans are faster than the rate of the prepayment assumption, the super-premium certificate may be retired before the certificate holder recovers its basis. If so, the certificate holder should be allowed to recognize a loss, but it is unclear exactly when the loss should be recognized under current law.

The Blue Book for the Tax Reform Act of 1986 indicates that the method of OID accrual prescribed by Code §1272(a)(6) should not allow for negative OID to be allocated to any accrual period.[54] Negative OID may be produced on a super-premium certificate when the prepayments of the mortgage loans occur faster than the rate of the prepayment assumption, thereby causing the sum of the present value of future payments to be made with respect to the certificate as of the end of an accrual period, plus payments made on the certificate during the accrual period, to be less than the adjusted issue price of the certificate at the

---

[53]For example, a certificate representing an IO strip.
[54]See the 1986 Blue Book, *supra* §105 note 5, at 426.

beginning of the accrual period.[55] The Blue Book indicates that this negative amount should be carried over to a subsequent accrual period until enough positive OID has accrued to fully offset the negative amount.[56] This requirement permits the inference that a super-premium certificate holder may recognize a loss under the accrual rules of Code §1272(a)(6) when, assuming the mortgage loans pay down based on their scheduled payments, it becomes impossible for the certificate holder to recover its entire basis. Under this analysis, a super-premium certificate holder should be able to recognize a loss currently only to the extent of the portion of its basis that will not be recovered.[57]

§107.2.4   Premium and Market Discount[58]

Premium. In the event that a certificate holder is considered to have purchased an undivided interest in a mortgage loan at a price that is greater than the certificate holder's undivided portion of the mortgage loan's remaining stated redemption price at maturity, the certificate holder may elect under Code §171 to amortize such excess (premium) under a constant-yield method based on the yield of such mortgage loan to the certificate holder, provided that the mortgage loan was originated after September 27, 1985.[59] If the mortgage loan was originated on or before September 27, 1985, any premium should be allocated among the principal payments on the mortgage loan and allowed as an ordinary loss deduction as principal payments are made.

If a certificate holder is eligible to elect to amortize premium with respect to its undivided interest in a mortgage loan under a constant yield method, it is not clear whether the method of amortization may account for prepayments on the mortgage loan in a manner consistent with the method of accruing OID under Code §1272(a)(6). The legislative history of the 1986 Act, however, may be read

---

[55]For example, suppose a super-premium certificate represents the right to receive 2 percent of all interest payments to be made on a pool of mortgage loans expected to be fully paid down in 12 years, and the entire pool (except for one mortgage loan) fully prepays at the end of the first monthly accrual period. The present value of all future payments at the end of the first accrual period would be de minimis and the amount of payments made with respect to the certificate during the first accrual period would be no more than one month's worth of interest (an amount substantially less than the purchase price). The adjusted issue price of the aggregated debt instrument at the beginning of the first accrual period is its purchase price. As a result, the certificate holder has incurred a loss approximately equal to the difference between its purchase price and the payments received during the first month.

[56]*Supra* note 54.

[57]Because the recovery of a super-premium certificate holder's basis depends on the rate of prepayment of the mortgage loans in the pool, the IRS may argue that the rules regarding contingent payments of principal should be applied to determine the accrual of interest income rather than the rules of Code §1272(a)(6).

[58]The rules regarding premium and market discount do not apply to stripped mortgage loans because stripped bonds and stripped coupons are treated as newly issued with OID each time they are purchased. See Code §1286(a).

[59]The 1986 Act amended the definition of a "bond" in Code §171(d) to include debt obligations of individuals (e.g., mortgage loans) issued after September 27, 1985. Before the 1986 Act, the definition of "bond" required issuance by a corporation.

to allow bond premium on an obligation subject to the rules of Code §1272(a)(6) to be amortized taking into account prepayments in a manner consistent with Code §1272(a)(6).[60]

Market discount. A certificate holder that acquires an undivided interest in lmortgage loans may be subject to the market discount rules of Code §§1276 through 1278 to the extent an undivided interest in a mortgage loan is considered to have been purchased at a market discount. In general, market discount will equal the excess of the certificate holder's allocable portion of the principal balance of the mortgage loan (or, in the case of a mortgage loan issued with OID, the revised issue price, i.e., the sum of the issue price plus accrued OID, reduced by payments of amounts included in the stated redemption price at maturity) over the certificate holder's purchase price.[61] Generally, unless a certificate holder elects to include market discount in income currently,[62] gain on the disposition of a mortgage loan with market discount is treated as ordinary income to the extent such gain does not exceed the accrued market discount not previously included in income.[63] Payments of amounts included in the stated redemption price at maturity will also be included in gross income to the extent such payments do not exceed accrued market discount not previously included in gross income.[64] With respect to a mortgage loan issued with OID, although unclear, payments of amounts included in the stated redemption price at maturity may first be considered accrued but unpaid OID and then accrued market discount not previously included in gross income to the extent of the remainder of the payment.[65]

According to the legislative history of the 1986 Act, until regulations are promulgated, a holder of a market discount bond entitled to installment payments of principal may elect to accrue market discount under one of the following alternatives:

(1)   The amount of market discount that accrues for an accrual period will be calculated on the basis of a constant interest rate (i.e., in a manner similar to the accrual of OID under Code §1272).

---

[60]See the 1986 Conf. Rep., *supra* §105 note 5, at II-842. See also the discussion at §107.2.1 and accompanying notes regarding the applicability of Code §1272(a)(6) to mortgage loans.

[61]Code §1278(a)(1), (a)(2)(A), and (a)(2)(B). The definition of "revised issue price" in Code §1278(a)(4) does not provide for an obligation that makes more than one principal payment (such as a mortgage loan) by subtracting payments of amounts included in the stated redemption price at maturity. In the case of an installment obligation, such as a mortgage loan, however, market discount may be artificially increased unless such a calculation is made.

Market discount will be considered to be zero if it is less than one-quarter of 1 percent of the stated redemption price at maturity of the market discount bond multiplied by the number of complete years to the maturity of the bond. Code §1278(a)(2)(C).

[62]See Code §1278(b).

[63]Code §1276(a)(1).

[64]See Code §1276(a)(3) and the 1986 Conf. Rep., *supra* §105 note 5, at II-842. The characterization rules of Code §1276 apply to market discount obligations issued after July 18, 1984. Code §1276(e). Pass-through certificate holders will therefore be subject to these rules only to the extent they own undivided interests in mortgage loans originated after July 18, 1984.

[65]Cf. Reg. §1.1275-2(a), which treats payments of amounts included in the stated redemption price at maturity first as a payment of accrued OID.

(2) For debt instruments with OID, the amount of market discount that accrues for an accrual period will be equal to the product of the total remaining market discount and a fraction, the numerator of which is the OID for the accrual period and the denominator of which is the total remaining OID at the beginning of the period.

(3) For market discount bonds that do not have OID, the amount of market discount deemed to accrue during an accrual period will be the amount of market discount that bears the same ratio to the total amount of remaining market discount as the amount of stated interest paid during the accrual period bears to the total amount of stated interest remaining to be paid as of the beginning of the accrual period.[66]

If a market discount bond would be subject to the OID accrual rules of Code §1272(a)(6) if it had OID, the prepayment assumption would be used in calculating the accrual of market discount.[67]

Presumably, if a mortgage loan is subject to the OID accrual rules of Code §1272(a)(6), then a certificate holder considered to have purchased an undivided interest in that mortgage loan at a market discount may accrue market discount in a manner similar to the OID accrual rules of Code §1272(a)(6).[68]

§108 TAX CONSEQUENCES TO FOREIGN CERTIFICATE HOLDERS

Consistent with its pass-through nature, interest paid to certificate holders who are foreign persons on a mortgage-backed pass-through certificate is exempt from 30 percent U.S. withholding tax to the extent the interest would be exempt if paid to the foreign investor directly. Thus, if the interest represents interest on a portfolio debt instrument with respect to a foreign investor, the tax exemption of Code §§871(h) and 881(c) and the withholding tax exemptions of Code §§1441(c)(9) and 1442(a) will apply. On the other hand, if the interest is not interest on a portfolio debt instrument, then the 30 percent tax rate (or lower treaty rate) will apply.[1] In order to avail itself of an exemption from U.S. withholding tax or obtain a lower

---

[66]See the 1986 Conf. Rep., *supra* §105 note 5, at II-842. See also Code §1276(b)(3).

[67]Id.

[68]If a certificate holder incurs indebtedness to purchase or carry the certificate, and the certificate holder is deemed to have purchased mortgage loans at a market discount, a portion of the certificate holder's interest deduction with respect to the indebtedness may be deferred. See Code §1277.

§108 [1]See Code §864(c)(2) for rules regarding when payments made with respect to interest on certificates will be considered income effectively connected with the conduct of a trade or business in the U.S. Code §§871(a)(1) and 881(a)(1). In Rev. Rul. 79-251, 1979-2 C.B. 271, the IRS ruled that a Ginnie Mae, mortgage-backed, pass-through certificate was a bond rather than a mortgage for purposes of the U.S.-Netherlands Treaty, as extended to the Netherlands Antilles. This was important because the treaty exempted interest on bonds, but not real estate mortgages, from U.S. withholding tax. The ruling is best viewed as an attempt to foster foreign investment in U.S. mortgages.

withholding rate provided for by a treaty, a foreign investor has to file a copy of IRS Form 1001.[2]

Thus, in structuring a pass-through for sale to foreign investors, the principal inquiry under the portfolio interest exemption is whether the underlying mortgages were issued before the July 18, 1984, effective date of the portfolio interest exemption.[3] Care should also be taken to ensure that no foreign investor owns, actually or constructively, 10 percent or more of the combined voting power of all classes of equity in the issuer of the mortgages[4] and that such holder is not a controlled foreign corporation within the meaning of Code §957 related to the issuer. This is typically only a concern in a transaction involving large commercial mortgages in which the purchaser of a pass-through certificate could be related to the obligor on one of the underlying mortgage loans.[5] Finally, if, as is generally the case, the certificate is a registered obligation, such holder must comply with certification procedures requiring the delivery of a statement on an IRS Form W-8 (or a substantially similar form) signed under penalties of perjury identifying such holder as a foreign person.[6] A domestic counterpart of IRS Form W-8 is IRS Form W-9, which is filed by certain nonexempt taxpayers in order to avoid U.S. backup withholding tax.[7]

§109   TREATMENT OF MORTGAGE PASS-THROUGH CERTIFICATES AS QUALIFYING ASSETS FOR CERTAIN TAXPAYERS INCLUDING THRIFTS AND REITs

Several Code sections provide beneficial treatment to certain taxpayers that invest in mortgage loans. For example, a domestic building and loan association,[1] a mutual savings bank,[2] or any cooperative bank without capital stock organized and operated for mutual purposes and without profit[3] may deduct each year a reasonable addition to a reserve for bad debts pursuant to Code §593(a)(1) provided, among other requirements, that it meets the requirements of Code

---

[2]See Appendix D for a copy of IRS Form 1001.

[3]See generally Reg. §35a.9999-5(e), Q&A 21. For a limited safe harbor from 30 percent withholding for mortgage pass-through certificates, see id., Q&A 22.

[4]Code §§871(h)(3) and 881(c)(3)(B). For purposes of this requirement, Code §871(h)(3) defines a "10-percent shareholder" with respect to a corporation or a partnership. Neither the Code, the regulations, nor the legislative history of the portfolio interest exemption indicate who the "issuer" of a certificate representing ownership of obligations issued by natural persons (e.g., mortgage loans) may be. Consequently, the "issuer" of the certificates may be considered the sponsor, the guarantor of the certificates, or the mortgagors.

[5]Code §881(C)(3)(C). For a discussion of the identity of the "issuer" for purposes of this requirement, see note 3, *supra*.

[6]Code §§871(h)(2)(B) and 881(c)(2)(B). See Appendix D for a copy of IRS Form W-8.

[7]See Appendix D for a copy of IRS Form W-9.

§109   [1]Code §593(a)(1)(A).

[2]Code §593(a)(l)(B).

[3]Code §593(a)(1)(C).

§7701(a)(19)(C).[4] This provision requires that at least 60 percent of the total assets of the domestic building and loan association must consist of cash and certain other obligations including "loans . . . secured by an interest in real property which is . . . residential real property. . . ."[5] If a pass-through certificate represents an interest in such loans, the owner of such certificate will be considered to own "loans secured by an interest in real property" for purposes of Code §7701(a)(19)(C).[6]

The size of the reasonable addition to a reserve for bad debts may be limited to a percentage of the total amount of "qualifying real property loans" held by an entity subject to Code §593.[7] If certificates represent undivided ownership interests in mortgage loans, the certificate holder will be considered to own "qualifying real property loans" within the meaning of Code §593(d).[8]

A certificate holder that is a REIT will also be entitled to "look through" the certificate for purposes of determining ownership of "real estate assets" within the meaning of Code §856(c)(5)(A).[9] In addition, the interest income from the underlying mortgage loans will be considered "interest on obligations secured by mortgages on real property" within the meaning of Code §856(c)(3)(B) for purposes of the gross income requirements applicable to REITs.[10]

Finally, a certificate holder that is a REMIC will be entitled to "look through" to the underlying mortgages to determine if substantially all its assets are qualified mortgages and certain other qualified assets under Code §860D(a)(4) and Code §860G(a)(3).

If certificates represent interests in stripped mortgage loans, no authority addresses whether the character of the stripped interests will be the same as that of the mortgage loans for purposes of the foregoing Code sections. While Code §1286 treats a stripped obligation as a separate obligation for purposes of the Code provisions regarding original issue discount, it is not clear whether this characterization would apply for purposes of the Code sections discussed above. Nevertheless, there is no policy reason not to treat certificates representing undivided ownership interests in stripped mortgage loans as representing interests in "qualifying real property loans" within the meaning of Code §593(d), "real estate assets" within the meaning of Code §856(c)(5)(A), and "loans . . . secured by an

---

[4]Code §593(a)(2).

[5]Code §7701(a)(19)(C).

[6]See e.g., Rev. Rul. 84-10, *supra* §103 note 5 (Fannie Mae certificates); Rev. Rul. 77-349, *supra* §103 note 5 (conventional mortgage-backed pass-through certificates backed by pool insurance); Rev. Rul. 71-399, *supra* §103 note 5 (Freddie Mac certificates); Rev. Rul. 70-545 and Rev. Rul. 70-544, *supra* §103 note 5 (Ginnie Mae certificates).

[7]Code §593(b)(2)(C).

[8]See e.g., Rev. Rul. 84-10, *supra* §103 note 5 (Fannie Mae certificates); Rev. Rul. 77-349, *supra* §103 note 5 (private pass-through certificates); Rev. Rul. 74-169, 1974-1 C.B. 147 (Ginnie Mae certificates), *modifying* Rev. Rul. 70-544 and Rev. Rul. 70-545, *supra* §103 note 5; and Rev. Rul. 71-399, *supra* §103 note 5 (Freddie Mac certificates).

[9]See Rev. Rul. 84-10, *supra* §103 note 5 (Fannie Mae certificates); Rev. Rul. 77-349, *supra* §103 note 5 (private pass-through certificates); Rev. Rul. 74-300, 1974-1 C.B. 169 (Freddie Mac certificates), *modifying* Rev. Rul. 71-399, *supra* §103 note 5; Rev. Rul. 70-545 and Rev. Rul. 70-544, *supra* §103 note 5; (Ginnie Mae certificates).

[10]Id.

interest in real property" within the meaning of Code §7701(a)(19)(C)(v), provided that the mortgage loans qualify for such treatment. Similarly, there is no policy reason not to treat interest income from the stripped obligations as "interest on obligations secured by mortgages on real property" within the meaning of Code §856(c)(3)(B), provided that the interest on the mortgage loans qualifies for such treatment. With respect to a REMIC, the 1986 Conference Report specifically provides that a stripped bond or a stripped coupon is a "qualified mortgage" if the underlying loan is a qualified mortgage.[11]

§110   REPORTING REQUIREMENTS

The trustee of a grantor trust holding mortgage loans is required to file a Form 1041 (U.S. Fiduciary Income Tax Return) with an attached statement identifying the certificate holders and showing the items of income and deduction attributable to the certificate holders.[1] In addition, the trustee is required to report to the IRS and the certificate holder the interest paid to the certificate holder as stated on the certificate (that is, the pass-through rate).[2] The trustee's obligation to report interest income is satisfied if the trustee files a Form 1041 with the IRS and sends a Form K-1 (Form 1041) to the certificate holders containing each certificate holder's allocable share of items of income and deduction.[3] Because neither the Code nor the regulations require the trustee to report the interest payments (including payments with respect to OID) to the certificate holder with respect to each mortgage loan held by the trust,[4] certificate holders may not be able to determine the amount of accrued OID on each mortgage loan unless the information is volunteered by the trustee or the servicer.[5]

Although unclear, the final OID regulations may require that a mortgage loan issued with OID must either (1) bear a legend on the face of the debt instrument, no later than the disposition of the mortgage loan by the first holder, which states the issue price, the amount of OID, the issue date, and the yield to maturity or (2) state the name and either the address or telephone number of a representative of the issuer who will promptly make such information available to holders upon

---

[11]See §307.1.2.

§110   [1]Reg. §1.671-4(a); see generally Rev. Rul. 77-349, *supra* §103 note 5. A certificate holder's actual income may be different because his or her own method of accounting determines the timing of income even though such income is first received by the trust. See also Appendix D for a copy of IRS Form 1041.

[2]Reg. §1.6049-5(a)(6). Under certain circumstances, the trustee is not required to report information with respect to foreign certificate holders. See generally Reg. §1.6049-5(b).

[3]Reg. §1.6049-5(a)(6). Usually, information reporting with respect to interest payments (including payments in respect of OID) required under Code §6049 is done on Form 1099. Form K-1 is used to report to trust beneficiaries.

[4]See Code §6049(b)(2)(A); see also Reg. §1.6049-5(a)(6).

[5]In addition, because no information is required to be provided with respect to each mortgage loan held by the trust, certificate holders may find it difficult if not impossible to properly allocate their bases for determining the amount and accrual of any market discount, the amortization of any premium, and the accrual of OID on stripped mortgage loans.

request. These information reporting requirements are not applicable to stripped bonds or coupons.[6] In addition, if certificates representing mortgage loans issued with OID are sold in a public offering, the trustee may be required to file a Form 8281 setting forth information regarding the size of the issue and the amount of OID.[7]

[6]Reg. §1.1275-3(a). Generally, the legends must set forth the amount of the OID, the issue date, the yield to maturity, and the amount of OID allocable to the short first accrual period. Reg. §1.1275-3(a). In informal discussions during the spring of 1989, the IRS indicated it is considering issuing a notice to clarify that no legending on stripped obligations is necessary.

[7]Reg. §1.1275-3(b)(2). See Stand. Fed. Tax Rep. (CCH) ¶32,844A. This reporting requirement does not apply with respect to a public offering of stripped bonds and stripped coupons. Reg. §1.1275-3(b)(4); see also IRS Announcement 86-22, I.R.B. 1986-9, at 34.

Other information reporting requirements to which a trustee may be subject are found in Code §6050H (returns relating to mortgage interest received in trade or business from individuals) and Code §6050J (returns relating to foreclosure and abandonment of security).

2

Collateralized Mortgage Obligations

§201 REASONS TO USE A CMO

There are typically two categories of transactions that are done as non-REMIC (real estate mortgage investment conduit) collateralized mortgage obligations (CMOs): (1) transactions that cannot be done as REMICs and (2) transactions in which the collateral consequences of making a REMIC election (chiefly recognition of gain) render the CMO a better alternative.

§201.1 Transactions that Cannot Be Done as REMICs

This class of transactions includes those in which the mortgage-backed securities (MBS) do not qualify as REMIC interests or in which the underlying collateral is not clearly a qualified mortgage under Code §860G(a)(3). Examples of the former group of transactions include those in which the interest rate on the proposed MBS is not clearly a fixed rate, a qualifying variable rate, or a qualified interest portion under Code §860G(a)(1)(B).[1] For example, an issuer may want to

---

§201 [1]See §305.

issue a REMIC regular interest when the interest rate increases with increases in the price of gold. An instrument with such a rate would not qualify as a regular interest.[2] Nevertheless, there is authority that an instrument with such an interest rate qualifies as a debt instrument for federal income tax purposes.[3]

Examples of transactions in which the underlying collateral is not clearly a qualified mortgage include transactions in which the collateral does not consist of mortgages at all (e.g., automobile loans) and transactions in which there is substantial non-real-estate security for the mortgage loan. Unlike the REMIC, a non-REMIC CMO can be structured using any sort of collateral.

§201.2   Transactions in Which the Collateral Consequences of a REMIC Election Are Undesirable

The CMO is particularly attractive when the holder of the mortgage loans does not want to recognize gain on the creation of the MBS. A REMIC election followed by a sale of some or all of the REMIC interests to the public triggers gain that is recognized either when the REMIC interests are sold or ratably over the life of the retained interests.[4] A non-REMIC CMO transaction, however, if properly structured, results in a financing for federal income tax purposes when no gain is recognized. This can be particularly helpful if the sponsor does not want to recognize immediate gain on the collateral or wants to defer a loss until a later year.

One classic example of an owner of mortgages that wants to issue CMOs rather than REMICs is a real estate investment trust (REIT) because the REIT will not be entitled to flow through tax treatment if more than 30 percent of its gross income is derived from the sale of real estate mortgages held less than four years.[5] Additionally, and more importantly, a pattern of sales raises an issue of whether the REIT is a dealer in mortgages. If so, any gain on the mortgage sales would be subject to a 100 percent prohibited transactions tax.[6] Thus, several REITs formed in the mid-1980s to originate mortgage loans and issue MBS issue only non-REMIC CMOs. Of course, a REIT is not precluded from purchasing either REMIC residual or regular interests and several REITs have been formed to make such purchases. Also, some REITs now use non-REIT affiliates to structure and move REMIC interests. These affiliates recognize gain or loss on creation of the REMIC and pay a corporate-level tax on their net income.

A CMO rather than a REMIC also may be attractive when the underlying mortgages are installment obligations originated prior to February 28, 1986, and the holder is a dealer in real estate that reports income on the installment method.[7]

---

[2] See §305.1.3.
[3] Reg. §1.1275-5 example (4).
[4] See *infra* §310.1.
[5] Code §856(c)(4).
[6] Code §857(b)(6).
[7] Code §453(b) now provides that the installment method is not available to dealers in real property, except certain dealers specified in Code §453(1)(2).

A REMIC election will result in the acceleration of the installment sale gain. Issuance of a CMO, however, will be treated as a financing for federal income tax purposes and installment sale gain will be recognized only as the principal on the mortgages is paid.

Finally, an issuer may be entitled to use a favorable method of accounting with respect to mortgage loans that it originates. If the loans are transferred to a REMIC rather than financed with a CMO, this method of accounting will be lost.

§202   TYPICAL CMO STRUCTURE

The typical CMO is a debt instrument issued by a single-purpose corporation or a trust (an "owner trust"). The corporation or trust uses the proceeds from the CMO offering to purchase mortgages. The mortgages in turn serve as security for the CMOs as well as the source of debt service on the CMOs. To perfect the CMO holder's security interest, the mortgage collateral is typically pledged by the issuer to an indenture trustee.

The CMO debt instruments, instead of having a single maturity, bear fast-pay, slow-pay maturities. This creates a degree of call protection for investors. The required tax transparency, that is, elimination of the potential corporate level tax, is achieved through Code §163 interest and original issue discount deductions on the CMOs.[1]

§203   KEY TAX ISSUE: STRUCTURING THE CMO ISSUE SO THAT IT IS RESPECTED AS A FINANCING FOR FEDERAL INCOME TAX PURPOSES

The typical CMO structure described in the previous section seems unobjectionable from a federal income tax standpoint. Thus, borrowing money to finance the purchase of interest-bearing assets is an everyday transaction that raises few significant federal income tax issues. The federal income tax issues in structuring a CMO, however, arise because the level of borrowing is substantial. To understand why, a little background may be helpful.

§203.1   Background

The preferred vehicle for issuing multiple-class MBS is not the CMO but rather the multiple-class pass-through trust. As described above,[1] such a trust is like the

---

§202   [1]CMOs are subject to the taxable mortgage pool rules discussed in Chapter 4.
§203   [1]See §104.2.

single class grantor trust (i.e., the simplest of MBS vehicles) except for the fast-pay, slow-pay feature. Such a multiple-class pass-through trust can be formed with a single pooling and servicing agreement, one trustee to hold the mortgages, no equity, and no mismatching between the timing of payments on the mortgages and payments on the pass-through certificates. Thus, it is the most economically efficient vehicle for reallocating cash flows from a mortgage pool. Moreover, for accounting, regulatory, and tax purposes, the sponsor treats the creation of the trust and sale of the certificates as a sale of the underlying mortgages, which is generally beneficial to the sponsor.

In the early 1980s, at least one taxpayer requested an IRS private letter ruling that a fast-pay, slow-pay trust was a grantor trust under Reg. §301.7701-4(c)(2) and Code §§671 through 679. That effort was unsuccessful, however, and as described above, the IRS first announced a no-ruling policy on multiple-class trusts[2] and then revised the regulations to provide that a multiple-class trust would be treated either as an association taxable as a corporation or as a partnership.[3] This thwarted attempts to form multiple-class pass-through trusts.

The solution to this problem was to use a corporation to purchase the mortgages and to issue fast-pay, slow-pay debt (i.e., CMOs) to finance the purchase. The economics of the transactions first proposed by investment bankers were strikingly similar to the economics of the multiple-class pass-through trust. That is, the most efficient way to structure the CMO was to have no mismatching between cash flows on the mortgages and cash flows on the CMOs. Furthermore, the corporate issuer would have no other equity interest in the mortgages, just as in a multiple-class pass-through trust. Instead, the economies would have been identical to a sale of the mortgages that could (except for the regulations mentioned above) be achieved through a multiple-class pass-through trust.

The two principal tax issues in the proposed transaction described above are still concerns today in structuring a CMO issue.[4] First, in the optimal, economically matched transaction, the CMO issuer's debt-equity ratio was infinite. This raised concerns about whether the CMOs could be viewed as a class of stock in the CMO issuer rather than as debt. Second, the proposed transaction appeared to rely solely on its form as a financing to achieve the desired tax result. A large body of case law holds that substance, not form, governs the treatment of a transaction for federal income tax purposes.[5] In addition, some specific authority

---

[2]Rev. Proc. 83-52, 1983-2 C.B. 569, *superseded by* Rev. Proc. 89-3, 1989-1 C.B. 761.
[3]See §104.2.
[4]Cf. the legislative history of the REMIC provisions:

> Present law is unclear whether interests in a corporation that are denominated as debt are properly treated as indebtedness of the corporation, where substantially all of the assets of the corporation are a single type of property, the corporation is thinly capitalized, and the rights of the owners of the interests mirror, in the aggregate, the characteristics of such property.

H.R. Rep. No. 841, 99th Cong. 2d Sess. (1986) II-222, n.4 (hereinafter referred to as the 1986 Conf. Rep.). Notwithstanding this statement, in a properly structured CMO most counsel will issue a favorable opinion on the tax consequences of the structure.

[5]Gregory v. Helvering, 293 U.S. 465, 35-1 U.S.T.C. ¶9043 (1935); Commissioner v. P.G. Lake, Inc., 356 U.S. 260, 265-267, 58-1 U.S.T.C. ¶9428 (1958); Commissioner v. Court Holding Co., 324 U.S. 331, 334, 45-1 U.S.T.C. ¶9125 (1945).

treated leveraged financings as sales of the underlying property.[6] The concern was that, in substance, the mortgages had been sold (rather than pledged) to the CMO holders using a multiple-class trust that would be treated as an association taxable as a corporation under Reg. §301.7701-4(c)(2).

Given this background, the key tax issues in structuring a CMO are to ensure that the CMOs are treated as debt rather than as equity for federal income tax purposes and that the CMO is not recharacterized as a multiple-class trust. Accordingly, in order to achieve the desired tax transparency, as discussed in detail below, the transaction must be tailored so that it is treated as a financing for federal income tax purposes.

§203.2 Necessity of Equity

The chief defense against both the debt-equity claim and the pledge versus sale claim is to ensure that the CMO issuer has a real economic interest in the underlying mortgage collateral. From a debt-equity standpoint this reduces the issuer's debt-equity ratio to a more reasonable range.[7] From the pledge versus sale standpoint, this equity is helpful in arguing that the issuer has retained enough of the economic bundle of rights in the mortgage collateral to be considered its owner for federal income tax purposes.[8]

Thus, equity becomes the key to structuring a CMO. A typical CMO will be structured so that the equity in the transaction has a minimum value.[9] This level of equity is measured by the value of the excess cash flow on the mortgages after the CMO debt service is paid. It can consist of (1) excess interest on the collateral over interest expense on the CMOs, (2) excess principal on the collateral over principal on the CMOs, or (3) anticipated reinvestment earnings on the collateral cash flows before they are distributed to the CMO owners. The value of this residual is simply what a third-party buyer would pay for it. A major problem in determining if residual value exists is if the residual interest is not sold to a third-party buyer; in such circumstances, the tax practitioner will typically look

---

[6]Elmer v. Commissioner, 65 F. Supp. 568, 3 U.S.T.C. ¶1114; Alworth-Washburn Co. v. Helvering, 67 F.2d 694, 3 U.S.T.C. ¶1167, Thomas Goggan & Bros. v. Commissioner, 45 B.T.A. 218 (1941).

[7]Whether an instrument is debt or equity for federal income tax purposes is a factual question. John Kelley Co. v. Commissioner, 326 U.S. 521, 46-1 U.S.T.C. ¶9133 (1946). Apart from the debt-equity ratio, however, a typical CMO bears all the indicia of "pure" debt. Thus, it has fixed principal and interest (see Code §385(b)(1)); it is usually triple-A rated because it is adequately secured (Code §385(b)(2)); it is nonconvertible (Code §385(b)(4)) and is usually held by independent creditors (Code §385(b)(5)). An instrument can be considered a debt instrument for federal income tax purposes even if the issuer has an extremely high debt-equity ratio. Byerlite Corp. v. Williams, 286 F.2d 285, 61-1 U.S.T.C. ¶9138 (1961); [16,500:1] W. H. Truschel v. Commissioner, 29 T.C. 433 (1957), acq., 1960-2 C.B. 7 [22,000:1].

[8]The distinction between a sale and a pledge of mortgages is discussed at §107.1.3. See also Simon, Selected Federal Income Tax Aspects of Securitizing Debt Obligations, 66 Taxes 897 (December 1988) for an excellent analysis of the pledge versus sale issue.

[9]The minimum value can vary from transaction to transaction according to various other features of the transaction, i.e., timing of collateral cash flow versus CMO cash flow, call features, the right to substitute loans, and other features. A practitioner that does several transactions may find it necessary to settle on a minimum level of equity applied consistently to all his or her clients' transactions.

to an expert to estimate value by discounting the excess cash flows by a discount rate he or she believes a buyer and seller would agree on in the market.

§203.3 What Is Equity?

The practitioners (and corporate lawyers) are often confused as to what constitutes "equity." Suppose, for example, that the sponsor transfers $1 million of cash to a corporation. The corporation then loans the $1 million back to the sponsor pursuant to a demand note. The corporation then issues $100 million of CMOs and uses the proceeds to buy $100 million of Ginnie Mae certificates. Tax equity is typically defined as a corporation's assets (determined based on fair market value) less its liabilities. Here, the corporation has $1 million of equity and a debt-equity ratio of 100 to 1. Historically, however, practitioners have not accepted this sort of structure. They are less concerned about actual cash being contributed to the issuer; instead, they want to see equity that represents the issuer's actual ownership in the mortgages. Such equity kills two birds with one stone: (1) the debt-equity ratio and (2) the pledge versus sale issue.

It is important to note that factors other than debt-equity bear on the tax analysis, including a mismatch of the timing of the cash flows and an ability to call the CMOs before the mortgages are paid off. Thus, while equity is an important consideration, it is not the only consideration.

§203.4 Other Factors

Apart from the equity in a CMO transaction, there are certain other ways to ensure that the IRS will not be successful in challenging the transaction. In general, these mechanisms ensure that the issuer will not be treated as having sold the collateral, that is, the pledge versus sale issue mentioned above.

One device used to avoid sale treatment is a call feature on the CMOs. A typical call feature gives the issuer the right to prepay the CMOs either on a date certain or when their principal balance declines to a predetermined amount. Presumably, the issuer would exercise the call (1) by selling the mortgage collateral and using the proceeds to repay the CMOs or (2) by refinancing the mortgage collateral and using the refinancing proceeds to repay the CMOs.

A call is significant from a federal income tax standpoint because it gives the issuer the ability to profit from a decline in interest rates, that is, it gives the issuer the opportunity to realize gain from the collateral.[10] For example, if a move in interest rates causes the mortgage collateral to be worth more than the face amount of the outstanding CMOs, the issuer can capture the difference as a profit by selling or refinancing the mortgage collateral. This ability to recognize the economic benefit of owning the collateral is an important sign that the issuer actually owns the collateral.

---

[10]Simon, *supra* note 8, at 907 n.84. In the early 1990s, many transactions done in the mid-80s were reaching their call dates. In a declining interest rate environment, the right to call the CMOs was quite valuable, and a semiactive market in these residual interests developed.

A call feature as described above only gives comfort on the ownership question if it is significant. Thus, it is generally thought that a call when only 10 percent of the mortgages are outstanding (i.e., a "clean-up call") gives the user very little "upside" potential. On the other hand, a right to call when between 20 and 40 percent of the mortgages remain is generally thought to be economically significant. Also, if a call premium must be paid to the CMO holders when the call is exercised, this can reduce or eliminate the economic benefit of a call. If the issuer has a right to call the CMOs when 40 percent or more of the collateral is outstanding, this is quite strong evidence of ownership. The price paid for such a call is a higher interest rate on the CMOs. A second method is to provide for mismatching of cash flows. This can involve timing mismatches or real economic mismatches.

A typical timing mismatch arises when payments are made quarterly or semiannually on the CMOs while payments on the collateral are received monthly. Thus, when mortgage principal and interest is received each month, it is invested in short-term instruments that mature before the next CMO payment date. Interest and principal from the mortgages, plus any reinvestment income from the temporary investments, is used to pay principal and interest on the CMOs on such date. If the issuer has been able to reinvest the mortgage principal and interest at a rate higher than that on the CMOs, the issuer is entitled to keep the difference. If the reinvestment rate is lower than the interest rate on the CMOs, then cash that would have otherwise gone to the issuer, typically cash flow from overcollateralization, must be used to pay the CMOs.

This timing mismatch serves two purposes. First, the CMOs look less like the underlying collateral if they pay principal and interest at different intervals. Second, the issuer's ability to make or lose money on the cash flows from the mortgages gives it a greater economic stake in the mortgages.

This timing mismatch, however, is usually undesirable for the same reasons. When a timing mismatch is suggested by the tax adviser, the sponsor will typically respond by suggesting that a guaranteed investment contract (GIC) be used to ensure sufficient cash to pay off the CMOs. A GIC is a contract with a third party who agrees to pay a predetermined interest rate on all money invested pursuant to the contract. For example, if the CMOs bear interest at 9 percent, the GIC would also provide for 9 percent interest. The issuer would be entitled to take monthly mortgage principal and interest, invest it in the GIC, and earn 9 percent until the next CMO payment date. Such a GIC obviously hurts the transaction from an economic mismatch standpoint. Thus, the mortgages and the GIC viewed together in this example mirror the CMOs. Of course, features in the transaction (such as equity or a call) may make it possible to use such a GIC.

The second type of cash flow mismatch is a real economic mismatch, involving different interest rates on the collateral versus the CMOs. Thus, for example, if the mortgages have a fixed interest rate and the CMOs have a floating interest rate, the potential for income or loss to the issuer is significant. This, in turn, is very strong evidence that the issuer owns the collateral.[11] Variations on this theme include, for example, issuing CMOs, half of which carry a floating rate against

[11]Rev. Rul. 78-118, 1978-1 C.B. 219.

fixed rate collateral. This can also be helpful, although obviously less so, as the differences decrease.

Another mismatch occurs when there are different principal amounts of the mortgage collateral and the CMO debt. This can be significant if it represents real economic overcollateralization (if it will be reflected in the value of the issuer's equity in the mortgages) but is much less significant if the values of the mortgages and the CMOs are exactly equal.

§204   CMO DEBT DOES NOT QUALIFY AS AN INTEREST IN THE UNDERLYING MORTGAGES

As a corporate or trust debt obligation, the CMO will not qualify as a real estate asset for various tax purposes including REIT qualification[1] and treatment as a qualified asset for purposes of determining qualification as a "domestic building and loan association" or whether a thrift institution can compute its bad debt deduction according to a percentage of taxable income method.[2] Additionally, CMO debt will not constitute a qualified mortgage for REMIC purposes.[3]

§205   STRUCTURING AN OWNER TRUST AS A TAX PARTNERSHIP

As can be seen from the discussion at §203, the issuer must have an equity interest in the mortgage collateral in order for the CMO to be treated as a financing for federal income tax purposes. A sponsor, however, may not want to own this equity because if it owns 100 percent of the equity, the sponsor will be required to consolidate the issuer's assets and liabilities on its balance sheet. Thus, for example, if the issuer is a corporation under state law and the sponsor owns 100 percent of the corporation's stock, the sponsor will be required to include the corporation's mortgages and CMO debt on its balance sheet. If the sponsor sells enough of the corporation's stock to deconsolidate (usually at least 50 percent), this solves the accounting problem. The sponsor, however, will not be permitted to file a consolidated federal income tax return with the issuer[1] and a corporate level income tax will be incurred on the residual income. The solution to this problem is the "owner trust."

The owner trust, like a corporate CMO issuer, issues CMOs backed by mortgages. It also issues certificates of beneficial ownership that represent ownership

§204   [1]Code §856(c)(3) and (c)(5).
[2]Code §§593(d) and 7701(a)(19)(C).
[3]Code §860G(a)(3); see §307.1.2.
§205   [1]Code §1504 generally requires ownership of at least 80 percent of a corporation's stock before a consolidated federal income tax return can be filed.

44

of the residual. The trust is structured so that it will be treated either as a grantor trust or a tax partnership if it has more than one owner. Therefore, investors can own trust certificates and avoid a corporate level tax on the residual income. Another benefit is that by selling at least 50 percent of the owner trust certificates, a CMO sponsor can remove the CMO debt from its balance sheet. If no one owns more than 50 percent of the trust certificates, the CMO debt effectively disappears for accounting purposes.

As long as only one class of ownership interest in the trust exists (properly structured CMO debt is excluded because it is not an ownership interest) and the trustee has no power to vary the investment of the residual holder (as is normally the case), the owner trust will probably be treated as a grantor trust for federal income tax purposes. Even when there are minor powers to vary the investment, the trust that is not an "investment trust" may still be considered a trust under the principles of Reg. §301.7701-4(a) and (b).[2]

To add certainty to this issue, however, most owner trusts are structured with a partnership "fallback" designed to ensure flow-through tax treatment under the partnership rules even if the trust is not considered a grantor trust. This involves adding three typical terms to the trust agreement:

(1)   Restricting transferability of the beneficial interests in the trust so that the trust is not considered to have free transferability under the partnership classification regulations.[3]
(2)   Specifically providing that the beneficial owners are liable for the debts of the trust so that the trust is not considered to have limited liability under the regulations.[4] The CMO debt is typically non-recourse so that the residual owners do not assume that liability.
(3)   Giving the residual owners (by majority vote) management control over key decisions that the owner trustee must make so that the trust does not have the corporate characteristic of centralized management under the regulations.[5] Typically, the owner trust documents provide that the owner trustee must seek directions from the owners whenever a decision must be made that is not merely ministerial.

Classification as a partnership results in flow-through tax treatment. Some ancillary complications arise such as Code §754 elections to adjust the inside basis of the assets on a transfer of residual interests and the fact that the partnership's rather than the partner's method of accounting governs the timing of income and expense at the partnership level. Nevertheless, these sorts of complications do not outweigh the benefit of achieving a single level of tax on the residual income.

---

[2]See Wyman Building Trust v. Commission, 45 B.T.A. 155 (1941), acq., 1941-2 C.B. 14; Anesthesia Service Medical Group Inc. v. Commissioner, 85 T.C. 1031 (1986), aff'd, 825 F.2d 241, 87-2 U.S.T.C. §9480 (9th Cir. 1987).
[3]See Reg. §301.7701-2(e).
[4]See Reg. §301.7701-2(d).
[5]See Reg. §301.7701-2(c).

3

Real Estate Mortgage Investment Conduits

§301 REASONS TO USE A REMIC

In deciding whether to use a real estate mortgage investment conduit (REMIC), mortgage-backed securities (MBS) transactions should be divided into three types: (1) single-class transactions in which the issuer can be classified as a grantor trust under the rules described at §103, (2) multiple-class transactions in which the issuer can be classified as a grantor trust, and (3) multiple-class transactions that will not qualify under the grantor trust rules and, if structured as multiple-class debt issued by an owner trust, will be treated as a taxable mortgage pool (TMP, as described in Chapter 4).

If the transaction is a single-class transaction that will qualify as a grantor trust ((1) above), a REMIC may not provide a significant advantage. First, the tax treatment to the holders of interests in a REMIC and to the holders of interests in a single-class grantor trust will be substantially similar. Moreover, the trustee's fee for administering a REMIC is generally higher than the trustee's fee for administering a grantor trust because of the additional tax filing requirements associated with a REMIC. A REMIC should be used, however, if (1) the underlying mortgages were issued before July 18, 1984; and (2) some or all of the REMIC's regular interests will be sold to foreign investors. This is because REMIC regular interests are automatically eligible for the portfolio interest exemption regardless of the date of origination of the underlying mortgages.[1] On the other hand, a REMIC will require a residual interest, which is not required with a single-class grantor trust.

If the transaction is a multiple-class transaction that will qualify as a grantor trust ((2) above), a REMIC may provide more of an advantage. Thus, if the multiple

___

§301 [1] H.R. Rep. No. 841, 99th Cong., 2d Sess. (1986) II-237-38, *et seq.* (hereinafter referred to as the 1986 Conf. Rep.).

classes are senior-subordinated classes, a REMIC gives the sponsor greater flexibility to allocate losses between the senior and subordinated classes than does a senior-subordinated grantor trust. In the case of a REMIC, a sponsor may provide that the principal balance of the subordinated class will be "written down" for principal losses on the mortgage loans. This principal write-down will have the effect of changing the percentage interest of the holders of the senior and subordinated classes in principal distributions for subsequent distribution periods. Although the same write-down should be allowed with respect to the subordinated class in a grantor trust, it is unclear under the Sears Regulations[2] whether the initial percentage interest of senior and subordinated certificate holders in a grantor trust must remain fixed (i.e., cannot be altered as a result of principal losses on the mortgage loans). As a result of this uncertainty, a REMIC provides more flexibility for varying sharing percentages with respect to losses than does a grantor trust.

EXAMPLE

An initial sharing ratio in a $100,000 REMIC pool is senior — 90 percent, and subordinated — 10 percent. If a $5,000 loan defaults before any principal payments are made and there is no recovery upon foreclosure, the senior certificate holder would be entitled to a $90,000/$95,000 interest in the remaining mortgages, and the subordinated certificate holder's interest in the mortgages would be reduced to $5,000/$95,000. Thus, in a REMIC, the senior certificate holders will be entitled to 90/95 percent of all principal distributions until the senior loss amount is recovered. In the senior-subordinated grantor trust, however, the sharing ratio of the senior and subordinated interests in the mortgages should remain 90 to 10 at all times. If losses occur, all principal (and, possibly, interest) distributions otherwise payable to the subordinated certificate holders will be payable to the senior certificate holders. These payments by the subordinated certificate holders to the senior certificate holders are payments in the nature of a guarantee. As such, the distribution is analyzed as though the subordinated certificate holders received their distributions of principal and interest equal to 10 percent of the total distribution and then paid this amount to the senior certificate holders.

An additional reason to elect to use a REMIC will exist if one or more of the multiple classes represent a coupon strip. Under the REMIC provisions, both interest-only (IO) and principal-only (PO) classes can be issued as regular interests and taxed as debt instruments under the original issue discount (OID) rules relating to certain prepayable, collateralized debt instruments.[3] The taxation of IO and PO certificates in a grantor trust is not as clear. Thus, the REMIC provides more tax certainty for the regular interest holder.

Finally, if the transaction is a multiple-class transaction that will not qualify as a grantor trust ((3) above), the REMIC probably provides a significant advantage

[2]For an explanation of the Sears Regulations, see §104.2.
[3]See §503.

over the alternative, the non-REMIC collateralized mortgage obligation (CMO). The REMIC probably should be used unless there are specific reasons for using a CMO, such as the ones enumerated at §201 (e.g., interests that will not qualify as REMIC interests, nonqualifying collateral, or installment sale or gain recognition concerns). Unlike a CMO, a REMIC requires no equity, allows exact matching of cash flows (i.e., monthly versus quarterly mismatch is not required), and provides qualifying asset treatment to investors such as thrifts, REITs, and other REMICs. Additionally, no call feature on the debt is required. Finally, as a result of the TMP rules (discussed in Chapter 4), the REMIC is now the sole vehicle for issuing multiple-class fast-pay, slow-pay debt instruments secured by mortgage loans.

The chief drawback to the REMIC election is the potential "toll charge" imposed by the REMIC statute. Thus, creation of a REMIC triggers gain (or loss) inherent in the underlying mortgage collateral. This gain or loss is then recognized over the REMIC's life, if REMIC interests are retained, or immediately, if REMIC interests are sold. Of course, the ability to recognize loss immediately on mortgage collateral can allow the REMIC sponsor some planning options.

§302   TYPICAL REMIC STRUCTURES

There are two typical REMIC structures. The first is a trust (like the owner trust described above) that owns mortgage collateral and issues debt instruments (also referred to as CMOs). The trust is formed pursuant to an owner trust agreement, in which an owner trustee appoints an indenture trustee to hold the collateral on behalf of the owners of the debt instruments. The debt instruments include multiple classes of REMIC regular interests and one class of a "securitized" REMIC residual interest. The latter interest is generally denominated as a bond for local law purposes, but it actually represents the difference between cash flows on the mortgages, if any, and cash flows on the regular interests.

The second typical structure is a multiple-class trust that holds mortgage loans. The trust is formed pursuant to a pooling and servicing agreement between the sponsor and a trustee. Credit enhancement is provided for the mortgage loans through a third party insurer or guarantor or through "internal" credit support such as a senior-subordinated arrangement or a reserve fund. The multiple classes of interest may be fast-pay, slow-pay or senior-subordinated, or they may represent stripped principal and interest on the underlying mortgage loans. They can also be issued in more exotic varieties, including classes of regular interests that relate only to some of the mortgage loans in the pool.

A third structure is the two-tier REMIC. The two-tier REMIC is normally formed if (1) the sponsor wishes to issue an IO regular interest based on a notional principal balance equal to the principal balance of a second class of regular interests,[1] or (2) it is less than perfectly clear that a one-tier structure qualifies under the REMIC rules. Although the REMIC Regulations clarified numerous uncertainties that formerly led to the use of two-tier REMICs, they did not totally

---

§302   [1]See §§305.1.8 and 314.

eliminate the need for two-tier REMICs. The special problems of two-tier REMICs are discussed at §314.

§303   REMIC REQUIREMENTS

In evaluating whether a particular MBS transaction should be done as a REMIC, the basic inquiry is whether it meets the six requirements for REMIC status set forth in Code §860D. Code §860D states that a REMIC is any entity (1) that elects to be treated as a REMIC for the tax year and all prior tax years; (2) in which all of the interests are regular or residual interests; (3) that has one (and only one) class of residual interests; (4) in which, as of the close of the third month beginning after the start-up day and at all times thereafter, substantially all of the assets of which consist of qualified mortgages and permitted investments; (5) that has a tax year that is a calendar year; and (6) with respect to which there are reasonable arrangements to ensure that (a) residual interests in such entity are not held by "disqualified organizations" and (b) information necessary for the application of the tax on disqualified organizations holding residual interests will be made available by the entity. Once it is clear a transaction meets those requirements, then, as discussed at §301, a REMIC should be used unless there is a specific reason for using either the grantor trust or the non-REMIC CMO.

The Code §860D requirements are discussed in more detail in the following paragraphs.

§304   ENTITY REQUIREMENT

A REMIC must be an entity.[1] The term "entity" is not defined in the statute but is very broad. Thus, it includes a partnership, corporation, or trust. It also includes a segregated pool of assets treated as if it were an entity.[2]

§305   REGULAR AND RESIDUAL INTERESTS

All of the interests in the REMIC must be regular or residual interests.[1] This requirement can be troublesome from two standpoints: first, ensuring that interests designed to be regular and residual interests actually meet the statutory definition, and second, ensuring that other rights to receive payments from the REMIC are not "interests" in the REMIC.

§304   [1]Code §860D(a).
[2]Reg. §1.860D-1(c).
§305   [1]Code §860D(a)(2).

§305.1   Regular Interests

A regular interest is defined to mean any interest in a REMIC that is issued on the start-up day with fixed terms and that is designated as a regular interest if:

(1)   such interest unconditionally entitles the holder to receive a specified principal amount (or other similar amount), and

(2)   interest payments (or other similar amounts), if any, with respect to such interest at or before maturity —

    (a)   are payable based on a fixed rate (or to the extent provided in regulations, at a variable rate), or

    (b)   consist of a specified portion of the interest payments on qualified mortgages and such portion does not vary during the period such interest is outstanding.[2]

A regular interest in a REMIC may be issued in the form of debt, stock, an interest in a partnership or trust, or any other form permitted by state law. If a regular interest is issued in a form other than debt, however, it must nevertheless entitle the holder of such interest to a specified amount that would, if the interest were debt, be identified as the fixed principal amount of the debt.[3]

The Technical and Miscellaneous Revenue Act of 1988 (TAMRA)[4] added the requirement that a regular interest be designated as such on the start-up day. The REMIC Regulations (defined at §305.1.1 below) state that this can be done by providing the IRS with certain information required by Reg. §1.860D-l(d)(ii).[5] Presumably, this can be done in the documents creating the regular interest and on the face of the bond or certificate. TAMRA also expanded the permissible interest rates to include an interest rate that consists of a fixed, specified portion of the interest payments on qualified mortgages; see subparagraph (2)(b) above. This permits certain types of interest strips to be treated as regular rather than residual interests.

The definition of "specified portion" is discussed in more detail at §305.1.8 below.

§305.1.1   Fixed-Rate Regular Interests

In the first type of permitted regular interest, the interest payments (or similar amounts) are payable *"based on* a fixed rate." This phrase is not otherwise defined in the Code. Thus, prior to the adoption of the final Treasury regulations issued with respect to REMICs on December 23, 1992 (the "REMIC Regulations"), several issues were open for consideration. The issues described below also exist with

---

[2]Code §860G(a)(1).

[3]Reg. §1.860G-1(b)(4).

[4]Pub. L. No. 100-647 (TAMRA).

[5]Reg. §1.860G-1(a)(i). See also §309 for a description of the information that is required to be reported for REMIC purposes.

respect to REMIC regular interests that have a permissible variable rate. The issues are discussed in this section only because, prior to the issuance of the REMIC Regulations, many tax counsel concluded that these issues did not cause a tax concern because the regular interest rate, although not fixed, was "based on a fixed rate."

The first issue is whether fixed-rate regular interests would qualify as regular interests "based on a fixed rate" if holders of such interests were entitled to call premiums. This issue will normally arise when the underlying mortgages are commercial loans, which themselves carry a call premium, either based on a fixed percentage of the principal amount of the mortgage or payable under a "yield maintenance" formula.[6]

Under the REMIC Regulations, an interest will fail to qualify as a regular interest if the interest entitles the holders to a premium that is determined based on the length of time that the regular interest is outstanding.[7] In contrast, an interest will not fail to qualify as a regular interest solely because the REMIC's organizational documents allocate and pay to its regular interest holders "customary prepayment penalties" that the REMIC receives with respect to its qualified mortgages.[8] Moreover, as long as the allocation is made in the REMIC's organizational documents, prepayment penalties can be paid to regular interest holders (including holders of IO regular interests) in any manner and need not be paid on a straight pass-through basis.[9]

Another issue under the "based on a fixed rate" requirement is whether default interest on a commercial mortgage note can be passed through to holders of fixed-rate regular interests. Prior to the issuance of the REMIC Regulations, strong arguments were advanced for treating a fixed-rate regular interest with rights to default interest as a rate "based on a fixed rate." Although paying default interest to holders of regular interests may be appropriate, the REMIC Regulations do not specifically provide that such payments are permissible. It is possible, however, that this omission is an oversight. To achieve maximum tax comfort, some tax counsel have recommended that default rate interest be "stripped" off the mortgage loans prior to the contribution of such loans to the REMIC. In such case, the "stripped" interest may be sold to the holders of the regular interests as a separate non-REMIC IO security.[10] In this structure, a holder's investment will include two components: (1) a REMIC regular interest (with a principal balance and a fixed interest rate) and (2) a right to the payments on the IO (with respect to default

---

[6]A yield maintenance formula is one where the prepayment premium is sufficient to allow the mortgagee to reinvest the premium payment plus the mortgage principal that is prepaid at current market interest rates and earn a return equal to the return it would have received had the mortgage not been prepaid.

[7]Reg. §1.860G-1(b)(1).

[8]Because tax counsel generally does not know whether a prepayment penalty is "customary," it is standard practice for tax counsel to rely on a representation letter from an underwriter or servicer stating that in the expert opinion of such party, the prepayment penalties with respect to the mortgage loans are customary in the industry. A sample representation letter is included at Appendix C.

[9]Id.

[10]The REMIC Regulations provide that this IO will not be treated as a separate interest in the REMIC. See §305.3.2 below. Payments on this IO to the holders of the regular interests should not be made from a REMIC account.

interest). A holder will be required to allocate a portion of his or her purchase price to the holder's right to receive default interest. As a result of such allocation, the regular interests may be deemed to be issued with OID.[11] Also, holders of such IOs will be required to determine whether the right to the default interest would be treated as "qualifying real property loans" within the meaning of Code §593(d) for holders that are mutual savings banks or domestic building and loan associations, or "real estate assets" within the meaning of Code §856(c)(6)(B) for holders that are REITs.

§305.1.2   Caps and Floors on Regular Interests

The REMIC Regulations provide that a cap or floor that establishes (1) a maximum or minimum rate or (2) a maximum or minimum number of basis points by which the rate may increase or decrease from one accrual or payment period to another (i.e., a periodic cap or floor) or, over the term of the interest (i.e., a lifetime cap or floor), is a permissible cap or floor that will not cause an interest rate to fail to be treated as a qualifying REMIC interest rate. Thus, a regular interest could have an interest rate equal to the weighted average of the interest rates on all the qualified mortgages held by the REMIC (which themselves bear qualifying fixed or variable rates) subject to a cap of 10 percent and a floor of 5 percent. Interest on the qualified mortgages above the cap could be paid to the residual interest holders.

The REMIC Regulations also provide that a qualifying variable rate includes a qualifying variable rate subject to a "funds-available cap."[12] A "funds-available cap" is a limit or ceiling on the amount of interest to be paid on a regular interest in any accrual or payment period that is based on the total amount available for distribution on such distribution date including both principal and interest received by an issuing entity on some or all of the qualified mortgages as well as amounts held in a reserve fund. Although the matter is not entirely clear, it appears that a funds-available cap has to be applied on a period-by-period basis. A funds-available cap will not be treated as a permissible cap, however, to the extent it is being used as a device for creating an otherwise impermissible rate.

One must consider all of the facts and circumstances in determining whether a cap or limit on interest payments is a funds-available cap and not a device for creating an impermissible rate. The following three factors are stated in the REMIC Regulations (or are implied from the relevant examples therein) as relevant in this determination: (1) whether the rate of interest payable to regular interest holders is below the rate payable on the REMIC's qualified mortgages on the start-up day; (2) whether, historically, the rate of interest payable to the regular interest holders has been consistently below that payable on the qualified mortgages; and (3) whether excess interest (the amount of interest collected on the

---

[11]For example, if a holder purchases its investment for $100x and the value on the REMIC's start-up day of the right to receive default interest is $1x, the issue price of the regular interest would be treated as $99x.

[12]Reg. §1.860G-1(a)(3)(v).

qualified mortgages over the amount required to be paid to regular interest holders on a given distribution date) is paid to regular interest holders as principal payments. Although not specifically prohibited, tax counsel have generally not permitted the funds-available cap if either the regular interests or the qualified mortgages bear interest at a fixed rate.

The following examples illustrate permissible and impermissible funds-available caps.

EXAMPLE 1

A sponsor contributes $100x of mortgage loans to a REMIC. The initial weighted average rate on the mortgage loans is the 11th District Cost of Funds Index (COFI) plus 200 basis points (net of servicing fees). The regular interests in the REMIC have a rate equal to the one-month London Interbank Offered Rate (LIBOR) plus 100 basis points and are subject to a funds-available cap. On the start-up day, the weighted average rate on the mortgage loans is 7.5 percent and the rate on the regular interests is 5 percent. In addition, based on historical data, the sponsor does not expect the rate on the regular interests to exceed the rate on the mortgage loans. Under such circumstances, the funds-available cap will be respected as a valid cap and not as a device.[13]

EXAMPLE 2

A sponsor contributes $100x of mortgage loans to a REMIC in return for all of the REMIC's regular and residual interests. The interest rate on the mortgage loans is a rate based on appreciation in the price of gold. The regular interests provide for interest payments at a rate equal to the Prime Rate and subject to a funds-available cap. On the start-up day, the prime rate is equal to 7 percent and the weighted average rate on the mortgage loans (based on the price of gold on such date) is 5 percent. In this instance, a funds-available cap will be considered a device for creating an impermissible rate since (1) the weighted average of the rates on the mortgage loans would not be a permissible rate or cap, and (2) the rate on the regular interests is in-the-money with respect to the cap on the REMIC's start-up day.

§305.1.3 Variable-Rate Regular Interests Treated as Qualified Floating Rates

In addition to an interest rate "based on a fixed rate," the Code also provides that regulations can authorize variable rates. The REMIC Regulations provide

---

[13]Reg. §1.860G-1(a)(3)(v) example 1.

that a qualifying variable rate for REMIC purposes is a "rate that is a 'qualifying variable rate' for purposes of sections 1271 through 1275 and the related regulations." At the time the REMIC Regulations were released, the OID regulations were not yet finalized and the proposed original issue discount regulations issued in December 1992 (the "Proposed OID Regulations")[14] did not use the term "qualifying variable rate." Thus, it was unclear for REMIC transactions in early 1993 whether the aforementioned REMIC provision was intended to permit REMIC regular interests with rates that would be characterized as "variable-rate debt instruments" (which include both qualified floating rates and objective rates) or only interests with rates that constitute "qualified floating rates" under the Proposed OID Regulations. If the "variable-rate debt instrument" definition was intended, a REMIC regular interest could have been issued with a rate based on the price of actively traded property (e.g., the S&P stock index). An additional ambiguity with regard to this provision was whether the definitions of "variable-rate debt instrument" and "qualified floating rate" in the Proposed OID Regulations could be relied upon because the REMIC Regulations refer to Code §§1271 through 1275 and the "related regulations," which implies only final OID regulations. Because of the uncertainty surrounding these issues the IRS issued Notice 93-11, which clarified that, solely for purposes of Code §860G(a)(1), only a qualified floating rate set at a current value would constitute a qualifying variable rate for REMIC regular interests.[15] The notice also specifically stated that taxpayers could rely on the notice until the Proposed OID Regulations were finalized.

On April 15, 1994, the IRS issued temporary and proposed regulations ("New Temporary Regulations" and "New Proposed Regulations," respectively, and together referred to as the "New Regulations") under the REMIC rules of the Code. The New Regulations (1) conform the definition of a "qualifying variable rate" included in the REMIC Regulations to the definition of a "qualified floating rate" included in the final OID regulations issued by the IRS on January 27, 1994 (the "Final OID Regulations"), and (2) clarify that IO regular interests may, in certain circumstances, be supported by other IO regular interests from a lower-tier REMIC.

As noted above, the New Temporary Regulations are designed to conform the definition of "qualifying variable rate" in the REMIC Regulations to the definition of a "qualified floating rate" under the meaning of the Final OID Regulations (without regard to rules in the Final OID Regulations regarding caps, floors, and certain multipliers). A "qualified floating rate" is defined in the Final OID Regulations as any variable rate in which variations in the value of such rate can reasonably be expected to measure contemporaneous variations in the cost of newly borrowed funds in the currency in which the debt instrument is denominated.

Based on the New Temporary Regulations, objective rates generally will not be qualifying variable rates for REMIC purposes. For example, a rate tied to the price of actively traded property (e.g., the S&P index) will not be a qualifying variable rate for REMIC purposes.

[14]Released by the IRS on December 21, 1992.
[15]Notice 93-11, IRB 1993-6, 42.

The New Proposed Regulations contain two basic parts. The first part incorpo-rates the New Temporary Regulations described above. The second part clarifies the definition of IO regular interests. Under the REMIC Regulations, IO regular interests must provide for interest equal to a specified portion of the interest payable on qualified mortgages that pay interest at a fixed rate or a qualifying variable rate (i.e., a qualified floating rate or a weighted average rate). Because this definition did not specifically cover IO regular interests in two-tier REMIC structures, tax lawyers asked the IRS to clarify that IO regular interests could qualify even if such interests pay interest based on a specified portion of the interest on other IO regular interests that are themselves based on fixed or qualify-ing variable rate qualified mortgages.

The New Proposed Regulations address this concern by providing that IO regular interests that pay a fixed percentage of the interest received on other IO regular interests ("Lower-Tier IOs") will qualify as valid REMIC regular interests if the Lower-Tier IOs bear a rate of interest that can be expressed as (1) a fixed percentage of the interest payable on qualified mortgages that themselves pay interest at a fixed rate or a qualifying variable rate, (2) a fixed number of basis points on all or some of the qualified mortgage loans, or (3) a fixed or a qualifying variable rate on some or all of the qualified mortgages in excess of a fixed number of basis points or in excess of a qualifying variable rate. The New Proposed Regulations therefore clarify that IO regular interests created in upper-tier REMICs that reflect 100 percent of the interest received on "WAC IOs" created in lower-tier REMICs are valid IO interest rates.

It should be noted, however, that the New Proposed Regulations only apply to IO regular interests issued by REMICs that consist solely of regular interests from other REMICs. Thus, REMICs that hold both regular interests and mortgage loans could not issue the type of IO regular interest described above. There is no apparent reason for this limitation. Accordingly, the authors expect that tax law-yers will comment on this aspect of the proposed regulation.

The New Proposed Regulations are proposed to be effective for entities whose start-up day is on or after November 12, 1991.

§305.1.3.1   *Weighted Average Regular Interests*

A second permissible variable rate under the REMIC Regulations is a rate based on a weighted average of the interest rates on some or all of the qualified mortgages held by the REMIC. The qualified mortgages taken into account, how-ever, must bear interest at a fixed or qualified floating rate. In addition, an interest rate is considered a qualifying weighted average rate even if, in determining that rate, the interest rate on some or all of the qualified mortgages is first subject to a cap or a floor or is first reduced by a number of basis points or a fixed percentage.[16]

---

[16]One issue that arises is whether a weighted average rate payable to REMIC regular interest holders on a 30/360 basis is permissible where the qualified mortgages in such REMIC have qualified floating or fixed rates calculated on a simple interest rate method. Such a rate is nonabusive and should be permitted although tax counsel may seek to modify the transaction slightly to avoid the issue altogether.

Finally, a weighted average rate that is net of any servicing spread, credit enhancement fees, or other expenses of the REMIC is a rate based on a weighted average rate for the qualified mortgages even if such rate reduction varies in amount from mortgage to mortgage.

§305.1.3.2   *Modified Variable-Rate Regular Interests*

In addition to a qualified floating rate and a weighted average rate, a qualifying variable rate for REMIC purposes also includes certain modified variable rates. Specifically, the REMIC Regulations provide that a variable rate can be expressed as (1) a fixed multiple of a qualifying variable rate (e.g., 2 × LIBOR); (2) a constant number of basis points more or less than a qualifying variable rate (e.g., LIBOR − 50 basis points); or (3) a fixed multiple (which may be either a positive or negative number) of a qualifying variable rate plus or minus a constant number of basis points (e.g., 2 × weighted average − 50 basis points).

§305.1.4   Combination of Rates

Under the REMIC Regulations, a rate will be treated as a qualifying variable rate if it is based on a fixed or qualifying variable rate during one or more accrual or payment periods and a different fixed or qualifying variable rate or rates in other periods.[17] Thus, the REMIC Regulations specifically permit stepped-rate regular interests including variable-rate index combinations (e.g., LIBOR plus 50 basis points in year one and prime plus 150 basis points thereafter). Although the matter is not entirely clear, tax counsel generally permit a combination rate only when the rate or rates following the initial rate will become unconditionally applicable on a specified date known as of the start-up day of the REMIC. Thus, tax counsel will generally not opine on transactions that include a regular interest rate that will switch based on a contingent event (e.g., on the day the Dow Jones Industrial Average exceeds 4,000 points, the rate will change from LIBOR plus 50 basis points to prime plus 150 basis points).

§305.1.5   Permitted Contingencies

The REMIC Regulations provide that the following seven contingencies are disregarded in determining whether a regular interest has fixed terms on the start-up day. Thus, an interest in a REMIC will not fail to qualify as a regular interest solely because (1) the timing of (but not the right to or amount of) principal

---

[17]Prior to the adoption of the REMIC Regulations, an issue existed with regard to whether stepped-rate regular interests could be characterized as fixed or qualifying variable rates. A stepped-rate regular interest is a regular interest, the interest rate on which increases (or decreases) according to a fixed formula over time. For example, a regular interest might provide for 6 percent interest for the first year, 7 percent interest for the second year, and 8 percent interest for the third year and thereafter until maturity.

payments is affected by the extent of prepayments on some or all of the qualified mortgages held by the REMIC or the amount of income from permitted investments; (2) the timing of interest and principal payments is affected by the payment of expenses incurred by the REMIC; (3) the amount or timing of principal or interest payments is affected by defaults on qualified mortgages and permitted investments, unanticipated expenses incurred by the REMIC, or lower than expected returns on permitted investments; (4) an interest bears a disproportionate share of the shortfalls resulting from any of the permitted contingencies under the REMIC Regulations; (5) the interest by its terms provides for the deferral of interest payments; (6) the amount of interest payments is affected by prepayment of the underlying mortgage loans (so-called prepayment interest shortfalls);[18] and (7) the amount or timing of principal or interest payments is subject to a contingency in which there is only a remote likelihood that the contingency will occur.[19]

§305.1.6   Senior-Subordinated Regular Interests

As noted above, one form of credit support for a transaction involving conventional mortgage loans is a senior-subordinated pass-through trust.

While the REMIC statute does not specifically address senior-subordinated regular interests, as noted above, the REMIC Regulations clearly provide that an interest will not fail to qualify as a regular interest solely because an interest bears a disproportionate share of the shortfalls resulting from credit losses on the mortgage loans and permitted investments, expenses of the REMIC or prepayment interest shortfalls.

Although senior-subordinated interests can be issued by grantor trusts, more complex senior-subordinated sharing formulas can be structured in a REMIC. For example, in a REMIC, the trust can use a "shifting interest" structure in which the senior certificates are entitled to a greater percentage of prepayments than their basic interest in the trust. This shifting interest mechanism serves to return the senior certificate holder's investment sooner and gives the senior certificate holder greater protection against subsequent defaults on the mortgage loans. In one typical formulation, the senior certificates are entitled to 100 percent of the scheduled principal payments and prepayments for the first five years of the trust's existence. Thereafter, this percentage declines over time. The shifting interest structure gives the senior certificate holders additional credit protection because the principal balance of the senior certificates decreases disproportionately faster than the principal balance of the subordinated certificates.

---

[18]When a mortgage is prepaid, interest on the mortgage stops accruing on the date of prepayment. As an economic matter a sponsor may decide to pass through this shortfall to investors. Alternatively, this shortfall may be made up by reducing the servicing fee for the same period. Under the REMIC Regulations, if a prepayment interest shortfall is passed through to the holders of REMIC regular interests, the interest rate on the regular interests will nevertheless be considered a permissible interest rate not subject to contingencies, even though the actual interest rate may vary on the REMIC certificate because of such prepayment interest shortfalls. Reg. §1.860G-1(b)(3).

[19]For example, cash-flow shortfalls that could arise as a result of the operation of the Soldiers and Sailors Civil Relief Act, 50 U.S.C. app. §526 (1988), will be treated as a remote contingency.

EXAMPLE

A company contributes $100,000 of mortgage loans to a trust that elects REMIC status. The REMIC issues Class A senior certificates with a principal balance of $90,000 and Class B subordinated certificates with a principal balance of $10,000. The Class A certificates will be entitled to all principal payments (including prepayments) until they are retired. Assume $50,000 of principal is paid on the mortgage loans. In such case, the Class A certificates would have a $40,000 principal balance and the Class B certificates would have a $10,000 principal balance. Thus, as a result of the special principal allocation, the Class A's percentage in the mortgage loans will have been reduced from 90 percent ($90,000÷$100,000) to 80 percent ($40,000÷$50,000). The allocation, therefore, has the effect of protecting the Class A certificates from future losses because their credit support (i.e., the Class B certificates) has increased from 10 percent ($10,000÷$100,000) to 20 percent ($10,000÷$50,000).

§305.1.7   Regular Interests Issued with Respect to a Portion of the REMIC's Qualified Mortgages

A regular interest can be issued which relates only to a portion of the qualified mortgages held by the REMIC. This may be a helpful device when the sponsor wishes to sell a group of non-government-guaranteed loans with different interest rates in one transaction. Thus, for example, assume that the sponsor owns $1 billion of conventional, single-family mortgage loans. Assume further that half the loans bear interest at 8 percent and half bear interest at 12 percent. The sponsor does not want to create two senior-subordinated REMICs (i.e., one for each mortgage loan group) because it wants to spread the risk of mortgage default over the entire $1 billion mortgage pool. On the other hand, the sponsor does not want to set up one senior-subordinated REMIC with a blended 10 percent pass-through rate because investors will not view favorably the blended prepayment rate that results. Instead, the sponsor wants to create regular interests that have separate prepayment risks but share common credit support.

To accomplish this, the mortgage loans held by the REMIC are divided into two mortgage loan groups: one for the 8 percent mortgages and one for the 12 percent mortgages. The REMIC issues three classes of regular interests: two senior regular interests and one subordinated regular interest. The senior regular interests each relates to one mortgage loan group. Thus, one class of the senior regular interests bears an 8 percent interest rate while the other class of senior regular interests bears a 12 percent interest rate. Prepayments on one mortgage loan group are to be paid to the corresponding regular interests. In addition, if desired, the senior regular interests could be divided into fast-pay or slow-pay classes.

From a credit standpoint, the senior regular interests are cross-collateralized. Thus, if in any payment period there is insufficient principal from the related mortgage loan group to pay principal on the senior regular interest, principal from the other mortgage loan group's subordinated interest is used to make up the shortfall. Distributions on the subordinated regular interest are made only after all principal payments are made on both senior regular interests.

Although not widely used, such regular interests are unobjectionable from a REMIC standpoint. Thus, each regular interest has a fixed principal amount and bears either interest based on a fixed rate or qualifying variable rate.

It is also permissible under the REMIC Regulations to give the senior regular interests relating to each mortgage loan group interest that is payable at a weighted average rate.[20] It is possible, however, that when the senior interests are fast-pay or slow-pay with the subordinated interests, the REMIC regular interests will lack fixed terms and the REMIC will fail. This latter point is illustrated by the following example:

EXAMPLE

Assume a REMIC is formed with two separate mortgage loan groups. Group A consists of $100x$ mortgage loans that pay interest based on LIBOR. Group B consists of $100x$ mortgage loans that pay interest based on a Prime Rate. The REMIC issues three classes of regular interests: two senior regular interests and one subordinated regular interest. The Class A and Class B senior regular interests relate to Group A and Group B mortgage loans, respectively. The Class C subordinated regular interests relate to both Group A and Group B loans. The Class A and Class B regular interests each have a principal balance of $90x$ and pay interest based on the weighted average of the Group A and Group B loans, respectively. The Class C regular interests have a principal balance of $20x$ and pay interest based on the weighted average of the Group A and Group B loans. Principal distributions on the Group A and Group B loans will be paid to the Class A and Class B regular interests, respectively, until such classes are retired.

The REMIC may not qualify as a REMIC because the Class C regular interests are not payable at their weighted average rate in all events. For example, if on the start-up day the Group A loans pay 6 percent and the Group B loans pay 12 percent, the Class C regular interests will be entitled to and will receive 9 percent interest on their $20x$ balance. If, however, $50x$ of principal is paid on the Group A loans, the Class C regular interests will be entitled to 10 percent interest (the weighted average rate of all the mortgage loans) on their $20x$ balance or $2x$. Yet, after paying interest on the Class A and Class B regular interests the REMIC will only have available $1.8x$ ($15x$ collections on the mortgage loans less $13.2x$ payments on the senior regular interests).

---

[20]Reg. §1.860G-1(a)(3)(ii).

§305.1.8   Regular Interests Done as Interest Strips

Code §860G(a)(1)(B) provides that a regular interest includes an interest in the REMIC that: (1) is issued on the start-up day with fixed terms; (2) is designated as a regular interest; and (3) has interest payments that (a) are payable based on a fixed rate (or to the extent provided in regulations, at a variable rate), or (b) consist of a specified portion of the interest payments on qualified mortgages and such portion does not vary during the period such interest is outstanding. TAMRA added the language in (3)(b) above to Code §860G(a)(1) in 1988, thereby authorizing the issuance of IO regular interests. Prior to TAMRA, an IO would only qualify as a residual interest. An IO regular interest entitles the holder to receive interest payments that are determined by reference to the interest payable on some or all of the qualified mortgages rather than by reference to the specified principal amount of a specific regular interest.

Under TAMRA, IO regular interests were relatively restricted. There were, in effect, three requirements that had to be met for the IO regular interest to qualify as such.

First, the IO regular interest had to entitle the holder to receive a specified principal amount (or other similar amount). Thus, a pure IO strip could not have been done as a regular interest. Generally, IO regular interests issued after TAMRA but before the issuance of the REMIC Regulations (including the Proposed REMIC Regulations, as defined below) had a $10,000 principal amount in order to meet this requirement.

Second, the IO regular interest had to be entitled to a specified portion of the interest payments on qualified mortgages. The apparent purpose of the statute was to permit regular interests with interest rates that resemble "stripped coupons" under Code §1286 and Reg. §301.7701-4.

Third, the specified portion of the interest payments on qualified mortgages could not vary during the period the IO regular interest was outstanding. For example, an IO regular interest could not be entitled to 50 percent of the interest on qualified mortgages until a prior class of regular interests was retired and then be entitled to 100 percent of the interest on the qualified mortgages.

The proposed REMIC regulations (the "Proposed REMIC Regulations") clarified that IO regular interests need not have a principal balance. However, Prop. Reg. §1.860G-l(a)(2)(i) retained the relatively restrictive definition of the term "specified portion" by defining it only as a right to receive interest payments that can be expressed as (1) a fixed percentage of the interest payable at either a fixed rate or at a qualified variable rate with respect to each qualified mortgage (e.g., 50 percent of the interest payable on a qualified mortgage) or (2) a fixed number of basis points (e.g., 100 basis points) of the interest payable with respect to each qualified mortgage.

The REMIC Regulations vastly expand the definition of "specified portion" beyond the two categories described above by including IO regular interests expressed as the interest payable at either a fixed rate or at a qualified variable rate on some or all of the qualified mortgages in excess of a fixed number of basis points or in excess of a qualified variable rate.[21] The types of IO regular interest rates permissible under the expanded definition of "specified portion" are illustrated by the following examples:

EXAMPLE 1

A REMIC holds $100 million of 8 percent Federal National Mortgage Association (FNMA) certificates. The REMIC issues Class A regular interests with a principal balance equal to $100 million and interest payable at LIBOR with a cap of 8 percent and Class S regular interests with no principal balance and interest payable equal to the difference between 8 percent and the LIBOR rate on the Class A regular interests. Although the Class S interest rate is "squeezed" as the LIBOR rate increases, the Class S interest rate is nevertheless a permissible IO regular interest rate under the REMIC Regulations because it is a fixed rate less a qualifying variable rate (i.e., LIBOR).

EXAMPLE 2

A REMIC holds $100 million of mortgage loans with interest rates equal to a Prime Rate plus spreads of 100 to 300 basis points. Each loan has a floor of 8 percent. The REMIC issues Class A regular interests with a principal balance of $100 million and a fixed rate of interest equal to 8 percent and Class S regular interests with no principal balance and interest payable equal to, on a loan by loan basis, the Prime Rate plus the relevant spread less 8 percent. The Class S interest rate is a permissible IO regular interest rate under the REMIC Regulations because it is a qualifying variable rate (i.e., the Prime Rate plus a fixed spread) less a fixed rate.

EXAMPLE 3

A REMIC holds the assets described in the preceding example. The REMIC issues Class A regular interests with a principal balance of $100 million and an interest rate equal to LIBOR (with a cap equal to the weighted average of the interest rates on the qualified mortgages) and Class S regular interests with no principal balance and interest payable equal to, on a loan-by-loan basis, the Prime Rate plus the relevant spread and LIBOR. The Class S interest rate is a permissible IO regular interest rate because it is a qualifying variable rate (i.e., the Prime Rate plus a fixed spread) less another qualifying variable rate (i.e., LIBOR).

---

[21] Reg. §1.860G-1(a)(2).

EXAMPLE 4

A REMIC holds the assets described in the first example. The REMIC issues Class A regular interests with a $50 million principal balance and an interest rate equal to LIBOR, Class B regular interests with a $50 million principal balance and an interest rate equal to 8 percent, and Class S regular interests with no principal balance, a notional principal balance equal to the principal balance of the Class A regular interests and an interest rate equal to 8 percent less LIBOR on its notional principal balance. All principal collections on the FNMA certificates will be payable first to the Class A regular interests until they are retired and then to the Class B regular interests. The Class S interest rate may *not* be a permissible IO regular interest rate because it is economically a specified portion of the interest on the Class A regular interests and not on the qualified mortgages of the REMIC.[22]

---

§305.1.9 Contractual Rights Coupled with Regular Interests

As noted previously, regular interests must be issued on the start-up day with fixed terms that unconditionally entitle the holder of such an interest to a fixed principal amount and interest payments that are payable at either a fixed or a qualifying variable rate. Thus, the stated interest rate on a regular interest must be payable in all events from the cash flow on the qualified mortgages, absent defaults or delinquencies on such mortgages. In certain REMIC transactions, this is achieved by capping the interest rate on a class of regular interests. For example, assume a REMIC owns $100 million of Fannie Mae 8 percent certificates and issues Class A and Class B regular interests and Class R residual interests. Assume further that the Class A regular interests pay interest at a fixed rate of 8 percent and that the Class B regular interests pay a rate of interest equal to LIBOR plus 1 percent. On the start-up day, LIBOR equals 4 percent and therefore the Class B regular interests can be supported by the cash flow on the qualified mortgages on such date. To ensure that the REMIC will always be able to pay interest on the Class B regular interests, such class must be capped at a rate of 8 percent.

The REMIC Regulations provide that a REMIC may issue a regular interest to a trustee of an investment trust for the benefit of trust certificate holders even where the trustee also holds for the benefit of such certificate holders other contractual rights. Most significantly, the REMIC Regulations permit this type of arrangement even where the contractual rights are created simultaneously with the formation of the REMIC and pursuant to a single set of organizational documents. This rule will only apply, however, when the trustee accounts for the contractual rights separate and apart from the regular interests (e.g., the purchase

---

[22]See §314 for an explanation of how the Class S regular interest could be structured in a two-tier REMIC.

price of such a certificate is allocated, for purposes of determining the issue price of the regular interests, between the regular interests and the contractual rights).[23] The effect of the aforementioned provision can be illustrated by the following example:

EXAMPLE

Assume a sponsor transfers $100 million of adjustable rate mortgages to a REMIC. The mortgages pay interest at a rate equal to the Prime Rate plus margins of 200 to 300 basis points. The REMIC wishes to issue $90 million Class A regular interests with a rate equal to the weighted average rate of the mortgage loans and $10 million Class B regular interests with a rate equal to LIBOR plus 100 basis points. If the REMIC sponsor does not wish to cap the rate to holders of Class B certificates at the weighted average of the interest rates on the mortgage loans, it could issue certificates which provide that the Class B certificates represent two separate units: (1) the Class B regular interests which bear a rate of LIBOR plus 100 basis points with a cap equal to the weighted average rate on the mortgage loans, and (2) a contractual right to receive payments from the REMIC's outside reserve fund equal to LIBOR plus 100 basis points with a cap of 15 percent.

§305.2 Residual Interests

A residual interest is an interest in a REMIC which is issued on the start-up day and which is designated as a residual interest.

§305.2.1 Small Residual Interests

In many cases, the sponsor will want the residual interest to be as small as possible. For example, in many pass-through structures there is no real economic need for the residual. Thus, all cash flows from the mortgages are typically dedicated to pay expenses and servicing fees and to provide for principal and interest distributions on the pass-through certificates (i.e., the regular interests).

EXAMPLE

A $100 million pool of 10 percent mortgages is contributed to a trust in exchange for a single class of pass-through certificates. If the servicing fee is .25 percent, the trust can issue $100 million of 9.75 percent pass-through

---

[23]See Appendix C for a copy of a certificate generally obtained from underwriters for purposes of determining the issue price of a regular interest held as part of a REMIC-related investment unit.

certificates. This is the optimal execution. To do this transaction as a REMIC, however, requires a residual interest.

In addition, the sponsor of the transaction may find that residuals are hard to sell because of their volatility. For example, a typical economic residual would represent the right to receive an interest-rate strip-off of the qualified mortgages. This strip behaves like the IO piece described above: If interest rates increase, it can increase significantly in value; however, if interest rates decrease, it can decrease significantly in value. Because of this volatility, these residuals are fairly risky instruments. While such residuals were purchased by thrifts and "residual" REITs beginning in 1986, by early 1989 thrift regulators had clamped down on the ability of a thrift to buy such a volatile instrument. Additionally, the poor performance of residual REITs had dampened the enthusiasm for such vehicles. Therefore, residuals with little or no economic value came into vogue.

Until the Joint Committee on Taxation issued its explanation of the 1986 Act,[24] there was some uncertainty about how large such a residual (or any residual) needed to be. In general, counsel required that a residual have a value somewhere between $10,000 and $100,000. Even though one of the goals of the REMIC legislation was to eliminate arbitrary distinctions about the size of residuals, counsel felt that the residual had to represent some economic interest in the REMIC.

The 1986 Blue Book however, tried to allay these fears. Thus, it provides that:

> The Congress intended that an interest in a REMIC could qualify as a residual interest regardless of its value. Thus, for example, an interest need not entitle the holder to any distributions in order to qualify as a residual interest.[25]

The REMIC Regulations confirm this interpretation because they do not require that residual interests have any economic value or entitle the residual owner to any distributions whatsoever. The REMIC Regulations are concerned only that the residual interests be designed as a "clean-up" mechanism to ensure that no income on the mortgage loans is lost as a result of repackaging the mortgage loans into a REMIC structure. Thus, as discussed below, once income from the mortgage loans has in effect been allocated to the regular interest holders, any excess is taxed to the residual interest holders.[26]

§305.2.2   Senior Residual Interests

In some cases, it may be advantageous to structure a residual that is senior in terms of credit priority to one or more regular interests, that is, a senior residual interest.

---

[24]See Staff of the Joint Comm. on Tax'n, General Explanation of the Tax Reform Act of 1986 (hereinafter referred to as the 1986 Blue Book).

[25]1986 Blue Book, *supra* note 24, at 416.

[26]In fact, most residuals have a negative economic value on an after-tax basis. This is because they represent the right to no economic distributions but require the residual owner to pay taxes on the REMIC's phantom income. As such, the sponsor may have to retain the residual (and treat the tax liability as an ongoing cost of the transaction) or pay a third party to take the residual.

For example, suppose that a governmental agency owns a pool of mortgage loans that it wants to sell. It could set up a senior-subordinated trust and sell senior interests in the trust to the public. It would retain the subordinated interest. It cannot structure the subordinated interest as a REMIC residual interest, however, because it is effectively prohibited from owning the residual interest under the Code §860D(a)(6) rules discussed below. If it structures a REMIC with a senior regular interest and a subordinated residual interest, the residual will be of extremely poor credit quality and, therefore, a potentially difficult instrument to sell. Instead of doing this, the trust could issue three classes of REMIC interests: a senior residual interest, a senior regular interest, and a subordinated regular interest. The senior residual interest would be an interest strip-off of the senior regular interest in the mortgage pool. The senior regular interest would represent the senior interest in the mortgage pool, less the residual interest strip. The subordinated regular interest would represent the subordinated interest in the mortgage pool. Making the residual interest senior to the subordinated regular interest gives the residual interest the credit support of the subordinated regular interest. This makes the residual interest easier to sell.

The residual interests in the foregoing example meet the definition of residual interests. Under the REMIC Regulations, "a residual interest is an interest in a REMIC that is issued on the start-up day and that is designated as a residual interest" in the operating documents of such REMIC.[27] Thus, if the residual interest is issued on the start-up day and properly designated as a residual interest, it will be treated as a residual interest for federal income tax purposes regardless of (1) its economic entitlements or (2) where it fits within the credit framework of the transaction.

§305.2.3 Requirement that the Residual Interest Not Be a Regular Interest

One of the two requirements for a residual interest is that it not be a regular interest. Under the REMIC Regulations it is clear that a residual interest need not be economically different from a regular interest. Therefore, if a residual interest is designated as a residual interest and not as a regular interest, it literally will qualify as one even if it economically resembles a regular interest.

§305.2.4 Super-Premium Regular Interests

The REMIC legislative history provides that certain interests with nominally fixed principal and interest payments may, in fact, be classified as residual interests, or part residual interests and part regular interests, because they are economically contingent. Thus, the 1986 Conference Report provides that:

> The Conferees intend that an interest in a REMIC may not qualify as a regular interest if the amount of interest (or similar payments) is disproportionate to the specified

---

[27] Reg. §1.860G-1(c).

principal amount. For example, if an interest is issued in the form of debt with a coupon rate of interest that is substantially in excess of prevailing market interest rates (adjusted for risk), the conferees intend that the interest would not qualify as a regular interest. Instead, the conferees intend that such an interest may be treated either as a residual interest or as a combination of a regular interest and a residual interest.[28]

The REMIC Regulations confirm that an interest will not qualify as a regular interest if the rate on such interest does not qualify as an IO regular interest rate and the amount of interest payable to the holder of such interest is disproportionately high relative to its specified principal amount (a "super-premium regular interest").[29] The REMIC Regulations provide that a regular interest will be treated as a super-premium regular interest if the issue price of such interest exceeds 125 percent of its specified principal amount.[30] Historically, the super-premium regular interest issue has arisen in connection with interests structured as leveraged inverse floaters that are often sold at a large premium relative to their stated principal amount. Generally, tax practitioners have restructured super-premium leveraged inverse floaters so that the upper-tier leveraged inverse floater can be characterized as an IO regular interest.

EXAMPLE

Assume Sponsor wishes to issue floater (F) and leveraged inverse floater (IF) regular interests with principal balances of $187,459,000 and $0.00, respectively, and interest rate formulas equal to LIBOR + .50 percent and 9.5 percent − LIBOR on a notional principal balance equal to the balance of the F, respectively. Because the IF has no principal balance and a significant market value, it would obviously be sold at a price greater than 125 percent of its principal balance and, therefore, must be structured as an IO regular interest and not as an inverse floater regular interest in a single-tier REMIC structure.

In order to issue IF as an IO regular interest, Sponsor forms REMIC I, which issues F Lower Tier (FLT) and IF Lower Tier (IFLT) regular interests. FLT and IFLT have principal balances of $124,972,666.67 and $62,486,333.33, respectively, and interest rate formulas of (LIBOR × 1.5) + 0.75 percent and 28.5 − (LIBOR × 3), respectively.[31] FLT and IFLT will then be contributed to REMIC II and will be treated as the sole qualified mortgages in REMIC II. REMIC II will issue F and IF as described in the preceding paragraph. However, for REMIC purposes, IF can now be characterized as an IO regular interest because it represents 100 percent of the interest on a qualified mort-

---

[28]1986 Conf. Rep., §301 note 1, at II-229.
[29]Reg. §1.860G-1(b)(5).
[30]Id.
[31]Tax counsel for issuers generally require the underwriters to provide a representation letter, in connection with two tier REMICs, that the regular interests structured from lower tier REMICs will not be treated themselves as super-premium regular interests.

gage (i.e., IFLT).[32] Since IF now qualifies as an IO regular interest, it will be treated as a valid regular interest for REMIC purposes and not as an impermissible super-premium regular interest.

§305.3   Permissible Interests in a REMIC

Code §860D provides that every interest in a REMIC must be either a regular interest or a residual interest. The REMIC Regulations clarify that although all interests in a REMIC must be either regular or residual, not every right to receive a payment from a REMIC is treated as an "interest" in the REMIC. Although not intended as an exclusive list, the REMIC Regulations identify certain rights to cash flow from a REMIC that will not be treated as REMIC interests.

§305.3.1   Reasonable Servicing Fees

The right to receive payments from a REMIC that represent reasonable compensation for services provided and that are expressed as a specified percentage of interest payments due on qualified mortgages or earnings from permitted investments will not be treated as an interest in the REMIC.[33]

§305.3.2   Stripped Interests

A stripped interest not held by the REMIC (i.e., a fixed, retained yield) will not be treated as an interest in the REMIC even if, in a transaction preceding or contemporaneous with the formation of the REMIC, such interest was created from the qualified mortgages in the REMIC.[34]

§305.3.3   Rights of Reimbursement

A right to be reimbursed from a REMIC pursuant to a credit enhancement contract is not an interest in a REMIC even if the credit enhancer is entitled to receive interest on the amounts advanced.[35] A credit enhancement contract is any agreement whereby a person agrees to guarantee full or partial payment of principal or interest payable on some or all of the qualified mortgages or full or partial payment on one or more classes of regular interests in the event of defaults

---

[32]It should be noted that 28.5 percent − (LIBOR × 3) on a notional principal balance equal to the principal balance of the IFLT is equal to 9.5 percent − LIBOR on a notional principal balance of $187,459,000.

[33]Reg. §1.860D-l(b)(2)(i).

[34]Reg. §1.860D-1(b)(2)(ii). See the discussion above at §305.1.1 with respect to passing through default-rate interest to holders of regular interests.

[35]Reg. §1.860D-1(b)(2)(iii).

or delinquencies on qualified mortgages or unanticipated losses or expenses incurred by the REMIC.[36] The REMIC Regulations clarify that certain servicer advances will likewise not constitute an interest in a REMIC.

§305.3.4 Certain Rights to Acquire Mortgages

The REMIC Regulations provide that the right or obligation to acquire mortgage loans from a REMIC (1) pursuant to a clean-up call (as defined below) or a qualified liquidation (as defined below) or (2) on conversion of a convertible mortgage, will not be treated as an interest in the REMIC.[37] The REMIC Regulations do not require that purchases of qualified mortgages pursuant to a clean-up call or a qualified liquidation be made at the greater of par or fair market value.

§305.3.5 De Minimis Interests

In addition to the specific rights listed above, the REMIC Regulations provide that any interest which is created to facilitate the formation of a REMIC and, as of the start-up day, has a fair market value which is less than the lesser of $1,000 or $1/1000$ of 1 percent of the aggregate fair market value of all the regular and residual interests in the REMIC, will not be treated as an interest in the REMIC.[38] This rule was principally designed to clarify that a small contribution (e.g., $10) in exchange for a nominal trust certificate needed to create a REMIC under state law does not create a second class of residual interest.

§306 ONE CLASS OF RESIDUAL INTERESTS

The third qualification requirement is that the REMIC have one and only one class of residual interests. In addition, distributions with respect to such interests must be pro rata.[1]

The single class of residual interest requirement exists to simplify the tax reporting of residual income. Apparently, the fear was that with several classes of residual interests, allocation of income and losses among them would be complicated. One obvious complication would result if the REMIC could allocate income and deductions in a manner similar to a partnership. This might encourage allocations of income to one class of residual interests held by savings and loan associations which could use their losses to offset REMIC excess inclusions.[2]

---

[36]Reg. §1.860G-2(c)(2).
[37]Id.
[38]Reg. §1.860D-1(b)(2)(iv).
§306 [1]Code §860D(a)(3).
[2]See §313.2.4 for a discussion of excess inclusions.

The single class of residual interest requirement would seem to prohibit any difference between residual owners.[3] For example, there should not be any difference between voting rights of the residual holders or the obligation to pay expenses of the REMIC. Clearly, things such as different priorities on timing of distributions or entitlement to cash flow are prohibited.

One way to avoid the single class of residual interest prohibition would be to form a partnership to hold the residual interest. The partnership could allocate cash flow, taxable income, tax losses, or other items. Of course, any such partnership allocations would need to have substantial economic effect under Code §704(b).

Also, a REIT created to own REMIC residual interests could issue several classes of stock with different timing priorities. Excess inclusions from the residual interests would be allocated among the REIT's shareholders according to the dividends received.[4]

§307   ASSET TEST

The fourth qualification test requires that on the last day of the third month beginning after the start-up day (the "test date") and continuously thereafter[1] substantially all of the REMIC's assets must consist of: (1) qualified mortgages and (2) permitted investments.[2]

§307.1   Qualified Mortgages and Permitted Investments

On and after the test date, "substantially all" of the REMIC's assets must consist of qualified mortgages and permitted investments. "Substantially all" is not defined in the Code. Although the REMIC legislative history states that "substantially all" should be defined so that no more than a de minimis amount of the REMIC's assets is considered nonqualified,[3] prior to the issuance of the REMIC Regulations, no one knew how to quantify "de minimis" for purposes of the qualified asset test. Therefore, tax counsel ensured that all assets in a REMIC on and after the test date would be treated as qualified mortgages and permitted investments.

Under a new safe harbor in the REMIC Regulations, nonqualifying assets in a REMIC will be treated as de minimis if the adjusted bases of those assets are less than 1 percent of the aggregate adjusted bases of all the REMIC's assets.[4] This safe harbor must be met on the test date and at all times thereafter. The REMIC

---

[3]In the one class of stock requirement found in subchapter S, any differences between classes (except with respect to voting rights) are prohibited. Code §1361(b)(1)(D) and (c)(4). Differences in voting rights are specifically allowed by statute.

[4]See text accompanying §313 note 36, *infra*.

§307 [1]The start-up day is the day designated by the REMIC on which regular and residual interests are issued. Code §860G(a)(9).

[2]Code §860D(a)(4).

[3]1986 Conf. Rep., §301 note 1, at II-226.

[4]Reg. §1.860D-1(b)(ii).

Regulations, however, do not foreclose the possibility that a de minimis amount could be an amount greater than 1 percent. In light of the safe harbor, however, having 1 percent or more of the REMIC's assets invested in other than qualified mortgages or permitted investments should be avoided.

It should also be noted that the qualified asset requirement need not be met during the 90-day period after the REMIC adopts a plan of liquidation.[5] This provision is necessary to protect a REMIC that has sold its assets and converted them to cash before liquidating.

§307.1.1   Qualified Mortgages

Qualified mortgages are real estate mortgages, certain substituted mortgages and regular (but not residual) interests in other REMICs.[6]

§307.1.2   Qualified Mortgage Definition

The first and predominant type of qualified mortgage is defined as:

[A]ny obligation (including any participation or certificate of beneficial ownership therein) which is principally secured by an interest in real property and which —
   (i) is transferred to the REMIC on the startup day in exchange for regular or residual interests in the REMIC, or
   (ii) is purchased by the REMIC within the 3-month period beginning on the start-up day if, except as provided in the regulations, such purchase is pursuant to a fixed-price contract in effect on the start-up day.[7]

Several things should be noted about the definition. First, as originally drafted, the statutory definition included the words "directly or indirectly" after the phrase "principally secured." Pursuant to this language, it was thought that a corporate bond secured solely by real estate mortgages was a qualified mortgage. Unfortunately, however, TAMRA deleted the words "directly or indirectly," and the intent of this provision was to delete from the qualified mortgage category corporate bonds secured by mortgages.[8] For example, a REMIC cannot be formed to buy non-REMIC CMOs.

The REMIC Regulations also provide an 80-percent test for determining whether a loan is "principally secured by an interest in real property." This test is met if the fair market value of the real estate securing the loan was at least equal to 80 percent of the loan's adjusted issue price (usually its principal amount) either: (1) upon origination or (2) at the time the sponsor contributes the loan to

---

[5]Code §860D(a), flush language.
[6]Code §860G(a)(3).
[7]Code §860G(a)(3)(A).
[8]1986 Blue Book, §305 note 24, at 413, note 67.

the REMIC.[9] In loan-to-value (LTV) terms, the 80-percent test equates with a 125-percent or less LTV.

Because the real estate's fair market value may not have been actually determined (either at origination or upon the REMIC's creation), the REMIC Regulations provide an alternative test for meeting the "principally secured" requirement. The alternative test is met if substantially all of the proceeds of the obligation were used to acquire or to improve or protect an interest in real property that, at the origination date, is the only security for the obligation. For purposes of the alternative test, U.S., state or local government guarantees and third party credit enhancement are not viewed as additional security for the obligation. Likewise, personal liability of the mortgagor is not considered other security for the obligation. The alternative test has been useful in securitizing loans in REMICs where the property is "construction-in-progress" and, on the start-up day of the REMIC, has an LTV in excess of 125 percent.[10] Finally, the REMIC Regulations provide a safe harbor for the 80-percent test. The safe harbor is met if the REMIC sponsor reasonably believes that the 80-percent test is met when the REMIC is created. This "reasonable belief" may be based on: (1) representations and warranties made by the originator of the loan; or (2) evidence indicating that (a) the originator of the obligation typically made loans in accordance with a set of established parameters (e.g., all loans had to have an LTV of 100 percent or less based on a recent appraisal) and (b) any mortgage loan originated in accordance with those parameters would meet the "qualified mortgage" standards for REMICs.

If the "reasonable belief" safe harbor is met, but it is ultimately discovered that the loan did not meet the 80-percent test, then the loan becomes a defective loan that must be removed from the REMIC within 90 days after such discovery.[11]

Second, under the Code any interests in mortgage pass-through grantor trusts will be qualified mortgages so long as the underlying assets qualify. Prior to the issuance of the REMIC Regulations, however, an issue arose with regard to the treatment of real property acquired through foreclosure and held by the trustee of a grantor trust. For example, suppose that a non-REMIC mortgage pool trust has been in existence for several years. Assume further that on the origination date of the trust all of the mortgage loans were performing loans and "qualified mortgages" for REMIC purposes. Suppose further that several of the loans in the trust have since defaulted and the mortgage pool trustee has taken title to the underlying real estate. Assume that a thrift institution owns a mortgage pass-through certificate representing an undivided ownership interest in the trust's assets. The thrift wants to contribute its pass-through certificate to a REMIC and sell regular interests to the public.

For federal income tax purposes, the REMIC would be considered to own an undivided ownership interest in all of the mortgage pass-through trust's assets, including the real estate. If the REMIC's ownership of the foreclosed real estate were treated as ownership of an asset that is not a qualified mortgage, a REMIC

---

[9]Fair market value is reduced by the full amount of any senior lien and by a pro rata share of the amount of any lien that is *pari passu* with the loan being tested. Reg. §1.860G-2(a)(2).

[10]It should be noted that construction-in-progress loans are sometimes secured by other assets (e.g., cash accounts) and therefore will not always meet the alternative test.

[11]Reg. §1.860G-2(a)(3)(iii).

qualification issue would result. Thus, if the adjusted basis of the real estate after the REMIC test date for qualified assets exceeded 1 percent of the adjusted bases of all the REMIC's assets on such date, the REMIC may be disqualified.

The REMIC Regulations eliminate this issue by treating mortgage pass-through certificates as "qualified mortgages" if: (1) the investment trust is classified as a trust under Reg. §301.7701-4(c); and (2) the certificate represents an undivided beneficial ownership in a pool of "qualified mortgages" and related assets that would be permitted investments if the trust were a REMIC.[12]

Third, the REMIC Regulations make it clear that stripped bonds and coupons are qualified mortgages so long as the underlying obligations are qualified mortgages.[13]

Fourth, a REMIC is not limited to single-family mortgages. Thus, any mortgage secured by real property qualifies. This includes second mortgages on residential real estate, home equity loans secured by residential real estate, mortgages on commercial real estate and mortgages on real estate located outside the United States. TAMRA also added loans secured by stock in a cooperative housing corporation as defined in Code §216 to the list of qualified mortgages.[14] Such loans are treated as loans secured by real property for other tax purposes,[15] so this technical correction was no surprise.

The REMIC Regulations define the terms "interests in real property" and "real property" for purposes of the REMIC rules by referencing the definitions of those terms set out in the REIT regulations.[16] The REMIC Regulations also modify the definition of interests in real property set out in Reg. §1.856-3(c) to also include certain timeshare interests. In addition, the REMIC Regulations provide that installment land sale contracts are qualified mortgages[17] and mortgages on loans secured by mobile homes are qualified mortgages so long as they meet the definition of a "single family residence"[18] set forth in Code §25(e)(10).[19]

The REMIC Regulations also provide that in addition to pass-through certificates guaranteed by Fannie Mae, Ginnie Mae and Freddie Mac, pass-through certificates guaranteed by the Canada Mortgage and Housing Corporation (CMHC) will be treated as obligations secured by interests in real property even

---

[12]It is unclear, however, whether the REMIC could issue regular interests that are supported by the value of this foreclosed real estate. For example, assume a non-REMIC mortgage pass-through trust certificate represents $80X of mortgage loans and $20X discounted fair market value of foreclosed real estate. Although the entire certificate can be contributed to the REMIC, the issue exists as to whether the REMIC can offer $100X principal balance of regular interests or only $80X principal balance of regular interests.

[13]Reg. §1.860G-2(a)(9).

[14]Code §860G(a)(3), flush language.

[15]Rev. Rul. 76-101, 1976-1 C.B. 186. This ruling holds that interest on loans secured by co-op stock is interest on obligations secured by real property for a REIT.

[16]Reg. §1.860G-2(a)(4). See also Reg. §1.856-3.

[17]Reg. §1.860G-2(a)(5).

[18]Code §25(e)(10) provides that a "single-family residence" includes any manufactured home that has a minimum of 400 square feet of living space and a minimum width in excess of 102 inches and that is of a kind customarily used at a fixed location.

[19]Reg. §1.860G-2(a)(5).

though CMHC certificates may not qualify as investment trusts under the Sears Regulations.[20]

Finally, the REMIC Regulations do not include partnership interests as qualified mortgages. Although a partnership interest in a partnership that holds qualified mortgages would presumably have qualified under the "directly or indirectly" language of the prior statute, it appears that the change in the qualified mortgage definition to the "principally secured" standard excludes partnership interests.

§307.1.3   Special Defeasance Rule

In some cases an obligor may seek a provision permitting it to "defease" a mortgage loan with Treasury securities or other non-real estate collateral. The REMIC Regulations provide that such a defeasance will not convert the mortgage into a disqualified mortgage if: (1) the new collateral consists solely of government securities as defined in the Investment Company Act of 1940; (2) the defeasance is pursuant to the mortgage documents; (3) the REMIC releases its lien to facilitate disposition of the underlying property; and (4) the defeasance is not within two years after the REMIC's start-up day.[21] The REMIC Regulations also provide, however, that the lien on real property can be released for reasons other than a mortgagor's disposition of the encumbered real property if the defeasance transaction is undertaken as part of a customary commercial transaction, and not as part of an arrangement to collateralize a REMIC offering with obligations that are not real estate mortgages.[22]

§307.1.4   Modifications

Commercial REMIC sponsors have been concerned that modification of a mortgage by the REMIC (e.g., in a workout) might, under general federal income tax principles, result in a deemed exchange of the mortgage for a new mortgage. If the exchange occurred more than two years after the REMIC's start-up day, the new mortgage would not be a "qualified mortgage," the REMIC could be disqualified and the mortgage interest would be subject to a 100-percent penalty tax.

The REMIC Regulations answer this concern with a special rule on modifications. The rule is that a "significant modification" (defined as one in which the new mortgage terms differ materially in kind or extent from the old) results in a new mortgage, which will only be a qualified mortgage if it meets the two-year qualified replacement rule.[23] A "significant modification" is any change in the

---

[20]CMHC certificates may not qualify as investment trusts under the Sears Regulations because the terms of the CMHC certificates permit the CMHC sponsor to substitute replacement mortgage loans for defective mortgage loans for a period beyond two years after the trust's formation.

[21]Reg. §1.860G-2(a)(8).

[22]Id.

[23]Reg. §1.860G-2(b)(1).

terms of an obligation that would be treated as an exchange of obligations under Code §1001 and the related regulations.[24]

The key to the new rule, however, is in a series of broad exceptions. If one of the exceptions is met, no new mortgage is created for REMIC purposes. The exceptions include: (1) a change in mortgage terms occasioned by default or reasonably foreseeable default; (2) assumption of the mortgage; (3) waiver of a due on sale clause; or (4) conversion of an interest rate by the obligor on a convertible ARM.[25] Under a special rule, modification of a mortgage loan backing a pass-through certificate held by the REMIC (e.g., a Ginnie Mae pass-through) is ignored so long as the pass-through was not structured to avoid the REMIC prohibited transaction rule.[26]

§307.1.5   Credit Support as an Incident of the Qualified Mortgages

Although credit enhancement is a staple of almost every mortgage-backed securities transaction, the original REMIC statute was silent on the treatment of credit enhancement arrangements. In fact, prior to the REMIC Regulations, the only legislative references to it were in the 1986 Conference Report, which, when discussing qualified reserve assets (see §307.2.1 below), states: "In determining whether the amount of the reserve is reasonable, the conferees believe that it is appropriate to take into account the credit-worthiness of the qualified mortgages and the extent and nature of any guarantees relating to the qualified mortgages." Additionally, the 1986 Blue Book clarified that even though "qualified reserve assets" must be intangible property held for investment, whose purpose is to provide for expenses and for additional security for payments on regular interests that would otherwise be delayed or defaulted because of defaults (including late payments) on qualified mortgages, "Congress intended that property would not fail to be considered to be held for investment, solely because the REMIC holds the property for these reasons."[27] The REMIC Regulations, however, provide a set of rules that, in effect, will permit a wide range of credit enhancement arrangements and techniques.

The general rule in the REMIC Regulations is that a credit enhancement contract (CEC) is an incident of the qualified mortgages and not a separate REMIC asset. What this rule means is that CECs do not have to be separately valued in determining REMIC qualification. Put another way, credit enhancement is REMIC neutral.

The REMIC Regulations also clarify that collateral securing a CEC is not treated as a REMIC asset. This is important, for example, where a sponsor guarantees payments on the REMIC's mortgage loans and supports the guarantee with a "spread account" funded from an interest strip or subordinated or residual cash flows.

---

[24]Reg. §1.860G-2(b)(2).
[25]Reg. §1.860G-2(b)(3).
[26]Reg. §1.860G-2(b)(6).
[27]1986 Blue Book, §305 note 24.

In addition, the REMIC Regulations clarify the definition of CECs in five ways. The REMIC Regulations provide that: (1) the term CEC includes arrangements that provide support for residual interests in a REMIC; (2) the term CEC includes an agreement between the REMIC and a third party whereby the third party agrees to make up cash flow shortfalls occasioned by lower than expected returns on cash flow investments; (3) certain arrangements to make advances to the REMIC are CECs even if those arrangements are between the REMIC and a third party other than the mortgage servicer; (4) certain agreements between a REMIC and a third party whereby the third party agrees to advance amounts to the REMIC to provide for the orderly administration of the REMIC, although technically not providing credit support, nonetheless are considered CECs; and (5) a guarantee or insurance arrangement does not fail to qualify as a CEC solely because the guarantor or insurer has the right to defer the guarantee or insurance payment that is to substitute for the amounts due on a defaulted mortgage, together with interest, according to the original payment schedule of the mortgage, or according to some other deferred payment schedule.[28]

Examples of CECs include pool insurance, certificate guarantee contracts, letters of credit, guarantees by either the REMIC sponsor or a third party, and certain mortgage servicer or third-party advances. Importantly, a CEC cannot guarantee prepayment speeds on the REMIC's qualified mortgages.

§307.1.6   Replacement Mortgages

A qualified mortgage is also deemed to include a qualified replacement mortgage.[29] This is simply a qualified mortgage that is transferred to the REMIC in exchange for another mortgage within certain limited time periods.[30] The principle is that when a mortgage pool is formed, some of the loans in the pool may not meet standards set by the parties. For example, the seller may represent that no mortgage is delinquent more than 30 days and that the mortgagor has obtained a title insurance policy. To the extent that these representations are found not to be true upon examination after closing, the seller would agree to substitute a qualified replacement mortgage for the defective mortgage.

The limited time period during which mortgages may be replaced with qualified replacement mortgages is the three-month period beginning on the start-up day for unlimited substitutions and the two-year period beginning on the start-up day for mortgages that are defective.

§307.1.7   Defective Mortgages

The REMIC Regulations contain special rules to determine when an obligation is "defective." This is important because: (1) if a loan is substituted outside

---

[28]Reg. §1.860G-2(c).
[29]Code §860G(a)(3)(B).
[30]Code §860G(a)(4).

the two-year defective loan safe harbor, the replacement loan is not a qualified replacement loan (and therefore not a qualified mortgage); and (2) a defective mortgage loan can be purchased from the REMIC by the sponsor at any time without a prohibited transaction tax.

A defective obligation under the REMIC Regulations is one: (1) that is in default or where a default is reasonably foreseeable; (2) that was fraudulently procured by the mortgagor; (3) which, in fact, failed the 80-percent test (or the alternative or safe harbor tests) for determining whether the mortgage is "principally secured" by an interest in real estate; or (4) which was transferred to the REMIC in violation of a customary representation or warranty given by the REMIC sponsor or prior owner of the mortgage. A representation as to prepayment rates is not a "customary" representation.

Special rules apply to certain defective loans. Specifically, if a defective obligation is discovered and the defect is one that if discovered before the start-up day would have prevented the mortgage from being a qualified mortgage, then the defect must be removed from the REMIC within 90 days after the date it is discovered. After the 90-day discovery period, the obligation ceases to be a qualified mortgage. It is, however, a qualified mortgage from the start-up day of the REMIC through the 90-day discovery period. This rule gives the REMIC the chance to remove the obligation without risking REMIC disqualification or a prohibited transaction tax on income from the disposition of such obligation by the REMIC.

If a defective obligation would still have been a qualified mortgage despite the defect, there is no need for the 90-day grace period. In this case, the sponsor could either: (1) cure the defect; (2) purchase the obligation from the REMIC without triggering any prohibited transaction tax; or (3) if permissible, leave the defect as is. It should be noted that the sponsor's failure to cure the defect does not mean the mortgage is no longer a qualified mortgage.

§307.1.8   Prefunding Accounts

A qualified mortgage also includes an obligation which is purchased by the REMIC within the three-month period beginning on the start-up day if such obligation is purchased pursuant to a fixed-price contract in effect on the start-up day.[31] REMIC transactions that include fixed-price contracts to acquire additional mortgage loans typically over-issue regular interests on the start-up day (i.e., issue regular interests with a principal balance in excess of the principal balance of the mortgages in the REMIC on the start-up day) and deposit a portion of the cash proceeds received from the sale of REMIC regular interests in a prefunding account.

A prefunding account is an account which holds cash or short term permitted investments and which is dedicated to purchasing additional mortgage collateral within a specified period of time on behalf of the REMIC. For example, on the start-up day a sponsor of mortgages transfers to the REMIC $100X of mortgage

---

[31]Code §860G(a)(3)(A)(ii).

loans and $100X of cash into a prefunding account. The REMIC issues $200X of regular and residual interests. Within the prescribed time period the REMIC purchases the additional mortgages in exchange for amounts held in the prefunding account.

Assuming there is a fixed-price contract to acquire the additional mortgages, the additional mortgages will be treated as qualified mortgages of the REMIC (assuming such mortgages otherwise meet the qualified mortgage definition). Although there is no specific definition of what constitutes a fixed-price contract, it appears that a fixed-price contract is a contract in which the price, the property, and the date of performance is specifically identified (e.g., delivery of $10 million of 7 percent fixed-rate, single-family mortgage loans with a 15-year term to be made on May 15, 1994) and one which does not allow the REMIC to take advantage of fluctuations in the market price of the additional mortgages. The legislative history to the REMIC statute provides that qualified mortgages may be considered to be purchased pursuant to a fixed-price contract despite the fact that the purchase price may be adjusted where the qualified mortgages are not delivered by the seller on the delivery date, provided that the adjustment is in the nature of damages for failure to deliver the qualified mortgages rather than as a result of fluctuations in market price between the closing date and the scheduled date of delivery.[32]

It should be noted, however, that if the prefunding account is an asset of the REMIC, amounts in the prefunding account will not be treated as qualified mortgages or permitted assets. The REMIC, therefore, will be subject to a 100 percent tax on any amounts earned from the investment of such amounts.[33] The first group of prefunded REMICs that were structured provided that the prefunding account was included in the REMIC. These amounts were maintained in non-interest bearing accounts so as to avoid the imposition of this 100 percent tax on the earnings of the prefunding REMIC account. As the market became more familiar with the use of the prefunding mechanism, prefunding accounts were established outside of the REMIC in interest bearing accounts. Contributions from those accounts to the REMIC to facilitate the purchase of additional mortgage loans are not treated as prohibited contributions provided all contributions are made in cash within the 90-day period after the start-up day.[34] All amounts in the outside prefunding account and earnings on such amounts will be taxed to the sponsor and not the REMIC. The sponsor will grant a security interest in the prefunding account to the REMIC but, as noted above, for tax purposes the sponsor will be the owner of those amounts.

Furthermore, because (1) the REMIC issues regular and residual interests equal to the sum of the principal balance of the mortgages and amounts held in the prefunding account, and (2) the amounts invested in the prefunding account are typically invested in "permitted investments" that earn a return less than the yield on the regular interests, on each monthly distribution date before the additional mortgages are purchased by the REMIC there will be an interest shortfall. In

[32]H. R. Rep. No. 795, 100th Cong., 2d Sess., pt. 2, at 81, note 42 (1988).
[33]Code §860F.
[34]Code §860G(d).

order to be able to pay stated interest on the regular interests, the sponsor must (1) establish an account on the start-up day and contribute to such account an amount of cash sufficient to pay the interest shortfall on the regular interests for the period of time before the additional mortgages are purchased (capitalized interest); or (2) create a stepped interest rate on the regular interests supported by the prefunded amount (i.e., the difference between the principal amount of regular interests and the principal balance of mortgage loans on the start-up day) (e.g., zero percent for the first three payment periods and 8 percent thereafter). If a capitalized interest account is maintained outside the REMIC, amounts contributed to the REMIC during the prefunding period may be supplemented by earnings on amounts deposited in the prefunding account.

§307.1.9 Permitted Investments

In addition to qualified mortgages, the only other type of qualifying asset for a REMIC is a permitted investment. A permitted investment includes the following three categories: (1) cash-flow investments; (2) qualified reserve assets; and (3) foreclosure properties.[35]

§307.2 Cash-Flow Investments

Cash-flow investments are temporary investments where the REMIC holds money it has received from qualified mortgages pending distribution to its interest holders. The REMIC Regulations provide that such investments must be passive, earning a return "in the nature of" interest.[36]

The investment in cash flow investments must be for a "temporary period."[37] This is not defined in the statute but the REMIC Regulations define "temporary" as that period from the time a REMIC receives payments on qualified mortgages to the time it distributes payments to interest holders.[38] The period, however, may not exceed 13 months under the REMIC Regulations.[39] Therefore, an investment held by the REMIC for more than 13 months is not a cash-flow investment. This period was picked in order to allow a REMIC to issue regular interests which provide for monthly, quarterly, semi-annual, or annual payments.

The key to the cash flow investment definition is determining what payments are "received on qualified mortgages." The REMIC Regulations include several categories: (1) principal and interest on qualified mortgages including prepayments of principal and payments under CECs; (2) proceeds from dispositions of qualified mortgages; (3) cash flow from foreclosure property and sales of foreclosure property; (4) a payment by either the REMIC sponsor or the prior

---

[35]Code §860G(a)(5).
[36]Reg. §1.860G-2(g)(1).
[37]Id.
[38]Reg. §1.860G-2(g)(1)(iii).
[39]Id.

owner of a defective obligation in lieu of repurchase upon breach of a customary warranty (e.g., a payment that makes up the difference between the interest rate as represented and the actual interest rate); and (5) prepayment penalties on qualified mortgages.

Finally, the REMIC Regulations explain that in determining the length of time that a REMIC has held an investment which is part of a commingled account or fund, the REMIC may employ any reasonable method of accounting (e.g., first-in, first-out (FIFO)).

The definition of cash-flow investment is broad enough to include most kinds of temporary investments that the REMIC makes, including short-term government securities, bank certificates of deposit, short-term repurchase agreements, and commercial paper.[40] It is also broad enough to include a guaranteed investment contract (GIC). A GIC is a contract whereby the REMIC agrees to invest all cash flows on the qualified mortgages with a third party, typically an insurance company, and the third party agrees to pay a fixed or specified floating rate of interest on all amounts invested during the contract term. The REMIC legislative history provides that the GIC should be one where the third party agrees to return the principal and agreed-upon interest at times coinciding with distributions on regular and residual interests.[41]

The chief restriction for cash-flow investments, however, is the prohibited transactions tax. Thus, any gain from the disposition of a cash-flow investment other than pursuant to a qualified liquidation is subject to a 100 percent prohibited transactions penalty tax.[42] This will prevent a REMIC from purchasing long-term investments or speculative investments such as debt futures or options as cash-flow investments.

§307.2.1 Qualified Reserve Assets

The next category of permitted investments is a qualified reserve asset.[43] Basically, these investments are those necessary to create reserves for various defined purposes. Again the goal is that the reserve be no more than necessary to do the job and that the assets be passive rather than active.

A qualified reserve asset must be: (1) intangible property; (2) held for investment; and (3) part of a qualified reserve fund.[44] The key to ensuring that an asset is a qualified reserve asset is to ensure that it is part of a qualified reserve fund. The Code provides that a qualified reserve fund is any reasonably required reserve used to provide for full payment of the REMIC's expenses or amounts due on regular interests in the event of defaults on qualified mortgages.[45] A qualified

---

[40]Code §860G(a)(6), thus, defines a cash-flow investment as ''any investment of amounts received under qualified mortgages for a temporary period before distribution to holders of interests in the REMIC.''

[41]1986 Conf. Rep., §301 note 1, at II-227.

[42]Code §860F(a)(2)(D).

[43]Code §860G(a)(7).

[44]Id.

[45]Code §860G(a)(7)(B).

reserve fund is any "reasonably required" reserve to provide for full payment of REMIC expenses or amounts due on regular or residual interests in the event of defaults on qualified mortgages, prepayment interest shortfalls, or lower than expected returns on cash flow investments. Importantly, the REMIC Regulations expand the qualified reserve fund definition to include reserves that protect residual interests. In contrast, the REMIC Regulations prohibit the practice (which is clearly permitted under the statute) of using residuals from one REMIC as qualified reserve assets in another REMIC.[46]

The "reasonably required" test is the key to qualified reserve fund status. The REMIC Regulations provide that to determine whether a reserve is reasonably required, it is appropriate to consider several things: (1) the credit quality of the qualified mortgages (e.g., first liens versus home equity loans); (2) the extent and nature of any guarantees; (3) expected REMIC expenses; and (4) expected availability of qualified mortgage payments to pay REMIC expenses.

The statute further provides that the reserve must be "promptly and appropriately reduced" as payments on qualified mortgages are received.[47] The REMIC Regulations clarify that the reserve may be increased by the addition of payments on qualified mortgages or by contributions of residual interest holders.

The REMIC Regulations provide a presumption that a qualified reserve is reasonable and is presumed to be promptly and appropriately reduced if it does not exceed: (1) the amount required by a nationally recognized rating agency to give the rating for the REMIC the sponsor desires; or (2) the amount required by a third-party insurer or guarantor who does not own, directly or indirectly, an interest in the REMIC, as a requirement for credit enhancement. A representation by an investment banking firm, while it may be useful, does not provide a presumption of reasonableness under the REMIC Regulations.

The presumption of reasonableness is just that: a presumption. It may be rebutted if the amounts required by a rating agency or a third-party insurer are not commercially reasonable considering the factors the IRS considers appropriate for sizing a reserve (listed above).[48]

A qualified reserve fund cannot derive significant gains from short-term trading. Thus, the Code provides that a reserve fund is not treated as a qualified reserve in any tax year in which more than 30 percent of the gross income from the reserve fund is derived from the sale or disposition of property held for less than three months.[49] Gain from dispositions necessary to prevent a default on a regular interest where the anticipated default would be caused by default on one or more qualifying mortgages is not counted for this purpose.[50]

The 30-percent test is similar to the "short-short" test applicable to regulated investment companies (RICs).[51] It is important to note that the test depends on gross and not net gains. Thus, gains from the sale of reserve assets are not reduced by losses from the sale of other reserve assets.

---

[46] Reg. §1.860G-2(g)(3).
[47] Id.
[48] Id.
[49] Code §860G(a)(7)(C).
[50] Id.
[51] Code §851(b)(3).

§307.2.2   Outside Reserve Funds

Outside reserve funds are commonly used in REMIC transactions for several reasons. One example would be a reserve initially funded by the sponsor where the sponsor will be reimbursed as payments are made on subordinated regular interests. Although commonly used, such outside reserves are not addressed in the REMIC statute.

The REMIC Regulations, however, provide a helpful rule that basically permits outside reserve funds to pay expenses of the REMIC or to make payments to REMIC interest holders.[52]

The REMIC Regulations provide that an outside reserve fund is not a REMIC asset, but only if the REMIC's organizational documents "clearly and expressly": (1) provide that the reserve fund is an outside reserve and not a REMIC asset; (2) identify the reserve fund owners by name or description of the class of owners; and (3) provide for all federal tax purposes that amounts transferred by the REMIC to the reserve are treated as distributed to the designated owner or owners or their transferees. Although not expressly stated, it appears that such owners therefore must be either regular or residual interest holders in the REMIC if amounts are distributed from the REMIC to fund the outside reserve (e.g., a reserve that funds over time).

The REMIC Regulations allow the use of outside reserve fund proceeds in situations where inside reserve fund proceeds may not be so used. For example, numerous REMIC transactions have used outside reserve funds to protect regular interest holders against "basis risk," i.e., the risk that the floating interest rate on their regular interest will exceed the rate produced by the REMIC's qualified mortgages.[53]

§307.2.3   Foreclosure Property

The last type of permitted investment is foreclosure property. This concept is borrowed from the REIT rules and is basically designed to deal with property that is acquired in a foreclosure of a qualified mortgage. Obviously, the concept is only important where the qualified mortgages are conventional and not government guaranteed mortgages.

Foreclosure property must meet the definition of foreclosure property under the REIT rules. Thus, foreclosure property is:[54]

> [A]ny real property (including interests in real property), and any personal property incident to such real property, acquired . . . as the result of [the REMIC] having bid in such property at foreclosure, or having otherwise reduced such property to ownership or possession by agreement or process of law, after there was a default (or default was imminent) . . . on an indebtedness which such property secured. Such term does not include property acquired . . . as a result of indebtedness arising

---

[52]Reg. §1.860G-2(h).
[53]See §305.1.2 above.
[54]Code §860G(a)(8).

from the sale or other disposition of property of the [REMIC] described in section 1221(1) which was not originally acquired as foreclosure property.[55]

Property ceases to be foreclosure property two years after it is acquired. The REIT provisions provide for extensions of this grace period. In addition, such extensions can be terminated, for example, if construction takes place on the property (other than a completion of a structure that was at least 10 percent complete at the time of default), or if a trade or business is conducted on the property more than 90 days after it is acquired by the REIT.[56]

The REIT rules also provide that property will not qualify as foreclosure property if the loan with respect to which default occurs (or is imminent) was acquired by the trust: (1) with an intent to foreclose; or (2) when the trust knew or had reason to know that default would occur (the "improper knowledge" test).[57] If a REMIC acquires a loan when it knew or had reason to know that the loan would default, the property securing the loan would not qualify as foreclosure property if the REMIC ultimately acquires the property. If more than one percent of the REMIC's assets consist of such property, the REMIC may cease to qualify as a REMIC.

In today's economic environment, however, it is fairly common to have some loans in a mortgage portfolio that are late in payment. Thus, there may be loans transferred to a REMIC that are one or more payments in arrears. In general, it is thought that such delinquencies do not necessarily mean that the mortgagor will ultimately not make the payments. Instead, most mortgage servicers allow a grace period before instituting collection or foreclosure proceedings. Unfortunately, however, the REIT rules do not draw a bright-line test (based on the number of payments a loan is delinquent) that can be used to determine when a REMIC has "improper knowledge" with respect to such a mortgage loan. In fact, the preamble to the REMIC Regulations specifically reserves comment on this topic.

In practice, tax counsel have generally felt comfortable including delinquent mortgage loans in a REMIC if such loans were less than three months delinquent as of the cut-off date for the pool. For example, if a REMIC transaction's start-up day is May 25, 1994 and the cut-off date for the REMIC pool is May 1, 1994, tax counsel will generally allow into the REMIC only those mortgage loans on which the February 1 payment had been made.

In order to apply the improper knowledge test in the REMIC context, it is important to understand how this test developed. In 1973, Congress amended the REIT rules to provide that income from foreclosure property (e.g., rents) constitutes qualifying REIT income regardless of whether the rent is based upon the net income of the tenant.[58] The amendment was designed to ensure that a REIT would not be disqualified merely because it became the owner of a property earning disqualifying REIT income (e.g., rents based on the tenant's net income)

---

[55]Code §856(e).

[56]Id. Code §860G(a)(8)(A) (parenthetical language).

[57]Reg. §1.856-6(b)(3).

[58]See Act of Jan. 3, 1975, Pub. L. No. 93-625, §6. Such income is subject to a corporate-level tax under Code §857(b)(4)(A).

through foreclosure. Congress was concerned, however, that a REIT might enter into mortgages with parties clearly incapable of making the mortgage payments. The REIT could then immediately foreclose and thereby acquire property that would pay rent based upon a calculation that would, absent the property's status as foreclosure property, be nonqualifying REIT income. Consequently, the Code §856(e) legislative history states that property would not qualify as foreclosure property if the loan with respect to which a default occurs (or is imminent) was acquired by the REIT with an intent to foreclose or when the REIT knew or had reason to know that default would occur.[59] The regulations under Code §856(e) adopted this statement as the Improper Knowledge Test.[60]

The concern underlying the enactment of the Improper Knowledge Test does not exist in the REMIC context. A REMIC will not acquire a delinquent loan in order to obtain the rental income on the underlying property upon foreclosure. Rather, investors in REMIC regular interests are interested in acquiring debt instruments with predictable yields based on periodic mortgage loan payments. Such investors would prefer that the REMIC never have to foreclose on a loan.

Since the perceived abuse underlying the improper knowledge test is not applicable in the REMIC context, practitioners expect that the IRS will ultimately provide a bright-line test generally as described above. There is some evidence that the IRS is thinking along these lines in the proposed taxable mortgage pool (TMP) regulations (see discussion in Chapter 4). Thus, residential mortgages that are more than 89 days delinquent and commercial mortgages that are more than 59 days delinquent are not considered real estate mortgages for TMP purposes.

The REIT rules relating to foreclosure property also require that a taxpayer make an election to treat property as foreclosure property on or before the due date (including extensions) for filing its tax return for the year in which the foreclosure property was acquired. The election is irrevocable. TAMRA amended Code §860G(a)(8) to make it clear that a REMIC is not required to make a specific election for property to be treated as foreclosure property.

The original REMIC statute provided that property would cease to be foreclosure property one year after the REMIC acquired the property. The concern, however, was that a REMIC might not sell its foreclosure property within one year, particularly if the property was commercial real estate. TAMRA, therefore, replaced the one-year rule with the less restrictive REIT rule described above (i.e., a two-year grace period plus extensions) and imposes a tax on the REMIC's net income from foreclosure property.[61] The tax is imposed at the highest rate applicable to a corporation. The net income from foreclosure property is defined by reference to the REIT rules. In general, this is the gain from sale or disposition of foreclosure property that is described in Code §1221(1), i.e., "dealer" property and gross income from foreclosure property (except such income as would be qualifying real estate related income for a REIT) less any deductions directly connected to the production of such income.[62] The REMIC statute also provides

---

[59]S. Rep. No. 1357, 93d Cong., 2d Sess., *reprinted in* 1974 U.S. Code Cong. & Admin. News 7478, 7490.
[60]See Reg. §1.856-6(b)(3).
[61]Code §860G(c).
[62]Code §857(b)(4)(B).

that the REMIC's taxable income is reduced by the amount of tax attributable to such income.[63]

§308 ARRANGEMENTS REASONABLY DESIGNED TO ENSURE THAT RESIDUALS WILL NOT BE HELD BY DISQUALIFIED ORGANIZATIONS

§308.1 Background

As discussed below, in 1986 Congress enacted the Code §860E excess inclusion rules to ensure that "phantom income" from a REMIC is always subject to federal income tax. Thus, among other things, excess inclusions are treated as unrelated business taxable income under Code §511. After the initial REMIC legislation, however, it became apparent that one way to avoid the excess inclusion rules was to have the residual interest held by a governmental entity such as the U.S. government or a state or local government, i.e., an entity that is not subject to the Code §511 tax on unrelated business taxable income.

To curb this perceived abuse, in October 1987 the Treasury Department proposed a set of amendments to the REMIC rules designed to ensure that residual interests could not be owned by government entities and certain other persons. As originally proposed, these rules would have imposed a tax on excess inclusions at the REMIC level to the extent that the REMIC had such entities as residual owners.

The October 1987 legislation caused some consternation among REMIC sponsors because of the difficulty of accurately determining who owns a REMIC residual interest. Most publicly traded residuals were held in "street name" through one or more layers of nominees and beneficial ownership was hard to determine. The problem was compounded by the existence of pooled investment vehicles such as REITs that might have government entities as owners. The attempt to impose an entity level tax on the REMIC also raised concerns because a public rating agency rating a transaction might assume that a tax would be paid on the entire amount of the REMIC's excess inclusion and would require reserve funds or other guarantees against such taxes.

As a result of these concerns, TAMRA contained a modified version of the October 1987 proposal. This proposal adopted a three-pronged stance to address the perceived abuse: (1) requiring the REMIC to adopt "reasonable arrangements" to ensure that "disqualified organizations" do not own any of the REMIC's residual interests; (2) imposing a tax on the transfer of a residual to a disqualified organization; and (3) imposing a tax on excess inclusions of "pass-through" entities such as REITs and RICs that had "disqualified organizations" as record (rather than beneficial) owners of shares (and imposing the tax on nominees for such shareholders who held RIC or REIT shares in "street name"). Although require-

---

[63]Code §860C(b)(1)(E).

ments (2) and (3) are not REMIC qualification requirements, they are discussed below so that the issues involving ownership by "disqualified organizations" can be considered together.

§308.2   The Reasonable Arrangements Requirement

The REMIC statute now provides that a REMIC will not qualify as such unless there are reasonable arrangements designed to ensure that: (1) residual interests in such REMIC are not held by "disqualified organizations"; and (2) information necessary for the application of the transferor tax (described below) will be made available by the REMIC.[1] A "disqualified organization" includes the United States, a state or political subdivision, a foreign government, any international organization, other organizations exempt from tax on unrelated business taxable income, and certain cooperatives.

As noted above, a REMIC is required to prohibit disqualified organizations from owning residual interests and to provide notice to residual owners of this restriction. The REMIC Regulations specify when arrangements to restrict transfer of residuals to disqualified organizations will be considered reasonable. The REMIC Regulations state that a registered residual interest combined with a clear and express prohibition in the REMIC's organizational documents on transfer to a disqualified organization will be reasonable, provided such prohibition is in a legend on the residual certificate or conspicuously stated in the residual offering document (e.g., a prospectus or private offering document).[2] Also, to qualify as a REMIC, the REMIC must agree to make available, upon request, information necessary to compute the transferor tax (described in the next section).[3] If requested, the information must be furnished to the requesting party and to the IRS within 60 days of the request.[4] The REMIC can charge a reasonable fee for providing the information.[5] This fee will not be treated as income derived from a prohibited transaction subject to the prohibited transaction tax.[6]

§308.3   Transferor Tax

In addition to the prohibition on ownership of REMIC residuals by disqualified organizations, the REMIC statute imposes a tax on any person that transfers a residual interest to a disqualified organization.[7]

As noted above, the tax is imposed on a transfer of a residual to a disqualified organization. It is paid by the transferor of the residual. If, however, the transfer is through an agent for the disqualified organization, then the agent is liable for the tax. The REMIC Regulations clarify that an agent includes a broker, nominee

---

§308   [1]Code §860D(a)(6).
[2]Reg. §1.860D-1(b)(5).
[3]Code §860D(a)(6)(B).
[4]Id.
[5]See Reg. §1.860E-2(a)(5).
[6]Id.
[7]Code §860E(e).

or other middleman. For example, if a disqualified organization has a brokerage account with a securities brokerage firm and the brokerage firm buys a REMIC residual on behalf of the disqualified organization, then the brokerage firm is liable for the tax.

The REMIC Regulations clarify some of the uncertainties surrounding the excise tax. First, the REMIC Regulations provide that the excise tax is due on April 15th of the year following the year of transfer.

The REMIC Regulations also clarify the method of calculating the excise tax. The tax equals the present value of the residual's excess inclusions, which is determined by discounting those excess inclusions back from the end of each calendar quarter remaining in the life of the REMIC to the date of transfer of the residual. The discount rate is the applicable federal rate that would apply to a debt instrument that was issued on the transfer date of the residual to the disqualified organization and whose term ended on the close of the last quarter in which excess inclusions were expected to accrue with respect to the residual interest.[8]

The anticipated excess inclusions must be determined as of the date the residual is transferred and must be based on: (1) events that have occurred in connection with the REMIC from the start-up day until the date of transfer; (2) the prepayment and reinvestment assumptions adopted under Code §1272(a)(6) (or such rules that would have been adopted had the REMIC's regular interests been issued with OID); and (3) any required or permitted clean-up calls or liquidations required in the REMIC's documents.

The transferor (or agent) is relieved of liability for the tax if it receives an affidavit from the transferee that the transferee is not a disqualified organization and, at the time of the transfer, it does not have actual knowledge that such an affidavit is false.[9] Although brokers generally do not acquire residuals as agents, if a broker were to acquire a residual it should obtain an affidavit from its client in order to avoid the tax on agents which is described above.

In the alternative, the REMIC Regulations allow the transferee simply to provide its social security number and to state under penalties of perjury that such number is the transferee's.[10]

The REMIC Regulations provide that transitory ownership of a residual by a disqualified organization will, however, be disregarded.[11] Thus, if the disqualified organization has a binding contract to sell the residual on the start-up day and the sale occurs within seven days of the start-up day, the transitory ownership by the disqualified organization will be disregarded.[12]

§308.4   Pass-Through Entities

Special rules apply to RICs, REITs, partnerships, common trust funds, and trusts and estates (pass-through entities).[13] Thus, a pass-through entity is not a

[8]Reg. §1.860E-2(a)(4).
[9]See Appendix C for a sample transferee affidavit.
[10]Reg. §1.860E-2(a)(7)(i)(B).
[11]Reg. §1.860E-2(a)(2).
[12]Id.
[13]Code §860E(e)(6).

disqualified organization. Accordingly, a transfer to a pass-through entity is not subject to the transferor tax. Instead, a pass-through entity is subject to a tax (again at the highest corporate rate) on REMIC excess inclusions for the taxable year to the extent interests in the pass-through entity are held by disqualified organizations.[14] For these purposes a pass-through entity is required to look only at record ownership of its residual interests.[15] Under these rules, the tax is thus borne by all the holders of an interest in such entity, unless it is specially allocated to the disqualified organizations that own interests in the pass-through entity. The REMIC Regulations provide that such a special allocation does not create a preferential dividend under Code §562(c) for a RIC or a REIT.[16]

The rule for pass-through entities also applies (except as provided in regulations) to nominees who hold an interest in a pass-through entity for another person.[17] Therefore, a nominee is subject to tax to the extent it holds an interest in a pass-through entity as a nominee for a disqualified organization.

The tax imposed on pass-through entities is deductible, but only against gross income from the residual interest to which the tax relates.[18]

The pass-through entity can avoid the disqualified organization tax with respect to its interests so long as the record holder of the interest provides an affidavit, stating that such record holder is not a disqualified organization, and so long as the pass-through entity does not have actual knowledge that the affidavit is false.[19]

Because of the foregoing rules, a pass-through entity such as a RIC or a REIT that intends to buy a substantial amount of REMIC residuals will typically include a provision in its charter providing that a disqualified organization cannot own its shares and that the pass-through entity can redeem any shares that are owned by a disqualified organization if the pass-through entity becomes aware of such ownership.

§308.5 Waiver Rules

The Code contains provisions whereby the Secretary of the Treasury (Secretary) may waive the transferor tax if: (1) after discovering a taxable transfer, steps are taken so that the residual is no longer held by a disqualified organization; and (2) such amounts as the Secretary prescribes are paid to the Secretary.[20]

§308.6 Effective Dates

The requirement of reasonable arrangements to ensure that no disqualified organization holds a residual interest applies to REMICs with start-up dates after

[14]Code §860E(e)(6)(A).
[15]Id.
[16]Reg. §1.860E-2(b)(4).
[17]Code §860E(e)(6)(B).
[18]Code §860E(e)(6)(C).
[19]Code §860E(e)(6)(D).
[20]Code §860E(e)(7).

March 31, 1988, unless the transfer was pursuant to a binding written contract in effect on such date.

The amendments relating to pass-through entities apply to excess inclusions for periods after March 31, 1988, but only to the extent such inclusions are allocable to an interest in a pass-through entity acquired after March 31, 1988, or attributable to a residual interest acquired after March 31, 1988. An interest in a pass-through entity (or a residual interest) acquired after March 31, 1988, pursuant to a binding written agreement entered into on or before March 31, 1988, is treated as acquired on or before March 31, 1988.

§309   ELECTION AND CALENDAR YEAR REQUIREMENTS

A REMIC may be formed as a state law entity or as a segregated pool of assets.[1] To constitute a REMIC, the assets identified as part of a segregated pool must be treated for all federal income tax purposes as assets of the REMIC and interests in the REMIC must be based solely on assets of the REMIC.[2]

A REMIC must elect to be treated as a REMIC for the tax year and all prior tax years. Thus, a REMIC cannot have been a subchapter C corporation, a partnership, or a trust that had a prior non-REMIC tax year.[3]

One concern this requirement raises is whether a trust will be considered to have a tax year that is a non-REMIC year. Thus, for example, it will usually be necessary to form a trust that will elect REMIC status prior to the REMIC's start-up day by making a small, initial contribution (for example, $200). If the trust is formed in one calendar year, but the REMIC start-up day occurs in a subsequent calendar year (e.g., a trust formed on December 31, 1989, whose REMIC start-up day is January 3, 1990), this should not be a problem if the trust conducts no significant activities and earns no income in 1989 which would prevent it from qualifying as a REMIC. One technical analysis of this issue is that the trust is a grantor trust for federal income tax purposes and that it does not have its own tax year because it does not exist separately from the grantor. The problem can also be avoided by designating the segregated pool of assets, exclusive of the initial contribution, as a REMIC. It should be noted, however, that the REMIC Regulations shed no light on this issue.

§309.1   Manner of Making Election

The REMIC election is made on the REMIC's return for its first tax year. Unless revoked, the election applies to all subsequent tax years.[4] Therefore, an election

§309   [1]Reg. §1.860D-1(c)(1).
[2]Id.
[3]Code §860(D)(a)(1).
[4]Code §860D(b)(1).

need not be made on the return after the first tax year, although it may be prudent to do so.

The REMIC Regulations provide that the election is made by timely filing, for the first tax year of its existence, a Form 1066 (U.S. Real Estate Mortgage Investment Conduit Income Tax Return) signed by a person authorized to sign that return under Reg. §1.860F-4(c).[5] In addition, for the first tax year of the REMICs existence the REMIC must provide, either on its return or in a separate statement attached to its return, the following:

(1) the REMIC's employer identification number (EIN) (which cannot be the same as the EIN of any other entity);

(2) information concerning the terms and conditions of the regular and residual interests of the REMIC or a copy of the offering circular or prospectus containing such information;

(3) a description of the prepayment and reinvestment assumptions made pursuant to Code §1272(a)(6) and the regulations thereunder, if any, including a statement supporting the selection of the prepayment assumption;

(4) the form of the electing entity under state law or if an election is made with respect to the segregated pool of assets within an entity, the form of the latter entity; and

(5) such other information required by the form.[6]

§309.2   *Termination of Election*

The REMIC election terminates if the REMIC ceases to meet the REMIC requirements at any time during the tax year. The termination applies to the tax year and all subsequent tax years. Thus, unlike the REIT rules,[7] the termination penalty is not limited to a five-year period.

The drastic nature of the termination requirement is alleviated somewhat because the Secretary has discretion to continue to treat the REMIC as a REMIC even after the termination event.[8] According to the REMIC legislative history, Congress intended that this relief was to be provided only where failure to meet the REMIC requirements was inadvertent and in good faith.

The statutory requirements for the relief are that: (1) the termination be inadvertent; (2) once the problem is discovered, action is taken to requalify; and (3) the entity and its interest holders agree to adjustments required by the Secretary, such as treatment of the REMIC as a C corporation during the termination period.[9]

---

[5]See Appendix A for a copy of IRS Form 1066.
[6]Reg. §1.860D-(d)(2).
[7]Code §856(g)(3).
[8]Code §860D(b)(2)(B).
[9]1986 Conf. Rep., §301 note 1, at II-229.

§309.3 Calendar Tax Year

The last REMIC requirement is that the REMIC must have a calendar tax year. This requirement, which is the same as that for REITs formed after 1976,[10] is designed to prevent deferral of income through the interaction of the REMIC's tax year with that of its residual holders.

§310 CONTRIBUTIONS TO THE REMIC

After meeting the qualification requirements, the next important topic is how contributions to the REMIC are treated for federal income tax purposes. In general, these rules are designed to treat, as closely as possible, the creation of the REMIC as the sale of the mortgage loans that comprise the REMIC by the sponsor who created the REMIC.

§310.1 Consequences to Transferor: Gain or Loss

The transferor does not recognize any gain or loss when property is transferred to the REMIC.[1] In most cases, this property will be qualified mortgages transferred by the REMIC sponsor. It may also include, however, assets that will comprise a qualified reserve fund.

The nonrecognition rule extends to transactions that are designated to avoid the rule. For example, assume that a bank owns mortgages which have a basis greater than their fair market value. No gain or loss would be recognized under Code §860F(b)(1)(A) if the bank transferred the mortgages directly to the REMIC in exchange for residual and regular interests. But, if it sold the mortgages to a third party (for example, an investment banking firm) for such cash and then used the cash to purchase regular interests in a REMIC created by the third party, it might argue that a gain or loss could be recognized. The REMIC Regulations, however, state that a sponsor will not be permitted to recognize a gain or loss in this manner.[2]

§310.1.1 Treatment of Nonrecognized Gain and Loss

The REMIC statute contains rules for inclusion or deduction of nonrecognized gain or loss to the transferor. As a practical matter, these rules are only a minor concern with respect to the regular interests because such interests are typically sold when the REMIC is formed. They are of greater concern to the holder of a residual interest that holds such residual interest rather than selling it.

---

[10] Code §859.
§310 [1] Code §860F(b)(1)(A).
[2] Reg. §1.860F-2(b)(2).

The amount of any nonrecognized gain or loss is the difference between the adjusted basis of the regular or residual interest and its issue price. Adjusted basis is computed in the manner described below.

Issue price for regular interests is determined under the rules that apply for original issue discount.[3] Therefore, such an amount includes underwriter's commissions. In addition, the issue price for each regular interest sold in a public offering is the same, regardless of the fact that some regular interests were purchased at different prices.

The issue price for a residual interest equals the amount of money paid for the residual interest or, in the case of a residual interest issued in exchange for property, the fair market value of the residual interest at the time of issuance.[4]

For a regular interest, the nonrecognized gain is includible in income as though it were market discount which the holder had elected under Code §1276(b) to include in income currently.[5] Presumably, in determining the proper accrual, a reasonable prepayment assumption could be used. Nonrecognized loss is allowed as a deduction as if it were an amortizable bond premium on the regular interest.[6] Again, although not entirely clear, a prepayment assumption should be permitted in computing the premium deduction.

For a residual interest the rules are even easier. Thus, nonrecognized gain or loss is included in income (or deducted) on a straight-line basis over the REMIC's anticipated weighted average life.[7] The anticipated weighted average life of a REMIC is the weighted average of the anticipated weighted average lives of all classes of interests in the REMIC.[8] This treatment is somewhat unrealistic, however, because the REMIC's anticipated weighted average life may be much longer than the residual's economic life. For example, in many transactions, the residual only represents the right to receive spread income while the first tranche of fast-pay or slow-pay regular interests is outstanding. Nevertheless, under a literal reading of the Code and REMIC Regulations, gain or loss will be recognized over the REMIC's entire weighted average life.

In computing the anticipated weighted average life of a regular interest, the residual holder should: (1) multiply the amount of each anticipated principal payment to be made on the interest by the number of years (including fractions) from the start-up day to the related principal payment date; (2) add the results; and (3) divide the sum by the total principal to be paid on the regular interest.[9]

§310.1.2   Basis

The REMIC statute provides that the total basis of regular and residual interests received by the transferor equals the total basis of the property transferred to the REMIC in exchange for such interests.[10]

---

[3]Code §1273.
[4]Reg. §1.860G-1(d)(1).
[5]Code §860F(b)(1)(C)(i); Reg. §1.860F-2(b)(4)(i).
[6]Code §860F(b)(1)(D)(i); Reg. §1.860F-2(b)(4)(ii).
[7]Code §860F(b)(C)(ii); Reg. §§1.860F-2(b)(4)(iii) and (iv).
[8]Reg. §1.860E-1(a)(3)(iv).
[9]Reg. §1.860E-l(a)(3)(iv)(B).
[10]Code §860F(b)(1)(B).

The basis in the regular and residual interests received, as determined under the above rule, is then allocated among the residual and regular interests according to their respective fair market values.[11]

EXAMPLE

Assume that the transferor's basis in qualified mortgages is $100. Further, assume that the transferor transfers the mortgages to a REMIC and receives, in return, regular and residual interests worth $101. The transferor's basis in the regular and residual interests is $100 — the basis in the qualified mortgages exchanged. This basis is split between the residual and regular interests according to their respective fair market values. Thus, assume that the residual's value is $2 and the regular interests are valued at $99. The transferor's basis in the residual equals 100 $\times$ ($2/101) or $1.98. His basis in the regular interest equals $100 $\times$ ($99/101) or $98.02.

The REMIC rules assume that the transferor always transfers mortgages in exchange for residual and regular interests. More often than not, however, this is not the case. Instead, the REMIC will sell regular interests to the public for cash and will then buy the mortgages from the sponsor using the cash. The REMIC Regulations state that the REMIC rules were intended to produce one result, regardless of the order of the steps by which qualified mortgages are received, and regular and residual interests are issued.[12] Therefore, even though the transaction is not structured as a contribution of mortgages in exchange for regular and residual interests, it will be treated as such and the results will be as described above.[13]

The key to the basis allocation is the valuation of the regular and residual interests received in the exchange. The fair market value of the regular interests should be the price at which they were sold to the public. Although not entirely clear, this should be the gross price to the public without reduction for costs of sale, including underwriting commissions. This amount may be different from the issue price of the regular interests as computed for original issue discount purposes because issue price is determined as a whole according to the price at which a substantial portion of the issue was sold to the public. On the other hand, it would appear that actual sale prices for all regular interests must be totalled to derive the fair market value of the regular interests.

The fair market value of the residual interests will be their purchase price (again not reduced by costs of sale) if the residual interests are sold as part of the transaction. If the residual interest is retained, then the value will be determined by reference to other residuals that have been sold. This may be somewhat difficult because each residual is different. One approach would be to determine what discount rate and prepayment assumption residual buyers were applying to residual cash flows at the time the residual was created. This discount rate would be used to compute the value of the residual by applying it to the cash flows expected

[11]Id.
[12]Reg. §1.860F-2(a)(1).
[13]Id.

to be generated by the residual based upon the prepayment assumption. This method does not take into account, however, the tax treatment of the residual holder which differs for each holder.[14] It also does not take into account that different buyers may use different prepayment assumptions in valuing the same residual.

§310.1.3 Syndication versus Organizational Expenses

The REMIC Regulations make a distinction between syndication and organizational expenses of the REMIC. This distinction, previously only found in the IRS rules on partnership syndication expenses, is primarily important in determining the sponsor's tax basis in regular or residual interests that it retains: organizational expenses are added to basis, syndication expenses are not.

The REMIC Regulations provide that the sponsor's basis in the residual and regular interests created on a REMIC's formation is equal to the sponsor's basis in the mortgages transferred to the REMIC, increased by organizational expenses.[15] This total basis is allocated among the residual and regular interests according to their relative fair market values on the date the transaction is priced,[16] or if no pricing occurs, on the start-up day.[17]

The REMIC Regulations define organizational expenses as expenses incurred by the sponsor or the REMIC that are directly related to the REMIC's creation.[18] Examples include: legal fees for services (e.g., preparation of a pooling and servicing agreement), accounting fees, and other administrative costs. Organizational expenses must be incurred during a period beginning a reasonable time before the start-up day and ending before the due date (without extensions) for the REMIC's first tax return. The term "reasonable time" is not defined.

Syndication expenses are expenses incurred by the sponsor or other person to market the REMIC interests.[19] Examples are brokerage fees, registration fees, fees of an underwriter or placement agent, prospectus or placement memorandum printing costs, and costs of other selling or promotional material. Syndication

---

[14]In certain cases, "phantom income" on the residual may make its value to a taxable holder zero, or even negative. In Priv. Ltr. Rul. 9228009 (Apr. 6, 1992), a corporation acquired non-economic residuals in which the present value of the tax costs associated with the residual exceeded the present value of the tax savings associated with the residual and the projected distributions. Nevertheless, the IRS ruled that the corporation's tax basis in the residual is zero and that the residual's adjusted issue price is also zero.

[15]Reg. §1.860F-2(b)(3)(ii).

[16]The pricing date for this purpose is defined in the REMIC Regulations as the date on which (1) the regular and residual interests' terms are fixed and (2) the prices at which a "substantial portion" of the regular interests will be sold are fixed. Reg. §1.860F-2(b)(3)(iii). Substantial portion is not defined although it may be interpreted by practitioners consistently with the OID rules in which 10 percent of the interests is generally considered a substantial portion.

[17]Use of pricing date values answers concerns that values of the regular and residual interests might change between the pricing date and the closing date (i.e., start-up day), thus affecting the basis allocation.

[18]Reg. §1.860F-2(b)(a)(ii)(A).

[19]Reg. §1.860F-2(b)(s)(ii)(B).

expenses do not increase basis in the regular and residual interests. Instead, they reduce the amount realized on the sale of the REMIC interests.

§310.1.4   Holding Period

There is no specific rule for the holding period of regular and residual interests that are received in exchange for transfers of qualified mortgages. Instead, assuming the transferred assets are capital assets or Code §1231 property, the general rule of Code §1223(1) will apply so that the holding period of the regular and residual interests will include the holding period for the qualified mortgages surrendered.

§310.1.5   Treatment of the REMIC

The REMIC should not recognize any gain or loss when it issues regular and residual interests in exchange for property.[20] The basis for the property received is its fair market value immediately after the transfer.[21]

The REMIC Regulations provide that the basis of a REMIC's qualified mortgages is equal to the aggregate of the issue prices of all regular and residual interests in the REMIC.[22] Under the Proposed OID Regulations, the issue price of a regular or residual interest differed depending on whether such interest was publicly offered, privately placed or retained by the sponsor. If the interest was publicly offered, the issue price was the initial offering price to the public at which a substantial amount of the interest was sold. If the interest was privately placed, the issue price was equal to the price paid by the first buyer.

The Final OID Regulations (see Chapter 5) have eliminated the distinction between publicly and non-publicly offered debt instruments for purposes of determining issue price. Thus, the first price at which a substantial amount (for example, 10 percent) of a class of regular interests is sold for a particular price will be treated as the issue price for such class regardless of whether such class is sold publicly or privately placed. Likewise, the Final OID Regulations provide that for both publicly and non-publicly offered regular interests, sales to bond houses, brokers or similar persons or organizations acting in the capacity of underwriters, placement agents or wholesalers will be ignored.

If the sponsor retains the interest, the issue price is the fair market value of the interest on the pricing date, if any, or the start-up day. The point of this is that normally a REMIC's regular interests are priced well before the REMIC is actually formed. Fluctuations in the market price of qualified mortgages after pricing should not affect the REMIC's basis in the qualified mortgages because, in effect, the REMIC owns the qualified mortgages immediately after the pricing.

---

[20]Although not expressly stated in the statute, this result seems proper by analogy to Code §1032 and because the regular interest is treated as a debt instrument for federal income tax purposes.

[21]Code §860F(b)(2).

[22]Reg. §1.860F-2(c).

While the REMIC Regulations are limited to qualified mortgages transferred to the REMIC by the sponsor, similar principles should apply to qualified mortgages purchased by a third party, such as an investment banking firm, prior to creation of the REMIC.

§311 TREATMENT OF DISTRIBUTIONS BY THE REMIC

The REMIC provisions also contain rules about distributions of property by the REMIC to residual and regular interest holders. This is not likely to occur, particularly because, as discussed below, REMIC liquidations are all-cash affairs. If it does happen, gain is recognized by the REMIC as though it had sold the property to the transferee for its fair market value.[1] Presumably, if this occurs, the gain will be subject to the prohibited transaction tax unless one of the safe harbors is met. Loss is not recognized.

§312 TAXATION OF THE REMIC

The tax treatment of the REMIC is relatively simple. Thus, the REMIC is not subject to tax, except in a few narrow instances. Instead, the REMIC's income, as computed under some special rules, is taxed to the holders of the regular and residual interests in the REMIC.

There are three primary exceptions to the rule that the REMIC itself is not subject to tax:[1] the prohibited transactions tax, the tax on contributions to the REMIC after the start-up day, and withholding taxes that may be imposed on the REMIC.

§312.1 Prohibited Transactions Tax

The prohibited transactions tax is a tax equal to 100 percent of the REMIC's net income from prohibited transactions.[2] Obviously, this is not a tax but a way to remove the economic incentive from certain types of transactions.

There are four types of prohibited transactions. The first is any disposition of a qualified mortgage, except a protected disposition. A protected disposition includes:

(1) Substitution of a qualified replacement mortgage for a qualified mortgage;

§311 [1]Code §860F(c)(1).
§312 [1]Code §860A.
[2]Code §860F(a)(1).

(2) Disposition "incident to" the foreclosure, default, or imminent default of the mortgage;

(3) The REMIC's bankruptcy or insolvency; and

(4) A qualified liquidation.[3]

A protected disposition also includes any disposition necessary to prevent default on a regular interest where the threatened default resulted from a default on one or more qualified mortgages.[4]

The second type of prohibited transaction is the receipt of any income from an asset that is not a qualified mortgage or a permitted investment.[5]

The third type of prohibited transaction is any amount representing a fee or other compensation for services.[6] This prevents a REMIC from earning any type of service income, for example, income for issuing a guarantee on mortgages owned by another REMIC. As noted above, a fee for supplying a residual interest holder with information about excess inclusions will not be considered prohibited transaction income.[7]

The last type of prohibited transaction income is any gain from the disposition of a cash-flow investment unless the disposition is pursuant to a qualified liquidation.[8] This rule is consistent with the treatment of a grantor trust — temporary investments must be held until maturity and not sold, at least not sold at a gain.

The REMIC is taxed on "net income" from its prohibited transactions. This is defined as the gross income less any deductions connected with the transaction that produced the gross income. Losses from prohibited transactions are not taken into account for this purpose.[9]

§312.2 Tax on Contributions After the Start-Up Day

TAMRA added a new tax on a REMIC for certain contributions to the REMIC after the start-up day. Although there is no explanation for the provision in the accompanying legislative history, the rule was apparently designed to ensure that the REMIC is not expanded after the start-up day by contributions of any property (including cash).

The basic rule (found in Code §860G(d)) is that if any amount is contributed to a REMIC after the start-up day, there is imposed a tax equal to 100 percent of the amount of the contribution received. The tax is paid with the REMIC's federal income tax return for the tax year in which the contribution is made.

The term "contribution" is not defined in the statute or the TAMRA legislative history. It is apparently not limited to contributions made by regular or residual interest holders in the REMIC, but is broad enough to include contributions by

---

[3]Code §860F(a)(1).
[4]Code §860F(a)(5)(A).
[5]Code §860F(a)(2)(B).
[6]Code §860F(a)(2)(C).
[7]See §308.2.
[8]Code §860F(a)(2)(D).
[9]Code §860F(a)(3).

any third party, including the REMIC sponsor. The term should not include proceeds of the sale of a qualified mortgage, or, of course, prepayments received on qualified mortgages. Although the statute refers to "any amount" contributed to the REMIC, the TAMRA legislative history applies the tax to "any property" contributed to the REMIC, e.g., cash or mortgages.

There are four exceptions to the contributions tax. The first is for any contribution to facilitate a clean-up call. The term "clean-up call" is not defined in the Code. However, the REMIC Regulations provide that a clean-up call is "the redemption of a class of regular interests when, by reason of prior payments with respect to those interests, the administrative costs associated with servicing that class outweigh the benefits of maintaining the class."[10] Thus, some transactions provide that each class of regular interests can be called when its principal balance is less than a specified percentage of its original principal balance. Money for the call can be provided by selling qualified mortgages or by the residual interest holder contributing money to the REMIC. This exception is designed to permit such a contribution. The REMIC Regulations list the following five factors to consider in evaluating whether a call is a permissible clean-up call: (1) the number of holders of that class of regular interests; (2) the frequency of payments to holders of that class; (3) the effect the redemption will have on the yield of that class; (4) the outstanding principal balance of that class; and (5) the percentage of the original principal balance of that class still outstanding.[11] The REMIC Regulations also provide a safe harbor clean-up call when the principal balance of a class is less than 10 percent of the original principal balance of such class.[12] It is also important to ensure that the call is not being exercised to profit from changes in interest rates.[13] Thus, if a clean-up call is to be exercised and it does not fit within the safe harbor, the tax advisor may want a representation that the call is being made to save administrative costs associated with keeping the class outstanding rather than to profit from changes in interest rates.

The next exception to the contributions tax is for any payment in the nature of a guarantee. The TAMRA legislative history requires that these be cash payments, a requirement not found in the statute, which probably poses little problem. The guarantee exception should cover servicer advances as well as payments to the REMIC under a surety bond, letter of credit or insurance policy. The statute is not limited to credit-related guarantees. Thus, payments pursuant to non-credit related guarantees should also be permitted. For example, a sponsor may guarantee that the REMIC's expenses will not exceed a particular dollar amount each year. A payment pursuant to such a guarantee should be considered "in the nature of a guarantee." Additionally, the exception should be broad enough to cover payments made pursuant to a liquidity contract between the sponsor and the REMIC which provides that a convertible mortgage will be repurchased if it is converted by the mortgagor. On the other hand, if the guarantee is a disguised method of making a contribution to the REMIC, a payment pursuant to such guarantee would be subject to the contributions tax.

[10]Reg. §1.860G-2(j)(1).
[11]Id.
[12]Reg. §1.860G-2(j)(3).
[13]See Reg. §1.860G-2(j)(2).

A third exception exists for any contribution during the three-month period beginning on the start-up day. This contribution must also be made in cash.[14] It is important to note that this 90-day period is different from the period for making sure that all the REMIC's assets are qualified assets described in Code §860D(a)(4) (such period begins on the start-up day and ends on "the close of the third month beginning after the start-up day").

A fourth and final exception exists for any contribution to a qualified reserve fund made by a holder of a residual interest. Thus, for example, the holder of a residual interest might be required to dedicate a portion of the cash flow on his residual interest to funding a reserve fund if certain conditions are met during the life of the REMIC. The TAMRA legislative history again requires that the contribution be made in cash.

Finally, the Secretary is empowered to write regulations permitting other types of contributions. No regulations have yet been issued.

§312.3 *Withholding Taxes*

The REMIC is also liable for withholding taxes. These will take two forms. First, a 30-percent or, if applicable, a lower treaty rate of withholding applies to payments made to holders of regular and residual interests. Under current law, however, assuming REMIC interest holders provide proper certifications, there will be few cases where withholding on regular interests is required. As discussed below, withholding may be required on residual interests.

The second type of withholding is 31-percent back-up withholding that applies in certain cases where the recipient does not properly certify that he is an exempt recipient and does not furnish the REMIC with an accurate taxpayer identification number.[15] The back-up withholding responsibilities as a practical matter will be handled by the financial institutions or brokers that make distributions on the REMIC's interests — they generally will not concern the REMIC.

§313   TAXATION OF REMIC INTEREST HOLDERS

§313.1 *Regular Interests*

A regular interest is treated as a debt instrument for federal income tax purposes. Thus, a regular interest holder is generally taxed as if he held a debt instrument with the same terms as the regular interest. There are three important differences, however.

---

[14]Recently, this exception has been utilized in conjunction with prefunding accounts established outside the REMIC that are invested pending the origination of mortgage loans used to satisfy a fixed-price contract. See §307.1.8 above. In such case, cash from the prefunding account is contributed by the sponsor to the REMIC and used to purchase qualified mortgages during a prefunding period beginning on the start-up day and ending 90 days thereafter.

[15]Code §3406.

§313.1.1   Automatic Accrual Method

First, the holder of a regular interest must report income on the regular interest according to the accrual method of accounting.[1] This treatment applies regardless of the regular interest holder's normal method of accounting and may result in an acceleration of income for a cash basis taxpayer. Such treatment will also make it necessary for the holder of a regular interest to report income even where the income is not yet paid, for example, in a default situation, unless it is clear the interest will never be paid.

§313.1.2   Special Gain Rule

The second difference is that the regular interest holder must treat part of the gain on sale of a regular interest as ordinary income even though it would otherwise be capital gain. The amount of gain so treated is equal to the excess of: (1) the amount the taxpayer would have reported as ordinary income on the regular interest if the regular interest yield was 110 percent of the applicable federal rate (determined as of the beginning of the taxpayer's holding period); over (2) the amount actually reported as income.[2] While the REMIC legislative history says that this is an additional amount of original issue discount that must be reported, the statute is not limited in this manner.[3] Thus, under the statute, even if the regular interest were not issued with OID, gain on sale would still be subject to the 110-percent rule.

The 110-percent rule apparently exists to ensure that gain recognized on a sale is treated as ordinary income and not capital gain up to some objective level. This rule is apparently a response to pre-REMIC concerns that holders of CMOs were reporting prepayments that accelerated OID income or gain on sale as capital gain rather than as ordinary income.[4] This rule, however, makes less sense in light of the rules that now apply to OID on CMO-type debt, discussed below.[5]

§313.1.3   Qualifying Asset Treatment

The third difference between a REMIC regular interest and other CMO debt instruments is that the holder of a regular interest is entitled to treat the regular interest as a direct ownership of the underlying mortgages for certain purposes of the Code. These special provisions include Code §593(d) relating to thrifts, Code §856(c)(6)(E) and Code §7701(a)(19)(C). The general rule is that if more than 95 percent of the REMIC's assets qualify under the relevant Code section, then the entire regular interest is treated as a qualifying asset under such provision.

§313   [1]Code §860B(b).
[2]Code §860B(c).
[3]See 1986 Conf. Rep., §301 note 1, at II-232; Code §860B(c); 1986 Blue Book, §305 note 24, at 420.
[4]See §502.
[5]See §503.

If less than 95 percent of the REMIC's assets qualify under the relevant Code section, the regular interest is only treated as a qualifying asset for purposes of such provision in the proportion that the qualified assets the REMIC owns bears to the REMIC's total assets.[6]

§313.2   Residual Interest Holders

The tax treatment of the residual interest holder is a little more interesting. In general, the residual interest holder includes the REMIC's net income or loss for the tax year in his income for federal income tax purposes. Special rules apply to tax "phantom income" that is generated by the REMIC. The residual interest holder is not taxed on cash distributed, unless such cash exceeds his adjusted basis in the residual interest.

§313.2.1   Inclusion of REMIC Net Income or Loss

As stated above, the residual interest holder includes the REMIC's net income or loss in his taxable income.[7] The holder is thus required to include the "daily portion" of such income or loss for each day during the tax year that he holds the residual interest.[8] The income or loss is treated as ordinary income or loss.[9]

The daily portion is computed by allocating to each day in the calendar quarter its *pro rata* share of the REMIC's taxable income or net loss for the quarter.[10] Amounts allocated to a day are then allocated to residual interest holders according to their respective interests on that day.[11]

Actual application of the rules may prove difficult. Thus, consider what happens when the REMIC has a loss for one quarter and income for another quarter that offsets the loss. For example, suppose that investor A holds 100 percent of a REMIC's residual interests for the first six months of 1994 and investor B holds 100 percent of the residual interests for the last six months of 1994. Assume further that the REMIC has $300,000 of taxable income for the first six months of 1994 and $300,000 of taxable loss for the last six months of 1994. The daily portion allocated to investor A for the first six months would be $1,666.66 of taxable income. The daily portion allocated to investor B for the second half of the year would be $1,666.66 of net loss. The REMIC itself would have no net income or loss for the tax year. This unique result becomes a particular problem where the residual holders during each part of the tax year, as in the example, are different. One taxpayer recognizes a gain and another recognizes a loss. Yet, there has been neither taxable gain nor loss at the REMIC level. While wide swings in income

[6]Code §§593(d), 856(c)(6)(E), and 7701(a)(19)(C).
[7]Code §860C(a).
[8]Code §860C(a)(1).
[9]Code §860C(e)(1).
[10]Code §860C(a)(2)(A).
[11]Code §860C(a)(2)(B).

are unlikely, they may occur in a REMIC that holds conventional mortgages where several such mortgages are found to be worthless during one quarter.

Net losses of the REMIC deducted by the residual holder cannot exceed the holder's basis in the residual interest as of the close of the calendar quarter.[12] If the residual interest is transferred during the quarter, the transfer date is treated as the end of the quarter for this purpose. Losses that are suspended are carried forward indefinitely but can only be used to offset income from the REMIC according to the REMIC legislative history.[13] Thus, no loss in excess of residual income is permitted even when the residual interest is retired.

Some special rules apply to determine the REMIC's taxable income or loss. In general, these rules are designed to coordinate the general principles of taxation under the Code with the REMIC rules.

These rules provide that the REMIC's taxable income is determined under an accrual method of accounting and in the same manner as an individual's, with certain exceptions.[14] First, the REMIC's regular interests are treated as the REMIC's debt.[15] Therefore, interest and original issue discount on such interests will be deductible by the REMIC. Second, market discount on any market discount bond owned by a REMIC is currently includible as it accrues.[16] The exact method for accrual is not set forth in the statute. Third, no item of income, gain, loss, or deduction from a prohibited transaction is taken into account.[17] Fourth, certain deductions such as personal exemptions, foreign taxes, charitable contributions, net operating losses, itemized deductions, and depletion are not allowed.[18] Fifth, as noted above, TAMRA added a provision that the tax imposed on net income from foreclosure property is deductible in computing the REMIC's taxable income.[19]

The REMIC Regulations generally follow the statute, with some important qualifications. First, the REMIC Regulations provide that gain and loss from the disposition of any REMIC asset is treated as ordinary gain or loss.[20] This is true even for assets that would otherwise be capital assets under the Code — for example, mortgages held for investment. One effect of this rule is that the rules limiting capital loss carryovers do not apply to a REMIC.

The REMIC Regulations also state that the REMIC is allowed a deduction without regard to the Code §163(d) interest expense limitation.[21] Furthermore, the REMIC Regulations provide that a REMIC's bad debt deductions are not treated as nonbusiness debts.[22] This is important because losses on nonbusiness debts are limited under the Code to wholly worthless debts.[23] Additionally, such

---

[12]Code §860C(e)(2)(A).
[13]1986 Conf. Rep., §301 note 1, at II-233.
[14]Code §860C(b)(1).
[15]Code §860C(b)(1)(A).
[16]Code §860C(b)(1)(B).
[17]Code §860C(b)(1)(C).
[18]Code §860C(b)(1)(D); the disallowed deductions are those listed in Code §703(a)(2).
[19]Code §860C(b)(1)(E).
[20]Reg. §1.860C-2(a).
[21]Reg. §1.860C-2(b)(2).
[22]Reg. §1.860C-2(b)(3).
[23]Code §166(d).

nonbusiness bad debt losses are treated as capital losses under Code §166(d). Accordingly, under the REMIC Regulations, a REMIC can claim a deduction for a partially worthless debt and such a deduction is an ordinary, rather than a capital, loss.

The REMIC Regulations also classify a REMIC's ordinary and necessary operating expenses as expenses deductible under Code §212, rather than Code §162.[24] For this purpose, Code §67 (which limits an individual's Code §212 expenses to those exceeding two percent of adjusted gross income) does not apply to the REMIC (although Code §67 does apply to REMIC residual holders that are individuals).

In addition, it should be noted that certain expenses incurred in connection with the REMIC's formation are not considered REMIC expenses under the REMIC Regulations. Instead, as described above, the REMIC Regulations treat such expenses as additions to the sponsor's basis in the regular and residual interests created upon the REMIC's formation.

Finally, the REMIC Regulations provide that a REMIC cannot deduct expenses and interest allocable to tax-exempt income.[25] Therefore, if a REMIC invests in tax-exempt bonds, the residual holder's share of the REMIC's net income will be the entire amount of interest on such bonds, rather than the income less interest deductions on regular interests and REMIC expenses. The Code provides that the residual holder's share of REMIC net income is ordinary income. The combination of these two rules would seem to produce inflated ordinary income amounts for the residual holder if the REMIC invests in tax-exempt bonds (and makes it fairly unlikely that a REMIC will do so, at least knowingly).

§313.2.2 Treatment of Distributions

Distributions by the REMIC are not included in the residual holder's gross income to the extent that they do not exceed the holder's basis in the residual interest.[26] If such distributions exceed the adjusted basis in the residual interest, they are treated as gain from the sale or exchange of the residual interest.[27]

The distribution rules thus reflect the fact that the residual holder, like a partner in a partnership, is taxed without regard to cash distributions.

§313.2.3 Basis Calculations

The residual holder's basis is determined in much the same way that a partner's basis in a partnership interest is determined. Thus, the residual holder's original basis is the cash or adjusted basis of property contributed to the REMIC. The residual holder's basis is increased by the taxable income of the REMIC allocated

[24]Reg. §1.860C-2(b)(4).
[25]Reg. §1.860C-2(b)(5).
[26]Code §860C(c)(1).
[27]Code §860C(c)(2).

to the holder[28] and by contributions under Code §860G(d)(2).[29] The residual holder's basis is decreased by allocated net losses and by the amount of any cash or the fair market value of any property distributions to such holder.[30] The residual holder's basis, however, cannot be reduced below zero.[31]

§313.2.4 Excess Inclusions

Perhaps the most difficult aspect of the residual interest holder's taxation is the treatment of excess inclusions. These rules are designed to ensure that "phantom income" from the REMIC is not diverted to a nontaxpaying entity.

Phantom income is a problem that has plagued the fast-pay or slow-pay mortgage vehicle from the start. As noted previously, it arises because interest income and market discount on mortgages held by the issuer accrue at a constant rate. Expenses relating to the fast-pay or slow-pay bonds, however, accrue at an ever-increasing rate. This is because the interest expense rises as lower yielding classes of bonds are retired. Phantom income arises because the cash attributable to the difference may be paid through to bondholders as principal. This leaves no cash for the residual owners.

Congress feared that without the excess inclusion rules, phony residual interests could be structured to siphon off phantom income. These residual interests could then be sold to persons that did not pay taxes, such as savings and loans with net operating losses, foreign taxpayers, and pension funds.

The excess inclusion rules are designed to eliminate this perceived abuse. They do this by providing that the taxable income of a holder will at least be equal to its share of the REMIC's excess inclusions for the tax year.[32] Thus, a taxpayer with a net operating loss cannot use its losses against excess inclusions. Additionally, excess inclusions are treated as unrelated business taxable income that is taxable to an otherwise tax-exempt pension trust.[33] Excess inclusion income is also subject to the full 30-percent U.S. withholding tax rate unreduced by any treaty.[34]

The excess inclusion rules do not apply to thrifts (to which Code §593(d) applies) that acquire REMIC residuals with "significant value" (as described below).[35]

Excess inclusions are calculated by computing a base return on the residual holder's investment in the residual interest. Any taxable income for the calendar quarter in excess of that amount is an excess inclusion.

The base return is computed by reference to the "daily accruals" on the residual interest during the calendar quarter. The daily accruals are computed each quarter by multiplying: (1) the residual's adjusted issue price at the start of the quarter by (2) 120 percent of the long-term Applicable Federal Rate (AFR).[36] The applicable

---

[28] Code §860C(d).
[29] Reg. §1.860C-1(b)(1).
[30] Reg. §1.860C-1(b)(2).
[31] Code §860C(d)(2).
[32] Code §860E(a)(1); Reg. §1.860E-1(a).
[33] Code §860E(b).
[34] Code §860G(b).
[35] Code §860E(a)(2).
[36] Code §860E(c)(2)(A).

long-term AFR is the long-term AFR in existence when the residual interest is issued. It is determined by compounding at the end of each quarter and is adjusted for the length of the quarter (for example, a short quarter may be caused by a newly formed REMIC, a liquidated REMIC or a transfer of a residual interest).[37] This amount is then allocated ratably to each day during the quarter.

The residual's adjusted issue price is the issue price of the residual interest, increased by daily accruals for prior quarters and decreased by any distributions made before the beginning of the quarter.[38] It is not reduced for any losses of the REMIC.

A special excess inclusion rule applies to REITs. Thus, the excess of all excess inclusions on all residual interests held by the REIT over the REIT's real estate investment trust taxable income (excluding any net capital gain) must be allocated among the REIT's shareholders according to the dividends received by such shareholders.[39] The amounts so allocated to REIT shareholders are treated by them as excess inclusions.[40] In effect, this rule operates so that the REIT dividend is first treated as an excess inclusion up to the amount of gross excess inclusion income at the REIT level. REIT expenses (e.g., management fees) apparently do not offset the excess inclusion income.

Before TAMRA, this rule applied only to REITs that held residual interests. TAMRA gives the IRS regulation authority to apply the rules to RICs. The REMIC Regulations reserve comment on the treatment of REITs, RICs, common trust funds and subchapter T cooperatives holding residual interests.[41]

§313.2.5   Significant Value Residuals: The 2/20 Rule

In the case of a residual interest that lacks "significant value," the Code provides that all income with respect to such interest will be treated as excess inclusion income.[42]

Although the REMIC legislative history provides that a residual interest would have significant value if its value is at least equal to 2 percent of the combined value of the regular and residual interests in the REMIC, it does not clearly identify at what point or points in time during the life of the REMIC such residual value must exist. The ambiguity with regard to this point led to the issuance in the early 1990s of so-called "burn-out" residuals where the residual has a 2 percent value on the start-up day but is paid off entirely within the first year or so of the REMIC's existence.

---

[37] Code §860E(c)(2)(A)(ii).
[38] Code §860E(c)(2)(B).
[39] Code §860E(d)(1).
[40] Code §860E(d)(2).
[41] Reg. §1.860E-1(b).
[42] Code §860E(c)(1). Although the Code provides that the income with respect to a residual interest lacking significant value is excess inclusion income "to the extent provided in regulations," tax counsel generally advise as to the treatment of the income on such residual interest even though the IRS has not issued any such regulations.

To address these instruments, the REMIC Regulations provide a "2/20 rule" for determining whether a residual has significant value.[43] Under the 2/20 rule a residual interest will have significant value if: (1) the aggregate of the issue prices of the residual interests is at least equal to 2 percent of the aggregate of the issue prices of all regular and residual interests in the REMIC; and (2) the anticipated weighted average life of the residual interests is at least 20 percent of the REMIC's weighted average anticipated life based on the prepayment and reinvestment assumptions used in pricing the transaction. Although not entirely clear, the REMIC Regulations apparently provide that the 2-percent value is required only on the start-up day. Thus, burn-out residuals are apparently restricted only by the requirement that the weighted average life of such a residual must be at least equal to 20 percent of the REMIC's anticipated weighted life.

The anticipated weighted average life of a REMIC is the weighted average of the anticipated weighted average lives of all classes of regular and residual interests.[44] The anticipated weighted average life of a regular interest with a principal balance and a market rate of interest is computed by multiplying the amount of each expected principal payment by the number of years (or fractions thereof) from the start-up day, adding these sums and dividing by the total principal expected to be paid on such regular interest[45] based on the relevant prepayment assumption, expected reinvestment income, any required or permitted clean-up calls, or any required qualified liquidations provided for in the REMIC's operative documents.[46] The anticipated weighted average life of: (1) a regular interest with either no specified principal balance or a principal balance and rights to interest payments disproportionate to such principal balance; or (2) a residual interest, would be computed under the formula described above but would include all payments expected on such interest instead of only the principal payments.[47]

The REMIC Regulations also provide for the order in which a thrift may use losses against excess inclusions. Under that rule, losses are first used against gross income that is not an excess inclusion, then against excess inclusions.[48] This is important because excess inclusions cannot be offset by losses of other members of a consolidated group while other income can be offset by group losses. For example, suppose a thrift has $100 of excess inclusion income, $100 of other gross income and a $100 loss. The REMIC Regulations provide that the $100 loss is used first to offset the $100 of non-excess inclusion income. The $100 excess inclusion remaining cannot be offset by group losses.

§313.2.6 Transfers of Noneconomic Residuals

The REMIC Regulations provide that a transfer of a noneconomic residual interest is disregarded for federal income tax purposes if a significant purpose of

---

[43]Reg. §1.860E-1(a)(3)(iii).
[44]Reg. §1.860E-1(a)(3)(iv).
[45]Reg. §1.860E-1(a)(3)(iv)(B).
[46]Reg. §1.860E-1(a)(3)(iv)(D).
[47]Reg. §1.860E-1(a)(3)(iv)(C).
[48]Reg. §1.860E-1(a)(3)(ii).

the transfer was to enable the transferor to impede the assessment or collection of tax.[49] A significant purpose to impede the assessment or collection of tax exists "if the transferor, at the time of the transfer, either knew or should have known that the transferee would be unwilling or unable to pay taxes due on its share of the taxable income of the REMIC."[50] A residual is defined as a non-economic residual unless, at the time it is transferred: (1) the present value of its expected future distributions at least equals the product of the present value of the anticipated excess inclusions and the highest rate of corporate tax for the year in which the transfer occurs; and (2) the transferor reasonably believes the transferee will receive distributions from the REMIC at or after the time at which the taxes accrue on the excess inclusions to satisfy the accrued taxes.[51] The purpose of this rule is to prevent the sale of residual interests to persons who are not expected to be able to pay the taxes with respect to excess inclusion income. A transferor of a noneconomic residual interest can establish a presumptive lack of improper knowledge by satisfying two conditions. First, the transferor conducts a reasonable investigation of the transferee and, as a result of that investigation, finds that the transferee has historically paid its debts as they come due and finds no significant evidence to indicate that the transferee will not continue to pay its debts as they come due in the future. Second, the transferor obtains from the transferee a representation that the transferee understands that the residual interest may generate tax liabilities in excess of cash flows and that the transferee intends to pay those tax liabilities as they come due. To protect transferors of noneconomic residual interests, tax counsel generally include in the transfer affidavit provided by transferees of residual interests the representation of the transferee that "the transferee does not have the intention to impede the assessment or collection of any federal, state or local taxes legally required to be paid with respect to the residual interest and the transferee hereby acknowledges that the residual interest may generate tax liabilities in excess of the cash flow associated with the residual interest and intends to pay such taxes associated with the residual interest when they become due."[52]

§313.2.7   Foreign Residual Owners

In 1991, the IRS made it clear that selling or placing residuals with foreign investors in order to avoid the imposition of tax will be outlawed by regulations. The REMIC Regulations provide that the transfer of a residual interest that has tax avoidance potential (TAP) is disregarded for all federal income tax purposes if the transferee is a foreign person.[53] This rule does not apply to residual income

---

[49]Reg. §1.860E-1(c)(1).
[50]Id.
[51]Reg. §1.860E-1(c)(2).
[52]See the sample transferee affidavit at Appendix C, representation #9.
[53]Reg. §1.860G-3(a)(1).

that is effectively connected to the residual holder's United States trade or business (in which case the residual holder is treated like a U.S. person).[54]

The TAP test is met unless, at the time the residual interest is transferred, the transferor reasonably expects that: (1) the future residual distributions will equal at least 30 percent of the anticipated excess inclusions; and (2) the transferor reasonably expects that the transferee will receive enough distributions at or after the time the residual's excess inclusions accrue and not later than the close of the calendar year following the calendar year of accrual to satisfy the expected tax and withholding liability with respect to the excess inclusions.[55] The REMIC Regulations modify the Proposed REMIC Regulations which specifically permitted a residual interest which "front-loads" excess inclusions but significantly "backloads" cash (for example, with a final distribution at the end of 30 years equal to 30 percent[56] of the sum of the residual's excess inclusion income). The REMIC Regulations do provide a safe harbor that a transferor will be deemed to have a reasonable expectation if the 30-percent test described above would be satisfied were the REMIC's qualified mortgages to prepay at each rate within a range of rates from 50 percent to 200 percent of the prepayment rate used in pricing the transaction.[57]

In order to prevent a foreign investor from transferring a residual interest of the type described in the previous paragraph to a U.S. person shortly before any tax is due, the REMIC Regulations provide that if the transfer has the effect of allowing the foreign person to avoid tax on accrued excess inclusions, the transfer is disregarded.[58] The foreign person thus continues to be treated as owner of the residual interest for withholding tax purposes. This rule may require a "chain of title" approach to residual transfers so a U.S. buyer can insure that the residual interest has never been held by a foreign investor.

§313.2.8   Marking Residual Interests to Market

The mark-to-market rules passed as part of the Revenue Reconciliation Act of 1993[59] (as new Code §475(a)) require "dealers in securities" to mark their securities to market at each year end. This provision appeared to require dealers to "mark to market" residual interests held in their dealer accounts regardless of whether or not the dealers held the residual interests as investments or as part of their inventory. When a security is marked to market, the holder is deemed to have sold the security for its fair market value on the last day of its taxable year and is required to recognize the gain or loss from the deemed sale. Accordingly, if residual interests were treated as securities for purposes of these provisions,

---

[54]Reg. §1.860G-3(a)(3). An exemption from withholding of tax on income that is effectively connected with the conduct of a trade or business in the United States is made on IRS Form 4224. See Appendix D for a copy of IRS Form 4224.

[55]Reg. §1.860G-3(a)(2)(i).

[56]Thirty percent is the U.S. withholding tax rate on excess inclusion income.

[57]Reg. §1.860G-3(a)(2)(ii).

[58]Reg. §1.860G-3(a)(4).

[59]Pub. L. No. 103-66.

dealers would be treated as having sold their residual interests for fair market value on the last business day of each taxable year in which they held such residual interests.

Generally, a "noneconomic" residual interest will generate excess inclusion income during the first several years of the REMIC's life. As a result of recognizing this income, the residual interest holder's basis in its residual interest will increase by an amount equal to the amount of such income. Because a noneconomic residual interest will always have a zero (or negative) fair market value, if residual interests were treated as securities under the mark-to-market provisions, dealers holding such residual interests would be entitled to a loss equal to the holder's adjusted tax basis in such residual interest at year end. As a result, the residual interest holder would generally have taxable income and an offsetting loss.[60]

On December 28, 1993, the IRS released temporary regulations relating to the requirement that a securities dealer mark to market securities held for sale to customers or otherwise held in its dealer account. The temporary regulations provided that for purposes of this mark-to-market requirement, the following items held by a dealer in securities were not securities and, therefore, were not subject to Code §475: (1) stock (including treasury stock) of the taxpayer and any option to buy or sell its stock (including treasury stock); (2) a liability of the taxpayer; or (3) a "negative value" REMIC residual interest. In general, a residual interest had negative value if, as of the date a taxpayer acquired the residual interest, the present value of the tax liabilities associated with holding the residual interest exceeded the sum of (1) the present value of the expected future distributions on the residual interest and (2) the present value of the anticipated tax savings associated with holding the interest as the REMIC generates losses. The amounts and present values of the anticipated tax liabilities, expected future distributions, and anticipated tax savings were all to be determined using (1) the prepayment and reinvestment assumptions adopted under Code §1272(a)(6), or that would have been adopted had the REMIC's regular interests been issued with original issue discount; (2) any required or permitted clean-up calls, or required qualified liquidation, provided for in the REMIC's organizational documents; and (3) a discount equal to the Applicable Federal Rate that would apply to a debt instrument issued on the date of acquisition of the residual interest. The temporary regulations provided the IRS Commissioner with the authority to treat as a "negative value" residual interest any residual interest having substantially the same economic effect as a "negative value" interest. The temporary regulations applied to taxable years ending on or after December 31, 1993.

On January 3, 1995, the IRS released proposed regulations under §475. The proposed regulations provide that any REMIC residual interest acquired after January 3, 1995, cannot be marked to market, regardless of the value of such REMIC residual interest. The temporary regulations described above still apply to any REMIC residual interest acquired on or prior to January 3, 1995. Thus, holders of positive value REMIC residual interests acquired on or prior to January 3, 1995, may continue to mark residual interests to market for the entire economic life of such interests.

---

[60]This loss could not have been used against the excess inclusion income generated by the residual and only could have been used to offset other income of the residual interest holder.

§313.2.9   Qualifying Asset Treatment

A residual interest is treated as a qualifying asset under the same rules that apply to regular interests. Thus, the entire residual interest is treated as a qualifying asset if more than 95 percent of the REMIC's assets are qualifying and a proportionate part of the residual interest is treated as qualifying if 95 percent or less of the REMIC's assets are qualifying.

§314   SPECIAL PROBLEMS OF TWO-TIER REMICS

A two-tier REMIC transaction is one where a REMIC is formed to hold the qualified mortgages and a second REMIC is formed to hold some or all of the regular interests in the first REMIC. Such transactions raise all the common REMIC issues discussed above, plus some unique ones.

§314.1   Reasons for Using a Two-Tier REMIC

The two-tier REMIC has been primarily used where it is not possible to use a single-tier REMIC or it is not entirely clear that one REMIC will meet the statutory rules. The classic example is the following transaction:

EXAMPLE

Assume that a REMIC owns $100X of fixed rate FNMA 8 percent certificates. The REMIC issues Class A, Class B and Class C regular interests with fixed rates of 6 percent, 8 percent and 10 percent, respectively. The regular interests are fast-pay or slow-pay interests and therefore pay sequentially. The sponsor would also like to issue a fourth class of regular interests with a notional principal balance equal to the balance of the Class A and interest equal to 1 percent of such balance. As noted above, an IO regular interest cannot be accomplished in a single-tier REMIC. If, however, the sponsor creates a two-tier REMIC, it can contribute the 6 percent Class A from the lower-tier REMIC to the upper-tier REMIC and crate a new 5 percent Class A and a 1 percent IO regular interest on the lower-tier Class A principal balance.

§314.2   Authority for the Two-Tier Structure

In the above example, if the lower-tier and upper-tier REMICs are treated as one entity, the entity would not qualify as a REMIC because it would have two residual interests. Therefore, it is important that the two REMICs in a two-tier REMIC are respected.

The Code seems to clearly contemplate "stacking" REMICs. Thus, the Code provides that a REMIC regular interest is a qualified mortgage under Code §860G(a)(3)(C).[1] Moreover, the 1988 TAMRA amendments adopt specific rules to deal with the treatment of qualified assets in layers of REMICs.

The REMIC Regulations provide that two or more REMICs may be created in a single set of organizational documents. This is true even if, for state law or federal securities law purposes, the documents create only one organization.[2] This rule is particularly helpful in light of concerns under the Investment Company Act of 1940 (1940 Act) that a "two-tier" REMIC might inadvertently create a 1940 Act investment company. The REMIC Regulations also permit two REMICs in one trust (i.e., a single state law organization) created pursuant to one pooling and servicing agreement.[3]

Accordingly, the REMIC Regulations adopt the view that from a policy standpoint, the chief consideration is that income from the mortgages is properly allocated to holders of regular and residual interests, which is the case with the two-tier REMIC. Therefore, two-tier REMICs are allowable.

§315   REMIC REPORTING REQUIREMENTS

§315.1   REMIC Return (Form 1066)

REMICs are required to make a return for each tax year on Form 1066.[1] The return is due on the fifteenth day of the fourth month following the end of the REMIC's tax year. Since all REMICs have to use the calendar year as their tax year, this Form 1066 is due on April 15. The information required to be set forth on the return is: (1) the amount of principal outstanding on each class of regular interests as of the close of the taxable year; (2) the amount of the daily accruals with respect to the class of residual interests determined under Code §860E(c); (3) the REMIC's employer identification number; and (4) such other information as is required by the form.[2] The obligation to file is on the REMIC, not on the holders of the residual interest.[3] The legislative history of TAMRA and the REMIC Regulations indicate that the REMIC return can be signed by a person who could sign the return if no REMIC election were made, e.g., if the REMIC were a trust, the trustee would sign the return. For REMICS which consist of a segregated pool of assets, the return would be signed by any person who could sign the return of the entity that owns the assets.[4]

---

§314 [1]Code §§593(d)(4), 856(c)(6)(E), and 7701(a)(19)(C). Each refers to REMICs that are part of a "tiered structure."

[2]Reg. §1.860F-2(a)(2)(i).

[3]Reg. §1.860F-2(a)(2)(ii).

§315 [1]Reg. §1.860F-4(b)(2); see Appendix A for a copy of IRS Form 1066.

[2]Id.

[3]Code §860F(e).

[4]H.R. Rep. No. 795, 100th Cong., 2d Sess., pt. 2, at 84 (1988); Reg. §1.860F-4(c).

§315.2   Reports to Residual Owners (Schedule Q)

In addition to the Form 1066, a REMIC must, for each quarter, provide to all holders of residual interests in the REMIC a Schedule Q (Form 1066)[5] setting forth the following information:

(1) the residual interest holder's share of the taxable income or net loss of the REMIC for the quarter;

(2) the amount of the excess inclusions for the quarter, if any, with respect to the residual interest;

(3) if the holder of the residual interest is a pass-through interest holder, the allocable investment expenses for the quarter; and

(4) whether at least 95 percent of the REMIC's assets are invested in certain types of assets,[6] and if not, the percentage of the REMIC's assets that are invested in such assets.[7]

The Schedule Q must be mailed no later than the last day of the month following the close of the calendar quarter.[8] A copy of Schedule Q for each residual interest holder and for each quarter must be attached to the REMIC's income tax return for that tax year.[9]

§315.3   Reporting for Regular Interests

IRS Notice 89-72 sets forth information reporting requirements for REMICs and issuers of collateralized debt obligations. The Notice provides that existing information reporting requirements apply to all issuers of collateralized debt obligations as well as to REMICs.[10] It also provides that only the nominee who holds the obligation for the actual owner (i.e., the last nominee in a chain of nominees) reports tax information to the IRS and to the actual owner.[11]

In order to assist the nominee in his information reporting requirements, issuers are now required to file Form 8811 (Information Return for Real Estate Mortgage Investment Conduits (REMICs) and Issuers of Collateralized Debt Obligations).[12] On that form, the issuer must provide its name, employer identification number, and the Committee on Uniform Security Identification Procedure (CUSIP) number

---

[5]See Appendix A for a copy of Schedule Q.

[6]See §313.1.3.

[7]Reg. §1.806F-4(e)(1)(i).

[8]Reg. §1.860F-4(e)(2)(i).

[9]Reg. §1.860F-4(e)(4).

[10]The debt instruments covered by the IRS Notice include REMIC regular interests and any other debt instrument described in Code §1272(a)(6)(C)(ii), i.e., debt instruments in which payments on the debt instrument can be accelerated by reason of prepayments of other obligations securing such debt instruments. Thus, the notice is not restricted to mortgage-backed debt but applies to other types of debt including debt collateralized by consumer receivables and automobile loans.

[11]Under temporary regulations issued in 1988, all "middlemen" in the chain were subject to reporting requirements.

[12]See Appendix A for a copy of IRS Form 8811.

assigned to each class of REMIC regular interest or collateralized debt obligation. The issuer must also provide the name, address and telephone number of a person who can be contacted by a broker or other middleman to obtain the tax information needed to fulfill its reporting obligation. The reporting requirement does not apply to REMICs all of whose regular interests are owned by another REMIC, i.e., the lower tier REMIC in a two-tier REMIC.

The information supplied to the IRS in Form 8811 will be compiled and published in January of each year in IRS Publication 938, Real Estate Mortgage Investment Conduits (REMICs) Reporting Information (Including Other Issuers of Collateralized Debt Obligations).

Generally, a REMIC must file Form 8811 within 30 days of its start-up day, and other issuers of collateralized debt obligations must file Form 8811 within 30 days of the issuance of those obligations.

As mentioned above, the Notice applies to all debt obligations described in Code §1272(a)(6)(C)(ii). However, although the Notice is unclear on this point, it appears that debt instruments issued prior to the effective date of Code §1272(a)(6)(C)(ii), December 31, 1986, are not covered by the IRS Notice.

§316 FUTURE REMIC REGULATIONS

The REMIC Regulations state that the IRS may provide future guidance with respect to the following seven items:

(1) Regulations under Code §1272(a)(6) concerning the application and scope of the OID rules to regular interests, qualified mortgages and other obligations.

(2) Rules concerning the proper tax treatment of a payment made by a transferor of a noneconomic residual interest to induce the transferee to acquire the interest.

(3) Regulation concerning the allocation of excess inclusions among interest holders in RICs and REITs.

(4) Clarification of the "improper knowledge" standard in Reg. §1.856-6(b)(3) for purposes of determining whether property acquired by a REMIC or a REIT in foreclosure will qualify as foreclosure property.

(5) Regulations concerning the financial information reporting requirements with respect to regular interests.

(6) Expansion of the class of persons that may be designated as tax matters persons.

(7) Regulations concerning withholding on distributions to foreign holders of residual interests to satisfy accrued tax liability due to excess inclusions.

4

Taxable Mortgage Pools

§401   REASONS FOR THE TAXABLE MORTGAGE POOL RULES

One of the controversies surrounding the real estate mortgage investment conduit (REMIC) legislation was the treatment of non-REMIC transactions. The original Senate version of the REMIC bill provided that non-REMIC multiple class mortgage pools would not be permitted after December 31, 1986.[1] The final legislation provided a five-year grace period in which REMICs and other non-REMIC transactions could coexist. Thereafter, i.e., after December 31, 1991, REMICs were intended to be the exclusive (or, as discussed below, nearly exclusive) method of issuing multiple class mortgage-backed securities (MBS). This is accomplished through the taxable mortgage pool (TMP) rules.[2]

---

§401   [1] S. Rep. No. 99-313, 99th Cong. 2d Sess., at 783, 800.
[2] Code §7701(i).

§402   EFFECT OF CLASSIFICATION AS A TAXABLE MORTGAGE POOL

The TMP rules provide that a TMP will be treated as a separate corporation that cannot be consolidated with another corporation in a consolidated federal income tax return.[1] In effect, this means that the TMP's net income will be subject to corporate-level tax under all circumstances. In most cases, and given the REMIC alternative, this will make non-REMIC transactions subject to the TMP rules impossible to do.

§403   DEFINITION OF A TAXABLE MORTGAGE POOL

A TMP is defined as an entity other than a REMIC if (1) substantially all of its assets consist of debt obligations (or interests therein), (2) more than 50 percent of the debt obligations are real estate mortgages (or interests therein), (3) the entity has issued debt obligations with two or more maturities, and (4) the terms of the payments on the multiple-class debt obligations bear a relationship to payments on the debt obligations owned by the entity.[1] TMP is thus a broad concept. It does not, however, include deals that could not be done as REMICs, e.g., receivables transactions. It also does not include senior-subordinated mortgage pools permitted under Reg. §301.7701-4(c)(2) example 2.

The TMP rules also provide that any part of an entity meeting the above requirements will be treated as a taxable mortgage pool.[2] Thus, for example, the rules cannot be circumvented by having a parent company issue the multiple-class, mortgage-backed debt directly rather than through a subsidiary.

§404   EXCEPTIONS TO THE TAXABLE MORTGAGE POOL RULES

There are two important exceptions to the TMP rules. First, the rules do not apply to domestic building and loan associations.[1] Such entities, therefore, can continue to issue collateralized mortgage obligations (CMOs) without incurring a corporate-level tax.

The second exception is for real estate investment trusts (REITs).[2] The TMP rules provide that for a REIT or a qualified REIT subsidiary no corporate-level tax will apply. Instead, amounts equivalent to the excess inclusions from the

---

§402   [1]Code §7701(i)(1).
§403   [1]Code §7701(i)(2)(A).
[2]Code §7701(i)(2)(B).
§404   [1]Code §7701(i)(2)(C).
[2]Code §7701(i)(3).

transaction will be passed through to the ultimate REIT shareholders. Therefore, REITs are able to continue to issue CMOs even after 1991. This exception was drafted as an accommodation to REITs that do not necessarily wish to recognize gain, under the rules described above, when a regular interest is sold. Nevertheless, such REITs may be at a disadvantage with respect to those investors that prefer purchasing REMIC regular interests.

§405   PROPOSED TAXABLE MORTGAGE POOL REGULATIONS

§405.1   General

Since the TMP rules took effect on January 1, 1992, there have been several transactions done that attempt, in one way or another, to provide for issuance of non-REMIC securities backed by mortgages. For example, one popular structure is to issue a single class of mortgage-backed debt. This avoids the multiple-class TMP restriction discussed at §403. Also, with the assistance of IRS private letter rulings, taxpayers have begun to explore when sale proceeds or discounted payoffs (as opposed to principal and interest payments) from an entity's delinquent commercial real estate mortgage loans can be used to service its multiple-class debt obligations.[1]

On December 23, 1992, the IRS issued proposed regulations (Proposed TMP Regulations) under the TMP rules. In general, the Proposed TMP Regulations are helpful in clarifying (1) which assets will be treated as real estate assets and (2) which structures will be permitted.

§405.1.1   Purpose of the TMP Rules

The Proposed TMP Regulations contain an interesting summary for the purpose of the TMP rules: "The purpose . . . is to prevent income generated by a pool of real estate mortgages from escaping Federal income taxation when the pool is used to issue multiple-class mortgage-backed securities."[2] Accordingly, the Proposed TMP Regulations state that they are to be applied in accordance with this purpose. This statement ignores other possible purposes for the TMP rules: (1) making REMIC the exclusive MBS vehicle and (2) preventing taxpayers from choosing between sale and financing treatment for economically identical transactions simply by electing or not electing REMIC status. Nevertheless, the Proposed TMP Regulations handily provide a single, succinct purpose to guide taxpayers in applying their provisions.

---

§405   [1]See, for example, Priv. Ltr. Rul. 9302024 (Oct. 20, 1992), in which the IRS ruled that a tax partnership formed by a government agency to liquidate nonperforming real estate loans was not a TMP, based on certain representations as to the structure of the tax partnership's debt and its operations.

[2]Prop. Reg. §301.7701(i)-1(a).

Contrary to what some practitioners had previously asserted, the Proposed TMP Regulations also make it clear that the TMP rules apply whether or not the entity could have qualified for REMIC treatment.

§405.1.2 "Substantially All" Requirement

As noted above, "substantially all" of an entity's assets must be debt obligations for it to be a TMP. The Proposed TMP Regulations provide that tax basis is used for this purpose. Furthermore, they state that "substantially all" is determined according to "all facts and circumstances." However, the Proposed TMP Regulations provide a safe harbor: if less than 80 percent of an entity's assets are debt obligations (or interests therein) then the "substantially all" test is not met and the entity will not be characterized as a TMP.

For purposes of the "substantially all" test, equity interests in pass-through entities are treated on a look-through basis. For example, if an entity owns shares in a REIT and the REIT owns mortgages, then the entity's adjusted basis in the REIT shares is considered to consist of mortgages in the same proportion as the REIT's mortgages bear to the REIT's other assets.

The Proposed TMP Regulations treat credit enhancement contracts as part of the loans or obligations they support rather than as separate assets in testing an entity's asset composition. In addition, if collateral supports credit enhancement (e.g., a reserve fund supporting a guarantee), then it is not treated as an asset of the entity. By excluding certain assets and treating others as real estate mortgages, these rules make it more difficult for an entity to avoid TMP status.

One of the classic TMP problems has been whether delinquent mortgages are debt obligations for purposes of the TMP rules. This is important because the REMIC rules effectively restrict the use of seriously delinquent mortgages in REMICs. The Proposed TMP Regulations, however, provide that "seriously impaired" mortgages are not debt obligations for purposes of the TMP rules. Therefore, under the Proposed TMP Regulations, the TMP rules would not apply to an entity if more than 20 percent of its obligations are "seriously impaired."

The determination of whether a mortgage loan is "seriously impaired" is based on all facts and circumstances. The Proposed TMP Regulations, however, provide a safe harbor whereby single family loans that are more than 89 days delinquent, and multi-family and commercial loans that are more than 59 days delinquent, are "seriously impaired."[3] This safe harbor does not apply if "an entity" is receiving or anticipates receiving (1) any payments of principal (including principal prepayments) or interest, if those payments are substantial and relatively certain as to amount, (2) payments from prearranged discount payoffs or foreclosures of the mortgage loans, or (3) payments from prearranged sales of the mortgage loans. For example, if an entity held a pool of "seriously impaired" commercial mortgage loans, the safe harbor would not apply if, prior to issuing debt obliga-

---

[3]It is unclear whether this test is applied based on the number of days a loan is delinquent to the cut-off date of a transaction or to the closing date of a transaction.

tions backed by the mortgages, the entity entered into contracts or any other arrangement to sell the mortgages or to receive discounted payoffs.

The application of this safe harbor raises several questions. First, seriously delinquent mortgage loans may have anticipated payments if 10 percent of a mortgage loan is insured (e.g., an FHA loan). Because the Proposed TMP Regulations do not define "substantial payments," it is unclear whether such a loan is excluded from the safe harbor. Furthermore, it is unclear whether seriously delinquent loans that are well seasoned and have a low current loan-to-value ratio (e.g., 50 percent LTV) would be considered loans upon which the entity expects principal payments regardless of how many days delinquent the loan may be.

§405.1.3   Real Estate Mortgage Definition

At least 50 percent of the debt obligations held by an entity must be real estate mortgages for it to be a TMP. The Proposed TMP Regulations define "real estate mortgages" to include (1) obligations (including participations or certificates of beneficial ownership) that are principally secured by an interest in real property, (2) REMIC regular and residual interests, and (3) stripped bonds and stripped coupons stripped from real estate mortgages.

Real property for this purpose is defined by reference to the REIT rules. This is the same cross-reference found in the REMIC rules. Also, manufactured housing (as defined in Code §25(e)(10)) is real property for this purpose, again consistent with the REMIC rules.

There are two tests for determining whether an obligation is "principally secured": (1) if the fair market value of the underlying real estate was at least 80 percent of the obligation's "adjusted issue price"[4] when it was originated (i.e., a loan-to-value ratio of 125 percent or less); or (2) if substantially all the proceeds were used to acquire, improve or protect an interest in real property that, at the origination date, was the only security for the property.[5]

For purposes of the 80 percent test, the value of the real estate is first reduced by the amount of senior liens and is also reduced by a proportionate amount of a pari-passu lien. Also, under the "use of proceeds" test ((2) above), government guarantees or other third party credit enhancements are not viewed as additional security.

In most cases, a mortgage would meet the 80 percent test and would be considered a "real estate mortgage." It is unclear, however, whether a loan could be retested upon restructuring; such a retesting might permit, for example, the loan to fail the 80 percent test if the value of real property collateral had declined but the value of personal property had increased or stayed constant.

---

[4]Adjusted issue price is usually the amount loaned where an obligation is originated for cash. Amounts paid by the borrower, however, may reduce the adjusted issue price under the OID Regulations. Reg. §1.1273-2(g)(2).

[5]The Proposed TMP Regulations, unlike the REMIC Regulations, do not include a safe harbor for the 80 percent test. See §307.1.2.

The Proposed TMP Regulations contain an anti-abuse rule whereby collateralized mortgage obligations issued after December 31, 1991, are treated as real estate mortgages. Tax attorneys had hoped that such obligations (which are not directly secured by real estate but only by mortgages) might escape the technical definition of a real estate mortgage. This, in turn, would have permitted an entity holding, for example, funding notes (i.e., notes secured by mortgages) to escape TMP classification. The Proposed TMP Regulations closed this potential loophole. In contrast, CMOs issued prior to 1992 are not treated as real estate mortgages under the Proposed TMP Regulations and therefore can be collateral for a non-REMIC multiple-class debt financing.

§405.1.4   Two or More Maturities

The entity's outstanding debt obligations must be of "two or more maturities" for it to be a TMP. The Proposed TMP Regulations provide that this requirement is met if the obligations (1) have different stated maturities or (2) if the holders possess different rights concerning acceleration or delay in the maturities of the obligations.

The Proposed TMP Regulations provide, however, that unequal credit risk allocation does not, by itself, create two or more maturities. Therefore, an entity could issue two classes of senior-subordinated debt with the same maturity. Credit risk for this purpose "is the risk that payments of principal or interest will be reduced or delayed because of a default on an asset that supports the debt obligations."[6]

An example in the Proposed TMP Regulations also illustrates that debt is treated as having only one maturity when the debt trustee may select at random particular bonds to be redeemed if mortgage cash flows are sufficient.[7] Another example shows that senior-subordinated bonds can have different interest rates and still be treated as debt with a single maturity date for TMP purposes.[8] The example also provides that a single class of debt still exists where the senior debt is accelerated if the issuer cannot make payments on the senior bonds as they become due.

§405.1.5   "Bear a Relationship" Test

To be a TMP, payments on the entity's outstanding debt (liability obligations) must bear a relationship to payments on the entity's debt obligations (asset obligations). The Proposed TMP Regulations clarify in several helpful ways how this somewhat vague test is met.

---

[6]Prop. Reg. §301.7701(i)-1(e)(2).

[7]Prop. Reg. §301.7701(i)-1(e)(3) example 1. This structure generally applies with respect to tax-exempt bonds and not classic taxable "retail" bonds where certain holders receive priority upon a call by lot. The Proposed TMP Regulations would appear to treat the latter structure as a TMP, although this may be unintentional.

[8]Prop. Reg. §301.7701(i)-1(e)(3) example 2.

The general rule is that the "bear a relationship" test is met if "under the terms of the liability obligations (or 'underlying arrangement') the timing and amount of payments on the liability obligations are in large part determined by the timing and amount of payments or projected payments on the asset obligations."[9] Any payment arrangement that achieves a substantially similar result also satisfies the test. Thus, payments on liability obligations based on payments on a group of assets (or an index of payments) that has an expected payment experience similar to that of the asset obligation should satisfy the "bear a relationship" test.

The important part of the "bear a relationship" test is determining whether something is a "payment" on the asset obligations. If it is not, it can support multiple classes of debt without running into the TMP definition. The Proposed TMP Regulations provide that a payment includes (1) principal and interest on asset obligations, including prepayments of principal and interest and payments under guarantees, but excluding payments arising from settlements at a substantial discount, (2) payments from prearranged settlements at a substantial discount, and (3) proceeds from prearranged sales of asset obligations.[10]

The Proposed TMP Regulations provide an important safe harbor for entities designed primarily to liquidate assets. This safe harbor could be helpful for entities formed to hold nonperforming mortgages which cannot be included in a REMIC. Under the safe harbor, payments on liability obligations do not "bear a relationship" if (1) the entity's organizational documents show clearly that it is formed for the primary purpose of liquidating its assets and distributing proceeds; (2) the entity's activities are all reasonably necessary to and consistent with the accomplishment of liquidating assets; (3) the entity plans to satisfy at least 50 percent of the liability obligations (as determined by issue price) having a different maturity with liquidation proceeds and not with scheduled payments on asset obligations; and (4) the terms of the liability obligations provide that the entity liquidates within three years after it first acquires assets to be liquidated or, if the entity does not so liquidate, the payments received on asset obligations after that time are paid through proportionately to debt holders based on their adjusted issue prices.[11]

This safe harbor would basically permit a nonperforming loan vehicle to issue multiple-class debt obligations and "fast-pay slow-pay" the obligations for three years. The rationale behind this safe harbor is that the IRS's phantom income concerns are relatively minimal where the debt will be paid off within three years or it ceases to be multiple-class debt after three years.

§405.1.6   Anti-Avoidance Rule

The Proposed TMP Regulations contain a general anti-avoidance rule that permits the IRS to disregard or make other adjustments to a transaction (or series of transactions) that technically avoids the TMP rules.[12] This authority permits

---

[9]Prop. Reg. §301.7701(i)-1(f)(1).
[10]Prop. Reg. §301.7701(i)-1(f)(2).
[11]Prop. Reg. §301.7701(i)-1(f)(3).
[12]Prop. Reg. §301.7701(i)-1(g)(1).

equity interests issued by a non-REMIC to be treated as debt.[13] Unfortunately, however, this authority is not further explained. Accordingly, tax practitioners generally do not opine on transactions that are structured with a single class of debt and multiple classes of "equity" that do not pay pro rata with the debt.

The Proposed TMP Regulations provide that interests in grantor trusts will never be treated as debt obligations for purposes of the anti-avoidance rule described in the preceding paragraph.[14] This clarifies that so long as an entity qualifies as a fixed investment trust it will not be a TMP. Thus, for example, senior-subordinated trusts or coupon stripping trusts would not be TMPs under this rule.

§405.1.7 "Portion of Entity" Rule

The Code gives the IRS authority to treat "portions of entities" as TMPs if they otherwise meet the TMP requirements. Thus, an entity that thought it had failed the "substantially all" or "50 percent real estate mortgage" tests might find itself nevertheless classified as a TMP under the "portion of entity" rule.

The Proposed TMP Regulations define a "portion" to "include all assets that support one or more of the same issues of debt obligations."[15] An asset supports a debt obligation if, under the debt's terms, the timing and amount of payments are "in large part" determined either directly or indirectly by the timing and amount of payments or projected payments on the asset or a group of assets that includes the asset. Unlike the "bear a relationship" test, "payments" for this purpose include all proceeds and receipts from an asset. Credit guarantees and assets unlikely to service debt obligations, however, are disregarded.[16]

As an example of the "portion of entity" rule, the Proposed TMP Regulations describe a corporation that owns an office building worth $10 million and $90 million of real estate mortgages. The corporation also has $900 million worth of other assets (presumably business assets). The corporation issues eight classes of bonds. Each class of bonds is secured by a letter of credit and a lien on the office building. In addition, one group of mortgages supports bond classes A though D, another supports classes E through G, and the third supports class H. Cash flows from each group of mortgages will service its related bonds. The example provides that the three groups of mortgages are each "portions" of the corporation. Moreover, no other asset (i.e., the office building or the corporation's business assets) is included in such portion. Accordingly, each portion would be tested separately under the TMP rules.[17]

---

[13]Id.
[14]Prop. Reg. §301.7701(i)-1(g)(2).
[15]Prop. Reg. §301.7701(i)-2(a).
[16]Prop. Reg. §301.7701(i)-2(b).
[17]Prop. Reg. §301.7701(i)-2(d).

§406 SPECIAL EXCEPTIONS TO THE TAXABLE MORTGAGE POOL RULES

§406.1 State and Local Governments

There has been some concern that the TMP rules might apply to certain tax-exempt bonds backed by real estate mortgages. The Proposed TMP Regulations provide, however, that an entity is not a TMP if (1) it is a State, the District of Columbia, or a political subdivision (as defined in Reg. §1.103-1(b)), or is empowered to issue obligations "on behalf of" one of these entities, (2) the entity issues debt obligations in the performance of its governmental purpose, and (3) until the debt is satisfied, the entity holds the remaining interest in any asset that supports those obligations.[1] The Proposed TMP Regulations provide that a governmental purpose does not include repackaging debt obligations for sale on the secondary market, even if profits from the sale are used in an essential governmental function.[2] The Proposed TMP Regulations give the IRS authority to determine that an entity with a similar purpose to an entity described in (1) through (3), above, is not a TMP.[3]

§406.1.1 Real Estate Investment Trusts

The Proposed TMP Regulations do not address the interaction of the REIT rules and the TMP provisions. As noted above, however, the Code and legislative history of the 1986 Act provide that a REIT (or a qualified REIT subsidiary) is not subject to the TMP rules, but that amounts similar to REMIC excess inclusions from a multiple-class mortgage-backed structure are passed through to the REIT's shareholders.

§406.1.2 S Corporations

The Proposed TMP Regulations provide that a TMP may not elect to be an S corporation or maintain S corporation status. Moreover, the Proposed TMP Regulations provide that an S corporation is not treated as part of an affiliated group merely because a portion of the S corporation is treated as a TMP.[4]

§407 EFFECTIVE DATE OF THE TAXABLE MORTGAGE POOL RULES

The Proposed TMP Regulations are proposed to be effective on the date that is 30 days after the date the regulations are published as final regulations.[1] Thus, a

---

§406 [1]Prop. Reg. §301.7701(i)-4(a)(1).
[2]Prop. Reg. §301.7701(i)-4(a)(2).
[3]Prop. Reg. §301.7701(i)-4(a)(3).
[4]Prop. Reg. §301.7701(i)-4(c).
§407 [1]Prop. Reg. §301.7701(i)-3(a).

tax opinion with respect to classification of an entity as a TMP that specifically relies on the Proposed TMP Regulations will note that the Proposed TMP Regulations are not yet effective and are possibly subject to change, which may be retroactive.[2]

Under the 1986 Act, the TMP rules do not apply to any entity in existence on December 31, 1991. However, if there is a substantial transfer of cash or other property to any entity after December 31, 1991, then the TMP rules apply as of the date of the transfer.[3] The Proposed TMP Regulations provide that there is a "substantial transfer" only if the transfer is on or after the date that is 30 days after the date the Proposed TMP Regulations are finalized and (1) the transfer is significant in amount and (2) the transfer is "connected to" the entity's issuance of "related debt obligations" that have different maturities.[4] A related debt obligation is one whose payments bear a relationship (within the meaning of the Proposed TMP Regulations) to payments on debt obligations that the entity holds as assets.[5]

The Proposed TMP Regulations also provide that an entity is classified as a TMP on the first "testing day" that it meets the TMP definition. A "testing day" is any day, on or after the date that is 30 days after the Proposed TMP Regulations are published as final regulations, on which an entity issues a related debt obligation that is significant in amount.[6] The Proposed TMP Regulations also provide that, once an entity is classified as a TMP, it remains a TMP through the day it retires its last related debt obligation.[7] Finally, the Proposed TMP Regulations clarify that a deemed termination of a partnership under the Code[8] will not trigger a "testing day."[9] Accordingly, such deemed terminations would be disregarded for purposes of the TMP effective date rules.

---

[2]Proposed regulations, however, are substantial authority for purposes of the substantial understatement penalty of Code §6662. Reg. §1.6662-4(d)(3)(iii).

[3]Prop. Reg. §301.7701(i)-3(b).

[4]Id.

[5]Prop. Reg. §301.7701(i)-3(b)(3).

[6]Prop. Reg. §301.7701(i)-3(c)(1).

[7]Prop. Reg. §301.7701(i)-3(c)(2).

[8]Code §708(b)(1)(B) provides that a partnership terminates if there is a sale or exchange of 50 percent or more of the total interest in partnership capital or profits within a 12-month period.

[9]Prop. Reg. §301.7701(i)-3(d).

5

Original Issue Discount

§501 OID ON CERTAIN MORTGAGE-BACKED DEBT AND REMIC REGULAR INTERESTS

As part of the real estate mortgage investment conduit (REMIC) legislation, Congress adopted rules to deal with original issue discount (OID) on REMIC regular interests and certain mortgage-backed debt instruments. To understand why these rules were necessary, it may be helpful to examine the tax treatment of asset-backed debt instruments before the REMIC legislation.

§502 PRE-1986 ACT RULES

Before the REMIC amendments, there were no rules on how to report OID on a debt instrument, such as a collateralized mortgage obligation (CMO), in which prepayments on an underlying pool of collateral accelerated principal payments on the debt instrument.

In a CMO, an investor could reasonably expect to be repaid sooner than the payment schedule indicated. For example, the following chart shows the differences in maturities of four classes of CMOs, assuming prepayments equal to a basic prepayment assumption (BPA)[1] and then assuming prepayments at 145 percent of a basic prepayment assumption:[2]

	0% BPA				145% BPA			
	Principal Amounts Outstanding				Principal Amounts Outstanding			
Date	Class A	Class B	Class C	Class D	Class A	Class B	Class C	Class D
July 30, 1987	100	100	100	100	100	100	100	100
July 25, 1988	98	100	100	110	86	100	100	110
July 25, 1989	95	100	100	120	69	100	100	120
July 25, 1990	92	100	100	132	53	100	100	132
July 25, 1991	89	100	100	144	38	100	100	144
July 25, 1992	86	100	100	158	24	100	100	158
July 25, 1993	82	100	100	173	11	100	100	173
July 25, 1994	78	100	100	190	0	92	100	190
July 25, 1995	73	100	100	208	0	34	100	208
July 25, 1996	68	100	100	228	0	0	91	228
July 25, 1997	63	100	100	250	0	0	68	250
July 25, 1998	56	100	100	273	0	0	46	273
July 25, 1999	50	100	100	300	0	0	25	300
July 25, 2000	42	100	100	328	0	0	4	328
July 25, 2001	34	100	100	360	0	0	0	302
July 25, 2002	25	100	100	394	0	0	0	267
July 25, 2003	15	100	100	432	0	0	0	234
July 25, 2004	4	100	100	473	0	0	0	204

§502 [1]The basic prepayment assumption (BPA) used in this example assumes that each mortgage loan underlying a certificate held by the issuer (regardless of interest rate, principal amount, original term to maturity, or geographic location) prepays in the first month after origination at an annual rate of .2 percent of its outstanding principal balance, that this prepayment rate increases each month through the thirtieth month after origination at an annual rate of .2 percent and remains constant in each month thereafter at 6 percent per annum.

[2]Prospectus Supplement dated June 9, 1987 to Prospectus dated June 9, 1987 for the Collateralized Mortgage Obligation Trust 32, Collateralized Mortgage Obligations.

| | 0% BPA | | | | 145% BPA | | | |
| | Principal Amounts Outstanding | | | | Principal Amounts Outstanding | | | |
Date	Class A	Class B	Class C	Class D	Class A	Class B	Class C	Class D
July 25, 2005	0	59	100	519	0	0	0	177
July 25, 2006	0	0	97	568	0	0	0	151
July 25, 2007	0	0	66	623	0	0	0	128
July 25, 2008	0	0	32	682	0	0	0	107
July 25, 2009	0	0	0	726	0	0	0	88
July 25, 2010	0	0	0	656	0	0	0	71
July 25, 2011	0	0	0	578	0	0	0	56
July 25, 2012	0	0	0	492	0	0	0	43
July 25, 2013	0	0	0	413	0	0	0	30
July 25, 2014	0	0	0	325	0	0	0	19
July 25, 2015	0	0	0	228	0	0	0	8
July 25, 2016	0	0	0	120	0	0	0	0
July 25, 2017	0	0	0	0	0	0	0	0
Weighted average life (years)*	11.1	18.3	20.6	26.5	3.4	7.8	11.0	19.3

*The weighted average life of a CMO is determined by (1) multiplying the amount of each principal payment by the number of years from the date of issuance to the related principal payment date, (2) summing the results, and (3) dividing the sum by the total principal paid on the CMO.

In this particular example, prepayments at 145 percent of BPA can be expected to shorten the maturity of the first CMO series, Class A, by 11 years (i.e., from July 25, 2004, to July 25, 1993). The second series, Class B, can be expected, at 145 percent of BPA, to be fully retired 10 years before its stated maturity (i.e., from July 25, 2005, to July 25, 1995). This difference between stated maturity and expected maturity is the reason that the OID rules under prior law[3] produced odd results when applied to CMOs.

The CMO's unique characteristics gave rise to two major questions: (1) how OID on a CMO was to be allocated between scheduled principal payments and (2) how prepayments on a CMO affected the issuer's deduction and the holder's inclusion of OID.

§502.1   Allocation of OID Among Scheduled Principal Payments

The Treasury regulations issued under Code §1232, as it existed prior to enactment of the Tax Equity and Fiscal Responsibility Act of 1982 (TEFRA),[4] provided that a serially maturing debt obligation, such as a CMO, was treated as a series of separate debt obligations, each issued with OID.[5] This rule was necessary

---

[3]Code §§1232 and 1232A of the Internal Revenue Code of 1954.
[4]Pub. L. No. 97-248 (TEFRA).
[5]Reg. §1.1232-3(b)(2)(iv).

because each principal payment on a serially maturing debt obligation was considered a partial retirement.[6]

Treasury regulations provided a mechanical "bond-years" method for allocating original issue discount among principal payments.[7] Under the bond-years method, the OID allocated to a payment was the OID on the entire debt obligation multiplied by a fraction, the numerator of which was the number of years from the issue date to the maturity date for the payment multiplied by the payment's face amount, and the denominator of which was the sum of the amounts determined under the preceding sentence for all payments on the debt obligation. This method served to allocate OID on a time-weighted basis. If all principal payments on a debt obligation were equal, the bond-years method slightly "backloaded" OID, that is, it resulted in an allocation of relatively less OID to earlier principal payments and relatively more OID to later principal payments.

The pre-TEFRA regulations ignored the possibility that if the principal payment amount, the total OID, and the yield on a debt obligation were known, an independent issue price could be mathematically established for each principal payment by subtracting from the scheduled payment amount the sum of the present values of the principal payment and the interest due thereon, discounted at the debt obligation's yield. Thus, by using what was essentially an economic principle of interest accrual, it would be rare if ever that the bond-years method would be used. Nevertheless, under the pre-TEFRA regulations, the economic accrual method for determining the issue price of a serial payment apparently was not permitted.

§502.1.1   Post-TEFRA

TEFRA adopted a new timing rule for deduction and inclusion of OID on most debt obligations.[8] The new rule was designed to correspond to the "actual economic accrual of interest."[9]

The mechanical bond-years method, used in the pre-TEFRA regulations to allocate OID between principal payments on a serially maturing debt obligation, was not consistent with the economic accrual of interest. Economically, the discount on any bond is the bond's face amount less the present value (discounted at the bond yield) of the future bond principal and interest payments. In turn, the OID allocated to each principal payment on a serially maturing debt obligation should be the principal payment's face amount less the present value of the principal payment and any stated interest payable thereon, discounted at the yield on the entire debt obligation. The OID allocated to the principal payment is subtracted from the payment's face amount to determine the principal payment's issue price.[10]

---

[6]Timken v. Commissioner, 6 T.C. 483 (1946), *acq.*

[7]Reg. §1.1232-3(b)(2)(iv)(d).

[8]1954 Code §1232A; 1954 Code §163(e).

[9]H.R. Rep. No. 760, 97th Cong., 2d Sess. 553 (1982).

[10]This method does not take into account the possibility that the yield on later-maturing principal payments may in fact be higher than on earlier payments. Rather, it assumes a constant yield for each principal payment. This may be slightly inaccurate from an economic standpoint because yields commonly increase with longer maturities. It seems necessary, however, from a practical standpoint, because the yield on a particular payment could only be accurately computed if it were sold and traded separately.

EXAMPLE

Assume that Corporation X issued a five-year, $100,000, 10 percent bond on January 1, 1989. The bond matures serially, with $20,000 payments due each December 31 and with the final $20,000 payment due on December 31, 1993. If the bond is issued at $80,000, then the bond yield (taking into account stated interest payments) would be 19.9436 percent. The OID allocated to each $20,000 principal payment would be that payment's face amount less the present value of the total of the payment and the interest due thereon, discounted to the issue date at the bond yield. Thus, the OID allocated to each payment would be:

Payment	Original Issue Discount
1	$1,658.06
2	3,040.41
3	4,192.91
4	5,153.78
5	5,954.88

Subtracting the allocated OID from the payment amount produces the issue price for each payment.[11]

Payment	Issue Price
1	$18,341.94
2	16,959.59
3	15,807.09
4	14,846.22
5	14,045.12
Total	$80,000.00

If the issue price (plus any prior adjustments) for any payment is compounded at the bond yield (19.9436 percent) for the number of periods in that payment's stated term, that amount less any stated interest (in each period) is the payment's face amount.

Thus, if $18,341.94, the issue price for payment 1, is multiplied by 19.9436 percent, the result is $3,658.04. The $18,341.94 plus $3,658.04 ($22,000), less stated interest of $2,000, produces the payment's $20,000 face amount.

Thus, under the economic accrual method, the issue price is an amount which, when compounded at the bond yield and reduced by stated interest, produces the payment's stated redemption price at maturity. TEFRA used the same formula to determine how much OID is includible or deductible on a bond each year.

In comparison to the bond-years method, the economic accrual method results in more OID allocated to earlier principal payments and less allocated to later principal payments for the same $100,000 bond:

---

[11]Discrepancies in cents are due to rounding.

	OID Allocated to Each Payment	
Payment	Bond-Years Method	Economic Accrual
1	$1,333.33	$1,658.06
2	2,667.67	3,040.41
3	4,000.00	4,192.91
4	5,333.33	5,153.78
5	6,667.67	5,954.88

The bond-years method tends to defer OID deduction and inclusion on an obligation when compared to the economic accrual method. The following chart shows the amount of OID deducted/included each year for the $100,000 obligation described previously under the two methods:

	OID Deducted/Included Each Year	
Payment	Bond-Years Method	Economic Accrual
1	$5,516.19	$5,954.86
2	5,012.17	5,153.76
3	4,291.45	4,192.89
4	3,284.02	3,040.39
5	1,896.17	1,658.04

§502.2   Prepayment Adjustments

The second uncertainty about the federal income tax treatment of OID on a CMO was whether the OID deducted by the issuer and included by the holder should be adjusted for principal prepayments.

The IRS had ruled privately that the scheduled payment date on an obligation whose maturity date could be accelerated by mortgage prepayments is the obligation's maturity date.[12] In the private letter ruling, the issuer guaranteed a particular prepayment rate on a mortgage-backed debt obligation. The holder, however, was also entitled to all mortgage prepayments if the mortgages paid off faster than the guaranteed rate.

If the principles of this letter ruling were applied to a CMO, however, undesirable results would be produced because of the disparity between the CMO's stated maturity date and its possibly accelerated maturity date. Thus, the CMO holder would include OID in income on a much slower basis than it accrues economically.

This timing disparity could also lead to the conversion of ordinary income into capital gain by the CMO's holder. Because the CMO is a corporate obligation, each principal payment was treated as an exchange. To the extent a CMO was prepaid subsequent to the first year, the OID yet to be included in the holder's income would be capital gain unless, under 1954 Code §1232(a)(2)(A), there was an intention to call the obligation before maturity.

[12]Priv. Ltr. Rul. 7725006 (Mar. 24, 1977), revoked on other grounds by Priv. Ltr. Rul. 8337016 (May 23, 1983).

There was no authority about whether the anticipated prepayment of a CMO evidenced an intention to call before maturity. Priv. Ltr. Rul. 7725006, however, states that there was no such intention to call a mortgage-backed debt obligation whose maturity was accelerated by mortgage principal payments. If this was so, then the entire difference between the CMO's face amount and the adjusted basis would be capital gain to the holder even though economically this difference represented discount.

EXAMPLE

Assume that after Corporation X has paid two principal payments of $20,000 each, it utilized an unscheduled $60,000 principal prepayment on December 31, 1989, to retire the balance of its five-year, $100,000, 10 percent bond used in the earlier example. On December 31, 1989, when Bondholder A receives a $60,000 unscheduled principal prepayment, A (who bought on the issue date) will have a basis of $54,023.09 in the bond. A has realized $60,000 and will recognize a gain of $5,976.91. Assuming X had no intention to call the bond before maturity, then, because the retirement of A's bond was an exchange under Code §1232(a), the $5,976.91 was long-term capital gain.

Corporation X, on the other hand, would deduct interest on the bond from its ordinary income. Thus, Reg. §1.163-4(c)(1) provided, in general, that if a bond issued with OID is redeemed at a price in excess of the issue price plus any OID previously deducted, the difference is deductible as interest for the taxable year. X would therefore deduct as interest the entire $5,976.91 of OID that A reported as long-term capital gain. Issuers and holders of CMOs were therefore able to resurrect the mismatching of ordinary income and capital gain that was one of the reasons behind the enactment of 1954 Code §1232.

§503   1986 ACT RULES

The REMIC provisions adopted rules intended to address the uncertainties described above with respect to CMOs and other asset-backed debt. They did this by adding Code §1272(a)(6), which prescribes a "level yield" method under which OID on a REMIC regular interest, and certain other prepayment-sensitive debt instruments, is computed.

The level-yield method prescribed is predicated on initially using a prepayment assumption to determine yield on the debt instrument. According to the Conference Report,[1] the prepayment assumption is generally used by the parties in pricing the particular transaction. In effect, this prepayment assumption is for the underlying mortgage collateral and takes into account any assumed rate of

---

§503   [1] H.R. Rep. No. 841, 99th Cong. 2d Sess. II-148 (1986).

reinvestment income. The pricing assumptions must be specified in the first tax return filed by the REMIC.[2]

Once the pricing assumption is determined and the debt instrument's yield to maturity is computed, the level-yield method is used to compute how much OID accrues during an accrual period. Pursuant to this method, the OID deemed to accrue during an accrual period is equal to the excess of the debt instrument's price at the end of the accrual period plus payments of the debt instrument's stated redemption price at maturity received during the accrual period over the debt instrument's adjusted issue price at the beginning of the accrual period.

The price of the debt instrument at the end of the accrual period is determined by projecting the debt instrument's future cash flows and then discounting the cash flows back at the debt instrument's original yield. To project the future cash flows, principal payments and prepayments during the accrual period are taken into account. The original prepayment assumption used in pricing the transaction is used to project future cash flows on the debt instrument.

The adjusted issue price of the debt instrument at the beginning of any accrual period equals the issue price of such instrument, increased by the aggregate amount of OID with respect to the instrument that accrued in all prior accrual periods, and reduced by the amount of distributions included in the instrument's stated redemption price at maturity made on the instrument in such prior periods.

The level-yield method is essentially a self-adjusting method for determining OID deductions and inclusions. Thus, by taking into account a prepayment assumption, OID deductions and inclusions will generally be accelerated when compared to scheduled maturities. Use of the level-yield calculation then serves to adjust the amount of OID, based on what actually happened during the accrual period. If prepayments occur faster than the prepayment assumption, then more OID will be deducted by the issuer and included by the holder. If prepayments are slower than the prepayment assumption, then less OID will be deducted by the issuer and included by the holder.

The Code §1272(a)(6) rule applies to all REMIC regular interests. It also applies to qualified mortgages held by a REMIC and any other debt instrument issued after December 31, 1986, if payments under such debt instrument may be accelerated by reason of prepayments of other obligations securing such debt instrument.[3]

§504   FINAL OID REGULATIONS

On January 27, 1994, the IRS issued final regulations (the "Final OID Regulations") under the Code's OID rules. The Final OID Regulations replace proposed OID regulations (the "Proposed OID Regulations") issued on December 22, 1992. The Final OID Regulations, however, specifically reserve comment on the application of Code §1272(a)(6) with respect to OID debt obligations subject to prepayment as a result of prepayment on collateral underlying such debt obligations. Neverthe-

[2]Reg. §1.860D-1(d)(2)(iii).
[3]Code §1272(a)(6)(C).

less, as discussed below, the Final OID Regulations do modify certain OID definitions and provide the tax treatment for regular interests characterized as variable-rate debt instruments.

§504.1 Issue Price

Under the Final OID Regulations, if a substantial amount of debt instruments in an issue is sold for money, the issue price of each instrument in the issue is the first price at which a substantial amount of the debt instruments is sold.[1] Thus, the Final OID Regulations eliminate the distinction between publicly and nonpublicly traded regular interests in determining issue price. Although the Final OID Regulations do not define "substantial amount," tax counsel generally treat 10 percent as substantial for these purposes. The Final OID Regulations also provide that the issue date of a debt instrument is the first settlement date or closing date, whichever is applicable, on which a substantial amount of the debt instruments in the issue is sold for money.[2]

For purposes of determining the issue price and issue date, the Final OID Regulations provide that sales to bond houses, brokers, or similar persons or organizations acting in the capacity of underwriters, placement agents, or wholesalers are ignored.[3] As with the determination of the issue price, the Final OID Regulations have eliminated the distinction between publicly and nonpublicly traded regular interests in this regard as well.

§504.2 Long First Accrual Periods

The Final OID Regulations confirm that accrual periods may be of any length and may even vary in length over the term of the instrument provided that each accrual period is no longer than one year.[4] This, coupled with some other changes, should finally end the long-running dispute about whether long first accrual periods result in OID.

§504.3 Qualified Stated Interest

Qualified stated interest (QSI) is generally interest "unconditionally payable" at a single fixed rate over a debt instrument's entire term.[5] Qualified stated interest with respect to a REMIC regular interest will be includible (or deductible) based on the accrual method of tax accounting and with respect to non-REMIC interests based on the taxpayer's method of tax accounting.

§504 [1]Reg. §1.1273-2(a)(1).
[2]Reg. §1.1273-2(a)(2).
[3]Reg. §1.1273-2(e).
[4]Reg. §1.1272-1(b)(1)(ii).
[5]Reg. §1.1273-1(c)(1)(i).

§504.4   Variable-Rate Debt Instruments

In general, the Final OID Regulations expand the definition of a variable rate debt instrument (VRDI) beyond the scope of the VRDI definition in the Proposed OID Regulations. Under the Proposed OID Regulations, a debt instrument would qualify as a VRDI if it (1) provided for total noncontingent principal payments at least equal to its issue price and (2) provided for stated interest, paid or compounded at least annually, at current values of (a) a single qualified floating rate, (b) a single qualified floating rate followed by a second qualified floating rate, (c) a single fixed rate followed by a single qualified floating rate, or (d) a single objective rate.[6] A "qualified floating rate" was generally defined as any floating rate in which variations in such rate could reasonably be expected to measure contemporaneous variations in the cost of newly borrowed funds (e.g., a Prime Rate or LIBOR).[7] An "objective rate" was generally defined as a rate that was not itself a qualified floating rate but which was determined using a single formula that was fixed throughout the term of the debt instrument and which was based upon one or more qualified floating rates (e.g., a multiple of a qualified floating rate or an inverse floating rate based upon a qualified floating rate), or which was based upon the price of actively traded property (other than foreign currency) or an index of the prices of such property.[8]

In contrast, under the Final OID Regulations, a debt instrument will qualify as a VRDI if (1) its issue price does not exceed the total noncontingent principal payments due under the debt instrument by more than a specified de minimis amount (generally, an amount equal to the lesser of (a) .015 multiplied by the product of the total noncontingent principal payments due under the debt instrument and the number of complete years to the debt instrument's maturity from its issue date or (b) 15 percent of the total noncontingent principal payments due under the debt instrument), and (2) it provides for stated interest, paid or compounded at least annually, at current values of (a) one or more qualified floating rates, (b) a single fixed rate and one or more qualified floating rates, (c) a single objective rate, or (d) a single fixed rate and a single objective rate that is a qualified inverse floating rate.[9] Thus, contrary to the Proposed OID Regulations, the Final OID Regulations allow the issue price of a VRDI to exceed the total noncontingent principal payments due under the debt instrument, provided that such excess is not greater than a specified de minimis amount. This enables a floating rate debt instrument to be issued at a de minimis premium and still qualify as a VRDI. Furthermore, the Final OID Regulations allow a VRDI to provide for stated interest at more than two qualified floating rates, whereas under the Proposed OID Regulations VRDIs were limited to two qualified floating rates. In addition, unlike the Proposed OID Regulations, the Final OID Regulations permit certain inverse floating rates tied to a qualified floating rate to be preceded by a fixed rate.

[6]Prop. Reg. §1.1275-5(a)(3).
[7]Prop. Reg. §1.1275-5(b).
[8]Prop. Reg. §1.1275-5(c).
[9]Prop. Reg. §1.1275-5(a).

§504.4.1 Qualified Floating Rates

A "qualified floating rate" is defined under the Final OID Regulations as any variable rate in which variations in the value of such rate can reasonably be expected to measure contemporaneous variations in the cost of newly borrowed funds in the currency in which the debt instrument is denominated.[10] In general, a multiple of a qualified floating rate is not a qualified floating rate. However, a variable rate equal to the product of a qualified floating rate and a fixed multiple that is greater than zero but not more than 1.35 will constitute a qualified floating rate under the Final OID Regulations.[11] Furthermore, under the Final OID Regulations a variable rate equal to the product of a qualified floating rate and a fixed multiple that is greater than zero but not more than 1.35, increased or decreased by a fixed rate, will also constitute a qualified floating rate.[12]

§504.4.2 Weighted Average Rate

Numerous REMIC transactions include regular interests with interest rates equal to the weighted average of the interest rates on some or all of the qualified mortgages. The Final OID Regulations do not specifically address the treatment of debt instruments with interest rates based on the weighted average of the interest rates on other debt instruments. There are, therefore, three possible approaches with respect to the tax treatment of such instruments.

One possible approach is to treat weighted average rates as qualified floating rates. This approach is based on the assumption that such rates "can reasonably be expected to measure contemporaneous variations in the cost of newly borrowed funds." This approach is most persuasive when the weighted average rate is based solely on debt instruments that pay interest at qualified floating rates. In contrast, a weighted average regular interest based on fixed rate mortgage loans issued a substantial period of time prior to the issue date of the weighted average regular interest may not be viewed as a cost of borrowing on the issue date of such debt.

A second approach would be to treat the weighted average regular interest as a contingent payment debt obligation. Such treatment generally requires an interest payment to be accrued when the amount of the payment is fixed. As a result, the timing for recognizing income on a weighted average regular interest treated as a contingent payment debt obligation could materially differ from the timing for recognizing such income if the instrument were taxed as described in the preceding paragraph.

A third approach would be for the holder of the weighted average regular interest to elect under the Final OID Regulations to treat all interest on such obligation as OID and accrue such income on a constant yield method (taking into account the prepayment assumption with respect to such regular interest).[13]

---

[10]Reg. §1.1275-5(b).
[11]Reg. §1.1275-5(b)(2)(i).
[12]Reg. §1.1275-5(b)(2)(ii).
[13]Reg. §1.1272-3.

§504.4.3   Interest-Only Regular Interests

The income tax treatment of interest-only (IO) regular interests is also not entirely clear. IO regular interests come in two formats: (1) interest payments based on a notional principal balance with no stated principal amount and (2) a super-premium regular interest issued at a price that significantly exceeds its stated principal balance. Tax counsel generally treat IO regular interests as debt obligations with no QSI payments. As such, the stated redemption price at maturity of IO regular interests is equal to the sum of all payments expected to be made on such interests (determined based on the prepayment assumption with respect to such interests), with the result that IO regular interests are treated as issued with OID. Treating IO regular interests as OID obligations results in accruals of income based on a constant yield method. This treatment may also, however, result in negative accruals of OID when the rate of prepayments on the qualified mortgages exceeds the rate of prepayments expected under the related prepayment assumption. Negative OID may not be deducted and may only be used to offset future accruals of OID.

An alternative approach to the taxation of IO regular interests would be to treat such interests as contingent payment debt obligations. In such case, holders of such interests would generally be required to accrue income on such instruments at a yield equal to the applicable federal rate.[14]

Finally, it should be noted that certain tax counsel are of the view that super-premium IO regular interests (category (2) in the second preceding paragraph) should be taxed as debt obligations issued at a premium in which the stated principal balance of such interests is treated as its stated redemption price at maturity.

§504.4.4   Objective Rates

Under the Final OID Regulations an "objective rate" is a rate that is not itself a qualified floating rate but one that is determined using a single fixed formula and is based upon (1) one or more qualified floating rates, (2) one or more rates in which each rate would be a qualified floating rate for a debt instrument denominated in a currency other than the currency in which the debt instrument is denominated, (3) either the yield or changes in the price of one or more items of actively traded personal property, or (4) a combination of objective rates.[15] The Final OID Regulations also provide that other variable rates may be treated as objective rates if so designated by revenue ruling or revenue procedure.[16] A "qualified inverse floating rate" is any objective rate in which such rate is equal to a fixed rate minus a qualified floating rate, as long as variations in the rate can reasonably be expected to inversely reflect contemporaneous variations in the cost of newly borrowed funds.[17]

---

[14]Prop. Reg. §1.1275-4(f).
[15]Reg. §1.1275-5(c)(1).
[16]Reg. §1.1275-5(c)(2).
[17]Reg. §1.1275-5(c)(3).

Although the Final OID Regulations generally expand the definition of an objective rate from the definition of such term in the Proposed OID Regulations, the Final OID Regulations do narrow the definition of an objective rate in certain respects. In particular, a variable rate will not qualify as an objective rate under the Final OID Regulations if it results in significant frontloading or backloading of interest.[18] As noted above, however, objective rates generally are not qualified variable rates for REMIC purposes.

§504.4.5 Combination Rates

Also contrary to the Proposed OID Regulations, the Final OID Regulations provide that if a debt instrument provides for stated interest at a fixed rate for an initial period of less than one year followed by either a qualified floating rate or an objective rate for a subsequent period, and if the value of the subsequent variable rate "on the issue date" is intended to approximate the fixed rate, then the fixed rate and the subsequent variable rate will constitute either a single qualified floating rate or an objective rate, as the case may be.[19] With respect to REMIC transactions, however, the fixed rate of interest for the initial accrual period is set a short time prior to the issue date. The Final OID Regulations further provide that a fixed rate and a subsequent variable rate will be conclusively presumed to qualify for this treatment if the value of the variable rate on the issue date does not differ from the value of the fixed rate by more than 25 basis points.[20] The Final OID Regulations also provide that two or more qualified floating rates will be treated as a single qualified floating rate if such rates can reasonably be expected to have approximately the same values throughout the term of the debt instrument.[21] Under the Final OID Regulations, if the values of such rates on the issue date are within 25 basis points of each other, then such rates are conclusively presumed to be reasonably expected to have approximately the same values throughout the term of the debt instrument.[22] Although the matter is not entirely clear, it is reasonable to conclude that if (1) the two rates are within 25 basis points of each other on the pricing date of the regular interests and (2) the pricing date is within a short period prior to the issue date (e.g., within 30 days), then the rates can be presumed to be reasonably expected to have the same values throughout the term of such regular interests.

§504.4.6 Qualified Stated Interest on a VRDI

The Final OID Regulations also revise and simplify the rules contained in the Proposed OID Regulations concerning the determination and accrual of OID and

[18]Reg. §1.1275-5(c)(4).
[19]Reg. §1.1275-5(a)(3)(ii).
[20]Id.
[21]Reg. §1.1275-5(b).
[22]Id.

the amount of qualified stated interest on a VRDI. Under the Final OID Regulations, if a VRDI provides for stated interest at either a single qualified floating rate or a single objective rate that is unconditionally payable in cash or property at least annually, then all stated interest on such debt instrument will constitute "qualified stated interest."[23] Under such circumstances, the debt instrument will only be issued with OID if it is issued at a "true" discount (i.e., if its stated principal amount exceeds its issue price by more than the de minimis amount). In general, all VRDIs are converted to "equivalent" fixed-rate debt instruments by converting any qualified floating rate provided for under the terms of the VRDI to a fixed rate equal to its value on the issue date and by assuming that any such rate will remain at such value.[24] Any objective rate provided for under the terms of the VRDI is converted to a fixed rate that reflects the yield that is reasonably expected for the instrument.[25] The general rules applicable to fixed-rate debt instruments are then applied to the "equivalent" fixed-rate debt instrument in order to determine the OID accruals and the amount of qualified stated interest payments on the VRDI. Appropriate adjustments to these amounts are made in each accrual period if the interest actually accrued or paid during such accrual period differs from the amount of interest assumed to have been accrued or paid under the "equivalent" fixed-rate debt instrument.

§504.5   *Election by Holders to Treat All Interest as OID*

The Final OID Regulations permit accrual (and cash) basis taxpayers to include all interest on a debt instrument in income using the constant-yield method applicable to OID.[26] The election applies to all income on the debt instrument including stated interest, OID, de minimis OID, acquisition discount, market discount, de minimis market discount and unstated interest. An adjustment is permitted for amortizable bond premium or acquisition premium. The Final OID Regulations provide that if a holder makes the election to accrue market discount currently under this provision, the holder is deemed to have made an election to accrue market discount currently on all market discount bonds that it holds.[27] A similar rule applies to amortizable bond premium.[28]

§504.6   *Inclusion/Deduction of De Minimis OID*

The Final OID Regulations retain the rule of the Proposed OID Regulations and provide that a holder includes de minimis OID ratably as principal payments on the debt instrument are made.[29] An issuer is permitted to use a straight-line

---

[23]Reg. §1.1275-5(e)(2).
[24]Id.
[25]Id.
[26]Reg. §1.1272-3.
[27]Reg. §1.1272-3(b)(2)(ii)(B).
[28]Reg. §1.1272-3(b)(2)(i)(B).
[29]Reg. §1.1273-1(d)(5).

method to deduct de minimis OID if it makes an election for the taxable year in which the debt instrument is issued.[30] The Final OID Regulations also permit an issuer to deduct de minimis OID at maturity or in proportion to stated interest payments on the debt.[31] A subsequent holder who purchases a debt instrument with de minimis OID at a discount must account for such discount under the market discount rules rather than the de minimis rules discussed above.[32]

§504.6.1 Subsequent Holders

For purposes of calculating OID accruals, acquisition premium, or market discount, the Final OID Regulations provide that a subsequent holder may determine the adjusted issue price of its debt instrument in any manner consistent with the Final OID Regulations.[33] This clarifies that a subsequent holder need not use the same accrual period as the prior holder to compute adjusted issue price.

§504.7 Investment Units

The Final OID Regulations clarify that the issue price of an investment unit is determined as if the investment unit were a debt instrument.[34] The issue price of the investment unit is determined under the general rules and is then allocated between the debt instrument and the property right or rights that comprise the unit based on their relative fair market values.[35] Generally, the issuer's allocation of the issue price of the investment unit is binding on all holders of the investment unit, unless the holder explicitly discloses that its allocation is different from the issuer's allocation.[36]

§504.8 Anti-Abuse Rule

The Final OID Regulations were accompanied by what may prove to be a controversial anti-abuse rule. This anti-abuse rule (promulgated in a temporary regulation) grants the IRS authority to "depart from" the Final OID Regulations in order to ensure reasonable results which are consistent with the purposes of the OID statute.[37] This determination is based on all the facts and circumstances. Of significance, the temporary regulation states that "[a] result will not be considered unreasonable, however, in the absence of a substantial effect on the present value of a taxpayer's tax liability."[38] The temporary regulation provides that the anti-

---

[30]Reg. §1.163-7(b)(2).
[31]Id.
[32]Reg. §1.1273-1(d)(5)(iii).
[33]Reg. §1.1275-1(b)(2).
[34]Reg. §1.1273-2(h).
[35]Id.
[36]Reg. §1.1273-2(h)(2).
[37]Temp. Reg. §1.1275-5T(g).
[38]Id.

abuse rule applies, for example, if the principal purpose of including an early call option, which is not expected to be exercised by the issuer, in a current-pay, increasing-rate note is to avoid the OID rules, and the effect of this structure is a substantial reduction in the present value of the holder's tax liability arising from the note.[39] This anti-abuse rule is obvious evidence of the IRS's frustration with taxpayers that seek to apply the law as written to achieve beneficial results. Whether it is an appropriate exercise of the government's regulatory authority is likely to be widely debated.

§504.9   *Effective Date of Final OID Regulations*

The Final OID Regulations are effective for debt instruments issued, and to lending transactions, sales, and exchanges that occur on or after April 4, 1994. Taxpayers may, however, rely on the Final OID Regulations with respect to all debt issued and lending transactions, sales, and exchanges that occurred after December 21, 1992.

The preamble to the Final OID Regulations provides that the IRS will treat (1) the Proposed OID Regulations as substantial authority for debt instruments issued and for lending transactions, sales, and exchanges that occurred after December 21, 1992, and (2) the Proposed OID Regulations issued in 1986 and 1991 as substantial authority for debt instruments issued and for lending transactions, sales, and exchanges that occurred prior to December 21, 1992.

§505   OID REPORTING REQUIREMENTS

Issuers of any debt instrument having OID are subject to two distinct types of reporting requirements: (1) information required to be provided to the purchaser of the debt instrument and (2) information required to be provided to the IRS. The purpose of the reporting requirements is to make available to debt holders the information necessary to calculate accruals of OID.

§505.1   *Legending*

The best way to provide information to a purchaser of a debt instrument is to set forth the information on the face of the debt instrument. Thus, the Code authorizes the Secretary to issue regulations requiring that the amount of OID and the issue date of a debt instrument be set forth on the instrument.[1] The regulations under Code §6049[2] require that any REMIC regular interest or collateralized debt instrument issued after April 8, 1988, that has OID must set forth on

---

[39]Id.
§505   [1]Code §1275(c)(1).
[2]Reg. §1.6049-7(g).

the face of such debt instrument (1) the amount of OID, (2) the issue date, (3) the rate on which interest is payable (if any) as of the issue date, (4) the yield to maturity, as well as the method used to calculate the yield if the instrument has a short accrual period, (5) the prepayment assumption used in pricing the regular interest or debt instrument, and (6) the amount of OID allocable to the short accrual period.[3] This information must be printed on the face of the debt instrument on the issue date or affixed by sticker to the face of the debt instrument within 10 days of the issue date.[4] Failure to legend the debt instrument properly will result in the imposition of a penalty of $50 for each instrument.[5] The penalty will not be imposed, however, if the issuer shows that the failure to legend is due to reasonable cause and not to willful neglect.[6]

The Final OID Regulations greatly simplify OID legending requirements and eliminate legending requirements on most types of publicly offered debt. The Final OID Regulations further provide that the legending requirements contained therein are not required for nonpublicly traded REMIC regular interests issued with OID. Although the Final OID Regulations eliminate the legending requirements under the proposed OID regulations issued in 1986,[7] the Final OID Regulations do not modify the reporting regulations for REMICS under Code §6049. Thus, absent further guidance from the IRS, it appears that issuers of REMIC regular interests must still comply with the legending requirements contained in Reg. §1.6049-7(g).

§505.2   *Reporting*

All issuers of a REMIC regular interest are required to report to the IRS on Form 8811 the following information: (1) the name, address, and taxpayer identification number of the REMIC; (2) the name, title, and address of the representative of the REMIC who can provide certain interest and OID information; (3) the start-up day of the REMIC; (4) the Committee on Uniform Security Identification Procedure (CUSIP) number for the instrument; (5) the name, title, address, and telephone number of the representative of the REMIC whom the IRS can contact; (6) any other information required by Form 8811.[8] Failure to furnish this information to the IRS may subject the issuer to a penalty of 1 percent of the aggregate issue price of the issue up to a maximum of $50,000.[9] The issuer will not be subject to the penalty if the failure to report is shown to be due to reasonable cause and not willful neglect.[10]

---

[3]Id.

[4]For debt instruments that are not publicly offered, the legend need not be attached until a disposition of the debt instrument. Reg. §1.1275-3(a). For convenience, however, an issuer may wish to afix the legend on the issue date.

[5]Code §6706(a).

[6]Id.

[7]Prop. Reg. §§1.1275-3(a) and 1.1272-1.

[8]Reg. §1.6049-7(b).

[9]Code §6706(b).

[10]Id.

Issuers of a REMIC regular interest who paid $10 or more of interest to a holder during the calendar year must deliver both to the IRS and to the holder of the instrument a Form 1099.[11] The information return must contain the following information: (1) the name, address, and taxpayer identification number of the holder; (2) the CUSIP number; (3) the aggregate amount of interest paid or deemed paid the holder during the calendar year; (4) any other information required by Form 1099.[12] In addition, if the regular interest was issued with OID, the Form 1099 must also state the aggregate amount of OID deemed paid to the holder during the calendar year.[13]

---

[11]Reg. §1.6049-7(b)(2).
[12]Reg. §1.6049-7(b)(2)(iii)(A).
[13]Reg. §1.6049-7(b)(2)(iii)(B). See Appendix D for a copy of Form 1099.

APPENDIX A

REMIC Tax Returns

FORM 1066: U.S. REAL ESTATE MORTGAGE INVESTMENT CONDUIT INCOME TAX RETURN AND SCHEDULE Q — QUARTERLY NOTICE TO RESIDUAL INTEREST HOLDER OF REMIC TAXABLE INCOME OR NET LOSS ALLOCATION

Form 1066 is used to report the income, deductions, and gains and losses from the operation of a REMIC. Additionally, Form 1066 is used by the REMIC to report and pay the taxes on net income from prohibited transactions, net income from foreclosure property, and contributions after the start-up day. It is filed by an entity that elects to be treated as a REMIC for its first tax year and meets the requirements of Code §860D(a). Schedule Q must be filed for each person who was a residual holder at any time during the tax year and for each quarter in which such person was a residual holder.

FORM 8811: INFORMATION RETURN FOR REAL ESTATE MORTGAGE INVESTMENT CONDUITS (REMICs) AND ISSUERS OF COLLATERALIZED DEBT OBLIGATIONS

Form 8811 is used by a REMIC or another issuer of an instrument to which Code §1272(a)(6) applies to provide the information required by the regulations under Code §6049. It is to be filed by entities that elect to be treated as REMICs and by issuers of collateralized debt obligations.

FORM 8281: INFORMATION RETURN FOR PUBLICLY OFFERED ORIGINAL ISSUE DISCOUNT INSTRUMENTS

Form 8281 is filed by the issuer of publicly offered debt instruments having OID. This form must be filed by issuers of publicly offered debt instruments within 30 days of the date of issuance of OID instruments to provide the information required by Code §1275(c).

FORM 8831: EXCISE TAXES ON EXCESS INCLUSIONS OF REMIC RESIDUAL INTERESTS

Form 8831 is to be filed to pay the Code §860E(e)(1) excise tax on certain transfers of a residual interest in a REMIC.

Appendix A.   REMIC Tax Returns

Form 1066

Department of the Treasury
Internal Revenue Service

U.S. Real Estate Mortgage Investment Conduit (REMIC) Income Tax Return
For calendar year 1994
▶ See separate instructions.

OMB No. 1545-1014

1994

Please Type or Print	Name	A Employer identification number
	Number, street, and room or suite no. (If a P.O. box, see page 3 of the instructions.)	B Date REMIC started
	City or town, state, and ZIP code	C Enter total assets at end of tax year $

D Check applicable boxes: (1) ☐ Final return   (2) ☐ Change in address   (3) ☐ Amended return

Section I—Computation of Taxable Income or Net Loss

Income (excluding amounts from prohibited transactions)

1	Taxable Interest	1	
2	Accrued market discount under section 860C(b)(1)(B)	2	
3	Capital gain (loss) (Schedule D)	3	
4	Ordinary gain (loss) (attach Form 4797)	4	
5	Other income (attach schedule)	5	
6	**Total** income (loss). Add lines 1 through 5	6	

Deductions (excluding amounts allocable to prohibited transactions)

7	Salaries and wages	7	
8	Rent	8	
9	Amount accrued to regular interest holders in the REMIC that is deductible as interest	9	
10	Other interest	10	
11	Taxes	11	
12	Depreciation (see instructions)	12	
13	Other deductions (attach schedule)	13	
14	**Total** deductions. Add lines 7 through 13	14	
15	Taxable income (net loss). Subtract line 14 from line 6. Enter here and on Schedule M, column (c)	15	

Section II—Tax and Payments

1	**Total tax.** Schedule J, line 13	1	
2	Tax paid with: ☐ Form 8736 ☐ Form 8800	2	
3	**Tax Due.** Enter excess of line 1 over line 2. (See instructions for Payment of Tax Due.) .	3	
4	**Overpayment.** Enter excess of line 2 over line 1	4	

Please Sign Here

Under penalties of perjury, I declare that I have examined this return, including accompanying schedules and statements, and to the best of my knowledge and belief, it is true, correct, and complete. Declaration of preparer (other than taxpayer) is based on all information of which preparer has any knowledge.

▶ Signature   ▶ Date

Paid Preparer's Use Only	Preparer's signature ▶	Date	Check if self-employed ☐	Preparer's social security number
	Firm's name (or yours if self-employed) and address ▶		E.I. No. ▶ ZIP code ▶	

For Paperwork Reduction Act Notice, see page 1 of the instructions.   Cat. No. 64383U   Form **1066** (1994)

Form 1066 (1994)   Page **2**

Schedule D   **Capital Gains and Losses**
   (Caution: *Use Form 4797 instead of Schedule D if the startup day was after November 11, 1991. See Instructions.*)

Part I—Short-Term Capital Gains and Losses—Assets Held One Year or Less

(a) Description of property (Example: 100 shares 7% preferred of "Z" Co.)	(b) Date acquired (mo., day, yr.)	(c) Date sold (mo., day, yr.)	(d) Sales price (see Instructions)	(e) Cost or other basis (see Instructions)		(f) Gain (loss) (col. (d) less (e))
1						
2 Short-term capital gain from installment sales from Form 6252					**2**	
3 Short-term capital loss carryover					**3**	
4 Net short-term capital gain (loss). Combine lines 1 through 3					**4**	

Part II—Long-Term Capital Gains and Losses—Assets Held More Than One Year

5						
6 Long-term capital gain from installment sales from Form 6252					**6**	
7 Capital gain distributions					**7**	
8 Enter gain, if applicable, from Form 4797					**8**	
9 Long-term capital loss carryover					**9**	
10 Net long-term capital gain (loss). Combine lines 5 through 9					**10**	

Part III—Summary of Parts I and II

11 Combine lines 4 and 10 and enter the net gain (loss) here	**11**	
12 If line 11 is a gain, enter here and also on line 3, Section I (page 1)	**12**	
13 If line 11 is a loss, enter here and as a loss on line 3, Section I (page 1), the **smaller** of:		
a The amount on line 11; or		
b $3,000	**13** (	)

Part IV—Computation of Capital Loss Carryovers From 1994 to 1995
   (Complete this part if the loss on line 11 is more than the loss on line 13.)

14 Enter loss shown on line 4. If none, enter -0- and skip lines 15 through 18	**14**	
15 Enter gain shown on line 10. If that line is blank or shows a loss, enter -0-	**15**	
16 Subtract line 15 from line 14	**16**	
17 Enter the smaller of line 13 or 16	**17**	
18 Subtract line 17 from line 16. This is your **short-term capital loss carryover from 1994 to 1995**	**18**	
19 Enter loss from line 10. If none, enter -0- and skip lines 20 through 23	**19**	
20 Enter gain shown on line 4. If line 4 is blank or shows a loss, enter -0-	**20**	
21 Subtract line 20 from line 19	**21**	
22 Subtract line 17 from line 13. (**Note:** *If you skipped lines 15 through 18, enter the amount from line 13.*)	**22**	
23 Subtract line 22 from line 21. This is your **long-term capital loss carryover from 1994 to 1995.**	**23**	

Appendix A. REMIC Tax Returns

Schedule J	Tax Computation

Part I—Tax on Net Income From Prohibited Transactions

1	Income—See instructions.			
a	Gain from certain dispositions of qualified mortgages	1a		
b	Income from nonpermitted assets	1b		
c	Compensation for services	1c		
d	Gain from the disposition of cash flow investments (except from a qualified liquidation) . . .	1d		
2	Total income. Add lines 1a through 1d	2		
3	Deductions directly connected with the production of income shown on line 2 (excluding amounts attributable to prohibited transactions resulting in a loss)	3		
4	Net income from prohibited transactions. Subtract line 3 from line 2	4		
5	Tax on net income from prohibited transactions. Enter 100% of line 4	5		

Part II—Tax on Net Income From Foreclosure Property (as defined in section 860G(a)(8)) (Caution: *See instructions before completing this part.*)

6	Net gain (loss) from the sale or other disposition of foreclosure property described in section 1221(1) (attach schedule)	6		
7	Gross income from foreclosure property (attach schedule)	7		
8	Total income from foreclosure property. Add lines 6 and 7	8		
9	Deductions directly connected with the production of income shown on line 8 (attach schedule)	9		
10	Net income from foreclosure property. Subtract line 9 from line 8	10		
11	Tax on net income from foreclosure property. Enter 35% of line 10	11		

Part III—Tax on Contributions After the Startup Day (*Do not complete this part if the startup day was before July 1, 1987. See instructions.*)

12	Amount of taxable contributions received during the calendar year after the startup day. See instructions (attach schedule)	12		

Part IV—Total Tax

13	Total tax. Add lines 5, 11, and 12. Enter here and on page 1, Section II, line 1	13		

Form 1066 (1994)   Page **4**

Designation of Tax Matters Person

Enter below the residual interest holder designated as the tax matters person (TMP) for the calendar year of this return.

Name of designated TMP ▶		Identifying number of TMP ▶	

Address of designated TMP ▶	

Additional Information

		Yes	No

E   What type of entity is this REMIC? Check box ▶   ☐ Corporation   ☐ Partnership   ☐ Trust   ☐ Segregated Pool of Assets

If you checked "Segregated Pool of Assets," enter the name and type of entity that owns the assets:
Name .... Type ....

F   Number of residual interest holders in this REMIC ▶ ....

G   Check this box if this REMIC is subject to the consolidated entity-level audit procedures of sections 6221 through 6231 . . . .

H   At any time during calendar year 1994, did the REMIC have an interest in or a signature or other authority over a financial account in a foreign country (such as a bank account, securities account, or other financial account)? (See the instructions for exceptions and filing requirements for Form TD F 90-22.1.) . . . .
If "Yes," enter name of foreign country ▶ ....

I   Was the REMIC the grantor of, or transferor to, a foreign trust that existed during the current tax year, whether or not the REMIC has any beneficial interest in it? If "Yes," you may have to file Forms 3520, 3520-A, or 926

J   Enter the amount of tax-exempt interest accrued during the year ▶ ....

K   Check this box if the REMIC had more than one class of regular interests . . . . ▶ ☐
If so, attach a schedule identifying the classes and principal amounts outstanding for each at the end of the year.

L   Enter the sum of the daily accruals determined under section 860E(c) for the calendar year ▶

Schedule L Balance Sheets	(a) Beginning of year		(b) End of year	
Assets				
1 Permitted investments (see instructions):				
a Cash flow investments				
b Qualified reserve assets				
c Foreclosure property				
2 Qualified mortgages				
3 Other assets (attach schedule)				
4 Total assets				
Liabilities and Capital				
5 Current liabilities (attach schedule)				
6 Other liabilities (attach schedule)				
7 Regular interests in REMIC				
8 Residual interest holders' capital accounts . . .				
9 Total liabilities and capital				

Schedule M Reconciliation of Residual Interest Holders' Capital Accounts						
(Show reconciliation of each residual interest holder's capital account quarterly on Schedule Q (Form 1066), Item E.)						
(a) Residual interest holders' capital accounts at beginning of year	(b) Capital contributed during year	(c) Taxable income (net loss) from Section I, line 15	(d) Nontaxable income	(e) Unallowable deductions	(f) Withdrawals and distributions	(g) Residual interest holders' capital accounts at end of year (combine cols. (a) through (f))
			(	)(	)	

♻ *Printed on recycled paper*

150

1994

Department of the Treasury
Internal Revenue Service

Instructions for Form 1066

U.S. Real Estate Mortgage Investment Conduit (REMIC) Income Tax Return

Section references are to the Internal Revenue Code unless otherwise noted.

Paperwork Reduction Act Notice

We ask for the information on this form to carry out the Internal Revenue laws of the United States. You are required to give us the information. We need it to ensure that you are complying with these laws and to allow us to figure and collect the right amount of tax.

The time needed to complete and file this form and related schedule will vary depending on individual circumstances. The estimated average times are:

	Form 1066	Schedule Q (Form 1066)
Recordkeeping	28 hr., 28 min.	6 hr., 13 min.
Learning about the law or the form	6 hr., 36 min.	1 hr., 16 min.
Preparing the form	9 hr., 13 min.	2 hr., 21 min.
Copying, assembling, and sending the form to the IRS	32 min.	16 min.

If you have comments concerning the accuracy of these time estimates or suggestions for making these forms simpler, we would be happy to hear from you. You can write to both the **Internal Revenue Service,** Attention: Tax Forms Committee, PC:FP, Washington, DC 20224; and the **Office of Management and Budget,** Paperwork Reduction Project (1545–1014), Washington, DC 20503. **DO NOT** send the tax form to either of these offices. Instead, see **Where To File** on page 2.

General Instructions

Purpose of Form

Form 1066 is used to report the income, deductions, and gains and losses from the operation of a real estate mortgage investment conduit (REMIC). In addition, the form is used by the REMIC to report and pay the taxes on net income from prohibited transactions, net income from foreclosure property, and contributions after the startup day.

Who Must File

An entity that elects to be treated as a REMIC for its first tax year (and for which the election is still in effect) **and** that meets the requirements of section 860D(a) must file Form 1066.

A REMIC is any entity:

1. To which an election to be treated as a REMIC applies for the tax year and all prior tax years,

2. All of the interests in which are regular interests or residual interests,

3. That has one (and only one) class of residual interests (and all distributions, if any, with respect to such interests are pro rata),

4. Substantially all of the assets of which consist of qualified mortgages

and permitted investments (as of the close of the 3rd month beginning after the startup day (defined in the instructions for **Item B,** on page 3) and at all times thereafter),

5. That has a tax year that is a calendar year, and

6. For which reasonable arrangements have been designed to ensure that **(a)** residual interests are not held by disqualified organizations (as defined in section 860E(e)(5)), and **(b)** information needed to apply section 860E(e) will be made available by the entity.

Note: *Paragraph 6 does not apply to REMICs with a startup day before April 1, 1988 (or those formed under a binding contract in effect on March 31, 1988).*

See section 860G for definitions and special rules. See section 860D(a) regarding qualification as a REMIC during a qualified liquidation.

Making the Election

The election to be treated as a REMIC is made by timely filing, for the first tax year of its existence, a Form 1066 signed by an authorized person. Once the election is made, it stays in effect for all years until it is terminated.

Cat. No. 64231R

First Tax Year

For the first tax year of a REMIC's existence, the REMIC must furnish the following in a separate statement attached to the REMIC's initial return:

1. Information concerning the terms of the regular interests and the designated residual interest of the REMIC, or a copy of the offering circular or prospectus containing such information, and

2. A description of the prepayment and reinvestment assumptions made in accordance with section 1272(a)(6) and its regulations, including documentation supporting the selection of the prepayment assumption.

Termination of Election

If any entity ceases to be a REMIC at any time during the tax year, the election to be a REMIC terminates for that year and all future years. An entity is considered to cease being a REMIC when it no longer meets the requirements of section 860D(a).

When To File

A REMIC must file Form 1066 by the 15th day of the 4th month following the close of its tax year. If the regular due date falls on a Saturday, Sunday, or legal holiday, file on the next business day (any day that is not a Saturday, Sunday, or legal holiday).

If you need more time to file a REMIC return, get **Form 8736,** Application for Automatic Extension of Time To File U.S. Return for a Partnership, REMIC, or for Certain Trusts, to request an automatic 3-month extension. You must file Form 8736 by the regular due date of the REMIC return.

If you have filed Form 8736 and you still need more time to file the REMIC return, get **Form 8800,** Application for Additional Extension of Time To File U.S. Return for a Partnership, REMIC, or for Certain Trusts, to request an additional extension of up to 3 months. To obtain this extension, you must show reasonable cause for the additional time you are requesting. Ask for the additional extension early so that if it is denied, the return can still be filed on time.

Form 1066.

Where To File

File Form 1066 with the Internal Revenue Service Center listed below.

If the REMIC's principal place of business or principal office or agency is located in	Use the following address
New Jersey, New York (New York City and counties of Nassau, Rockland, Suffolk, and Westchester)	Holtsville, NY 00501
New York (all other counties), Connecticut, Maine, Massachusetts, New Hampshire, Rhode Island, Vermont	Andover, MA 05501
Florida, Georgia, South Carolina	Atlanta, GA 39901
Indiana, Kentucky, Michigan, Ohio, West Virginia	Cincinnati, OH 45999
Kansas, New Mexico, Oklahoma, Texas	Austin, TX 73301
Alaska, Arizona, California (counties of Alpine, Amador, Butte, Calaveras, Colusa, Contra Costa, Del Norte, El Dorado, Glenn, Humboldt, Lake, Lassen, Marin, Mendocino, Modoc, Napa, Nevada, Placer, Plumas, Sacramento, San Joaquin, Shasta, Sierra, Siskiyou, Solano, Sonoma, Sutter, Tehama, Trinity, Yolo, and Yuba), Colorado, Idaho, Montana, Nebraska, Nevada, North Dakota, Oregon, South Dakota, Utah, Washington, Wyoming	Ogden, UT 84201
California (all other counties), Hawaii	Fresno, CA 93888
Illinois, Iowa, Minnesota, Missouri, Wisconsin	Kansas City, MO 64999
Alabama, Arkansas, Louisiana, Mississippi, North Carolina, Tennessee	Memphis, TN 37501
Delaware, District of Columbia, Maryland, Pennsylvania, Virginia	Philadelphia, PA 19255

Accounting Method

A REMIC must compute its taxable income (or net loss) using the accrual method of accounting. See section 860C(b).

Under the accrual method, an amount is includible in income when all the events have occurred that fix the right to receive the income and the amount can be determined with reasonable accuracy.

Generally, an accrual basis taxpayer can deduct accrued expenses in the tax year that all events occurred that determine the liability and the amount of the liability can be determined with reasonable accuracy. However, all the events that establish liability for the amount are treated as occurring only

Page 2

when economic performance takes place. There are exceptions for recurring items. See section 461(h).

Rounding Off to Whole Dollars

You may round off cents to the nearest whole dollar on the return and schedules. To do so, drop any amount less than 50 cents and increase any amount from 50 cents through 99 cents to the next higher dollar.

Recordkeeping

The REMIC records must be kept as long as their contents may be material in the administration of any Internal Revenue law. Copies of the filed tax returns should also be kept as part of the REMIC's records. See Pub. 583, Taxpayers Starting a Business, for more information.

Final Return

If the REMIC ceases to exist during the year, check the box at item D(1), page 1, Form 1066.

Amended Return

If after the REMIC files its return it later becomes aware of any changes it must make to income, deductions, etc., the REMIC should file an amended Form 1066 and amended Schedule Q (Form 1066), Quarterly Notice to Residual Interest Holder of REMIC Taxable Income or Net Loss Allocation, for each residual interest holder. Check the box at item D(3), page 1, Form 1066. Give corrected Schedules Q (Form 1066) labeled "Amended" to each residual interest holder.

Note: If a REMIC does not meet the small REMIC exception under sections 860F(e) and 6231, and related regulations, or if a REMIC makes the election described in section 6231(a)(1)(B)(ii) not to be treated as a small REMIC, the amended return will be a request for administrative adjustment, and Form 8082, Notice of Inconsistent Treatment or Amended Return (Administrative Adjustment Request (AAR)), must be filed by the Tax Matters Person. See sections 860F(e) and 6227 for more information.

If the REMIC's Federal return is changed for any reason, it may affect its state return. This would include changes made as a result of an examination of the REMIC return by the IRS. Contact the state tax agency where the state return is filed for more information.

Attachments

If you need more space on the forms or schedules, attach separate sheets. Use the same size and format as on the printed forms. But show the totals on

the printed forms. Be sure to put the REMIC's name and employer identification number on each sheet.

You must complete every applicable entry space on Form 1066. If you attach statements, do not write "See Attached" instead of completing the entry spaces on this form.

Other Forms and Returns That May Be Required

Form 1096, Annual Summary and Transmittal of U.S. Information Returns. Use this form to summarize and send information returns to the Internal Revenue Service Center.

Form 1098, Mortgage Interest Statement. This form is used to report the receipt from any individual of $600 or more of mortgage interest and points in the course of the REMIC's trade or business.

Forms 1099-A, B, C, INT, MISC, OID, R and S. You may have to file these information returns to report abandonments and acquisitions through foreclosure, proceeds from broker and barter exchange transactions, discharge of indebtedness, interest payments, medical and dental health care payments, miscellaneous income, original issue discount, distributions from pensions, annuities, retirement or profit-sharing plans, IRAs, insurance contracts, etc., and proceeds from real estate transactions. Also, use these returns to report amounts that were received as a nominee on behalf of another person.

For more details, see the Instructions for Forms 1099, 1098, 5498, and W-2G.

Note: Generally, a REMIC must file Forms 1099-INT and 1099-OID, as appropriate, to report accrued income of $10 or more of regular interest holders. See Regulations section 1.6049-7. Also, every REMIC must file Forms 1099-MISC if it makes payments of rents, commissions, or other fixed or determinable income (see section 6041) totaling $600 or more to any one person in the course of its trade or business during the calendar year.

Form 8300, Report of Cash Payments Over $10,000 Received in a Trade or Business. Generally, this form is used to report the receipt of more than $10,000 in cash or foreign currency in one transaction (or a series of related transactions).

Cashier's checks, bank drafts, and money orders with face amounts of $10,000 or less are considered cash under certain circumstances. For more information, see Form 8300 and Regulations section 1.60501-1(c).

Form 8811, Information Return for Real Estate Mortgage Investment Conduits (REMICs) and Issuers of Collateralized

Appendix A. REMIC Tax Returns

Form 1066.

Debt Obligations. A REMIC uses this form to provide the information required by Regulations section 1.6049-7(b)(1)(ii). The information will be published in **Pub. 938,** Real Estate Mortgage Investment Conduits (REMICs) Reporting Information. This publication contains a directory of REMICs.

Form 8822, Change of Address, may be used to inform the IRS of a new REMIC address if the change is made after filing Form 1066.

Payment of Tax Due

The REMIC must pay the tax due (line 3, Section II, page 1) in full by the 15th day of the 4th month following the end of the tax year. Attach to Form 1066 a check or money order for the amount due payable to the "Internal Revenue Service."

Interest and Penalties

Interest and penalty charges are described below. If a REMIC files late or does not pay the tax when due, it may be liable for penalties unless it can show that failure to file or pay was due to reasonable cause and not willful neglect.

Interest.—Interest is charged on taxes not paid by the due date, even if an extension of time to file is granted. Interest is also charged on penalties imposed for failure to file, negligence, fraud, gross valuation overstatement, and substantial understatement of tax from the due date (including extensions) to the date of payment. The interest charge is figured at a rate determined under section 6621.

Late filing penalty.—A penalty may be charged if **(a)** the return is filed after the due date (including extensions), or **(b)** the return does not show all the information required. However, the penalty will not be charged if you can show reasonable cause for the late filing or for the failure to include the required information on the return.

If no tax is due, the amount of the penalty is $50 for each month or part of a month (up to 5 months) the return is late, multiplied by the total number of persons who were residual interest holders in the REMIC during any part of the REMIC's tax year for which the return is due. If tax is due, the penalty is the amount stated above plus 5% of the unpaid tax for each month or part of a month the return is late, up to a maximum of 25% of the unpaid tax. If the return is more than 60 days late, the minimum penalty is $100 or the balance of the tax due on the return, whichever is smaller.

Late payment penalty.—The penalty for not paying the tax when due is usually ½ of 1% of the unpaid tax for each month or part of a month the tax is unpaid. The penalty cannot exceed 25% of the unpaid tax. The penalty will not

be charged if you can show reasonable cause for not paying on time.

Other penalties.—Penalties can also be imposed for negligence, substantial understatement of tax, and fraud. See sections 6662 and 6663.

Contributions to the REMIC

Generally, no gain or loss is recognized by the REMIC or any of the regular or residual interest holders when property is transferred to the REMIC in exchange for an interest in the REMIC. The adjusted basis of the interest received equals the adjusted basis of the property transferred to the REMIC.

The basis to the REMIC of property transferred by a regular or residual interest holder is its fair market value immediately after its transfer.

If the issue price of a regular interest is more than its adjusted basis, the excess is included in income by the regular interest holder as accrued market discount for the applicable tax years under the rules of section 1276(b). If the issue price of a residual interest is more than its adjusted basis, the excess is amortized and included in the residual interest holder's income ratably over the anticipated life of the REMIC.

If the adjusted basis of a regular interest is more than its issue price, the regular interest holder treats the excess as amortizable bond premium subject to the rules of section 171. If the adjusted basis of a residual interest is more than its issue price, the excess is deductible ratably over the life of the REMIC.

Payments Subject to Withholding at Source

If there are any nonresident alien individuals, foreign partnerships, or foreign corporations as regular interest holders or residual interest holders, and the REMIC has items of gross income from sources within the United States (see sections 861 through 865), see **Form 1042,** Annual Withholding Tax Return for U.S. Source Income of Foreign Persons.

Who Must Sign

Startup day after November 9, 1988.— For a REMIC with a startup day after November 9, 1988, Form 1066 may be signed by any person who could sign the return of the entity in the absence of the REMIC election. Thus, the return of a REMIC that is a corporation or trust would be signed by a corporate officer or a trustee, respectively. For REMICs with only segregated pools of assets, the return would be signed by any person who could sign the return of the entity owning the assets of the REMIC under applicable state law.

Startup day before November 10, 1988.—A REMIC with a startup day

before November 10, 1988, may elect to apply the rules for REMICs with a startup day after November 9, 1988. Otherwise, Form 1066 must be signed by a residual interest holder or, as provided in section 6903, by a fiduciary as defined in section 7701(a)(6) who is acting for the REMIC and who has furnished adequate notice as described in Regulations section 301.6903-1(b).

Paid preparer's information.—If someone prepares the return and does not charge the REMIC, that person should not sign the return.

Generally, anyone who is paid to prepare the REMIC return must sign the return and fill in the Paid Preparer's Use Only area of the return.

The preparer required to sign the REMIC's return **must** complete the required preparer information and:

● Sign it, by hand, in the space provided for the preparer's signature. (Signature stamps or labels are not acceptable.)

● Give the REMIC a copy of the return in addition to the copy to be filed with the IRS.

Specific Instructions

General Information

Name, address, and employer identification number.—Print or type the REMIC's legal name and address on the appropriate lines. Include the suite, room, or other unit number after the street address. If the Post Office does not deliver mail to the street address and the REMIC has a P.O. box, show the box number instead of the street address.

Note: *Each REMIC must have its own employer identification number.*

Show the correct employer identification number (EIN) in Item A on page 1 of Form 1066. If the REMIC does not have an EIN, get **Form SS-4,** Application for Employer Identification Number, for details on how to obtain an EIN immediately by telephone. If the REMIC has previously applied for an EIN, but has not received it by the time the return is due, write "Applied for" in the space for the EIN. Do not apply for an EIN more than once. See Pub. 583 for details.

Item B—Date REMIC started.—Enter the "startup day" selected by the REMIC.

The startup day is the day on which the REMIC issued all of its regular and residual interests. However, a sponsor may contribute property to a REMIC in exchange for regular and residual interests over any period of 10 consecutive days and the REMIC may designate any one of those 10 days as the startup day. The day so designated is then the startup day, and all interests are treated as issued on that day.

Page 3

Form 1066.

Item C—Total assets at end of tax year.—Enter the total assets of the REMIC. If there are no assets at the end of the tax year, enter the total assets as of the beginning of the tax year.

Section I

Line 1—Taxable Interest.—Enter the total taxable interest. "Taxable interest" is interest that is included in ordinary income from all sources except interest exempt from tax and interest on tax-free covenant bonds. You may elect under section 171(e) to reduce the amount of interest accrued on taxable bonds acquired after 1987 by the amount of amortizable bond premium on those bonds attributable to the current tax year. There is also an election for taxable bonds acquired on or after October 23, 1986.

Line 2—Accrued market discount under section 860C(b)(1)(B).—Enter the amount of market discount attributable to the current tax year determined on the basis of a constant interest rate under the rules of section 1276(b)(2).

Line 3—Capital gain (loss).—Enter the amount shown on line 12 or 13 (if any), from Schedule D, page 2.

Line 4—Ordinary gain (loss).—Enter the net gain (loss) from line 20, Part II, Form 4797.

Line 5—Other income.—Enter any other taxable income not listed above and explain it on an attached schedule. If the REMIC issued regular interests at a premium, the net amount of the premium is income that must be prorated over the term of these interests. Include this income on this line.

Deductions—(Lines 7–14).—Include only deductible amounts on lines 7–14. A REMIC is not allowed any of the following deductions in computing its taxable income:

● The net operating loss deduction;

● The deduction for taxes paid or accrued to foreign countries and U.S. possessions;

● The deduction for charitable contributions;

● The deduction for depletion under section 611 for oil and gas wells; and,

● Losses or deductions allocable to prohibited transactions.

Line 9—Amount accrued to regular interest holders in the REMIC that is deductible as interest.—Regular interests in the REMIC are treated as indebtedness for Federal income tax purposes. Enter the amount of interest, including original issue discount, paid or accrued to regular interest holders for the tax year. Do not deduct any amounts paid or accrued for residual interests in the REMIC.

Line 10—Other Interest.—Do not include interest deducted on line 9 or

Page 4

interest on indebtedness incurred or continued to purchase or carry obligations on which the interest is wholly exempt from income tax. You may elect to include amortization of bond premium on taxable bonds acquired before 1988 unless you elected to offset amortizable bond premium against the interest accrued on the bond (see the Section I, line 1, instructions). Do not include any amount attributable to a tax-exempt bond.

Line 11—Taxes.—Enter taxes paid or accrued during the tax year but do not include the following:

● Federal income taxes (except the tax on net income from foreclosure property);

● Foreign or U.S. possession income taxes;

● Taxes not imposed on the REMIC; or

● Taxes, including state or local sales taxes, that are paid or incurred in connection with an acquisition or disposition of property (such taxes must be treated as a part of the cost of the acquired property or, in the case of a disposition, as a reduction in the amount realized on the disposition).

Note: *If you have to pay tax on net income from foreclosure property, you should include this tax (from line 11 of Schedule J) here on line 11.*

See section 164(d) for apportionment of taxes on real property between the seller and purchaser.

Line 12—Depreciation.—See the Instructions for Form 4562 or **Pub. 534,** Depreciation, to figure the amount of depreciation to enter on this line. You must complete and attach **Form 4562,** Depreciation and Amortization, if the REMIC placed property in service during 1994, claims a section 179 expense deduction, or claims depreciation on any car or other listed property.

Line 13—Other deductions.—Enter any other allowable deductions for which no line is provided on Form 1066.

Schedule D

General Instructions

Purpose of schedule.—For a REMIC with a startup day before November 12, 1991, use Schedule D to report the sale or exchange of capital assets. To report sales or exchanges of property other than capital assets, see Form 4797 and its instructions.

A REMIC with a startup day after November 11, 1991, must use Form 4797 instead of Schedule D because all of its gains and losses from the sale or exchange of any property are treated as ordinary gains and losses.

For amounts received from an installment sale, the holding period rule in effect in the year of sale will determine the treatment of amounts

received as long-term or short-term capital gain.

Report every sale or exchange of property in detail, even though there is no gain or loss.

For details, see **Pub. 544,** Sales and Other Dispositions of Assets.

Capital gain distributions.—On line 7, report as long-term capital gain distributions: **(a)** a capital gain dividend, and **(b)** the REMIC's share of the undistributed capital gain from a mutual fund or other regulated investment company.

For details, see **Pub. 564,** Mutual Fund Distributions.

Losses on worthless securities.—If any securities that are capital assets become worthless during the tax year, the loss is a loss from the sale or exchange of capital assets as of the last day of the tax year.

Losses from wash sales.—The REMIC cannot deduct losses from a wash sale of stock or securities. A wash sale occurs if the REMIC acquires (by purchase or exchange), or has a contract or option to acquire, substantially identical stock or securities within 30 days before or after the date of the sale or exchange. See section 1091 for details.

Installment sales.—If the REMIC sold property (except publicly traded stock or securities) at a gain and will receive any payment in a tax year after the year of sale, it must use the installment method and **Form 6252,** Installment Sale Income, unless it elects not to use the installment method.

If the REMIC wants to elect out of the installment method, it must report the full amount of the gain on a timely filed return (including extensions).

Specific Instructions

Column (d)—Sales price.—Enter either the gross sales price or the net sales price from the sale. On sales of stocks and bonds, report the gross amount as reported to the REMIC by the REMIC's broker on **Form 1099-B,** Proceeds From Broker and Barter Exchange Transactions, or similar statement. However, if the broker advised the REMIC that gross proceeds (gross sales price) minus commissions and option premiums were reported to the IRS, enter that net amount in column (d).

Column (e)—Cost or other basis.—In general, the cost or other basis is the cost of the property plus purchase commissions and improvements, minus depreciation. If the REMIC got the property in a tax-free exchange, involuntary conversion, or wash sale of stock, it may not be able to use the actual cash cost as the basis. If the REMIC uses a basis other than cash cost, attach an explanation.

Appendix A. REMIC Tax Returns

Form 1066.

When selling stock, adjust the basis by subtracting all the nontaxable distributions received before the sale. This includes nontaxable dividends from utility company stock and mutual funds. Also, adjust the basis for any stock splits.

See section 852(f) for the treatment of certain load charges incurred in acquiring stock in a mutual fund with a reinvestment right.

Increase the cost or other basis by any expense of sale, such as broker's fee, commission, and option premium, before making an entry in column (e), unless the REMIC reported net sales price in column (d).

For details, see Pub. 551, Basis of Assets.

Schedule J

Part I—Tax on Net Income from Prohibited Transactions

Do not net losses from prohibited transactions against income or gains from prohibited transactions in determining the amounts to enter on lines 1a through 1d. These losses are not deductible in computing net income from prohibited transactions.

Note: *For purposes of lines 1a and 1d below, the term "prohibited transactions" does not include any disposition that is required to prevent default on a regular interest where the threatened default resulted from a default on one or more qualified mortgages, or to facilitate a clean-up call. A clean-up call is the redemption of a class of regular interests when, by reason of prior payments with respect to those interests, the administrative costs associated with servicing that class outweigh the benefits of maintaining the class. It does not include the redemption of a class in order to profit from a change in interest rates.*

Line 1a—Gain from certain dispositions of qualified mortgages.—Enter the amount of gain from the disposition of any qualified mortgage transferred to the REMIC other than a disposition from:

1. The substitution of a qualified replacement mortgage for a qualified mortgage (or the repurchase in lieu of substitution of a defective obligation).

2. The foreclosure, default, or imminent default of the mortgage.

3. The bankruptcy or insolvency of the REMIC.

4. A qualified liquidation.

See section 860F(a) for details and exceptions.

Line 1b—Income from nonpermitted assets.—Enter the amount of any income received or accrued during the year attributable to any asset other than a qualified mortgage or permitted

investment. See section 860G(a) for definitions.

Line 1c—Compensation for services.—Enter the amount of fees or other compensation for services received or accrued during the year.

Line 1d—Gain from the disposition of cash flow investments (except from a qualified liquidation).—Enter the amount of gain from the disposition of any "cash flow investment" except from a qualified liquidation. A cash flow investment is any investment of amounts received under qualified mortgages for a temporary period (not more than 13 months) before distribution to holders of interests in the REMIC. See section 860F(a)(4) for the definition of a qualified liquidation.

Line 3—Deductions directly connected with the production of income shown on line 2.—Enter the total amount of allowable deductions directly connected with the production of the income shown on lines 1a through 1d except for those deductions connected with prohibited transactions resulting in a loss.

Part II—Tax on Net Income From Foreclosure Property

For a definition of foreclosure property, see instructions on page 6 for Schedule L, line 1c. Net income from foreclosure property must also be included in the computation of taxable income (or net loss) shown in Section I, page 1, Form 1066.

Line 7—Gross income from foreclosure property.—Do not include on line 7 amounts described in section 856(c)(3)(A), (B), (C), (D), (E) or (G).

Line 9—Deductions.—Only those expenses which are proximately related to earning the income shown on line 8 may be deducted to figure net income from foreclosure property. Allowable deductions include depreciation on foreclosure property, interest paid or accrued on debt of the REMIC attributable to the carrying of foreclosure property, real estate taxes, and fees charged by an independent contractor to manage foreclosure property. **Do not** deduct general overhead and administrative expenses.

Line 11—Tax on net income from foreclosure property.—The REMIC is allowed a deduction for the amount of tax shown on this line. Include this amount in computing the deduction for taxes to be entered on line 11, Section I, page 1, Form 1066.

Part III—Tax on Contributions After the Startup Day

Do not complete this part if the startup day was before July 1, 1987. For this purpose "startup day" means any day selected by a REMIC which is on or

before the first day on which interests in the REMIC are issued.

The tax imposed by section 860G(d) is 100% of the amount shown on line 12.

Line 12—Amount of taxable contributions.—Enter the amount of contributions received during the calendar year after the startup day (as defined above). Do not include cash contributions described below:

1. Any contribution to facilitate a clean-up call or a qualified liquidation.

2. Any payment in the nature of a guarantee.

3. Any contribution during the 3-month period beginning on the startup day.

4. Any contribution to a qualified reserve fund by any holder of a residual interest in the REMIC.

Attach a schedule showing your computation.

Designation of Tax Matters Person (TMP)

A REMIC may designate a tax matters person in the same manner that a partnership may designate a tax matters partner under Temporary Regulations section 301.6231(a)(7)-1T. When applying that section, treat all holders of a residual interest in the REMIC as general partners. The designation may be made by completing the **Designation of Tax Matters Person** section on page 4 of Form 1066.

Additional Information

Be sure to answer the questions and provide other information in items E through L.

Item E—Type of entity.—Check the box for the entity type of the REMIC recognized under state or local law. If the REMIC is not a separate entity under state or local law, check the box for "Segregated Pool of Assets," and state the name and type of entity which owns the assets in the spaces provided.

Item F—Number of residual interest holders.—Enter the number of persons who were residual interest holders at any time during the tax year.

Item G—Consolidated REMIC proceedings.—Generally, the tax treatment of REMIC items is determined at the REMIC level in a consolidated REMIC proceeding, rather than in separate proceedings with individual residual interest holders.

Check the box for Item G if any of the following applies:

● The REMIC had more than 10 residual interest holders at any time during the tax year.

● Any residual interest holder was a nonresident alien or was other than a natural person or estate, **unless** there

Page 5

155

Form 1066.

was at no time during the tax year more than one holder of the residual interest.

● The REMIC has elected to be subject to the rules for consolidated REMIC proceedings.

"Small REMICs," as defined in sections 860F(e), 6231(a)(1)(B), and the regulations of both, are not subject to the rules for consolidated REMIC proceedings but may make an irrevocable election to be covered by them.

For details on the consolidated entity-level audit procedures, see "Examination of Partnerships and S Corporations" in **Pub. 556,** Examination of Returns, Appeal Rights, and Claims for Refund, and sections 860F(e) and 6231.

Item H—Foreign accounts.—Check "Yes" if either **1** OR **2** below applies:

1. At any time during calendar year 1994, the REMIC had an interest in or signature or other authority over a bank account, securities account, or other financial account in a foreign country, and

● The combined value of the accounts was more than $10,000 at any time during the calendar year, and

● The accounts were not with a U.S. military banking facility operated by a U.S. financial institution.

2. The REMIC owns more than 50% of the stock in any corporation that would answer the question "Yes" to Item **1** above.

Get **Form TD F 90-22.1,** Report of Foreign Bank and Financial Accounts, to see if the REMIC is considered to have an interest in or signature or other authority over a bank account, securities account, or other financial account in a foreign country.

If you checked "Yes" for Item H, file Form TD F 90-22.1 by June 30, 1995, with the Department of the Treasury at the address shown on the form. Form TD F 90-22.1 is not a tax return. **Do not file it with Form 1066.**

Item I—Foreign trusts.—Check "Yes" if the REMIC was a grantor of, or a transferor to, a foreign trust that existed during the tax year.

A U.S. REMIC that has (at any time) transferred property to a foreign trust may have to include the income from that property in the REMIC's taxable income if the trust had a U.S. beneficiary during 1994. (See section 679.)

If the REMIC transfers property to a foreign corporation as paid-in surplus or as a contribution to capital, or to a foreign estate or trust, or to a foreign partnership, an excise tax is imposed

under section 1491 (see **Form 926,** Return by a U.S. Transferor of Property to a Foreign Corporation, Foreign Estate or Trust, or Foreign Partnership). To avoid this excise tax, the REMIC may choose to treat the transfer as a taxable sale or exchange as specified in section 1057.

Item L—Sum of the daily accruals.—Enter the total of the daily accruals for all residual interests for the calendar year. See section 860E(c)(2) for details.

Schedule L—Balance Sheets

The amounts shown should agree with the REMIC's books and records. Attach a statement explaining any differences.

Line 1a.—Cash flow investments are any investments of amounts received under qualified mortgages for a temporary period (not more than 13 months) before distribution to holders of interests in the REMIC.

Line 1b.—Qualified reserve assets include any intangible property that is held for investment and as part of any reasonably required reserve to provide for full payment of expenses of the REMIC or amounts due on regular interests in the event of defaults on qualified mortgages or lower than expected returns on cash flow investments. No more than 30% of the gross income from such assets may be derived from the sale or disposition of property held less than 3 months. See section 860G(a)(7)(C) for details and exceptions.

Line 1c.—Foreclosure property is any real property (including interests in real property), and any personal property incident to such real property, acquired by the REMIC as a result of the REMIC's having bid in the property at foreclosure, or having otherwise reduced the property to ownership or possession by agreement or process of law, after there was a default or imminent default on a qualified mortgage held by the REMIC. Generally, this property ceases to be foreclosure property 2 years after the date that the REMIC acquired the property. See sections 860G(a)(8), 856(e), and Regulations section 1.856-6 for more details.

Note: Solely for purposes of section 860D(a), the determination of whether any property is foreclosure property will be made without regard to section 856(e)(4).

Line 7.—Regular interests are interests in the REMIC that are issued on the startup day with fixed terms and that are designated as regular interests, if:

1. Such interest unconditionally entitles the holder to receive a specified

principal amount or other similar amounts; and

2. Interest payments (or similar amounts), if any, with respect to the interest at or before maturity are payable based on a fixed rate (or at a variable rate described in Regulations section 1.860G-1(a)(3) and section 1.860G-1T), or consist of a specified portion of the interest payments on qualified mortgages and this portion does not vary during the period that the interest is outstanding.

The interest will meet the requirements of 1 above even if the timing (but not the amount) of the principal payments (or other similar amounts) is contingent on the extent of prepayments on qualified mortgages and the amount of income from permitted investments.

Schedule M—Reconciliation of Residual Interest Holders' Capital Accounts

Show what caused the changes in the residual interest holders' capital accounts during the tax year.

The amounts shown should agree with the REMIC's books and records and the balance sheet amounts. Attach a statement explaining any differences.

Include in column (d) tax-exempt interest income, other tax-exempt income, income from prohibited transactions, income recorded on the REMIC's books but not included on this return, and allowable deductions not charged against book income this year.

Include in column (e) capital losses over the $3,000 limitation (for a REMIC with a startup day before November 12, 1991), other nondeductible amounts (such as losses from prohibited transactions and expenses connected with the production of tax-exempt income), deductions allocable to prohibited transactions, expenses recorded on books not deducted on this return, and taxable income not recorded on books this year.

Schedule Q—Quarterly Notice to Residual Interest Holder of REMIC Taxable Income or Net Loss Allocation

Attach a separate Copy A, Schedule Q (Form 1066), to Form 1066 for each person who was a residual interest holder at any time during the tax year and for each quarter in which each person was a residual interest holder.

Appendix A. REMIC Tax Returns

SCHEDULE Q (Form 1066) (Rev. October 1992) Department of the Treasury Internal Revenue Service	**Quarterly Notice to Residual Interest Holder of REMIC Taxable Income or Net Loss Allocation** For calendar quarter ended .... , 19 .... (Complete for each residual interest holder—See instructions on back of Copy C.)	OMB No. 1545-1014 Expires 10-31-95 **Copy C—For REMIC's Records**

Residual interest holder's identifying number	REMIC's identifying number
Residual interest holder's name, address, and ZIP code	REMIC's name, address, and ZIP code

A What type of entity is this residual interest holder? ▶ ....

B Enter residual interest holder's percentage of ownership of all residual interests:
  1 Before change ▶ .... %
  2 End of quarter ▶ .... %

C Enter the percentage of the REMIC's assets for the quarter represented by each of the following:
  1 Qualifying real property loans under section 593(d)(1) ▶ .... %
  2 Real estate assets under section 856(c)(6)(B) ▶ .... %
  3 Assets described in section 7701(a)(19)(C) (relating to the
     definition of a domestic building and loan association) ▶ .... %

D IRS Center where REMIC files return ▶

E Reconciliation of residual interest holder's capital account

(a) Capital account at beginning of quarter	(b) Capital contributed during quarter	(c) Taxable income (net loss) from line 1b below	(d) Nontaxable income	(e) Unallowable deductions	(f) Withdrawals and distributions	(g) Capital account at end of quarter (combine cols. (a) through (f))
			( )	( )	( )	

Caution: *See the Instructions for Residual Interest Holder on back of Copy B before entering information from this schedule on your tax return.*

1a Taxable income (net loss) of the REMIC for the calendar quarter . . . . . .

  b Your share of the taxable income (net loss) for the calendar quarter . . . .

2a Sum of the daily accruals under section 860E for all residual interests for the calendar quarter . . . .

  b Sum of the daily accruals under section 860E for your interest for the calendar quarter . . . . . .

  c Excess inclusion for the calendar quarter for your residual interest (subtract line 2b from line 1b, but do not enter less than zero) . . . .

3 **Residual interest holders who are individuals or other pass-through interest holders. (See instructions.) Not required to be completed for other entities.**

  a Section 212 expenses of the REMIC for the calendar quarter . . . .

  b Your share of section 212 expenses for the calendar quarter. (If you are an individual, this amount must be included in gross income in addition to the amount shown on line 1b. See instructions for treatment of this amount as a miscellaneous itemized deduction.) . . . .

For Paperwork Reduction Act Notice, see Form 1066 instructions.   **Schedule Q (Form 1066)** (Rev. 10-92)

Schedule Q (Form 1066).

Instructions for Residual Interest Holder

(Section references are to the Internal Revenue Code unless otherwise noted.)

Purpose of Form

The real estate mortgage investment conduit (REMIC) uses Schedule Q to notify you of your share of the REMIC's quarterly taxable income (or net loss), the excess inclusion with respect to your interest, and your share of the REMIC's section 212 expenses for the quarter.

Keep your copy of this schedule for your records. Do not file it with your tax return.

General Instructions

Tax treatment of REMIC items.—Although the REMIC is not subject to income tax (except on net income from prohibited transactions, net income from foreclosure property, and contributions made after the startup day), you are liable for tax on your share of the REMIC's taxable income, whether or not distributed, and you must include your share on your tax return. Generally, you must report REMIC items shown on your Schedule Q (and any attached schedules) or similar statement consistent with the way the REMIC treated the items on the return it filed. This rule does not apply if your REMIC falls within the "small REMIC" exception and does not elect to be subject to the consolidated entity-level audit procedures.

If your treatment on your original or amended return is (or may be) inconsistent with the REMIC's treatment, or if the REMIC was required to file but has not filed a return, you must file **Form 8082**, Notice of Inconsistent Treatment or Amended Return (Administrative Adjustment Request (AAR)), with your original or amended return to identify and explain the inconsistency (or to note that a REMIC return has not been filed). See sections 860F(e) and 6222 for the inconsistent treatment rules.

Errors.—If you believe the REMIC has made an error on your Schedule Q, notify the REMIC and ask for a corrected Schedule Q. Do not change any items on your copy. Be sure that the REMIC sends a copy of the corrected Schedule Q to the IRS. If you are unable to reach an agreement with the REMIC about the inconsistency, you must file Form 8082 as explained in the previous paragraph.

Limitation on losses.—Generally, you may not claim your share of the quarterly net loss from a REMIC that is greater than the adjusted basis of your residual interest in the REMIC at the end of the calendar quarter (determined without regard to your share of the net loss of the REMIC for that quarter). Any loss disallowed because it exceeds your adjusted basis is treated as incurred by the REMIC in the following quarter, but only for the purpose of offsetting your share of REMIC taxable income for that quarter.

Items that increase your basis are:

1. Money and your adjusted basis in property contributed to the REMIC.

2. Your share of the REMIC's taxable income.

3. Any income reported under section 860F(b)(1)(C)(ii).

Items that decrease your basis are:

1. Money and the fair market value of property distributed to you.

2. Your share of the REMIC's losses.

3. Any deduction claimed under section 860F(b)(1)(D)(ii).

Passive activity limitations under section 469.—Amounts includible in income (or deductible as a loss) by a residual interest holder are treated as portfolio income (loss). Such income (or loss) is not taken into account in determining the loss from a passive activity under section 469.

Specific Instructions

Item C—REMIC assets.—This information is provided only for the use of a residual interest holder that qualifies as a domestic building and loan association, mutual savings bank, cooperative bank subject to section 593, or real estate investment trust.

Line 1b—Your share of the taxable income (net loss) for the calendar quarter.—

Calendar year taxpayers and fiscal year taxpayers whose tax years end with a calendar quarter: If you are an individual, you must report, as ordinary income or loss, the total of the amounts shown on line 1b of Schedule Q for each quarter included in your tax year, after applying any basis limitations, on Schedule E (Form 1040), Part IV, column (d). If you are not an individual, report the amounts as instructed on your tax return.

Fiscal year taxpayers whose tax years do not end with a calendar quarter: You must figure the amount to report based on your tax year. For each calendar quarter that overlaps the beginning or end of your tax year, divide the amount shown on line 1a by the number of days in that quarter. Multiply the result by your percentage of ownership of all residual interests for each day of your tax year included in that quarter. Total the daily amounts of taxable income (net loss) for the overlapping quarters. Add these amounts to the amounts shown on line 1b for the full quarters included in your tax year. Report the resulting income or loss in the same manner as explained above for calendar year taxpayers.

Line 2c. Excess inclusion for the calendar quarter for your residual interest.—

Calendar year taxpayers and fiscal year taxpayers whose tax years end with a calendar quarter: The total of the amounts shown on line 2c for all quarters included in your tax year is the smallest amount of taxable income you may report for that year. The preceding sentence does not apply to a financial institution to which section 593 applies, except where necessary or appropriate to prevent avoidance of Federal income tax. (Special rules apply to members of affiliated groups filing consolidated returns. See sections 860E(a)(3) and (4).) The line 2c amount is treated as "unrelated business taxable income" if you are an exempt organization subject to the unrelated business tax under section 511. If you are an individual, enter this amount as an item of information on Schedule E (Form 1040), Part IV, column (c). If you must also report this amount as your taxable income, enter the amount shown on line 2c on the taxable income line of your return and write "Sch. Q" on the dotted line to the left of the entry space.

Fiscal year taxpayers whose tax years do not end with a calendar quarter: The same rules explained above for calendar year taxpayers apply, except that you must figure the excess inclusion based on your tax year. For each calendar quarter that overlaps the beginning or end of your tax year, divide the amount shown on line 2a by the number of days in that quarter. Multiply the result by your percentage of ownership of all residual interests for each day of your tax year included in that quarter. Total the daily amounts for the overlapping quarter. Subtract this total from your share of the taxable income for the part of the quarter included in your tax year, as previously figured. Add the resulting amounts for the overlapping quarters to the amounts shown on line 2c for the full quarters included in your tax year and report it in the same manner as explained above for calendar year taxpayers.

Line 3b. Your share of section 212 expenses for the calendar quarter. —

Calendar year taxpayers and fiscal year taxpayers whose tax years end with a calendar quarter: If you are an individual or other pass-through interest holder (as defined in Temporary Regulations section 1.67-3T), you must report as ordinary income the total of the amounts shown on line 3b of Schedule Q for each quarter included in your tax year. This amount must be reported in addition to your share of taxable income (net loss) determined above. If you are an individual, report this total on Schedule E (Form 1040), Part IV, column (e). If you are not an individual, report the amounts as instructed on your tax return.

If you are an individual and itemize your deductions on your return, you may be able to deduct the total as a miscellaneous itemized deduction. It should be included with the other miscellaneous deductions that are subject to the 2% of adjusted gross income limit.

Fiscal year taxpayers whose tax years do not end with a calendar quarter: The same rules explained above for calendar year taxpayers apply, except that you must figure your share of section 212 expenses based on your tax year. For each calendar quarter that overlaps the beginning or end of your tax year, divide the amount shown on line 3a by the number of days in that quarter. Multiply the result by your percentage of ownership of all residual interests for each day of your tax year included in that quarter. Total the daily amounts of section 212 expenses for the overlapping quarters. Add these amounts to the amounts shown on line 3b for the full quarters included in your tax year. Report the resulting amount in the same manner as explained above for calendar year taxpayers.

Appendix A.   REMIC Tax Returns

Schedule Q (Form 1066).

Instructions for REMIC

(Section references are to the Internal Revenue Code unless otherwise noted.)

Purpose of Form

Schedule Q (Form 1066) shows each residual interest holder's share of the REMIC's quarterly taxable income (net loss), the excess inclusion for the residual interest holder's interest, and the residual interest holder's share of the REMIC's section 212 expenses for the quarter.

Although the REMIC is not subject to income tax (except on net income from prohibited transactions, net income from foreclosure property, and contributions made after the startup day), the residual interest holders are liable for tax on their shares of the REMIC's taxable income, whether or not distributed, and must include their shares on their tax returns.

General Instructions

Complete Schedule Q (Form 1066) for each person who was a residual interest holder at any time during the calendar quarter. File Copy A with Form 1066. Give Copy B to the residual interest holder by the last day of the month following the month in which the calendar quarter ends. Keep Copy C with a copy of Form 1066 as part of the REMIC's records.

Specific Instructions

On each Schedule Q, enter the names, addresses, and identifying numbers of the residual interest holder and REMIC. For each residual interest holder that is an individual, you must enter the residual interest holder's social security number. For all other residual interest holders, you must enter the residual interest holder's employer identification number. However, if a residual interest holder is an individual retirement arrangement (IRA), enter the identifying number of the IRA trust. Do not enter the social security number of the individual for whom the IRA is maintained.

Item A—What type of entity is this residual interest holder?— State on this line whether the residual interest holder is an individual, a corporation, a fiduciary, a partnership, an exempt organization, a nominee (custodian), or another REMIC. If the residual interest holder is a nominee, use the following codes to indicate in parentheses the type of entity the nominee represents.

I – Individual; C – Corporation; F – Fiduciary; P – Partnership; E – Exempt Organization; R – REMIC; or IRA – Individual Retirement Arrangement.

Item B—Residual interest holder's percentage of ownership.— Enter in item B(2) the percentage at the end of the calendar quarter. However, if a residual interest holder's percentage of ownership changed during the quarter, enter in item B(1) the percentage immediately before the change. If there are multiple changes in the percentage of ownership during the quarter, attach a statement giving the date and percentage before each change.

Item C—REMIC assets.—Enter in Item C the percentage of the REMIC's assets during the calendar quarter represented by each of the following three categories of assets:

1. Qualifying real property loans under section 593(d)(1);

2. Real estate assets under section 856(c)(6)(B); and

3. Assets described in section 7701(a)(19)(C) (relating to the definition of a domestic building and loan association).

These percentages must be computed using the average adjusted basis of the assets held during the calendar quarter. To do this, the REMIC must make the appropriate computation as of the close of each month, week, or day and then average the monthly, weekly, or daily percentages for the quarter. The monthly, weekly, or daily computation period must be applied uniformly during the calendar quarter to all categories of assets and gross income, and may not be changed in succeeding calendar quarters without IRS consent. If the percentage of the REMIC's assets for any category is at least 95%, the REMIC may show "95 or more" for that category in item C.

Note: *If less than 95% of the assets of the REMIC are real estate assets (as defined in section 856(c)(6)(B)), the REMIC must also report to any real estate investment trust that holds a residual interest the information specified in Regulations section 1.860F-4(e)(1)(ii)(B).*

Item E—Reconciliation of residual interest holder's capital account.— See the instructions for Schedule M of Form 1066.

Line 1a—Taxable income (net loss) of the REMIC for the calendar quarter.—Enter the REMIC's taxable income (net loss) for the calendar quarter. The sum of the totals for the 4 quarters in the calendar year must equal the amount shown on line 15, section I of Form 1066.

Line 1b—Your share of the taxable income (net loss) for the calendar quarter.—Enter the residual interest holder's share of the taxable income (net loss) shown on line 1a (determined by adding the holder's daily portions under section 860C(a)(2) for each day in the quarter the holder held the residual interest). If line 1a is a loss, enter the residual interest holder's full share of the loss, without regard to the adjusted basis of the residual interest holder's interest in the REMIC.

Line 2a—Sum of the daily accruals under section 860E for all residual interests for the calendar quarter.—Enter the product of the sum of the adjusted issue prices of all residual interests at the beginning of the quarter and 120% of the long-term Federal rate (determined on the basis of compounding at the end of each quarter and properly adjusted for the length of such quarter). See section 860E(c) for details.

Line 2b—Sum of the daily accruals under section 860E for your interest.—Enter zero if line 2a is zero. Otherwise, divide the amount shown on line 2a by the number of days in the quarter. Multiply the result by the residual interest holder's percentage of ownership for each day in the quarter that the residual interest holder owned the interest. Total the daily amounts and enter the result.

Line 3—Complete lines 3a and 3b only for residual interest holders who are individuals or other pass-through interest holders (as defined in Temporary Regulations section 1.67-3T).

Line 3a—Section 212 expenses of the REMIC for the calendar quarter.—Enter the REMIC's allocable section 212 expenses for the calendar quarter. The term "allocable section 212 expenses" means the aggregate amount of the expenses paid or accrued in the calendar quarter for which a deduction is allowable under section 212 in determining the taxable income of the REMIC for the calendar quarter.

Section 212 expenses generally include operational expenses such as rent, salaries, legal and accounting fees, the cost of preparing and distributing reports and notices to interest holders, and litigation expenses.

Line 3b—Your share of section 212 expenses for the calendar quarter.—Enter the residual interest holder's share of the amount shown on line 3a.

159

Form **8811**
(Rev. November 1994)
Department of the Treasury
Internal Revenue Service

**Information Return for Real Estate
Mortgage Investment Conduits (REMICs)
and Issuers of Collateralized Debt Obligations**

OMB No. 1545-1099

1 Name of REMIC or issuer of a collateralized debt obligation	2 Employer identification number

3 Address (Number, street, and room or suite no., or P.O. box no., city or town, state, and ZIP code)

4 Name and title of the representative to be contacted by the public (see instructions)	5 Telephone number of representative (optional) ( )

6 Address of the representative to be contacted by the public (if different from REMIC's or issuer's)

7 CUSIP number(s) (see instructions)	8 Startup day or issue date
9 Name and title of the representative to be contacted by the IRS (see instructions)	10 Telephone number of representative ( )

11 Address of the representative to be contacted by the IRS

Please Sign Here

Under penalties of perjury, I declare that I have examined this return, including accompanying statements, and to the best of my knowledge and belief, it is true, correct, and complete.

▶ _____ _____ ▶ _____
Signature (see instructions)   Date   Title

Paperwork Reduction Act Notice

We ask for the information on this form to carry out the Internal Revenue laws of the United States. You are required to give us the information. We need it to ensure that you are complying with these laws and to allow us to figure and collect the right amount of tax.

The time needed to complete and file this form will vary depending on individual circumstances. The estimated average time is:

Recordkeeping . . 2 hr., 38 min.

Learning about the law or the form . . . . . 24 min.

Preparing, copying, assembling, and sending the form to the IRS . . . . . 27 min.

If you have comments concerning the accuracy of these time estimates or suggestions for making this form simpler, we would be happy to hear from you. You can write to both the **Internal Revenue Service**, Attention: Tax Forms Committee, PC:FP, Washington, DC 20224, and the **Office of Management and Budget**, Paperwork Reduction Project (1545-1099), Washington, DC 20503. **DO NOT** send the tax form to either of these offices. Instead, see **Where To File** on page 2.

General Instructions

Section references are to the Internal Revenue Code.

Purpose of Form

A REMIC or another issuer of an instrument to which section 1272(a)(6) applies (collateralized debt obligation) uses Form 8811 to provide the information required by Regulations section 1.6049-7(b)(1)(ii). The information in Box 1 and Boxes 3 through 8 will be published in **Pub. 938**, Real Estate Mortgage Investment Conduits (REMICs) Reporting Information. This publication contains a directory of REMICs and issuers of collateralized debt obligations.

Who Must File

Entities that elect to be treated as a REMIC and issuers of a collateralized debt obligation must file Form 8811.

When To File

File Form 8811 no later than 30 days after **(a)** the startup day of the REMIC or **(b)** the issue date of the collateralized debt obligation.

The REMIC or issuer of a collateralized debt obligation must file a new Form 8811 within 30 days after the change of any of the information provided on a previously filed Form 8811. If the REMIC or other issuer ceases to have interests outstanding, file Form 8811 with the word "VOID" written across the form. The IRS will delete the information on this REMIC or issuer from Pub. 938.

Cat. No. 10460C

Form **8811** (Rev. 11-94)

Appendix A. REMIC Tax Returns

Where To File

Send Form 8811 to REMIC Publication Project, Internal Revenue Service, 1111 Constitution Avenue, N.W., Room 5607, Washington, DC 20224.

Signatures

REMIC with a startup day after November 9, 1988.—For a REMIC with a startup day after November 9, 1988, Form 8811 must be signed by a person who could sign the return of the entity in the absence of the REMIC election. Thus, the return of a REMIC that is a corporation or trust must be signed by a corporate officer or a trustee, respectively. For REMICs that consist of segregated pools of assets, the return must be signed by a person who could sign the return of the entity that owns the assets of the REMIC under applicable state law.

REMIC with a startup day before November 10, 1988.—A REMIC with a startup day before November 10, 1988, may elect to apply the rules applicable to REMICs with a startup day after November 9, 1988. Otherwise, Form 8811 must be signed by a residual interest holder or, as provided in section 6903, by a fiduciary who is acting for the REMIC and who has given adequate notice as prescribed in Regulations section 301.6903-1(b). The term "fiduciary" means a guardian, trustee, executor, administrator, receiver, conservator, or any person acting in any fiduciary capacity for any person.

Issuer of a collateralized debt obligation.—Form 8811 must be signed by a person who could sign the return of the issuer of the collateralized debt obligation.

Specific Instructions

Boxes 4, 5, and 6

Enter the name, title, and either the address or the address and telephone number of the official or representative designated by the REMIC or issuer of the collateralized debt obligation to provide information necessary to figure the amount of interest and original issue discount (OID) that the holder is required to report on the appropriate tax return.

Box 7

Enter the Committee on Uniform Security Identification Procedure (CUSIP) number assigned to each class of REMIC regular interest or to each collateralized debt obligation.

Box 8

The startup day is the day on which the REMIC issued all of its regular and residual interests. However, a sponsor may contribute property to a REMIC in exchange for regular and residual interests over any period of 10 consecutive days and the REMIC may designate any one of those 10 days as the startup day. The day so designated is then the startup day, and all interests are treated as issued on that day. For non-REMIC debt obligations, the "issue date" is defined in section 1275(a)(2).

Boxes 9, 10 and 11

Enter the name and title, address and telephone number of the official or representative of the REMIC or issuer of the collateralized debt obligation whom the IRS may contact with questions concerning this form. This information will not appear in Pub. 938.

161

Form **8281**
(Rev. July 1994)
Department of the Treasury
Internal Revenue Service

**Information Return for Publicly Offered
Original Issue Discount Instruments**

OMB No. 1545-0887

1 Issuer's name	2 Issuer's taxpayer identification number

Present address (including number, street, apt. or suite no., or P.O. box, city or town, state, and ZIP code)

3a Name of representative (See instructions.)	3b Telephone number ( )

Present address (if different from issuer's)

4 CUSIP number	5 Issue date	6 Maturity date

7 Type of instrument (See instructions.)	8 Issue price (percent of principal amount)	9 Stated interest rate (See instructions.)—Check if variable ▶ ☐

10 Interest payment dates

11 Amount of OID for entire issue	12 Yield to maturity	13 Stated redemption price at maturity of the entire issue (if the redemption price of each debt instrument within the issue is other than $1,000, indicate the stated redemption price of each debt instrument.)

14 Description of debt instruments. (See instructions.) Attach a schedule of OID per $1,000 principal amount for the life of the instrument. If the principal amount is other than $1,000, indicate the actual OID per principal amount per year. The schedule must be based on a 6-month accrual period. It must show the daily portion of OID for each accrual period and the total OID for each calendar year.

Under penalties of perjury, I declare that I have examined this return, including accompanying schedules and statements, and, to the best of my knowledge and belief, it is true, correct, and complete.

Signature ▶   Title ▶   Date ▶

For Paperwork Reduction Act Notice, see back of form.   Cat. No. 62024G   Form **8281** (Rev. 7-94)

162

Appendix A.   REMIC Tax Returns

Form 8281.

General Instructions

Section references are to the Internal Revenue Code.

Paperwork Reduction Act Notice

We ask for the information on this form to carry out the Internal Revenue laws of the United States. You are required to give us the information. We need it to ensure that you are complying with these laws and to allow us to figure and collect the right amount of tax.

The time needed to complete and file this form will vary depending on individual circumstances. The estimated average time is:

Recordkeeping	5 hr., 16 min.
Learning about the law or the form	18 min.
Preparing, copying, assembling, and sending the form to the IRS . .	23 min.

If you have comments concerning the accuracy of these time estimates or suggestions for making this form more simple, we would be happy to hear from you. You can write to both the **Internal Revenue Service,** Attention: Reports Clearance Officer, PC:FP, Washington, DC 20224; and the **Office of Management and Budget,** Paperwork Reduction Project (1545-0887), Washington, DC 20503. **DO NOT** send this form to either of these offices. Instead, see **Where To File** on this page.

Purpose of Form

Use Form 8281 if you are the issuer of publicly offered debt instruments having original issue discount (OID) to provide the information required by section 1275(c).

Who Must File

An issuer of a publicly offered debt instrument (obligation) having OID, such as a bond, debenture, or note, must file Form 8281. Publicly offered debt instruments also may include:

1. Serial obligations.

2. Exchanges of one debt instrument for another debt instrument, or exchanges of debt instruments for stock.

3. Investment unit offerings consisting of a debt instrument sold together with options or warrants.

4. Sinking fund instruments.

5. Convertible instruments.

Exceptions.—DO NOT FILE this form for the following:

1. Regular interests of a real estate mortgage investment conduit (REMIC) or collateralized debt obligations. REMICs and issuers of collateralized debt obligations must file **Form 8811,** Information Return for Real Estate Mortgage Investment Conduits (REMICs) and Issuers of Collateralized Debt Obligations.

2. Instruments on which OID is de minimis, as defined in section 1273(a)(3).

3. Tax-exempt obligations (the interest on which is not taxable).

4. Short-term obligations (those that mature in 1 year or less).

5. Certificates of deposit (CDs) issued by banks or other financial institutions.

6. CDs that are sold by brokers or other middlemen.

7. A public offering of stripped bonds or stripped coupons, including instruments issued under the Department of the Treasury's STRIPS program and instruments that constitute ownership interests in U.S. Treasury securities.

When To File

File Form 8281 within 30 days of the date of issuance of an OID instrument. File a separate Form 8281 for each issue.

Where To File

Send Form 8281 to Internal Revenue Service Data Center, Attn: OID, P.O. Box 331200, Detroit, MI 48232-7200.

Definitions

Original issue discount means the excess of the stated redemption price at maturity over the issue price.

Stated redemption price at maturity means the amount fixed by the last modification of the purchase agreement and includes interest and other amounts payable at maturity (other than interest based on a fixed rate and payable unconditionally at fixed periodic intervals of 1 year or less during the entire term of the debt instrument).

Issue price, in the case of publicly offered instruments not issued for property, means the initial offering price to the public (excluding bond houses and brokers) at which a substantial amount of such instruments was sold.

For more information about OID instruments and the OID reporting requirements, see Pub. 1212, List of Original Issue Discount Instruments.

Penalty

An issuer who fails to timely file Form 8281 will be subject to a penalty of 1% of the aggregate issue price of the debt instruments, unless such failure is due to reasonable cause and not willful neglect. The maximum penalty with respect to any issue is $50,000.

Specific Instructions

For serial obligations, complete Items 1 through 3 and attach a list showing the information for Items 4 through 14 for each obligation within the series. For all other obligations, complete all items.

To revise a form, write "Revised" across the top of this form and staple a copy of the previously filed form to this form. Complete all items on this form.

Items 3a and 3b.—Enter the name, address, and telephone number of an official or representative of the issuing company who has personal knowledge of this offering and who can be contacted if additional information is needed.

Item 4.—Enter the Committee on Uniform Security Identification Procedures (CUSIP) number assigned to the instruments.

Item 5.—Enter the date on which the issue was first sold to the public at the issue price.

Item 7.—Enter the type of instrument issued, such as unsecured public issue, an instrument backed by Treasury obligations, or foreign issue.

Item 8.—Enter the issue price as a percent of the principal amount. For example, XYZ bonds were first offered to the public at $900 with a principal amount of $1,000. The issue price of $900 expressed as a percent of principal is 90. If the percent is 100 or more, explain in Item 14.

If the instrument is part of an investment unit or exchange offering, attach a description of the method used to determine the issue price.

Item 9.—Enter the annual stated (or coupon) interest rate. If zero, enter "0." If the interest rate is variable, check the box and indicate the rate for the first year. If the rate is determined annually, check the box and explain in Item 14 how the annual rate will be determined. If any terms or conditions under the offering could change the stated interest rate, check the box and attach an explanation or a copy of the prospectus or offering circular containing such information.

Item 10.—Enter the interest payment dates.

Item 11.—Enter the amount of OID for the entire issue. For example, if the issue price for the entire issue totals $890,000, and the stated redemption price at maturity totals $1 million, the OID for the entire issue is $110,000.

Item 12.—Enter the yield to maturity as a percent. For example, if the annual yield is 9% and the yield to maturity is 9.6%, enter 9.6%. If the interest rate is determined annually, do not complete this item.

Item 14.—Please provide a description of the instruments including any terms and conditions that provide for payments of principal before maturity or early retirement. Also indicate whether the instruments are:

1. Part of an investment unit.

2. Issued in an exchange offering described in section 368(a).

3. Part of a serial issue.

You may provide a copy of the prospectus or offering circular instead of the required description.

To compute the OID allocable to a debt instrument having a short accrual period, you may use any reasonable method. **Please indicate what method you used.**

You must attach a schedule of OID per $1,000 principal amount for the life of the instrument. However, if the principal amount is other than $1,000, indicate the actual OID per principal amount per year and specify the actual principal amount. The schedule must be based on a 6-month accrual period. It must show the daily portion of OID for each accrual period and the total OID for each calendar year.

| Form **8831**
(Rev. January 1994)
Department of the Treasury
Internal Revenue Service | **Excise Taxes on Excess Inclusions of
REMIC Residual Interests** | OMB No. 1545-1379
Expires 3-31-96 |

Please Type or Print	Name	Identifying number
	Number, street, and room or suite no. (If a P.O. box, see instructions.)	
	City or town, state, and ZIP code	

Part I Transfers to Disqualified Organizations

Section A—Information on the Transfer

1 Enter the date the residual interest was transferred to a disqualified organization . . . . ▶ ___ / ___ / ___

2 Within a reasonable time after discovering this transfer was subject to tax under section 860E(e)(1), were steps taken so that the residual interest you transferred is no longer held by a disqualified organization? ▶ ☐ Yes ☐ No

3 If you answered "Yes" to question 2, enter the date the disqualified organization disposed of the residual interest . . . . ▶ ___ / ___ / ___

If you answered "Yes" to question 2, the tax due under section 860E(e)(1) will be waived if you pay the amount due under Regulations section 1.860E-2(a)(7)(ii). Skip Section B and go to Section C to figure the amount due.

If you answered "No" to question 2, use Section B to figure the tax due under section 860E(e)(1). Do not complete Section C.

Section B—Tax Due Under Section 860E(e)(1). Complete this section ONLY if you answered "No" to question 2.

4 Enter the present value of the excess inclusions allocable to the residual interest you transferred that are expected to accrue in each calendar quarter (or part thereof) following the transfer of that interest to the disqualified organization (see instructions) . . . . | **4** |

5 Tax due. Multiply line 4 by 35% (see **Caution** under Specific Instructions) . . . . | **5** |

Section C—Amount Due Under Regulations Section 1.860E-2(a)(7)(ii). Complete this section ONLY if you answered "Yes" to question 2.

6 Enter the amount of excess inclusions allocable to the residual interest you transferred that accrued during the period the disqualified organization held that interest . . . . | **6** |

7 Amount due. Multiply line 6 by 35% (see **Caution** under Specific Instructions) . . . . . . | **7** |

Part II Tax on Pass-Through Entities With Interests Held by Disqualified Organizations

8 Enter the ending date of the pass-through entity's tax year for which this return is being filed . . . . ▶ ___ / ___ / ___

9 Enter the amount of excess inclusions allocable to interests in the pass-through entity for which the record holder is a disqualified organization . . . . | **9** |

10 Tax due. Multiply line 9 by 35% (see **Caution** under Specific Instructions) . . . . | **10** |

Part III Tax and Payments

11 Enter the amount from line 5, 7, or 10, whichever applies . . . . | **11** |

12 Less: Amount paid with Form 2758 . . . . | **12** |

13 Amount due. Enter the excess of line 11 over line 12 . . . . | **13** |

14 Overpayment. Enter the excess of line 12 over line 11 . . . . | **14** |

Under penalties of perjury, I declare that I have examined this return, including accompanying schedules and statements, and to the best of my knowledge and belief, it is true, correct, and complete.

▶ _____ ▶ _____ ▶ _____
Signature   Date   Title (if any)

General Instructions

(Section references are to the Internal Revenue Code unless otherwise noted.)

Privacy Act and Paperwork Reduction Act Notice

We ask for the information on this form to carry out the Internal Revenue laws of the United States. The Internal Revenue Code requires this information under sections 860E, 6001, 6011, and 6109 and their regulations. We need it to figure and collect the right amount of tax. Routine uses of this information include giving it to the Department of Justice for civil and criminal litigation and to cities, states and the District of Columbia for use in administering their tax laws. If you fail to provide this information, you may be charged penalties and, in certain cases, you may be subject to criminal prosecution.

The time needed to complete and file this form will vary depending on individual circumstances. The estimated average time is: **Recordkeeping, 4 hr., 32 min.; Learning about the law or the form, 1 hr., 5 min.; Preparing and sending the form to the IRS, 1 hr., 13 min.**

If you have comments concerning the accuracy of these time estimates or suggestions for making this form more simple, we would be happy to hear from you. You can write to both the Internal Revenue Service, Attention: Reports Clearance Officer, PC:FP, Washington, DC 20224; and the Office of Management and Budget, Paperwork Reduction Project (1545-1379), Washington, DC 20503. DO NOT send this form to either of these offices. Instead, see **Where To File** on page 2.

Purpose of Form

Use Form 8831 to report and pay:

● The excise tax due under section 860E(e)(1) on any transfer of a residual interest in a REMIC to a disqualified organization;

● The amount due under Regulations section 1.860E-2(a)(7)(ii) if the tax under section 860E(e)(1) is to be waived; or

● The excise tax due under section 860E(e)(6) on pass-through entities with interests held by disqualified organizations.

Cat. No. 13377A   Form **8831** (Rev. 1-94)

Appendix A. REMIC Tax Returns

Form 8831.

Definitions

Disqualified organization.—A "disqualified organization" is:

1. The United States, any state or subdivision thereof, any foreign government, any international organization, or any of their agencies (except for certain taxable instrumentalities described in section 168(h)(2)(D) and the Federal Home Loan Mortgage Corporation);

2. Any tax-exempt organization (other than a farmers' cooperative described in section 521), unless that organization is subject to the unrelated business income tax; and

3. Any cooperative described in section 1381(a)(2)(C).

Pass-through entity.—A "pass-through entity" is a regulated investment company, real estate investment trust, common trust fund, partnership, trust, estate, or a cooperative described in section 1381. A person holding an interest in a pass-through entity as a nominee for another person is also treated as a pass-through entity.

Who Must File

You must file Form 8831 if you are liable for the excise tax due under section 860E(e)(1) (or the amount due under Regulations section 1.860E-2(a)(7)(ii)) because you transferred a residual interest in a REMIC to a disqualified organization after March 31, 1988 (unless the transfer was made under a binding contract in effect on that date).

You will not be treated as having transferred your interest to a disqualified organization if you obtain an affidavit from the transferee signed under penalties of perjury that either furnishes his or her social security number or states that the transferee is not a disqualified organization, provided you do not have actual knowledge at the time of the transfer that the affidavit is false.

A pass-through entity must file Form 8831 if it is liable for the tax due under section 860E(e)(6). The entity must pay this tax if, at any time during the entity's tax year, excess inclusions from a residual interest in a REMIC are allocable to an interest in the entity for which the record holder is a disqualified organization. The tax applies to excess inclusions for periods after March 31, 1988, but only to the extent the inclusions are allocable either to an interest in the pass-through entity acquired after March 31, 1988, OR to a residual interest acquired by the pass-through entity after March 31, 1988. Any interest acquired under a binding contract in effect on March 31, 1988, is treated as acquired before that date. A real estate investment trust, regulated investment company, common trust fund, or publicly traded partnership is subject to the tax due under section 860E(e)(6) ONLY for tax years beginning after 1988.

A pass-through entity is not subject to the excise tax under section 860E(e)(6) if it obtains an affidavit from the record holder signed under penalties of perjury that either furnishes his or her social security number or states that the record holder is not a disqualified organization, provided the pass-through entity does not have actual knowledge at the time of the transfer that the affidavit is false.

A pass-through entity that owes both the excise tax due under section 860E(e)(1) (or the amount due under Regulations section 1.860E-2(a)(7)(ii)) and the excise tax due under section 860E(e)(6) must file a separate form for each tax.

When To File

For the excise tax due under section 860E(e)(1), file Form 8831 and pay the tax by April 15 of the year following the calendar year in which the residual interest is transferred to a disqualified organization. A pass-through entity must file Form 8831 and pay the tax due under section 860E(e)(6) by the 15th day of the 4th month following the close of its tax year. If the regular due date falls on a Saturday, Sunday, or legal holiday, file on the next business day. A business day is any day that is not a Saturday, Sunday, or legal holiday.

If more time is needed, use **Form 2758**, Application for Extension of Time To File Certain Excise, Income, Information, and Other Returns, to request an extension of time to file Form 8831. However, Form 2758 does not extend the time for payment of tax.

Where To File

File Form 8831 with the Internal Revenue Service Center used for filing your income tax return. If you have no legal residence, principal place of business, or office or agency in the United States, file Form 8831 with the Internal Revenue Service Center, Philadelphia, PA 19255.

Rounding Off to Whole Dollars

Money items may be shown on the return as whole dollars. To do so, drop any amount less than 50 cents and increase any amount from 50 cents through 99 cents to the next higher dollar.

Amended Return

To amend a previously filed Form 8831, file a corrected Form 8831 marked "Amended" at the top of the form.

Signature

See the instructions for the "Signature" section of your Federal income tax return.

Interest and Penalties

Interest.—Interest is charged on taxes not paid by the due date at a rate determined under section 6621.

Late filing of return.—A penalty of 5% a month or part of a month, up to a maximum of 25%, is imposed on the net amount due if the excise tax return is not filed when due.

Late payment of tax.—Generally, the penalty for not paying tax when due is ½ of 1% of the unpaid amount, up to a maximum of 25%, for each month or part of a month the tax remains unpaid. The penalty is imposed on the net amount due.

Specific Instructions

Caution: *The Revenue Reconciliation Act of 1993 increased the tax rate from 34% to 35% on lines 5 and 7 for transfers in tax years beginning after 1992. This rate increase also applies on line 10 for tax years of pass-through entities beginning after 1992. For tax years ending before 1993, use 34% instead of 35% to figure your tax. For tax years beginning before 1993 that include January 1, 1993, use a weighted average of these rates to figure your tax. See section 15 for details.*

Name and Address

Enter the name shown on your most recently filed Federal income tax return. Include the suite, room, apartment, or other unit number after the street address. If the Post Office does not deliver mail to the street address

and you have a P.O. box, show the box number instead of the street address.

Identifying Number

If you are an individual, enter your social security number. Other filers, enter your employer identification number.

Line 4

The excess inclusions expected to accrue must be determined as of the date the residual interest is transferred and must be based on (a) events that have occurred up to the time of the transfer, (b) the prepayment and reinvestment assumptions adopted under section 1272(a)(6) (or that would have been adopted if the REMIC's regular interests had been issued with original issue discount), and (c) any required or permitted clean-up calls, or required qualified liquidation provided under the REMIC's organizational documents.

The present value of the excess inclusions expected to accrue is determined by discounting all remaining excess inclusions expected to accrue on the residual interest from the end of each calendar quarter in which those inclusions are expected to accrue to the date the disqualified organization acquired the residual interest. The discount rate to be used in this computation is the applicable Federal rate under section 1274(d)(1) that would apply to a debt instrument issued on the date the disqualified organization acquired the residual interest and with a term that ends on the last day of the last quarter in which excess inclusions are expected to accrue for the interest.

The REMIC must furnish the information needed to figure the amount on line 4 upon your request. The information must be furnished within 60 days of the request. The REMIC may charge a fee for this information.

Line 6

Enter the amounts reported on Schedule Q (Form 1066), Quarterly Notice to Residual Interest Holder of REMIC Taxable Income or Net Loss Allocation, line 2c, to the disqualified organization for the period it held the residual interest.

Line 9

Enter the amounts reported on Schedule Q (Form 1066), line 2c, for the tax year of the pass-through entity that are allocable to all disqualified organizations that held an interest in the entity.

Line 10

You may deduct the amount on line 10 in figuring the amount of ordinary income of the pass-through entity. For example, the tax is deductible by a real estate investment trust in figuring its real estate investment trust taxable income under section 857(b)(2).

Line 12

If you filed Form 2758, enter the amount paid, if any, when you filed that form.

Line 13

Full payment of the amount due must accompany Form 8831. Make your check or money order payable to the "Internal Revenue Service." Write your name, address, identifying number, and "Form 8831" on the check or money order.

Line 14

The IRS will refund the amount on line 14 if you owe no other taxes.

APPENDIX B

REMIC Tax Law

CODE PROVISIONS 860A THROUGH 860G

SEC. 860A. TAXATION OF REMIC's.

(a) *General Rule.* — Except as otherwise provided in this part, a REMIC shall not be subject to taxation under this subtitle (and shall not be treated as a corporation, partnership, or trust for purposes of this subtitle).

(b) *Income Taxable To Holders.* — The income of any REMIC shall be taxable to the holders of interests in such REMIC as provided in this part.

SEC. 860B. TAXATION OF HOLDERS OF REGULAR INTERESTS.

(a) *General Rule.* — In determining the tax under this chapter of any holder of a regular interest in a REMIC, such interest (if not otherwise a debt instrument) shall be treated as a debt instrument.

(b) *Holders Must Use Accrual Method.* — The amounts includible in gross income with respect to any regular interest in a REMIC shall be determined under the accrual method of accounting.

(c) *Portion Of Gain Treated As Ordinary Income.* — Gain on the disposition of a regular interest shall be treated as ordinary income to the extent such gain does not exceed the excess (if any) of —

(1) the amount which would have been includible in the gross income of the taxpayer with respect to such interest if the yield on such interest were

110 percent of the applicable Federal rate (as defined in section 1274(d) without regard to paragraph (2) thereof) as of the beginning of the taxpayer's holding period, over

(2) the amount actually includible in gross income with respect to such interest by the taxpayer.

(d) *Cross Reference* —

For special rules in determining inclusion of original issue discount on regular interests, see section 1272(a)(6).

SEC. 860C.   TAXATION OF RESIDUAL INTERESTS.

(a) *Pass-Thru Of Income Or Loss.* —

(1) *In General.* — In determining the tax under this chapter of any holder of a residual interest in a REMIC, such holder shall take into account his daily portion of the taxable income or net loss of such REMIC for each day during the taxable year on which such holder held such interest.

(2) *Daily Portion.* — The daily portion referred to in paragraph (1) shall be determined —

(A) by allocating to each day in any calendar quarter its ratable portion of the taxable income (or net loss) for such quarter, and

(B) by allocating the amounts so allocated to any day among the holders (on such day) of residual interests in proportion to their respective holdings on such day.

(b) *Determination Of Taxable Income Or Net Loss.* — For purposes of this section —

(1) *Taxable Income.* — The taxable income of a REMIC shall be determined under an accrual method of accounting and, except as provided in regulations, in the same manner as in the case of an individual, except that —

(A) regular interests in such REMIC (if not otherwise debt instruments) shall be treated as indebtedness of such REMIC,

(B) market discount on any market discount bond shall be included in gross income for the taxable years to which it is attributable as determined under the rules of section 1276(b)(2) (and sections 1276(a) and 1277 shall not apply),

(C) there shall not be taken into account any item of income, gain, loss, or deduction allocable to a prohibited transaction,

(D) the deductions referred to in section 703(a)(2) (other than any deduction under section 212) shall not be allowed, and

(E) the amount of the net income from foreclosure property (if any) shall be reduced by the amount of the tax imposed by section 860G(c).

(2) *Net Loss.* — The net loss of any REMIC is the excess of —

(A) the deductions allowable in computing the taxable income of such REMIC, over

(B) its gross income.

Such amount shall be determined with the modifications set forth in paragraph (1).

(c) *Distributions.* — Any distribution by a REMIC —

(1) shall not be included in gross income to the extent it does not exceed the adjusted basis of the interest, and

(2) to the extent it exceeds the adjusted basis of the interest, shall be treated as gain from the sale or exchange of such interest.

(d) *Basis Rules.* —

(1) *Increase In Basis.* — The basis of any person's residual interest in a REMIC shall be increased by the amount of the taxable income of such REMIC taken into account under subsection (a) by such person with respect to such interests.

(2) *Decreases In Basis.* — The basis of any person's residual interest in a REMIC shall be decreased (but not below zero) by the sum of the following amounts:

(A) any distributions to such person with respect to such interest, and

(B) any net loss of such REMIC taken into account under subsection (a) by such person with respect to such interest.

(e) *Special Rules.* —

(1) *Amounts Treated As Ordinary.* — Any amount taken into account under subsection (a) by any holder of a residual interest in a REMIC shall be treated as ordinary income or ordinary loss, as the case may be.

(2) *Limitation On Losses.* —

(A) *In General* — The amount of the net loss of any REMIC taken into account by a holder under subsection (a) with respect to any calendar quarter shall not exceed the adjusted basis of such holder's residual interest in such REMIC as of the close of such calendar quarter (determined without regard to the adjustment under subsection (d)(2)(B) for such calendar quarter).

(B) *Indefinite Carryforward.* — Any loss disallowed by reason of subparagraph (A) shall be treated as incurred by the REMIC in the succeeding calendar quarter with respect to such holder.

(3) *Cross Reference.* —

For special treatment of income in excess of daily accruals, see section 860E.

SEC. 860D.   REMIC DEFINED.

(a) *General Rule.* — For purposes of this title, the terms "real estate mortgage investment conduit" and "REMIC" mean any entity —

(1) to which an election to be treated as a REMIC applies for the taxable year and all prior taxable years,

(2) all of the interests in which are regular interests or residual interests,

(3) which has 1 (and only 1) class of residual interests (and all distributions, if any, with respect to such interests are pro rata),

(4) as of the close of the 3rd month beginning after the startup day and at all times thereafter substantially all of the assets of which consist of qualified mortgages and permitted investments,

(5) which has a taxable year which is a calendar year, and

(6) with respect to which there are reasonable arrangements designed to ensure that —

(A) residual interests in such entity are not held by disqualified organizations (as defined in section 860E(e)(5)), and

(B) information necessary for the application of section 860E(e) will be made available by the entity.

In the case of a qualified liquidation (as defined in section 860F(a)(4)(A)), paragraph (4) shall not apply during the liquidation period (as defined in section 860F(a)(4)(B)).

(b) *Election.* —

(1) *In General.* — An entity (otherwise meeting the requirements of subsection (a)) may elect to be treated as REMIC for its 1st taxable year. Such an election shall be made on its return for such 1st taxable year. Except as provided in paragraph (2), such an election shall apply to the taxable year for which made and all subsequent taxable years.

(2) *Termination.* —

(A) *In General.* — If any entity ceases to be a REMIC at any time during the taxable year, such entity shall not be treated as a REMIC for such taxable year or any succeeding taxable year.

(B) *Inadvertent Terminations.* — If —

(i) an entity ceases to be a REMIC,

(ii) the Secretary determines that such cessation was inadvertent,

(iii) no later than a reasonable time after the discovery of the event resulting in such cessation, steps are taken so that such entity is once more a REMIC, and

(iv) such entity, and each person holding an interest in such entity at any time during the period specified pursuant to this subsection, agrees to make such adjustments (consistent with the treatment of such entity as a REMIC or a C corporation) as may be required by the Secretary with respect to such period,

then, notwithstanding such terminating event, such entity shall be treated as continuing to be a REMIC (or such cessation shall be disregarded for purposes of subparagraph (A)) whichever the Secretary determines to be appropriate.

SEC. 860E.   TREATMENT OF INCOME IN EXCESS OF DAILY ACCRUALS ON RESIDUAL INTERESTS.

(a) *Excess Inclusions May Not Be Offset By Net Operating Losses.* —

(1) *In General.* — Except as provided in paragraph (2), the taxable income of any holder of a residual interest in a REMIC for any taxable year shall in no event be less than the excess inclusion for such taxable year.

(2) *Exception For Certain Financial Institutions.* — Paragraph (1) shall not apply to any organization to which section 593 applies. The Secretary may by regulations provide that the preceding sentence shall not apply where necessary or appropriate to prevent avoidance of tax imposed by this chapter.

(3) *Special Rule For Affiliated Groups.* — All members of an affiliated group filing a consolidated return shall be treated as 1 taxpayer for purposes of this subsection, except that paragraph (2) shall be applied separately with respect to each corporation which is a member of such group and to which section 593 applies.

(4) *Treatment Of Certain Subsidiaries.* —

(A) *In General.* — For purposes of this subsection, a corporation to which section 593 applies and each qualified subsidiary of such corporation shall be treated as a single corporation to which section 593 applies.

(B) *Qualified Subsidiary.* — For purposes of this subsection, the term "qualified subsidiary" means any corporation —

(i) all the stock of which, and substantially all the indebtedness of which, is held directly by the corporation to which section 593 applies, and

(ii) which is organized and operated exclusively in connection with the organization and operation of 1 or more REMIC's.

(5) *Coordination With Section 172.* — Any excess inclusion for any taxable year shall not be taken into account —

(A) in determining under section 172 the amount of any net operating loss for such taxable year, and

(B) in determining taxable income for such taxable year for purposes of the 2nd sentence of section 172(b)(2).

(b) *Organizations Subject To Unrelated Business Tax.* — If the holder of any residual interest in a REMIC is an organization subject to the tax imposed by section 511, the excess inclusion of such holder for any taxable year shall be treated as unrelated business taxable income of such holder for purposes of section 511.

(c) *Excess Inclusion.* — For purposes of this section —

(1) *In General.* — The term "excess inclusion" means, with respect to any residual interest in a REMIC for any calendar quarter, the excess (if any) of —

(A) the amount taken into account with respect to such interest by the holder under section 860C(a), over

(B) the sum of the daily accruals with respect to such interest for days during such calendar quarter while held by such holder.

To the extent provided in regulations, if residual interests in a REMIC do not have significant value, the excess inclusions with respect to such interests shall be the amount determined under subparagraph (A) without regard to subparagraph (B).

(2) *Determination Of Daily Accruals. —*

(A) *In General. —* For purposes of this subsection, the daily accrual with respect to any residual interest for any day in any calendar quarter shall be determined by allocating to each day in such quarter its ratable portion of the product of —

(i) the adjusted issue price of such interest at the beginning of such quarter, and

(ii) 120 percent of the long-term Federal rate (determined on the basis of compounding at the close of each calendar quarter and properly adjusted for the length of such quarter).

(B) *Adjusted Issue Price. —* For purposes of this paragraph, the adjusted issue price of any residual interest at the beginning of any calendar quarter is the issue price of the residual interest (adjusted for contributions) —

(i) increased by the amount of daily accruals for prior quarters, and

(ii) decreased (but not below zero) by any distribution made with respect to such interest before the beginning of such quarter.

(C) *Federal Long-Term Rate. —* For purposes of this paragraph, the term "Federal long-term rate" means the Federal long-term rate which would have applied to the residual interest under section 1274(d) (determined without regard to paragraph (2) thereof) if it were a debt instrument.

(d) *Treatment Of Residual Interests Held By Real Estate Investment Trusts. —* If a residual interest in a REMIC is held by a real estate investment trust, under regulations prescribed by the Secretary —

(1) any excess of —

(A) the aggregate excess inclusions determined with respect to such interests, over

(B) the real estate investment trust taxable income (within the meaning of section 857(b)(2), excluding any net capital gain),

shall be allocated among the shareholders of such trust in proportion to the dividends received by such shareholders from trust, and

(2) any amount allocated to a shareholder under paragraph (1) shall be treated as an excess inclusion with respect to a residual interest held by such shareholder.

Rules similar to the rules of the preceding sentence shall apply also in the case of regulated investment companies, common trust funds, and organizations to which part I of subchapter T applies.

(e) *Tax On Transfers Of Residual Interest To Certain Organizations, Etc.* —

(1) *In General.* — A tax is hereby imposed on any transfer of a residual interest in a REMIC to a disqualfied organization.

(2) *Amount Of Tax.* — The amount of the tax imposed by paragraph (1) on any transfer of a residual interest shall be equal to the product of —

(A) the amount (determined under regulations) equal to the present value of the total anticipated excess inclusions with respect to such interest for periods after such transfer, multiplied by

(B) the highest rate of tax specified in section 11(b)(1).

(3) *Liability.* — The tax imposed by paragraph (1) on any transfer shall be paid by the transferor; except that, where such transfer is through an agent for a disqualified organization, such tax shall be paid by such agent.

(4) *Transferee Furnishes Affidavit.* — The person (otherwise liable for any tax imposed by paragraph (1)) shall be relieved of liability for the tax imposed by paragraph (1) with respect to any transfer if —

(A) the transferee furnishes to such person an affidavit that the transferee is not a disqualified organization, and

(B) as of the time of the transfer, such person does not have actual knowledge that such affidavit is false.

(5) *Disqualified Organization.* — For purposes of this section, the term, "disqualified organization" means —

(A) the United States, any State or political subdivision thereof, any foreign government, any international organization, or any agency or instrumentality of any of the foregoing,

(B) any organization (other than a cooperative described in section 521) which is exempt from tax imposed by this chapter unless such organization is subject to the tax imposed by section 511, and

(C) any organization described in section 1381(a)(2)(C).

For purposes of subparagraph (A), the rules of section 168(h)(2)(D) (relating to treatment of certain taxable instrumentalities) shall apply; except that, in the case of the Federal Home Loan Mortgage Corporation, clause (ii) of such section shall not apply.

(6) *Treatment Of Pass-Thru Entities.* —

(A) *Imposition Of Tax.* — If, at any time during any taxable year of a pass-thru entity, a disqualified organization is the record holder of an interest in such entity, there is hereby imposed on such entity for such taxable year a tax equal to the product of —

(i) the amount of excess inclusions for such taxable year allocable to the interest held by such disqualfied organization, multiplied by

(ii) the highest rate of tax specified in section 11(b)(1).

(B) *Pass-Thru Entity.* — For purposes of this paragraph, the term "pass-thru entity" means —

(i) any regulated investment company, real estate investment trust, or common trust fund,

(ii) any partnership, trust, or estate, and

(iii) any organization to which part I of subchapter T applies.

Except as provided in regulations, a person holding an interest in a pass-thru entity as a nominee for another person shall, with respect to such interest, be treated as a pass-thru entity.

(C) *Tax To Be Deductible.* — Any tax imposed by this paragraph with respect to any excess inclusion of any pass-thru entity for any taxable year shall, for purposes of this title (other than this subsection), be applied against (and operate to reduce) the amount included in gross income with respect to the residual interest involved.

(D) *Exception Where Holder Furnishes Affidavit.* — No tax shall be imposed by subparagraph (A) with respect to any interest in a pass-thru entity for any period if —

(i) the record holder of such interest furnishes to such pass-thru entity an affidavit that such record holder is not a disqualifed organization, and

(ii) during such period, the pass-thru entity does not have actual knowledge that such affidavit is false.

(7) *Waiver* — The Secretary may waive the tax imposed by paragraph (1) on any transfer if —

(A) within a reasonable time after discovery that the transfer was subject to tax under paragraph (1), steps are taken so that the interest is no longer held by the disqualified organization, and

(B) there is paid to the Secretary such amounts as the Secretary may require.

(8) *Administrative Provisions.* — For purposes of subtitle F, the taxes imposed by this subsection shall be treated as excise taxes with respect to which the deficiency procedures of such subtitle apply.

(f) *Treatment Of Variable Insurance Contracts.* — Except as provided in regulations, with respect to any variable contract (as defined in section 817), there shall be no adjustment in the reserve to the extent of any excess inclusion.

SEC. 860F.   OTHER RULES.

(a) *100 Percent Tax On Prohibited Transactions.* —

(1) *Tax Imposed.* — There is hereby imposed for each taxable year of a REMIC a tax equal to 100 percent of the net income derived from prohibited transactions.

(2) *Prohibited Transaction.* — For purposes of this part, the term "prohibited transaction" means —

(A) *Disposition Of Qualified Mortgage.* — The disposition of any qualified mortgage transferred to the REMIC other than a disposition pursuant to —

(i) the substitution of a qualified replacement mortgage for a qualified mortgage (or the repurchase in lieu of substitution of a defective obligation),

(ii) a disposition incident to the foreclosure, default, or imminent default of the mortgage,

(iii) the bankruptcy or insolvency of the REMIC, or

(iv) a qualified liquidation.

(B) *Income From Nonpermitted Assets.* — The receipt of any income attributable to any asset which is neither a qualified mortgage nor a permitted investment.

(C) *Compensation For Services.* — The receipt by the REMIC of any amount representing a fee or other compensation for services.

(D) *Gain From Disposition Of Cash Flow Investments.* — Gain from the disposition of any cash flow investment other than pursuant to any qualified liquidation.

(3) *Determination Of Net Income.* — For purposes of paragraph (1), the term "net income derived from prohibited transactions" means the excess of the gross income from prohibited transactions over the deductions allowed by this chapter which are directly connected with such transactions; except that there shall not be taken into account any item attributable to any prohibited transaction for which there was a loss.

(4) *Qualified Liquidation.* — For purposes of this part —

(A) *In General.* — The term "qualified liquidation" means a transaction in which —

(i) the REMIC adopts a plan of complete liquidation,

(ii) such REMIC sells all its assets (other than cash) within the liquidation period, and

(iii) all proceeds of the liquidation (plus the cash), less assets retained to meet claims, are credited or distributed to holders of regular or residual interests on or before the last day of the liquidation period.

(B) *Liquidation Period.* — The term "liquidation period" means the period —

(i) beginning on the date of the adoption of the plan of liquidation, and

(ii) ending at the close of the 90th day after such date.

(5) *Exceptions.* — Notwithstanding subparagraphs (A) and (D) of paragraph (1), the term "prohibited transaction" shall not include any disposition —

(A) required to prevent default on a regular interest where the threatened default resulted from a default on 1 or more qualified mortgages, or

(B) to facilitate a clean-up call (as defined in regulations).

(b) *Treatment Of Transfers To The REMIC.* —

(1) *Treatment Of Transferor.* —

(A) *Nonrecognition Gain Or Loss.* — No gain or loss shall be recognized to the transferor on the transfer of any property to a REMIC in exchange for regular or residual interests in such REMIC.

(B) *Adjusted Bases Of Interests.* — The adjusted bases of the regular and residual interests received in a transfer described in subparagraph (A) shall be equal to the aggregate adjusted bases of the property transferred in such transfer. Such amount shall be allocated among such interests in proportion to their respective fair market values.

(C) *Treatment Of Nonrecognized Gain.* — If the issue price of any regular or residual interest exceeds its adjusted basis as determined under subparagraph (B), for periods during which such interest is held by the transferor (or by any other person whose basis is determined in whole or in part by reference to the basis of such interest in the hand of the transferor) —

(i) in the case of a regular interest, such excess shall be included in gross income (as determined under rules similar to rules of section 1276(b)), and

(ii) in the case of a residual interest, such excess shall be included in gross income ratably over the anticipated period during which the REMIC will be in existence.

(D) *Treatment Of Nonrecognized Loss.* — If the adjusted basis of any regular or residual interest received in a transfer described in subparagraph (A) exceeds its issue price, for periods during which such interest is held by the transferor (or by any other person whose basis is determined in whole or in part by reference to the basis of such interest in the hand of the transferor) —

(i) in the case of a regular interest, such excess shall be allowable as a deduction under rules similar to the rules of section 171, and

(ii) in the case of a residual interest, such excess shall be allowable as a deduction ratably over the anticipated period during which the REMIC will be in existence.

(2) *Basis To REMIC.* — The basis of any property received by a REMIC in a transfer described in paragraph (1)(A) shall be its fair market value immediately after such transfer.

(c) *Distributions Of Property.* — If a REMIC makes a distribution of property with respect to any regular or residual interest —

(1) notwithstanding any other provision of this subtitle, gain shall be recognized to such REMIC on the distribution in the same manner as if it had sold such property to the distributee at its fair market value, and

(2) the basis of the distributee in such property shall be its fair market value.

(d) *Coordination With Wash Sale Rules.* — For purposes of section 1091 —

(1) any residual interest in a REMIC shall be treated as a security, and

(2) in applying such section to any loss claimed to have been sustained on the sale or other disposition of a residual interest in a REMIC —

(A) except as provided in regulations, any residual interest in any REMIC and any interest in a taxable mortgage pool (as defined in section 7701(i)) comparable to a residual interest in a REMIC shall be treated as substantially identical stock or securities, and

(B) subsection (a) and (e) of such section shall be applied by substituting "6 months" for "30 days" each place it appears.

(e) *Treatment Under Subtitle F.* — For purposes of subtitle F, a REMIC shall be treated as a partnership (and holders of residual interests in such REMIC shall be treated as partners). Any return required by reason of the preceding sentence shall include the amount of the daily accruals determined under section 860E(c). Such return shall be filed by the REMIC. The determination of who may sign such return shall be made without regard to the first sentence of this subsection.

SEC. 860G.   OTHER DEFINITIONS AND SPECIAL RULES.

(a) *Definitions.* — For purposes of this part —

(1) *Regular Interest.* — The term "regular interest" means any interest in a REMIC which is issued on the startup day with fixed terms and which is designated as a regular interest if —

(A) such interest unconditionally entitles the holder to receive a specified principal amount (or other similar amount), and

(B) interest payments (or other similar amount), if any, with respect to such interest at or before maturity —

(i) are payable based on a fixed rate (or the extent provided in regulations, at a variable rate), or

(ii) consist of a specified portion of the interest payments on qualified mortgages and such portion does not vary during the period such interest is outstanding.

The interest shall not fail to meet the requirements of subparagraph (A) merely because the timing (but not the amount) of the principal payments (or other similar amounts) may be contingent on the extent of prepayments on qualified mortgages and the amount of income from permitted investments.

(2) *Residual Interest.* — The term "residual interest" means an interest in a REMIC which is issued on the startup day, which is not a regular interest, and which is designated as a residual interest.

(3) *Qualified Mortgage.* — The term "qualified mortgage" means —

(A) any obligation (including any participation or certificate of beneficial ownership therein) which is principally secured by an interest in real property and which —

(i) is transferred to the REMIC on the startup day in exchange for regular or residual interests in the REMIC, or

(ii) is purchased by the REMIC within the 3-month period beginning on the startup day if, except as provided in the regulations, such purchase is pursuant to a fixed price contract in effect on the startup day,

(B) any qualified replacement mortgage, and

(C) any regular interest in another REMIC transferred to the REMIC on the startup day in exchange for regular or residual interests in the REMIC.

For purposes of subparagraph (A) any obligation secured by stock held by a person as a tenant-stockholder (as defined in section 216) in a cooperative housing corporation (as so defined) shall be treated as secured by an interest in real property.

(4) *Qualified Replacement Mortgage.* — The term "qualified replacement mortgage" means any obligation —

(A) which would be a qualified mortgage if transferred on the startup day in exchange for regular or residual interests in the REMIC, and

(B) which is received for —

(i) another obligation within the 3-month period beginning on the startup day, or

(ii) a defective obligation within the 2-year period beginning on the startup day.

(5) *Permitted Investments.* — The term "permitted investments" means any —

(A) cash flow investment,

(B) qualified reserve asset, or

(C) foreclosure property.

(6) *Cash Flow Investment.* — The term "cash flow investment" means any investment of amounts received under qualified mortgages for a temporary period before distribution to holders of interests in the REMIC.

(7) *Qualified Reserve Asset.* —

(A) *In General.* — The term "qualified reserve asset" means any intangible property which is held for investment and as part of a qualified reserve fund.

(B) *Qualified Reserve Fund.* — For purposes of subparagraph (A), the term "qualified reserve fund" means any reasonably required reserve to provide for full payment of expenses of the REMIC or amounts due on regular interests in the event of defaults on qualified mortgages or lower than expected returns on cash-flow investments. The amount of any such reserve shall be promptly and appropriately reduced as payments of qualified mortgages are received.

(C) *Special Rule.* — A reserve shall not be treated as a qualified reserve for any taxable year (and all subsequent taxable years) if more than 30 percent of the gross income from the assets in such fund for the taxable year is derived from the sale or other disposition of property held for less than 3 months. For purposes of the preceding sentence, gain on the disposition of a qualified reserve asset shall not be taken into account if the disposition giving rise to such gain is required to prevent default on a regular interest where the threatened default resulted from a default on 1 or more qualified mortgages.

(8) *Foreclosure Property.* — The term "foreclosure property" means property —

(A) which would be foreclosure property under section 856(e) (without regard to paragraph (5) thereof) if acquired by a real estate investment trust, and

(B) which is acquired in connection with the default or imminent default of a qualified mortgage held by the REMIC.

Solely for purposes of section 860D(a), the determination of whether any property is foreclosure property shall be made without regard to section 856(e)(4).

(9) *Startup Day.* — The term "startup day" means the day on which the REMIC issues all of its regular and residual interests. To the extent provided in regulations, all interests issued (and all transfers to the REMIC) during any period (not exceeding 10 days) permitted in such regulations shall be treated as occurring on the day during such period selected by the REMIC for purposes of this paragraph.

(10) *Issue Price.* — The issue price of any regular or residual interest in a REMIC shall be determined under section 1273(b) in the same manner as if such interest were a debt instrument; except that if the interest is issued for property, paragraph (3) of section 1273(b) shall apply whether the requirements of such paragraph are met.

(b) *Treatment Of Nonresident Aliens And Foreign Corporations.* — If the holder of a residual interest in a REMIC is a nonresident alien individual or a foreign corporation, for purposes of sections 871(a), 881, 1441, and 1442 —

(1) amounts includible in the gross income of such holder under this part shall be taken into account when paid or distributed (or when the interest is disposed of), and

(2) no exemption from the taxes imposed by such sections (and no reduction in the rates of such taxes) shall apply to any excess inclusion.

The Secretary may by regulations provide that such amounts shall be taken into account earlier than as provided in paragraph (1) where necessary or appropriate to prevent the avoidance of tax imposed by this chapter.

(c) *Tax On Income From Foreclosure Property.* —

Appendix B.   REMIC Tax Law

(1) *In General.* — A tax is hereby imposed for each taxable year on the net income from foreclosure property of each REMIC. Such tax shall be computed by multiplying the net income from foreclosure property by the highest rate of tax specified in section 11(b).

(2) *Net Income From Foreclosure Property.* — For purposes of this part, the term "net income from foreclosure property" means the amount which would be the REMIC's net income from foreclosure property under section 857(b)(4)(B) if the REMIC were a real estate investment trust.

(d) *Tax On Contributions After Startup Date.* —

(1) *In General.* — Except as provided in paragraph (2), if any amount is contributed to a REMIC after the startup day, there is hereby imposed a tax for the taxable year of the REMIC in which the contribution is received equal to 100 percent of the amount of such contribution.

(2) *Exceptions.* — Paragraph (1) shall not apply to any contribution which is made in cash and is described in any of the following subparagraphs:

(A) Any contribution to facilitate a cleanup call (as defined in regulations) or a qualified liquidation.

(B) Any payment in the nature of a guarantee.

(C) Any contribution during the 3-month period beginning on the startup day.

(D) Any contribution to a qualified reserve fund by any holder of a residual interest in the REMIC.

(E) Any other contribution permitted in regulations.

(e) *Regulations.* — The Secretary shall prescribe such regulations as may be necessary or appropriate to carry out the purposes of this part, including regulations —

(1) to prevent unreasonable accumulations of assets in a REMIC,

(2) permitting determination of the fair market value of property transferred to a REMIC and issue price of interest in a REMIC to be made earlier than otherwise provided,

(3) requiring reporting to holders of residual interests of such information as frequently as is necessary or appropriate to permit such holders to compute their taxable income accurately,

(4) providing appropriate rules for treatment of transfers of qualified replacement mortgages to the REMIC where the transferor holds any interest in the REMIC, and

(5) providing that a mortgage will be treated as a qualified replacement mortgage only if it is part of a bona fide replacement (and not part of a swap of mortgages).

REMIC REGULATIONS

Real Estate Mortgage Investment Conduits

§1.860A-0. Outline of REMIC provisions. — This section lists the paragraphs contained in §§ 1.860A-1 through 1.860G-3.

§ 1.860A-1. Effective dates and transition rules.
  (a) In general.
  (b) Exceptions.
    (1) Reporting regulations.
    (2) Tax avoidance rules.
      (i) Transfers of certain residual interests.
      (ii) Transfers to foreign holders.
      (iii) Residual interests that lack significant value.
    (3) Excise taxes.

§ 1.860C-1. Taxation of holders of residual interests.
  (a) Pass-thru of income or loss.
  (b) Adjustments to basis of residual interests.
    (1) Increase in basis.
    (2) Decrease in basis.
    (3) Adjustments made before disposition.
  (c) Counting conventions.

§ 1.860C-2. Determination of REMIC taxable income or net loss.
  (a) Treatment of gain or loss.
  (b) Deductions allowable to a REMIC.
    (1) In general.
    (2) Deduction allowable under section 163.
    (3) Deduction allowable under section 166.
    (4) Deduction allowable under section 212.
    (5) Expenses and interest relating to tax-exempt income.

§ 1.860D-1. Definition of a REMIC.
  (a) In general.
  (b) Specific requirements.
    (1) Interests in a REMIC.
      (i) In general.
      (ii) De minimis interests.
    (2) Certain rights not treated as interests.
      (i) Payments for services.
      (ii) Stripped interests.
      (iii) Reimbursement rights under credit enhancement contracts.
      (iv) Rights to acquire mortgages.
    (3) Asset test.
      (i) In general.
      (ii) Safe harbor.
    (4) Arrangements test.
    (5) Reasonable arrangements.

(i) Arrangements to prevent disqualified organizations from holding residual interests.

(ii) Arrangements to ensure that information will be provided.

(6) Calendar year requirement.

(c) Segregated pool of assets.

(1) Formation of REMIC.

(2) Identification of assets.

(3) Qualified entity defined.

(d) Election to be treated as a real estate mortgage investment conduit.

(1) In general.

(2) Information required to be reported in the REMIC's first taxable year.

(3) Requirement to keep sufficient records.

§ 1.860E-1. *Treatment of taxable income of a residual interest holder in excess of daily accruals.*

(a) Excess inclusion cannot be offset by otherwise allowable deductions.

(1) In general.

(2) Affiliated groups.

(3) Special rule for certain financial institutions.

(i) In general.

(ii) Ordering rule.

(A) In general.

(B) Example.

(iii) Significant value.

(iv) Determining anticipated weighted average life.

(A) Anticipated weighted average life of the REMIC.

(B) Regular interests that have a specified principal amount.

(C) Regular interests that have no specified principal amount or that have only a nominal principal amount, and all residual interests.

(D) Anticipated payments.

(b) Treatment of a residual interest held by REITs, RICs, common trust funds, and subchapter T cooperatives. [Reserved]

(c) Transfers of noneconomic residual interests.

(1) In general.

(2) Noneconomic residual interest.

(3) Computations.

(4) Safe harbor for establishing lack of improper knowledge.

(d) Transfers to foreign persons.

§ 1.860E-2. *Tax on transfers of residual interest to certain organizations.*

(a) Transfers to disqualified organizations.

(1) Payment of tax.

(2) Transitory ownership.

(3) Anticipated excess inclusions.

(4) Present value computation.

(5) Obligation of REMIC to furnish information.

(6) Agent.

(7) Relief from liability.

(i) Transferee furnishes information under penalties of perjury.

(4) Default by the person obligated to purchase a convertible mortgage.

(5) Convertible mortgage.

(e) Prepayment interest shortfalls.

(f) Defective obligations.

    (1) Defective obligation defined.

    (2) Effect of discovery of defect.

(g) Permitted investments.

    (1) Cash flow investment.

        (i) In general.

        (ii) Payments received on qualified mortgages.

        (iii) Temporary period.

    (2) Qualified reserve funds.

    (3) Qualified reserve asset.

        (i) In general.

        (ii) Reasonably required reserve.

            (A) In general.

            (B) Presumption that a reserve is reasonably required.

            (C) Presumption may be rebutted.

(h) Outside reserve funds.

(i) Contractual rights coupled with regular interests in tiered arrangements.

    (1) In general.

    (2) Example.

(j) Clean-up call.

    (1) In general.

    (2) Interest rate changes.

    (3) Safe harbor.

(k) Startup day.

§ 1.860G-3. *Treatment of foreign persons.*

    (a) Transfer of a residual interest with tax avoidance potential.

    (1) In general.

    (2) Tax avoidance potential.

        (i) Defined.

        (ii) Safe harbor.

    (3) Effectively connected income.

    (4) Transfer by a foreign holder.

    (b) [Reserved]

§ 1.860A-1. **Effective dates and transition rules.** — (a) *In general.* Except as otherwise provided in paragraph (b) of this section, the regulations under sections 860A through 860G are effective only for a qualified entity (as defined in § 1.860D-1(c)(3)) whose startup day (as defined in section 860G(a)(9) and § 1.860G-2(k)) is on or after November 12, 1991.

(b) *Exceptions* — (1) *Reporting regulations* — (i) Sections 1.860D-1(c)(1) and (3), and § 1.860D-1(d)(1) through (3) are effective after December 31, 1986.

(ii) Sections 1.860F-4(a) through (e) are effective after December 31, 1986 and are applicable after that date except as follows:

(A) Section 1.860F-4(c)(1) is effective for REMICs with a startup day on or after November 10, 1988.

(B) Sections 1.860F-4(e)(1)(ii)(A) and (B) are effective for calendar quarters and calendar years beginning after December 31, 1988.

(C) Section 1.860F-4(e)(1)(ii)(C) is effective for calendar quarters and calendar years beginning after December 31, 1986 and ending before January 1, 1988.

(D) Section 1.860F-4(e)(1)(ii)(D) is effective for calendar quarters and calendar years beginning after December 31, 1987 and ending before January 1, 1990.

(2) *Tax avoidance rules* — (i) *Transfers of certain residual interests.* Section 1.860E-1(c) (concerning transfers of noneconomic residual interests) and § 1.860G-3 (a)(4) (concerning transfers by a foreign holder to a United States person) are effective for transfers of residual interests on or after September 27, 1991.

(ii) *Transfers to foreign holders.* Generally, § 1.860G-3(a) (concerning transfers of residual interests to foreign holders) is effective for transfers of residual interests after April 20, 1992. However, § 1.860G-3(a) does not apply to a transfer of a residual interest in a REMIC by the REMIC's sponsor (or by another transferor contemporaneously with formation of the REMIC) on or before June 30, 1992, if —

(A) The terms of the regular interests and the prices at which regular interests were offered had been fixed on or before April 20, 1992;

(B) On or before June 30, 1992, a substantial portion of the regular interests in the REMIC were transferred, with the terms and at the prices that were fixed on or before April 20, 1992, to investors who were unrelated to the REMIC's sponsor at the time of the transfer; and

(C) At the time of the transfer of the residual interest, the expected future distributions on the residual interest were equal to at least 30 percent of the anticipated excess inclusions (as defined in § 1.860E-2(a)(3)), and the transferor reasonably expected that the transferee would receive sufficient distributions from the REMIC at or after the time at which the excess inclusions accrue in an amount sufficient to satisfy the taxes on the excess inclusions.

(iii) *Residual interests that lack significant value.* The significant value requirement in § 1.860E-1(a)(1) and (3) (concerning excess inclusions accruing to organizations to which section 593 applies) generally is effective for residual interests acquired on or after September 27, 1991. The significant value requirement in 1.860E-1(a)(1) and (3) does not apply, however, to residual interests acquired by an organization to which section 593 applies as a sponsor at formation of a REMIC in a transaction described in § 1.860F-2(a)(1) if more than 50 percent of the interests in the REMIC (determined by reference to issue price) were sold to unrelated investors before November 12, 1991. The exception from the significant value requirement provided by the preceding sentence applies only so long as the sponsor owns the residual interests.

(3) *Excise taxes.* Section 1.860E-2(a)(1) is effective for transfers of residual interests to disqualified organizations after March 31, 1988. Section 1.860E-2(b)(1) is effective for excess inclusions accruing to pass-thru entities after March 31, 1988.

§ 1.860C-1. Taxation of holders of residual interests. — (a) *Pass-thru of income or loss.* Any holder of a residual interest in a REMIC must take into account the holder's daily portion of the taxable income or net loss of the REMIC for each day during the taxable year on which the holder owned the residual interest.

(b) *Adjustments to basis of residual interests* — (1) *Increase in basis.* A holder's basis in a residual interest is increased by —

(i) The daily portions of taxable income taken into account by that holder under section 860C(a) with respect to that interest; and

(ii) The amount of any contribution described in section 860G(d)(2) made by that holder.

(2) *Decrease in basis.* A holder's basis in a residual interest is reduced (but not below zero) by —

(i) First, the amount of any cash or the fair market value of any property distributed to that holder with respect to that interest; and

(ii) Second, the daily portions of net loss of the REMIC taken into account under section 860C(a) by that holder with respect to that interest.

(3) *Adjustments made before disposition.* If any person disposes of a residual interest, the adjustments to basis prescribed in paragraph (b)(1) and (2) of this section are deemed to occur immediately before the disposition.

(c) *Counting conventions.* For purposes of determining the daily portion of REMIC taxable income or net loss under section 860C(a)(2), any reasonable convention may be used. An example of a reasonable convention is "30 days per month/90 days per quarter/360 days per year."

§ 1.860C-2. Determination of REMIC taxable income or net loss. — (a) *Treatment of gain or loss.* For purposes of determining the taxable income or net loss of a REMIC under section 860C(b), any gain or loss from the disposition of any asset, including a qualified mortgage (as defined in section 860G(a)(3)) or a permitted investment (as defined in section 860G(a)(5) and § 1.860G-2(g)), is treated as gain or loss from the sale or exchange of property that is not a capital asset.

(b) *Deductions allowable to a REMIC* — (1) *In general.* Except as otherwise provided in section 860C(b) and in paragraph (b)(2) through (5) of this section, the deductions allowable to a REMIC for purposes of determining its taxable income or net loss are those deductions that would be allowable to an individual, determined by taking into account the same limitations that apply to an individual.

(2) *Deduction allowable under section 163.* A REMIC is allowed a deduction, determined without regard to section 163(d), for any interest expense accrued during the taxable year.

(3) *Deduction allowable under section 166.* For purposes of determining a REMIC's bad debt deduction under section 166, debt owed to the REMIC is not treated as nonbusiness debt under section 166(d).

(4) *Deduction allowable under section 212.* A REMIC is not treated as carrying on a trade or business for purposes of section 162. Ordinary and necessary operating expenses paid or incurred by the REMIC during the taxable year are deductible under section 212, without regard to section 67. Any expenses that are incurred in connection with the formation of the REMIC and that relate to the organization of the REMIC and the issuance of regular and residual interests are not treated as expenses of the REMIC for which a deduction is allowable under section 212. See § 1.860F-2(b)(3)(ii) for treatment of those expenses.

(5) *Expenses and interest relating to tax-exempt income.* Pursuant to section 265(a), a REMIC is not allowed a deduction for expenses and interest allocable to tax-exempt income. The portion of a REMIC's interest expense that is allocable to tax-exempt interest is determined in the manner prescribed in section 265(b)(2), without regard to section 265(b)(3).

§ 1.860D-1. Definition of a REMIC. — (a) *In general.* A real estate mortgage investment conduit (or REMIC) is a qualified entity, as defined in paragraph (c)(3) of this section, that satisfies the requirements of section 860D(a). See paragraph (d)(1) of this section for the manner of electing REMIC status.

(b) *Specific requirements* — (1) *Interests in a REMIC* — (i) *In general.* A REMIC must have one class, and only one class, of residual interests. Except as provided in paragraph (b)(1)(ii) of this section, every interest in a REMIC must be either a regular interest (as defined in section 860G(a)(1) and § 1.860G-1(a)) or a residual interest (as defined in section 860G(a)(2) and § 1.860G-1(c)).

(ii) *De minimis interests.* If, to facilitate the creation of an entity that elects REMIC status, an interest in the entity is created and, as of the startup day (as defined in section 860G(a)(9) and § 1.860G-2(k)), the fair market value of that interest is less than the lesser of $1,000 or 1/1,000 of one percent of the aggregate fair market value of all the regular and residual interests in the REMIC, then, unless that interest is specifically designated as an interest in the REMIC, the interest is not treated as an interest in the REMIC for purposes of section 860D(a)(2) and (3) and paragraph (b)(1)(i) of this section.

(2) *Certain rights not treated as interests.* Certain rights are not treated as interests in a REMIC. Although not an exclusive list, the following rights are not interests in a REMIC.

(i) *Payments for services.* The right to receive from the REMIC payments that represent reasonable compensation for services provided to the REMIC in the ordinary course of its operation is not an interest in the REMIC. Payments made by the REMIC in exchange for services may be expressed as a specified percentage of interest payments due on qualified mortgages or as a specified percentage of earnings from permitted investments. For example, a mortgage servicer's right to receive reasonable compensation for servicing the mortgages owned by the REMIC is not an interest in the REMIC.

(ii) *Stripped interests.* Stripped bonds or stripped coupons not held by the REMIC are not interests in the REMIC even if, in a transaction preceding or contemporaneous with the formation of the REMIC, they and the REMIC's qualified mortgages were created from the same mortgage obligation. For example, the right of a mortgage servicer to receive a servicing fee in excess of reasonable compensation from payments it receives on mortgages held by a REMIC is not an interest in the REMIC. Further, if an obligation with a fixed principal amount provides for interest at a fixed or variable rate and for certain contingent payment rights (e.g., a shared appreciation provision or a percentage of mortgagor profits provision), and the owner of the obligation contributes the fixed payment rights to a REMIC and retains the contingent payment rights, the retained contingent payment rights are not an interest in the REMIC.

(iii) *Reimbursement rights under credit enhancement contracts.* A credit enhancer's right to be reimbursed for amounts advanced to a REMIC pursuant to the terms of a credit enhancement contract (as defined in § 1.860G-2(c)(2)) is not an interest in the REMIC even if the credit enhancer is entitled to receive interest on the amounts advanced.

(iv) *Rights to acquire mortgages.* The right to acquire or the obligation to purchase mortgages and other assets from a REMIC pursuant to a clean-up call (as defined in § 1.860G-2(j)) or a qualified liquidation (as defined in section 860F(a)(4)), or on conversion of a convertible mortgage (as defined in § 1.860G-2(d)(5)), is not an interest in the REMIC.

(3) *Asset test* — (i) *In general.* For purposes of the asset test of section 860D(a)(4), substantially all of a qualified entity's assets are qualified mortgages and permitted investments if the qualified entity owns no more than a de minimis amount of other assets.

(ii) *Safe harbor.* The amount of assets other than qualified mortgages and permitted investments is de minimis if the aggregate of the adjusted bases of those assets is less than one percent of the aggregate of the adjusted bases of all of the REMIC's assets. Nonetheless, a qualified entity that does not meet this safe harbor may demonstrate that it owns no more than a de minimis amount of other assets.

(4) *Arrangements test.* Generally, a qualified entity must adopt reasonable arrangements designed to ensure that —

(i) Disqualified organizations (as defined in section 860E(e)(5)) do not hold residual interests in the qualified entity; and

(ii) If a residual interest is acquired by a disqualified organization, the qualified entity will provide to the Internal Revenue Service, and to the persons specified in section 860E(e)(3), information needed to compute the tax imposed under section 860E(e) on transfers of residual interests to disqualified organizations.

(5) *Reasonable arrangements* — (i) *Arrangements to prevent disqualified organizations from holding residual interests.* A qualified entity is considered to have adopted reasonable arrangements to ensure that a disqualified organization (as defined in section 860E(e)(5)) will not hold a residual interest if —

(A) The residual interest is in registered form (as defined in § 5f.103-1(c) of this chapter); and

(B) The qualified entity's organizational documents clearly and expressly prohibit a disqualified organization from acquiring beneficial ownership of a residual interest, and notice of the prohibition is provided through a legend on the document that evidences ownership of the residual interest or through a conspicuous statement in a prospectus or private offering document used to offer the residual interest for sale.

(ii) *Arrangements to ensure that information will be provided.* A qualified entity is considered to have made reasonable arrangements to ensure that the Internal Revenue Service and persons specified in section 860E(e)(3) as liable for the tax imposed under section 860E(e) receive the information needed to compute the tax if the qualified entity's organizational documents require that it provide to the Internal Revenue Service and those persons a computation showing the present value of the total anticipated excess inclusions with respect to the residual interest for periods after the transfer. See § 1.860E-2(a)(5) for the obligation to furnish information on request.

(6) *Calendar year requirement.* A REMIC's taxable year is the calendar year. The first taxable year of a REMIC begins on the startup day and ends on December 31 of the same year. If the startup day is other than January 1, the REMIC has a short first taxable year.

(c) *Segregated pool of assets* — (1) *Formation of REMIC.* A REMIC may be formed as a segregated pool of assets rather than as a separate entity. To constitute a REMIC, the assets identified as part of the segregated pool must be treated as a separate entity. To constitute a REMIC, the assets identified as part of the segregated pool must be treated for all Federal income tax purposes as assets of the REMIC and interests in the REMIC must be based solely on assets of the REMIC.

(2) *Identification of assets.* Formation of the REMIC does not occur until —

(i) The sponsor identifies the assets of the REMIC, such as through execution of an indenture with respect to the assets; and

(ii) The REMIC issues the regular and residual interests in the REMIC.

(3) *Qualified entity defined.* For purposes of this section, the term "qualified entity" includes an entity or a segregated pool of assets within an entity.

(d) *Election to be treated as a real estate mortgage investment conduit* — (1) *In general.* A qualified entity, as defined in paragraph (c)(3) of this section, elects to be treated as a REMIC by timely filing, for the first taxable year of its existence, a Form 1066, U.S. Real Estate Mortgage Investment Conduit Income Tax Return, signed by a person authorized to sign that return under § 1.860F-4(c). See § 1.9100-1 for rules regarding extensions of time for making elections. Once made, this election is irrevocable for that taxable year and all succeeding taxable years.

(2) *Information required to be reported in the REMIC's first taxable year.* For the first taxable year of the REMIC's existence, the qualified entity, as defined in paragraph (c)(3) of this section, must provide either on its return or in a separate statement attached to its return —

(i) The REMIC's employer identification number, which must not be the same as the identification number of any other entity,

(ii) Information concerning the terms and conditions of the regular interests and the residual interest of the REMIC, or a copy of the offering circular or prospectus containing such information,

(iii) A description of the prepayment and reinvestment assumptions that are made pursuant to section 1272(a)(6) and the regulations thereunder, including a statement supporting the selection of the prepayment assumption,

(iv) The form of the electing qualified entity under State law or, if an election is being made with respect to a segregated pool of assets within an entity, the form of the entity that holds the segregated pool of assets, and

(v) Any other information required by the form.

(3) *Requirement to keep sufficient records.* A qualified entity, as defined in paragraph (c)(3) of this section, that elects to be a REMIC must keep sufficient records concerning its investments to show that it has complied with the provisions of sections 860A through 860G and the regulations thereunder during each taxable year.

§ 1.860E-1. **Treatment of taxable income of a residual interest holder in excess of daily accruals.** — (a) *Excess inclusion cannot be offset by otherwise allowable deductions* — (1) In general. Except as provided in paragraph (a)(3) of this section, the taxable income of any holder of a residual interest for any taxable year is in no event less than the sum of the excess inclusions attributable to that holder's residual interests for that taxable year. In computing the amount of a net operating loss (as defined in section 172(c)) or the amount of any net operating loss carryover (as defined in section 172(b)(2)), the amount of any excess inclusion is not included in gross income or taxable income. Thus, for example, if a residual interest holder has $100 of gross income, $25 of which is an excess inclusion, and $90 of business deductions, the holder has taxable income of $25, the amount of the excess inclusion, and a net operating loss of $15 ($75 of other income - $90 of business deductions).

(2) *Affiliated groups.* If a holder of a REMIC residual interest is a member of an affiliated group filing a consolidated income tax return, the taxable income of the affiliated group cannot be less than the sum of the excess

inclusions attributable to all residual interests held by members of the affiliated group.

(3) *Special rule for certain financial institutions* — (i) *In general.* If an organization to which section 593 applies holds a residual interest that has significant value (as defined in paragraph (a)(3)(iii) of this section), section 860E(a)(1) and paragraph (a)(1) of this section do not apply to that organization with respect to that interest. Consequently, an organization to which section 593 applies may use its allowable deductions to offset an excess inclusion attributable to a residual interest that has significant value, but, except as provided in section 860E(a)(4)(A), may not use its allowable deductions to offset an excess inclusion attributable to a residual interest held by any other member of an affiliated group, if any, of which the organization is a member. Further, a net operating loss of any other member of an affiliated group of which the organization is a member may not be used to offset an excess inclusion attributable to a residual interest held by that organization.

(ii) *Ordering rule* — (A) *In general.* In computing taxable income for any year, an organization to which section 593 applies is treated as having applied its allowable deductions for the year first to offset that portion of its gross income that is not an excess inclusion and then to offset that portion of its income that is an excess inclusion.

(B) *Example.* The following example illustrates the provisions of paragraph (a)(3)(ii) of this section:

Example. Corp. X, a corporation to which section 593 applies, is a member of an affiliated group that files a consolidated return. For a particular taxable year, Corp. X has gross income of $1,000, and of this amount, $150 is an excess inclusion attributable to a residual interest that has significant value. Corp. X has $975 of allowable deductions for the taxable year. Corp. X must apply its allowable deductions first to offset the $850 of gross income that is not an excess inclusion, and then to offset the portion of its gross income that is an excess inclusion. Thus, Corp. X has $25 of taxable income ($1,000 - $975), and that $25 is an excess inclusion that may not be offset by losses sustained by other members of the affiliated group.

(iii) *Significant value.* A residual interest has significant value if —

(A) The aggregate of the issue prices of the residual interests in the REMIC is at least 2 percent of the aggregate of the issue prices of all residual and regular interests in the REMIC; and

(B) The anticipated weighted average life of the residual interests is at least 20 percent of the anticipated weighted average life of the REMIC.

(iv) *Determining anticipated weighted average life* — (A) *Anticipated weighted average life of the REMIC.* The anticipated weighted average life of a REMIC is the weighted average of the anticipated weighted average lives of all classes of interests in the REMIC. This weighted average is determined under the formula in paragraph (a)(3)(iv)(B) of this section, applied by treating all payments taken into account in computing the anticipated weighted average lives of regular and residual interests in the REMIC as principal payments on a single regular interest.

(B) *Regular interests that have a specified principal amount.* Generally, the anticipated weighted average life of a regular interest is determined by —

(1) Multiplying the amount of each anticipated principal payment to be made on the interest by the number of years (including fractions thereof) from the startup day (as defined in section 860G(a)(9) and § 1.860G-2(k)) to the related principal payment date;

(2) Adding the results; and

(3) Dividing the sum by the total principal paid on the regular interest.

(C) *Regular interests that have no specified principal amount or that have only a nominal principal amount, and all residual interests.* If a regular interest has no specified principal amount, or if the interest payments to be made on a regular interest are disproportionately high relative to its specified principal amount (as determined by reference to § 1.860G-1(b)(5)(i)), then, for purposes of computing the anticipated weighted average life of the interest, all anticipated payments on that interest, regardless of their designation as principal or interest, must be taken into account in applying the formula set out in paragraph (a)(3)(iv)(B) of this section. Moreover, for purposes of computing the weighted average life of a residual interest, all anticipated payments on that interest, regardless of their designation as principal or interest, must be taken into account in applying the formula set out in paragraph (a)(3)(iv)(B) of this section.

(D) *Anticipated payments.* The anticipated principal payments to be made on a regular interest subject to paragraph (a)(3)(iv)(B) of this section, and the anticipated payments to be made on a regular interest subject to paragraph (a)(3)(iv)(C) of this section or on a residual interest, must be determined based on —

(1) The prepayment and reinvestment assumptions adopted under section 1272(a)(6), or that would have been adopted had the REMIC's regular interests been issued with original issue discount; and

(2) Any required or permitted clean up calls or any required qualified liquidation provided for in the REMIC's organizational documents.

(b) *Treatment of residual interests held by REITs, RICs, common trust funds, and subchapter T cooperatives.* [Reserved]

(c) *Transfers of noneconomic residual interests* — (1) *In general.* A transfer of a noneconomic residual interest is disregarded for all Federal tax purposes if a significant purpose of the transfer was to enable the transferor to impede the assessment or collection of tax. A significant purpose to impede the assessment or collection of tax exists if the transferor, at the time of the transfer, either knew or should have known (had "improper knowledge") that the transferee would be unwilling or unable to pay taxes due on its share of the taxable income of the REMIC.

(2) *Noneconomic residual interest.* A residual interest is a noneconomic residual interest unless, at the time of the transfer —

(i) The present value of the expected future distributions on the residual interest at least equals the product of the present value of the anticipated excess inclusions and the highest rate of tax specified in section 11(b)(1) for the year in which the transfer occurs; and

(ii) The transferor reasonably expects that, for each anticipated excess inclusion, the transferee will receive distributions from the REMIC at or after the time at which the taxes accrue on the anticipated excess inclusion in an amount sufficient to satisfy the accrued taxes.

(3) *Computations.* The present value of the expected future distributions and the present value of the anticipated excess inclusions must be computed under the procedure specified in § 1.860E-2(a)(4) for determining the present value of anticipated excess inclusions in connection with the transfer of a residual interest to a disqualified organization.

(4) *Safe harbor for establishing lack of improper knowledge.* A transferor is presumed not to have improper knowledge if —

(i) The transferor conducted, at the time of the transfer, a reasonable investigation of the financial condition of the transferee and, as a result of the investigation, the transferor found that the transferee had historically paid its debts as they came due and found no significant evidence to indicate that the transferee will not continue to pay its debts as they come due in the future; and

(ii) The transferee represents to the transferor that it understands that, as the holder of the noneconomic residual interest, the transferee may incur tax liabilities in excess of any cash flows generated by the interest and that the transferee intends to pay taxes associated with holding the residual interest as they become due.

(d) *Transfers to foreign persons*. Paragraph (c) of this section does not apply to transfers of residual interests to which § 1.860G-3(a)(1), concerning transfers to certain foreign persons, applies.

§ 1.860E-2. Tax on transfers of residual interests to certain organizations. — (a)

Transfers to disqualified organizations — (1) *Payment of tax*. Any excise tax due under section 860E(e)(1) must be paid by the later of March 24, 1993, or April 15th of the year following the calendar year in which the residual interest is transferred to a disqualified organization. The Commissioner may prescribe rules for the manner and method of collecting the tax.

(2) *Transitory ownership*. For purposes of section 860E(e) and this section, a transfer of a residual interest to a disqualified organization in connection with the formation of a REMIC is disregarded if the disqualified organization has a binding contract to sell the interest and the sale occurs within 7 days of the startup day (as defined in section 860G(a)(9) and § 1.860G-2(k)).

(3) *Anticipated excess inclusions*. The anticipated excess inclusions are the excess inclusions that are expected to accrue in each calendar quarter (or portion thereof) following the transfer of the residual interest. The anticipated excess inclusions must be determined as of the date the residual interest is transferred and must be based on —

(i) Events that have occurred up to the time of the transfer;

(ii) The prepayment and reinvestment assumptions adopted under section 1272(a)(6), or that would have been adopted had the REMIC's regular interests been issued with original issue discount; and

(iii) Any required or permitted clean up calls, or required qualified liquidation provided for in the REMIC's organizational documents.

(4) *Present value computation*. The present value of the anticipated excess inclusions is determined by discounting the anticipated excess inclusions from the end of each remaining calendar quarter in which those excess inclusions are expected to accrue to the date the disqualified organization acquires the residual interest. The discount rate to be used for this present value computation is the applicable Federal rate (as specified in section 1274(d)(1)) that would apply to a debt instrument that was issued on the date the disqualified organization acquired the residual interest and whose term ended on the close of the last quarter in which excess inclusions were expected to accrue with respect to the residual interest.

(5) *Obligation of REMIC to furnish information.* A REMIC is not obligated to determine if its residual interests have been transferred to a disqualified organization. However, upon request of a person designated in section 860E(e)(3), the REMIC must furnish information sufficient to compute the present value of the anticipated excess inclusions. The information must be furnished to the requesting party and to the Internal Revenue Service within 60 days of the request. A reasonable fee charged to the requestor is not income derived from a prohibited transaction within the meaning of section 860F(a).

(6) *Agent.* For purposes of section 860E(e)(3), the term "agent" includes a broker (as defined in section 6045(c) and § 1.6045-1(a)(1)), nominee, or other middleman.

(7) *Relief from liability* — (i) *Transferee furnishes information under penalties of perjury.* For purposes of section 860E(e)(4), a transferee is treated as having furnished an affidavit if the transferee furnishes —

(A) A social security number, and states under penalties of perjury that the social security number is that of the transferee; or

(B) A statement under penalties of perjury that it is not a disqualified organization.

(ii) *Amount required to be paid.* The amount required to be paid under section 860E(e)(7)(B) is equal to the product of the highest rate specified in section 11(b)(1) for the taxable year in which the transfer described in section 860E(e)(1) occurs and the amount of excess inclusions that accrued and were allocable to the residual interest during the period that the disqualified organization held the interest.

(b) *Tax on pass-thru entities* — (1) *Tax on excess inclusions.* Any tax due under section 860E(e)(6) must be paid by the later of March 24, 1993, or by the fifteenth day of the fourth month following the close of the taxable year of the pass-thru entity in which the disqualified person is a record holder. The Commissioner may prescribe rules for the manner and method of collecting the tax.

(2) *Record holder furnishes information under penalties of perjury.* For purposes of section 860E(e)(6)(D), a record holder is treated as having furnished an affidavit if the record holder furnishes —

(i) A social security number and states, under penalties of perjury, that the social security number is that of the record holder; or

(ii) A statement under penalties of perjury that it is not a disqualified organization.

(3) *Deductibility of tax.* Any tax imposed on a pass-thru entity pursuant to section 860E(e)(6)(A) is deductible against the gross amount of ordinary

income of the pass-thru entity. For example, in the case of a REIT, the tax is deductible in determining real estate investment trust taxable income under section 857(b)(2).

(4) *Allocation of tax.* Dividends paid by a RIC or by a REIT are not preferential dividends within the meaning of section 562(c) solely because the tax expense incurred by the RIC or REIT under section 860E(e)(6) is allocated solely to the shares held by disqualified organizations.

§ 1.860F-1. **Qualified liquidations.** — A plan of liquidation need not be in any special form. If a REMIC specifies the first day in the 90-day liquidation period in a statement attached to its final return, then the REMIC will be considered to have adopted a plan of liquidation on the specified date.

§ 1.860F-2. **Transfers to a REMIC.** — (a) *Formation of a REMIC* — (1) *In general.* For Federal income tax purposes, a REMIC formation is characterized as the contribution of assets by a sponsor (as defined in paragraph (b)(1) of this section) to a REMIC in exchange for REMIC regular and residual interests. If, instead of exchanging its interest in mortgages and related assets for regular and residual interests, the sponsor arranges to have the REMIC issue some or all of the regular and residual interests for cash, after which the sponsor sells its interests in mortgages and related assets to the REMIC, the transaction is, nevertheless, viewed for Federal income tax purposes as the sponsor's exchange of mortgages and related assets for regular and residual interests, followed by a sale of some or all of those interests. The purpose of this rule is to ensure that the tax consequences associated with the formation of a REMIC are not affected by the actual sequence of steps taken by the sponsor.

(2) *Tiered arrangements* — (i) *Two or more REMICs formed pursuant to a single set of organizational documents.* Two or more REMICs can be created pursuant to a single set of organizational documents even if for state law purposes or for Federal securities law purposes those documents create only one organization. The organizational documents must, however, clearly and expressly identify the assets of, and the interests in, each REMIC, and each REMIC must satisfy all of the requirements of section 860D and the related regulations.

(ii) A REMIC and one or more investment trusts formed pursuant to a single set of documents. A REMIC (or two or more REMICs) and one or more investment trusts can be created pursuant to a single set of organizational documents and the separate existence of the REMIC(s) and the investment trust(s) will be respected for Federal income tax purposes even if for state law purposes or for Federal securities law purposes those documents create only one organization. The organizational documents for the REMIC(s) and the investment trust(s) must, however, require both the REMIC(s) and the investment trust(s) to account for items of income and ownership of assets for Federal tax purposes in a manner that respects the separate existence of the multiple entities. See § 1.860G-2(i) concerning issuance of regular interests coupled with other contractual rights for an illustration of the provisions of this paragraph.

(b) *Treatment of sponsor* — (1) *Sponsor defined.* A sponsor is a person who directly or indirectly exchanges qualified mortgages and related assets for regular and residual interests in a REMIC. A person indirectly exchanges interests in qualified mortgages and related assets for regular and residual interests in a REMIC if the person transfers, other than in a nonrecognition transaction, the mortgages and related assets to another person who acquires a transitory ownership interest in those asets before exchanging them for interests in the REMIC, after which the transitory owner then transfers some or all of the interests in the REMIC to the first person.

(2) *Nonrecognition of gain or loss.* The sponsor does not recognize gain or loss on the direct or indirect transfer of any property to a REMIC in exchange for regular or residual interests in the REMIC. However, the sponsor, upon a subsequent sale of the REMIC regular or residual interests, may recognize gain or loss with respect to those interests.

(3) *Basis of contributed assets allocated among interests* — (i) *In general.* The aggregate of the adjusted bases of the regular and residual interests received by the sponsor in the exchange described in paragraph (a) of this section is equal to the aggregate of the adjusted bases of the property transferred by the sponsor in the exchange, increased by the amount of organizational expenses (as described in paragraph (b)(3)(ii) of this section). That total is allocated among all the interests received in proportion to their fair market values on the pricing date (as defined in paragraph (b)(3)(iii) of this section) if any, or, if none, the startup day (as defined in section 860G(a)(9) and § 1.860G-2(k)).

(ii) *Organizational expenses* — (A) *Organizational expense defined.* An organizational expense is an expense that is incurred by the sponsor or by the REMIC and that is directly related to the creation of the REMIC. Further, the organizational expense must be incurred during a period beginning a reasonable time before the startup day and ending before the date prescribed by law for filing the first. REMIC tax return (determined without regard to any extensions of time to file). The following are examples of organizational expenses: legal fees for services related to the formation of the REMIC, such as preparation of a pooling and servicing agreement and trust indenture; accounting fees related to the formation of the REMIC; and other administrative costs related to the formation of the REMIC.

(B) *Syndication expenses.* Syndication expenses are not organizational expenses. Syndication expenses are those expenses incurred by the sponsor or other person to market the interests in a REMIC, and, thus, are applied to reduce the amount realized on the sale of the interests. Examples of syndication expenses are brokerage fees, registration fees, fees of an underwriter or placement agent, and printing costs of the prospectus or placement memorandum and other selling or promotional material.

(iii) *Pricing date.* The term "pricing date" means the date on which the terms of the regular and residual interests are fixed and the prices at which a substantial portion of the regular interests will be sold are fixed.

(4) *Treatment of unrecognized gain or loss* — (i) *Unrecognized gain on regular interests.* For purposes of section 860F(b)(1)(C)(i), the sponsor must include in gross income the excess of the issue price of a regular interest over the sponsor's basis in the interest as if the excess were market discount (as defined in section 1278(a)(2)) on a bond and the sponsor had made an election under section 1278(b) to include this market discount currently in gross income. The sponsor is not, however, by reason of this paragraph (b)(4)(i), deemed to have made an election under section 1278(b) with respect to any other bonds.

(ii) *Unrecognized loss on regular interests.* For purposes of section 860F(b)(1)(D)(i), the sponsor treats the excess of the sponsor's basis in a regular interest over the issue price of the interest as if that excess were amortizable bond premium (as defined in section 171(b)) on a taxable bond and the sponsor had made an election under section 171(c). The sponsor is not, however, by reason of this paragraph (b)(4)(ii), deemed to have made an election under section 171(c) with respect to any other bonds.

(iii) *Unrecognized gain on residual interests.* For purposes of section 860F(b)(1)(C)(ii), the sponsor must include in gross income the excess of the issue price of a residual interest over the sponsor's basis in the interest ratably over the anticipated weighted average life of the REMIC (as defined in § 1.860E-1(a)(3)(iv)).

(iv) *Unrecognized loss on residual interests.* For purposes of section 860F(b)(1)(D)(ii), the sponsor deducts the excess of the sponsor's basis in a residual interest over the issue price of the interest ratably over the anticipated weighted average life of the REMIC.

(5) *Additions to or reductions of the sponsor's basis.* The sponsor's basis in a regular or residual interest is increased by any amount included in the sponsor's gross income under paragraph (b)(4) of this section. The sponsor's basis in a regular or residual interest is decreased by any amount allowed as a deduction and by any amount applied to reduce interest payments to the sponsor under paragraph (b)(4)(ii) of this section.

(6) *Transferred basis property.* For purposes of paragraph (b)(4) of this section, a transferee of a regular or residual interest is treated in the same manner as the sponsor to the extent that the basis of the transferee in the interest is determined in whole or in part by reference to the basis of the interest in the hands of the sponsor.

(c) *REMIC's basis in contributed assets.* For purposes of section 860F(b)(2), the aggregate of the REMIC's bases in the assets contributed by the sponsor to the REMIC in a transaction described in paragraph (a) of this section is equal to the aggregate of the issue prices (determined under section 860G(a)(10) and § 1.860G-1(d)) of all regular and residual interests in the REMIC.

§ 1.860F-4, REMIC reporting requirements and other administrative rules. — (a) *In general.* Except as provided in paragraph (c) of this section, for purposes of subtitle F of the Internal Revenue Code, a REMIC is treated as a partnership and any holder of a residual interest in the REMIC is treated as a partner. A REMIC is not subject, however, to the rules of subchapter C of chapter 63 of the Internal Revenue Code, relating to the treatment of partnership items, for a taxable year if there is at no time during the taxable year more than one holder of a residual interest in the REMIC.

(b) *REMIC tax return* — (1) *In general.* To satisfy the requirement under section 6031 to make a return of income for each taxable year, a REMIC must file the return required by paragraph (b)(2) of this section. The due date and any extensions for filing the REMIC's annual return are determined as if the REMIC were a partnership.

(2) *Income tax return.* The REMIC must make a return, as required by section 6011(a), for each taxable year on Form 1066, U.S. Real Estate Mortgage Investment Conduit Income Tax Return. The return must include —

(i) The amount of principal outstanding on each class of regular interests as of the close of the taxable year,

(ii) The amount of the daily accruals determined under section 860E(c), and

(iii) The information specified in § 1.860D-1(d)(2)(i), (iv), and (v).

(c) *Signing of REMIC return* — (1) *In general.* Although a REMIC is generally treated as a partnership for purposes of subtitle F, for purposes of determining who is authorized to sign a REMIC's income tax return for any taxable year, the REMIC is not treated as partnership and the holders of residual interests in the REMIC are not treated as partners. Rather, the REMIC return must be signed by a person who could sign the return of the entity absent the REMIC election. Thus, the return of a REMIC that is a corporation or trust under applicable State law must be signed by a corporate officer or a trustee, respectively. The return of a REMIC that consists of a segregated pool of assets must be signed by a person who could sign the return of the entity that owns the assets of the REMIC under applicable State law.

(2) *REMIC whose startup day is before November 10, 1988* — (i) *In general.* The income tax return of a REMIC whose startup day is before November 10, 1988, may be signed by any person who held a residual interest during the taxable year to which the return relates, or, as provided in section 6903, by a fiduciary, as defined in section 7701(a)(6), who is acting for the REMIC and who has furnished adequate notice in the manner prescribed in § 301.6903-1(b) of this chapter.

(ii) *Startup day.* For purposes of paragraph (c)(2) of this section, startup day means any day selected by a REMIC that is on or before the first day on which interests in such REMIC are issued.

(iii) *Exception.* A REMIC whose startup day is before November 10, 1988, may elect to have paragraph (c)(1) of this section apply, instead of paragraph (c)(2) of this section, in determining who is authorized to sign the REMIC return. See section 1006(t)(18)(B) of the Technical and Miscellaneous Revenue Act of 1988. (102 Stat. 3426) and § 5h.6(a)(1) of this chapter for the time and manner for making this election.

(d) *Designation of tax matters person.* A REMIC may designate a tax matters person in the same manner in which a partnership may designate a tax matters partner under § 301.6231(a)(7)-1T of this chapter. For purposes of applying that section, all holders of residual interests in the REMIC are treated as general partners.

(e) *Notice to holders of residual interests* — (1) *Information required.* As of the close of each calendar quarter, a REMIC must provide to each person who held a residual interest in the REMIC during that quarter notice on Schedule Q (Form 1066) of information specified in paragraphs (e)(1)(i) and (ii) of this section.

(i) *In general.* Each REMIC must provide to each of its residual interest holders the following information —

(A) That person's share of the taxable income or net loss of the REMIC for the calendar quarter;

(B) The amount of the excess inclusion (as defined in section 860E and the regulations thereunder), if any, with respect to that person's residual interest for the calendar quarter;

(C) If the holder of a residual interest is also a pass-through interest holder (as defined in § 1.67-3T(a)(2)), the allocable investment expenses (as defined in § 1.67-3T(a)(4)) for the calendar quarter, and

(D) Any other information required by Schedule Q (Form 1066).

(ii) *Information with respect to REMIC assets* — (A) *95 percent asset test.* For calendar quarters after 1988, each REMIC must provide to each of its residual interest holders the following information —

(1) The percentage of REMIC assets that are qualifying real property loans under section 593,

(2) The percentage of REMIC assets that are assets described in section 7701(a)(19), and

(3) The percentage of REMIC assets that are real estate assets defined in section 856(c)(6)(B),

computed by reference to the average adjusted basis (as defined in section 1011) of the REMIC assets during the calendar quarter (as described in paragraph (e)(1)(iii) of this section). If the percentage of REMIC assets represented by a category is at least 95 percent, then the REMIC need only specify that the percentage for that category was at least 95 percent.

(B) *Additional information required if the 95 percent test not met.* If, for any calendar quarter after 1988, less than 95 percent of the assets of the REMIC are real estate assets defined in section 856(c)(6)(B), then, for that calendar quarter, the REMIC must also provide to any real estate investment trust (REIT) that holds a residual interest the following information —

(1) The percentage of REMIC assets described in section 856(c)(5)(A), computed by reference to the average adjusted basis of the REMIC assets during the calendar quarter (as described in paragraph (e)(1)(iii) of this section),

(2) The percentage of REMIC gross income (other than gross income from prohibited transactions defined in section 860F(a)(2)) described in section 856(c)(3)(A) through (E), computed as of the close of the calendar quarter, and

(3) The percentage of REMIC gross income (other than gross income from prohibited transactions defined in section 860F(a)(2)) described in section 856(c)(3)(F), computed as of the close of the calendar quarter. For purposes of this paragraph (e)(1)(ii)(B)(3), the

term "foreclosure property" contained in section 856(c)(3)(F) has the meaning specified in section 860G(a)(8).

In determining whether a REIT satisfies the limitations of section 856(c)(2), all REMIC gross income is deemed to be derived from a source specified in section 856(c)(2).

(C) *For calendar quarters in 1987*. For calendar quarters in 1987, the percentages of assets required in paragraphs (e)(1)(ii)(A) and (B) of this section may be computed by reference to the fair market value of the assets of the REMIC as of the close of the calendar quarter (as described in paragraph (e)(1)(iii) of this section), instead of by reference to the average adjusted basis during the calendar quarter.

(D) *For calendar quarters in 1988 and 1989*. For calendar quarters in 1988 and 1989, the percentages of assets required in paragraphs (e)(1)(ii)(A) and (B) of this section may be computed by reference to the average fair market value of the assets of the REMIC during the calendar quarter (as described in paragraph (e)(1)(iii) of this section), instead of by reference to the average adjusted basis of the assets of the REMIC during the calendar quarter.

(iii) *Special provisions*. For purposes of paragraph (e)(1)(ii) of this section, the percentage of REMIC assets represented by a specified category computed by reference to average adjusted basis (or fair market value) of the assets during a calendar quarter is determined by dividing the average adjusted bases (or for calendar quarters before 1990, fair market value) of the assets in the specified category by the average adjusted basis (or, for calendar quarters before 1990, fair market value) of all the assets of the REMIC as of the close of each month, week, or day during that calendar quarter. The monthly, weekly, or daily computation period must be applied uniformly during the calendar quarter to all categories of assets and may not be changed in succeeding calendar quarters without the consent of the Commissioner.

(2) *Quarterly notice required* — (i) *In general*. Schedule Q must be mailed (or otherwise delivered) to each holder of a residual interest during a calendar quarter no later than the last day of the month following the close of the calendar quarter.

(ii) *Special rule for 1987*. Notice to any holder of a REMIC residual interest of the information required in paragraph (e)(1) of this section for any of the four calendar quarters of 1987 must be mailed (or otherwise delivered) to each holder no later than March 28, 1988.

(3) *Nominee reporting* — (i) *In general*. If a REMIC is required under paragraphs (e)(1) and (2) of this section to provide notice to an interest holder

who is a nominee of another person with respect to an interest in the REMIC, the nominee must furnish that notice to the person for whom it is a nominee.

(ii) *Time for furnishing statement.* The nominee must furnish the notice required under paragraph (e)(3)(i) of this section to the person for whom it is a nominee no later than 30 days after receiving this information.

(4) *Reports to the Internal Revenue Service.* For each person who was a residual interest holder at any time during a REMIC's taxable year, the REMIC must attach a copy of Schedule Q to its income tax return for that year for each quarter in which that person was a residual interest holder. Quarterly notice to the Internal Revenue Service is not required.

(f) *Information returns for persons engaged in a trade or business.* See § 1.6041-1(b)(2) for the treatment of a REMIC under sections 6041 and 6041A.

§ 1.860G-1. Definition of regular and residual interests. — (a) *Regular interest* — (1) *Designation as a regular interest.* For purposes of section 860G(a)(1), a REMIC designates an interest as a regular interest by providing to the Internal Revenue Service the information specified in § 1.860D-1(d)(2)(ii) in the time and manner specified in § 1.860D-1(d)(2).

(2) *Specified portion of the interest payments on qualified mortgages* — (i) *In general.* For purposes of section 860G(a)(1)(B)(ii), a specified portion of the interest payments on qualified mortgages means a portion of the interest payable on qualified mortgages, but only if the portion can be expressed as —

(A) A fixed percentage of the interest that is payable at either a fixed rate or at a variable rate described in paragraph (a)(3) of this section on some or all of the qualified mortgages;

(B) A fixed number of basis points of the interest payable on some or all of the qualified mortgages; or

(C) The interest payable at either a fixed rate or at a variable rate described in paragraph (a)(3) of this section on some or all of the qualified mortgages in excess of a fixed number of basis points or in excess of a variable rate described in paragraph (a)(3) of this section.

(ii) *Specified portion cannot vary.* The portion must be established as, of the startup day (as defined in section 860G(a)(9) and § 1.860G-2(k)) and , except as provided in paragraph (a)(2)(iii) of this section, it cannot vary over the period that begins on the startup day and ends on the day that the interest holder is no longer entitled to receive payments.

(iii) *Defaulted or delinquent mortgages*. A portion is not treated as varying over time if an interest holder's entitlement to a portion of the interest on some or all of the qualified mortgages is dependent on the absence of defaults or delinquencies on those mortgages.

(iv) *No minimum specified principal amount is required*. If an interest in a REMIC consists of a specified portion of the interest payments on the REMIC's qualified mortgages, no minimum specified principal amount need be assigned to that interest. The specified principal amount can be zero.

(v) *Examples*. The following examples, each of which describes a pass-thru trust that is intended to qualify as a REMIC, illustrate the provisions of this paragraph (a)(2).

Example 1. (i) A sponsor transferred a pool of fixed rate mortgages to a trustee in exchange for two classes of certificates. The Class A certificate holders are entitled to all principal payments on the mortgages and to interest on outstanding principal at a variable rate based on the current value of One-Month LIBOR, subject to a lifetime cap equal to the weighted average rate payable on the mortgages. The Class B certificate holders are entitled to all interest payable on the mortgages in excess of the interest paid on the Class A certificates. The Class B certificates are subordinate to the Class A certificates so that cash flow shortfalls due to defaults or delinquencies on the mortgages will be borne first by the Class B certificate holders.

(ii) The Class B certificate holders are entitled to all interest payable on the pooled mortgages in excess of a variable rate described in paragraph (a)(3)(vi) of this section. Moreover, the portion of the interest payable to the Class B certificate holders is not treated as varying over time solely because payments on the Class B certificates may be reduced as a result of defaults or delinquencies on the pooled mortgages. Thus, the Class B certificates provide for interest payments that consist of a specified portion of the interest payable on the pooled mortgages under paragraph (a)(2)(i)(C) of this section.

Example 2. (i) A sponsor transferred a pool of variable rate mortgages to a trustee in exchange for two classes of certificates. The mortgages call for interest payments at a variable rate based on the current value of the One-Year Constant Maturity Treasury: Index (hereinafter "CMTI") plus 200 basis points, subject to a lifetime cap of 12 percent. Class C certificate holders are entitled to all principal payments on the mortgages and interest on the outstanding principal at a variable rate based on the One-Year CMTI plus 100 basis points, subject to a lifetime cap of 12 percent. The interest rate on the Class C certificates is reset at the same time the rate is reset on the pooled mortgages.

(ii) The Class D certificate holders are entitled to all interest payments on the mortgages in excess of the interest paid on the Class C certificates. So long as the One-Year CMTI is at 10 percent or lower, the Class D certificate holders are entitled to 100 basis points of interest on the pooled mortgages. If, however, the index exceeds 10 percent on a reset date, the Class D certificate holders' entitlement shrinks, and it disappears if the index is at 11 percent or higher.

(iii) The Class D certificate holders are entitled to all interest payable on the pooled mortgages in excess of a qualified variable rate described in paragraph (a)(3) of this section. Thus, the Class D certificates provide for interest payments that consist of a specified portion of the interest payable on the qualified mortgages under paragraph (a)(2)(i)(C) of this section.

Example 3. (i) A sponsor transferred a pool of fixed rate mortgages to a trustee in exchange for two classes of certificates. The fixed interest rate payable on the mortgages varies from mortgage to mortgage, but all rates are between 8 and 10 percent. The Class E certificate holders are entitled to receive all principal payments on the mortgages and interest on outstanding principal at 7 percent. The Class F certificate holders are entitled to receive all interest on the mortgages in excess of the interest paid on the Class E certificates.

(ii) The Class F certificates provide for interest payments that consist of a specified portion of the interest payable on the mortgages under paragraph (a)(2)(i) of this section. Although the portion of the interest payable to the Class F certificate holders varies from mortgage to mortgage, the interest payable can be expressed as a fixed percentage of the interest payable on each particular mortgage.

(3) *Variable rate.* A regular interest may bear interest at a variable rate. For purposes of section 860G(a)(1)(B)(i), a variable rate of interest is a rate described in this paragraph (a)(3).

(i) *Rate based on index.* A rate that is a qualifying variable rate for purposes of sections 1271 though 1275 and the related regulations is a variable rate. For example, a rate based on the average cost of funds of one or more financial institutions is a variable rate. Further, a rate equal to the highest, lowest, or average of two or more objective interest indices is a variable rate for purposes of this section.

(ii) *Weighted average rate* — (A) *In general.* A rate based on a weighted average of the interest rates on some or all of the qualified mortgages held by a REMIC is a variable rate. The qualified mortgages taken into account must, however, bear interest at a fixed rate or at a rate described in this paragraph (a)(3). Generally, a weighted average interest rate is a rate that, if applied to the aggregate outstanding principal balance of a pool of mortgage loans for an accrual period, produces an amount of interest that equals the sum of the interest payable on the pooled loans for that accrual period. Thus, for an accrual period in which a pool of mortgage loans comprises $300,000 of loans bearing a 7 percent interest rate and $700,000 of loans bearing a 9.5 percent interest rate, the weighted average rate for the pool of loans is 8.75 percent.

(B) *Reduction in underlying rate.* For purposes of paragraph (a)(3)(ii)(A) of this section, an interest rate is considered to be based on a weighted average rate even if, in determining that rate, the interest rate on some or all of the qualified mortgages is first subject to a cap or a floor, or is first reduced by a number of basis points or a fixed percentage. A rate determined by taking a weighted average of the interest rates on the qualified mortgage loans net of any servicing spread, credit enhancement fees, or other expenses of the REMIC is a rate based on a weighted average rate for the qualified mortgages. Further, the amount of any rate reduction described above may vary from mortgage to mortgage.

(iii) *Additions, subtractions, and multiplications.* A rate is a variable rate if it is —

(A) Expressed as the product of a rate described in paragraph (a)(3)(i) or (ii) of this section and a fixed multiplier;

(B) Expressed as a constant number of basis points more or less than a rate described in paragraph (a)(3)(i) or (ii) of this section; or

(C) Expressed as the product, plus or minus a constant number of basis points, of a rate described in paragraph (a)(3)(i) or (ii) of this section and a fixed multiplier (which may be either a positive or a negative number).

(iv) *Caps and floors.* A rate is a variable rate if it is a rate that would be described in paragraph (a)(3)(i) through (iii) of this section except that it is —

(A) Limited by a cap or ceiling that establishes either a maximum rate or a maximum number of basis points by which the rate may increase from one accrual or payment period to another or over the term of the interest; or

(B) Limited by a floor that establishes either a minimum rate or a maximum number of basis points by which the rate may decrease from one accrual or payment period to another or over the term of the interest.

(v) *Funds-available caps* — (A) *In general*. A rate is a variable rate if it is a rate that would be described in paragraph (a)(3)(i) through (iv) of this section except that it is subject to a "funds-available" cap. A funds-available cap is a limit on the amount of interest to be paid on an instrument in any accrual or payment period that is based on the total amount available for the distribution, including both principal and interest received by an issuing entity on some or all of its qualified mortgages as well as amounts held in a reserve fund. The term "funds-available cap" does not, however, include any cap or limit on interest payments used as a device to avoid the standards of paragraph (a)(3)(i) through (iv) of this section.

(B) *Facts and circumstances test*. In determining whether a cap or limit on interest payments is a funds-available cap within the meaning of this section and not a device used to avoid the standards of paragraph (a)(3)(i) through (iv) of this section, one must consider all of the facts and circumstances. Facts and circumstances that must be taken into consideration are —

(1) Whether the rate of the interest payable to the regular interest holders is below the rate payable on the REMIC's qualified mortgages on the start-up day; and

(2) Whether, historically, the rate of interest payable to the regular interest holders has been consistently below that payable on the qualified mortgages.

(C) *Examples*. The following examples, both of which describe a pass-thru trust that is intended to qualify as a REMIC, illustrate the provisions of this paragraph (a)(3)(v).

Example 1. (i) A sponsor transferred a pool of mortgages to a trustee in exchange for two classes of certificates. The pool of mortgages has an aggregate principal balance of $100x. Each mortgage in the pool provides for interest payments based on the eleventh district cost of funds index (hereinafter COFI) plus a margin. The initial weighted average rate for the pool is COFI plus 200 basis points. The trust issued a Class X certificate that has a principal amount of 100x$ and that provides for interest payments at a rate equal to One-Year LIBOR plus 100 basis points, subject to a cap described below. The Class R certificate, which the sponsor designated as the residual interest, entitles its holder to all funds left in the trust after the Class X certificates have been retired. The Class R certificate holder is not entitled to current distributions.

(ii) At the time the certificates were issued, COFI equalled 4.874 percent and One-Year LIBOR equalled 3.375 percent. Thus, the initial weighted average pool rate was 6.874 percent and the Class X certificate rate was 4.375 percent. Based on historical data, the sponsor does not expect the rate paid on the Class X certificate to exceed the weighted average rate on the pool.

(iii) Initially, under the terms of the trust instrument, the excess of COFI plus 200 over One-Year LIBOR plus 100 (excess interest) will be applied to pay expenses of the trust, to fund any required reserves, and then to reduce the principal balance on the Class X certificate. Consequently, although the aggregate principal balance of the mortgages initially matched the principal balance of the Class X certificate, the principal balance on the Class X certificate will pay down faster than the principal balance on the mortgages as long as the weighted average rate on the mortgages is greater than One-Year LIBOR plus 100. If, however, the rate on the Class X certificate (One-Year LIBOR plus 100) ever exceeds the weighted average rate on the mortgages, then the Class X certificate holders will receive One-Year LIBOR plus 100 subject to a cap based on the current funds that are available for distribution.

(iv) The funds available cap here is not a device used to avoid the standards of paragraph (a)(3)(i) through (iv) of this section. First, on the date the Class X certificates were issued, a significant spread existed between the weighted average rate payable on the mortgages and the rate payable on the Class X certificate. Second, historical data suggest that the weighted average rate payable on the mortgages will continue to exceed the rate payable on the Class X certificate. Finally, because the excess interest will be applied to reduce the outstanding principal balance of the Class X certificate more rapidly than the outstanding principal balance on the mortgages is reduced, One-Year LIBOR plus 100 basis points would have to exceed the weighted average rate on the mortgages by an increasingly larger amount before the funds available cap would be triggered. Accordingly, the rate paid on the Class X certificates is a variable rate.

Example 2. (i) The facts are the same as those in Example 1, except that the pooled mortgages are commercial mortgages that provide for interest payments based on the gross profits of the mortgagors, and the rate on the Class X certificates is 400 percent of One-Year LIBOR (a variable rate under paragraph (a)(3)(iii) of this section), subject to a cap equal to current funds available to the trustee for distribution.

(ii) Initially, 400 percent of One-Year LIBOR exceeds the weighted average rate payable on the mortgages. Furthermore, historical data suggest that there is a significant possibility that, in the future, 400 percent of One-Year LIBOR will exceed the weighted average rate on the mortgages.

(iii) The facts and circumstances here indicate that the use of 400 percent of One-Year LIBOR with the above-described cap is a device to pass through to the Class X certificate holder contingent interest based on mortgagor profits. Consequently, the rate paid on the Class X certificate here is not a variable rate.

(vi) *Combination of rates.* A rate is a variable rate if it is based on —

(A) One fixed rate during one or more accrual or payment periods and a different fixed rate or rates, or a rate or rates described in paragraph (a)(3)(i) through (v) of this section, during other accrual or payment periods; or

(B) A rate described in paragraph (a)(3)(i) through (v) of this section during one or more accrual or payment periods and a fixed rate or rates, or a different rate or rates described in paragraph (a)(3)(i) through (v) of this section in other periods.

(4) *Fixed terms on the startup day.* For purposes of section 860G(a)(1), a regular interest in a REMIC has fixed terms on the startup day if, on the startup day, the REMIC's organizational documents irrevocably specify —

(i) The principal amount (or other similar amount) of the regular interest;

(ii) The interest rate or rates used to compute any interest payments (or other similar amounts) on the regular interest; and

(iii) The latest possible maturity date of the interest.

(5) *Contingencies prohibited.* Except for the contingencies specified in paragraph (b)(3) of this section, the principal amount (or other similar amount) and the latest possible maturity date of the interest must not be contingent.

(b) *Special rules for regular interests* — (1) *Call premium.* An interest in a REMIC does not qualify as a regular interest if the terms of the interest entitle the holder of that interest to the payment of any premium that is determined with reference to the length of time that the regular interest is outstanding and is not described in paragraph (b)(2) of this section.*sma*

(2) *Customary prepayment penalties received with respect to qualified mortgages.* An interest in a REMIC does not fail to qualify as a regular interest solely because the REMIC's organizational documents provide that the REMIC must allocate among and pay to its regular interest holders any customary prepayment penalties that the REMIC receives with respect to its qualified mortgages. Moreover, a REMIC may allocate prepayment penalties among its classes of interests in any manner specified in the REMIC's organizational documents. For example, a REMIC could allocate all or substantially all of a prepayment penalty that it receives to holders of an interest-only class of

interests because that class would be most significantly affected by prepayments.

(3) *Certain contingencies disregarded.* An interest in a REMIC does not fail to qualify as a regular interest solely because it is issued subject to some or all of the contingencies described in paragraph (b)(3)(i) through (vi) of this section.

(i) *Prepayments, income, and expenses.* An interest does not fail to qualify as a regular interest solely because —

(A) The timing of (but not the right to or amount of) principal payments (or other similar amounts) is affected by the extent of prepayments on some or all of the qualified mortgages held by the REMIC or the amount of income from permitted investments (as defined in § 1.860G-2(g)); or

(B) The timing of interest and principal payments is affected by the payment of expenses incurred by the REMIC.

(ii) *Credit losses.* An interest does not fail to qualify as a regular interest solely because the amount or the timing of payments of principal or interest (or other similar amounts) with respect to a regular interest is affected by defaults on qualified mortgages and permitted investments, unanticipated expenses incurred by the REMIC, or lower than expected returns on permitted investments.

(iii) *Subordinated interests.* An interest does not fail to qualify as a regular interest solely because that interest bears all, or a disproportionate share, of the losses stemming from cash flow shortfalls due to defaults or delinquencies on qualified mortgages or permitted investments, unanticipated expenses incurred by the REMIC, lower than expected returns on permitted investments, or prepayment interest shortfalls before other regular interests or the residual interest bear losses occasioned by those shortfalls.

(iv) *Deferral of interest.* An interest does not fail to qualify as a regular interest solely because that interest, by its terms, provides for deferral of interest payments.

(v) *Prepayment interest shortfalls.* An interest does not fail to qualify as a regular interest solely because the amount of interest payments is affected by prepayments of the underlying mortgages.

(vi) *Remote and incidental contingencies.* An interest does not fail to qualify as a regular interest solely because the amount or timing of payments of principal or interest (or other similar amounts) with respect to the interest is subject to a contingency if there is only a remote likelihood that the contingency will occur. For example, an interest could qualify as a regular interest even though full payment of principal and interest on that interest is contingent upon the absence of significant cash flow shortfalls due to the operation of the Soldiers and Sailors Civil Relief Act, 50 U.S.C. app. § 526 (1988).

(4) *Form of regular interest.* A regular interest in a REMIC may be issued in the form of debt, stock, an interest in a partnership or trust, or any other form permitted by state law. If a regular interest in a REMIC is not in the form of debt, it must, except as provided in paragraph (a)(2)(iv) of this section, entitle the holder to a specified amount that would, were the interest issued in debt form, be identified as the principal amount of the debt.

(5) *Interest disproportionate to principal* — (i) *In general.* An interest in a REMIC does not qualify as a regular interest if the amount of interest (or other similar amount) payable to the holder is disproportionately high relative to the principal amount or other specified amount described in paragraph (b)(4) of this section (specified principal amount). Interest payments (or other similar amounts) are considered disproportionately high if the issue price (as determined under paragraph (d) of this section) of the interest in the REMIC exceeds 125 percent of its specified principal amount.

(ii) *Exception.* A regular interest in a REMIC that entitles the holder to interest payments consisting of a specified portion of interest payments on qualified mortgages qualifies as a regular interest even if the amount of interest is disproportionately high relative to the specified principal amount.

(6) *Regular interest treated as a debt instrument for all Federal income tax purposes.* In determining the tax under chapter 1 of the Internal Revenue Code, a REMIC regular interest (as defined in section 860G(a)(1) is treated as a debt instrument that is an obligation of the REMIC. Thus, sections 1271 through 1288, relating to bonds and other debt instruments, apply to a regular interest. For special rules relating to the accrual of original issue discount on regular interests, see section 1272(a)(6).

(c) *Residual interest.* A residual interest is an interest in a REMIC that is issued on the startup day and that is designated as a residual interest by providing the information specified in § 1.860D-1(d)(2)(ii) at the time and in the manner provided in § 1.860D-1(d)(2). A residual interest need not entitle the holder to any distributions from the REMIC.

(d) *Issue price of regular and residual interests* — (1) *In general.* The issue price of any REMIC regular or residual interest is determined under section 1273(b) as if the interest were a debt instrument and, if issued for property, as if the requirements of section 1273(b)(3) were met. Thus, if a class of interests is publicly offered, then the issue price of an interest in that class is the initial offering price to the public at which a substantial amount of the class is sold. If the interest is in a class that is not publicly offered, the issue price is the price paid by the first buyer of that interest regardless of the price paid for the remainder of the class. If the interest is in a class that is retained by the sponsor, the issue price is its fair market value on the pricing date (as defined in § 1.860F-2(b)(3)(iii)), if any, or, if none, the startup day, regardless of whether the property exchanged therefor is publicly traded.

(2) *The public.* The term "the public" for purposes of this section does not include brokers or other middlemen, nor does it include the sponsor who acquires all of the regular and residual interests from the REMIC on the startup day in a transaction described in § 1.860F-2(a).

§ 1.860G-2. Other rules. — (a) *Obligations principally secured by an interest in real property* — (1) *Tests for determining whether an obligation is principally secured.* For purposes of section 860G(a)(3)(A), an obligation is principally secured by an interest in real property only if it satisfies either the test set out in paragraph (a)(1)(i) or the test set out in paragraph (a)(1)(ii) of this section.

(i) *The 80-percent test.* An obligation is principally secured by an interest in real property if the fair market value of the interest in real property securing the obligation —

(A) Was at least equal to 80 percent of the adjusted issue price of the obligation at the time the obligation was originated (see paragraph (b)(1) of this section concerning the origination date for obligations that have been significantly modified); or

(B) Is at least equal to 80 percent of the adjusted issue price of the obligation at the time the sponsor contributes the obligation to the REMIC.

(ii) *Alternative test.* For purposes of section 860G(a)(3)(A), an obligation is principally secured by an interest in real property if substantially all of the proceeds of the obligation were used to acquire or to improve or protect an interest in real property that, at the origination date, is the only security for the obligation. For purposes of this test, loan guarantees made by the United States or any state (or any political subdivision, agency, or instrumentality of the United States or of any state), or other third party credit enhancement are not viewed as additional security for a loan. An obligation is not considered to be secured by property other than real property solely because the obligor is personally liable on the obligation.

(2) *Treatment of liens.* For purposes of paragraph (a)(1)(i) of this section, the fair market value of the real property interest must be first reduced by

the amount of any lien on the real property interest that is senior to the obligation being tested, and must be further reduced by a proportionate amount of any lien that is in parity with the obligation being tested.

(3) *Safe harbor* — (i) *Reasonable belief that an obligation is principally secured.* If, at the time the sponsor contributes an obligation to a REMIC, the sponsor reasonably believes that the obligation is principally secured by an interest in real property within the meaning of paragraph (a)(1) of this section, then the obligation is deemed to be so secured for purposes of section 860G(a)(3). A sponsor cannot avail itself of this safe harbor with respect to an obligation if the sponsor actually knows or has reason to know that the obligation fails both of the tests set out in paragraph (a)(1) of this section.

(ii) *Basis for reasonable belief.* For purposes of paragraph (a)(3)(i) of this section, a sponsor may base a reasonable belief concerning any obligation on —

(A) Representations and warranties made by the originator of the obligation; or

(B) Evidence indicating that the originator of the obligation typically made mortgage loans in accordance with an established set of parameters, and that any mortgage loan originated in accordance with those parameters would satisfy at least one of the tests set out in paragraph (a)(1) of this section.

(iii) *Later discovery that an obligation is not principally secured.* If, despite the sponsor's reasonable belief concerning an obligation at the time it contributed the obligation to the REMIC, the REMIC later discovers that the obligation is not principally secured by an interest in real property, the obligation is a defective obligation and loses its status as a qualified mortgage 90 days after the date of discovery. See paragraph (f) of this section, relating to defective obligations.

(4) *Interests in real property; real property.* The definition of "interests in real property" set out in § 1.856-3(c), and the definition of "real property" set out in § 1.856-3(d), apply to define those terms for purposes of section 860G(a)(3) and paragraph (a) of this section.

(5) *Obligations secured by an interest in real property.* Obligations secured by interests in real property include the following: mortgages, deeds of trust, and installment land contracts; mortgage pass-thru certificates guaranteed by GNMA, FNMA, FHLMC, or CMHC (Canada Mortgate and Housing Corporation); other investment trust interests that represent undivided beneficial ownership in a pool of obligations principally secured by interests in real property and related assets that would be considered to be permitted investments if the investment trust were a REMIC, and provided the invest-

ment trust is classified as a trust under § 301.7701-4(c) of this chapter; and obligations secured by manufactured housing treated as single family residences under section 25(e)(10) (without regard to the treatment of the obligations or the properties under state law).

(6) *Obligations secured by other obligations; residual interests.* Obligations (other than regular interests in a REMIC) that are secured by other obligations are not principally secured by interests in real property even if the underlying obligations are secured by interests in real property. Thus, for example, a collateralized mortgage obligation issued by an issuer that is not a REMIC is not an obligation principally secured by an interest in real property. A residual interest (as defined in section 860G(a)(2)) is not an obligation principally secured by an interest in real property.

(7) *Certain instruments that call for contingent payments are obligations.* For purposes of section 860G(a)(3) and (4), the term "obligation" includes any instrument that provides for total noncontingent principal payments that at least equal the instrument's issue price even if that instrument also provides for contingent payments. Thus, for example, an instrument that was issued for $100x and that provides for noncontingent principal payments of $100x, interest payments at a fixed rate, and contingent payments based on a percentage of the mortgagor's gross receipts, is an obligation.

(8) *Defeasance.* If a REMIC releases its lien on real property that secures a qualified mortgage, that mortgage ceases to be a qualified mortgage on the date the lien is released unless —

(i) The mortgagor pledges substitute collateral that consists solely of government securities (as defined in section 2(a)(16) of the Investment Company Act of 1940 as amended (15 U.S.C. 80a-1));

(ii) The mortgage documents allow such a substitution;

(iii) The lien is released to facilitate the disposition of the property or any other customary commercial transaction, and not as part of an arrangement to collateralize a REMIC offering with obligations that are not real estate mortgages; and

(iv) The release is not within 2 years of the startup day.

(9) *Stripped bonds and coupons.* The term "qualified mortgage" includes stripped bonds and stripped coupons (as defined in section 1286(e)(2) and (3)) if the bonds (as defined in section 1286(e)(1)) from which such stripped bonds or stripped coupons arose would have been qualified mortgages.

(b) *Assumptions and modifications — (1) Significant modifications are treated as exchanges of obligations.* If an obligation is significantly modified in a manner or under circumstances other than those described in paragraph (b)(3) of this section, then the modified obligation is treated as one that was newly issued in exchange for the unmodified obligation that it replaced. Consequently —

(i) If such a significant modification occurs after the obligation has been contributed to the REMIC and the modified obligation is not a qualified replacement mortgage, the modified obligation will not be a qualified mortgage and the deemed disposition of the unmodified obligation will be a prohibited transaction under section 860F(a)(2); and

(ii) If such a significant modification occurs before the obligation is contributed to the REMIC, the modified obligation will be viewed as having been originated on the date the modification occurs for purposes of the tests set out in paragraph (a)(1) of this section.

(2) *Significant modification defined.* For purposes of paragraph (b)(1) of this section, a "significant modification" is any change in the terms of an obligation that would be treated as an exchange of obligations under section 1001 and the related regulations.

(3) *Exceptions.* For purposes of paragraph (b)(1) of this section, the following changes in the terms of an obligation are not significant modifications regardless of whether they would be significant modifications under paragraph (b)(2) of this section —

(i) Changes in the terms of the obligation occasioned by default or a reasonably foreseeable default;

(ii) Assumption of the obligation;

(iii) Waiver of a due-on-sale clause or a due on encumbrance clause; and

(iv) Conversion of an interest rate by a mortgagor pursuant to the terms of a convertible mortgage.

(4) *Modifications that are not significant modifications.* If an obligation is modified and the modification is not a significant modification for purposes of paragraph (b)(1) of this section, then the modified obligation is not treated as one that was newly originated on the date of modification.

(5) *Assumption defined.* For purposes of paragraph (b)(3) of this section, a mortgage has been assumed if —

(i) The buyer of the mortgaged property acquires the property subject to the mortgage, without assuming any personal liability;

(ii) The buyer becomes liable for the debt but the seller also remains liable; or

(iii) The buyer becomes liable for the debt and the seller is released by the lender.

(6) *Pass-thru certificates.* If a REMIC holds as a qualified mortgage a pass-thru certificate or other investment trust interest of the type described in paragraph (a)(5) of this section, the modification of a mortgage loan that backs the pass-thru certificate or other interest is not a modification of the pass-thru certificate or other interest unless the investment trust structure was created to avoid the prohibited transaction rules of section 860F(a).

(c) *Treatment of certain credit enhancement contracts* — (1) *In general.* A credit enhancement contract (as defined in paragraph (c)(2) and (3) of this section) is not treated as a separate asset of the REMIC for purposes of the asset test set out in section 860D(a)(4) and § 1.860D-1(b)(3), but instead is treated as part of the mortgage or pool of mortgages to which it relates. Furthermore, any collateral supporting a credit enhancement contract is not treated as an asset of the REMIC solely because it supports the guarantee represented by that contract. See paragraph (g)(1)(ii) of this section for the treatment of payments made pursuant to credit enhancement contracts as payments received under a qualified mortgage.

(2) *Credit enhancement contracts.* For purposes of this section, a credit enhancement contract is any arrangement whereby a person agrees to guarantee full or partial payment of the principal or interest payable on a qualified mortgage or on a pool of such mortgages, or full or partial payment on one or more classes of regular interests or on the class of residual interests, in the event of defaults or delinquencies on qualified mortgages, unanticipated losses or expenses incurred by the REMIC, or lower than expected returns on cash flow investments. Types of credit enhancement contracts may include, but are not limited to, pool insurance contracts, certificate guarantee insurance contracts, letters of credit, guarantees, or agreements whereby the REMIC sponsor, a mortgage servicer, or other third party agrees to make advances described in paragraph (c)(3) of this section.

(3) *Arrangements to make certain advances.* The arrangements described in this paragraph (c)(3) are credit enhancement contracts regardless of whether, under the terms of the arrangement, the payor is obligated, or merely permitted, to advance funds to the REMIC.

(i) *Advances of delinquent principal and interest.* An arrangement by a REMIC sponsor, mortgage servicer, or other third party to advance to the REMIC out of its own funds an amount to make up for delinquent payments on qualified mortgages is a credit enhancement contract.

(ii) *Advances of taxes, insurance payments, and expenses.* An arrangement by a REMIC sponsor, mortgage servicer, or other third party to pay taxes and hazard insurance premiums on, or other expenses incurred to protect the REMIC's security interest in, property securing a qualified mortgage in the event that the mortgagor fails to pay such taxes, insurance premiums, or other expenses is a credit enhancement contract.

(iii) *Advances to ease REMIC administration.* An agreement by a REMIC sponsor, mortgage servicer, or other third party to advance temporarily to a REMIC amounts payable on qualified mortgages before such amounts are actually due to level out the stream of cash flows to the REMIC or to provide for orderly administration of the REMIC is a credit enhancement contract. For example, if two mortgages in a pool have payment due dates on the twentieth of the month, and all the other mortgages have payment due dates on the first of each month, an agreement by the mortgage servicer to advance to the REMIC on the fifteenth of each month the payments not yet received on the two mortgages together with the amounts received on the other mortgages is a credit enhancement contract.

(4) *Deferred payment under a guarantee arrangement.* A guarantee arrangement does not fail to qualify as a credit enhancement contract solely because the guarantor, in the event of a default on a qualified mortgage, has the option of immediately paying to the REMIC the full amount of mortgage principal due on acceleration of the defaulted mortgage, or paying principal and interest to the REMIC according to the original payment schedule for the defaulted mortgage, or according to some other deferred payment schedule. Any deferred payments are payments pursuant to a credit enhancement contract even if the mortgage is foreclosed upon and the guarantor, pursuant to subrogation rights set out in the guarantee arrangement, is entitled to receive immediately the proceeds of foreclosure.

(d) *Treatment of certain purchase agreements with respect to convertible mortgages* — (1) *In general.* For purposes of sections 860D(a)(4) and 860G(a)(3), a purchase agreement (as described in paragraph (d)(3) of this section) with respect to a convertible mortgage (as described in paragraph (d)(5) of this section) is treated as incidental to the convertible mortgage to which it relates. Consequently, the purchase agreement is part of the mortgage or pool of mortgages and is not a separate asset of the REMIC.

(2) *Treatment of amounts received under purchase agreements.* For purposes of sections 860A through 860G and for purposes of determining the accrual of original issue discount and market discount under sections 1272(a)(6) and 1276, respectively, a payment under a purchase agreement described in paragraph (d)(3) of this section is treated as a prepayment in full of the mortgage to which it relates. Thus, for example, a payment under a purchase agreement with respect to a qualified mortgage is considered a payment received under a qualified mortgage within the meaning of section 860G(a)(6) and the transfer of the mortgage is not a disposition of the mortgage within the meaning of section 860F(a)(2)(A).

(3) *Purchase agreement.* A purchase agreement is a contract between the holder of a convertible mortgage and a third party under which the holder agrees to sell and the third party agrees to buy the mortgage for an amount equal to its current principal balance plus accrued but unpaid interest if and when the mortgagor elects to convert the terms of the mortgage.

(4) *Default by the person obligated to purchase a convertible mortgage.* If the person required to purchase a convertible mortgage defaults on its obligation to purchase the mortgage upon conversion, the REMIC may sell the mortgage in a market transaction and the proceeds of the sale will be treated as amounts paid pursuant to a purchase agreement.

(5) *Convertible mortgage.* A convertible mortgage is a mortgage that gives the obligor the right at one or more times during the term of the mortgage to elect to convert from one interest rate to another. The new rate of interest must be determined pursuant to the terms of the instrument and must be intended to approximate a market rate of interest for newly originated mortgages at the time of the conversion.

(e) *Prepayment interest shortfalls.* An agreement by a mortgage servicer or other third party to make payments to the REMIC to make up prepayment interest shortfalls is not treated as a separate asset of the REMIC and payments made pursuant to such an agreement are treated as payments on the qualified mortgages. With respect to any mortgage that prepays, the prepayment interest shortfall for the accrual period in which the mortgage prepays is an amount equal to the excess of the interest that would have accrued on the mortgage during that accrual period had it not prepaid, over the interest that accrued from the beginning of that accrual period up to the date of the prepayment.

(f) *Defective obligations* — (1) *Defective obligation defined.* For purposes of sections 860G(a)(4)(B)(ii) and 860F(a)(2), a defective obligation is a mortgage subject to any of the following defects.

(i) The mortgage is in default, or a default with respect to the mortgage is reasonably foreseeable.

(ii) The mortgage was fraudulently procured by the mortgagor.

(iii) The mortgage was not in fact principally secured by an interest in real property within the meaning of paragraph (a)(1) of this section.

(iv) The mortgage does not conform to a customary representation or warranty given by the sponsor or prior owner of the mortgage regarding the characteristics of the mortgage, or the characteristics of the pool of mortgages of which the mortgage is a part. A representation that payments on a qualified mortgage will be received at a rate no less than a specified minimum or no greater than a specified maximum is not customary for this purpose.

(2) *Effect of discovery of defect.* If a REMIC discovers that an obligation is a defective obligation, and if the defect is one that, had it been discovered before the startup day, would have prevented the obligation from being a qualified mortgage, then, unless the REMIC either causes the defect to be cured or disposes of the defective obligation within 90 days of discovering the defect, the obligation ceases to be a qualified mortgage at the end of that 90 day period. Even if the defect is not cured, the defective obligation is, nevertheless, a qualified mortgage from the startup day through the end of the 90 day period. Moreover, even if the REMIC holds the defective obligation beyond the 90 day period, the REMIC may, nevertheless, exchange the defective obligation for a qualified replacement mortgage so long as the requirements of section 860G(a)(4)(B) are satisfied. If the defect is one that does not affect the status of an obligation as a qualified mortgage, then the obligation is always a qualified mortgage regardless of whether the defect is or can be cured. For example, if a sponsor represented that all mortgages transferred to a REMIC had a 10 percent interest rate, but it was later discovered that one mortgage had a 9 percent interest rate, the 9 percent mortgage is defective, but the defect does not affect the status of that obligation as a qualified mortgage.

(g) *Permitted investments* — (1) *Cash flow investment* — (i) *In general.* For purposes of section 860G(a)(6) and this section, a cash flow investment is an investment of payments received on qualified mortgages for a temporary period between receipt of those payments and the regularly scheduled date for distribution of those payments to REMIC interest holders. Cash flow investments must be passive investments earning a return in the nature of interest.

(ii) *Payments received on qualified mortgages.* For purposes of paragraph (g)(1) of this section, the term "payments received on qualified mortgages" includes —

(A) Payments of interest and principal on qualified mortgages, including prepayments of principal and payments under credit enhancement contracts described in paragraph (c)(2) of this section;

(B) Proceeds from the disposition of qualified mortgages;

(C) Cash flows from foreclosure property and proceeds from the disposition of such property;

(D) A payment by a sponsor or prior owner in lieu of the sponsor's or prior owner's repurchase of a defective obligation, as defined in paragraph (f) of this section, that was transferred to the REMIC in breach of a customary warranty; and

(E) Prepayment penalties required to be paid under the terms of a qualified mortgage when the mortgagor prepays the obligation.

(iii) *Temporary period.* For purposes of section 860G(a)(6) and this paragraph (g)(1), a temporary period generally is that period from the time a REMIC receives payments on qualified mortgages and permitted investments to the time the REMIC distributes the payments to interest holders. A temporary period may not exceed 13 months. Thus, an investment held by a REMIC for more than 13 months is not a cash flow investment. In determining the length of time that a REMIC has held an investment that is part of a commingled fund or account, the REMIC may employ any reasonable method of accounting. For example, if a REMIC holds mortgage cash flows in a commingled account pending distribution, the first-in, first-out method of accounting is a reasonable method for determining whether all or part of the account satisfies the 13 month limitation.

(2) *Qualified reserve funds.* The term qualified reserve fund means any reasonably required reserve to provide for full payment of expenses of the REMIC or amounts due on regular or residual interests in the event of defaults on qualified mortgages, prepayment interest shortfalls (as defined in paragraph (e) of this section), lower than expected returns on cash flow investments, or any other contingency that could be provided for under a credit enhancement contract (as defined in paragraph (c)(2) and (3) of this section).

(3) *Qualified reserve asset* — (i) *In general.* The term "qualified reserve asset" means any intangible property (other than a REMIC residual interest) that is held both for investment and as part of a qualified reserve fund. An asset need not generate any income to be a qualified reserve asset.

(ii) *Reasonably required reserve* — (A) *In general.* In determining whether the amount of a reserve is reasonable, it is appropriate to consider the credit quality of the qualified mortgages, the extent and nature of any guarantees relating to either the qualified mortgages or the regular and residual interests, the expected amount of expenses of the REMIC, and the expected availability of proceeds from qualified mortgages to pay the expenses. To the extent that a reserve exceeds a reasonably required amount, the amount of the reserve must be promptly and appropriately reduced. If at any time, however, the amount of the reserve fund is less than is reasonably required, the amount of the reserve fund may be increased by the addition of payments received on qualified mortgages or by contributions from holders of residual interests.

(B) *Presumption that a reserve is reasonably required.* The amount of a reserve fund is presumed to be reasonable (and an excessive reserve is presumed to have been promptly and appropriately reduced) if it does not exceed —

(1) The amount required by a nationally recognized independent rating agency as a condition of providing the rating for REMIC interests desired by the sponsor; or

(2) The amount required by a third party insurer or guarantor, who does not own directly or indirectly (within the meaning of section 267(c)) an interest in the REMIC (as defined in § 1.860D-1(b)(1)), as a condition of providing credit enhancement.

(C) *Presumption may be rebutted.* The presumption in paragraph (g)(3)(ii)(B) of this section may be rebutted if the amounts required by the rating agency or by the third party insurer are not commercially reasonable considering the factors described in paragraph (g)(3)(ii)(A) of this section.

(h) *Outside reserve funds.* A reserve fund that is maintained to pay expenses of the REMIC, or to make payments to REMIC interest holders is an outside reserve fund and not an asset of the REMIC only if the REMIC's organizational documents clearly and expressly —

(1) Provide that the reserve fund is an outside reserve fund and not an asset of the REMIC;

(2) Identify the owner(s) of the reserve fund, either by name, or by description of the class (e.g., subordinated regular interest holders) whose membership comprises the owners of the fund; and

(3) Provide that, for all Federal tax purposes, amounts transferred by the REMIC to the fund are treated as amounts distributed by the REMIC to the designated owner(s) or transferees of the designated owner(s).

(i) *Contractual rights coupled with regular interests in tiered arrangements* — (1) *In general.* If a REMIC issues a regular interest to a trustee of an investment trust for the benefit of the trust certificate holders and the trustee also holds for the benefit of those certificate holders certain other contractual rights, those other rights are not treated as assets of the REMIC even if the investment trust and the REMIC were created contemporaneously pursuant to a single set of organizational documents. The organizational documents must, however, require that the trustee account for the contractual rights as property that the trustee holds separate and apart from the regular interest.

(2) *Example.* The following example, which describes a tiered arrangement involving a pass-thru trust that is intended to qualify as a REMIC and a pass-thru trust that is intended to be classified as a trust under § 301.7701-4(c) of this chapter, illustrates the provisions of paragraph (i)(1) of this section.

Example. (i) A sponsor transferred a pool of mortgages to a trustee in exchange for two classes of certificates. The pool of mortgages has an aggregate principal balance of $100x. Each mortgage in the pool provides for interest payments based on the eleventh district cost of funds index (hereinafter COFI) plus a margin. The trust (hereinafter REMIC trust) issued a Class N bond, which the sponsor designates as a regular interest, that has a principal amount of $100x and that provides for interest payments at a rate equal to One-Year LIBOR plus 100 basis points, subject to a cap equal to the weighted average pool rate. The Class R interest, which the sponsor designated as the residual interest, entitles its holder to all funds left in the trust after the Class N bond has been retired. The Class R interest holder is not entitled to current distributions.

(ii) On the same day, and under the same set of documents, the sponsor, also created an investment trust. The sponsor contributed to the investment trust the Class N bond together with an interest rate cap contract. Under the interest rate cap contract, the issuer of the cap contract agrees to pay to the trustee for the benefit of the investment trust certificate holders the excess of One-Year LIBOR plus 100 basis points over the weighted average pool rate (COFI plus a margin) times the outstanding principal balance of the Class N bond in the event One-Year LIBOR plus 100 basis points ever exceeds the weighted average pool rate. The trustee (the same institution that serves as REMIC trust trustee), in exchange for the contributed assets, gave the sponsor certificates representing undivided beneficial ownership interests in the Class N bond and the interest rate cap contract. The organizational documents require the trustee to account for the regular interest and the cap contract as discrete property rights.

(iii) The separate existence of the REMIC trust and the investment trust are respected for all Federal income tax purposes. Thus, the interest rate cap contract is an asset beneficially owned by the several certificate holders and is not an asset of the REMIC trust. Consequently, each certificate holder must allocate its purchase price for the certificate between its undivided interest in the Class N bond and its undivided interest in the interest rate cap contract in accordance with the relative fair market values of those two property rights.

(j) *Clean-up call* — (1) *In general.* For purposes of section 860F (a)(5)(B), a clean-up call is the redemption of a class of regular interests when, by reason of prior payments with respect to those interests, the administrative costs associated with servicing that class outweigh the benefits of maintaining the class. Factors to consider in making this determination include —

(i) The number of holders of that class of regular interests;

(ii) The frequency of payments to holders of that class;

(iii) The effect the redemption will have on the yield of that class of regular interests;

(iv) The outstanding principal balance of that class; and

(v) The percentage of the original principal balance of that class still outstanding.

(2) *Interest rate changes.* The redemption of a class of regular interests undertaken to profit from a change in interest rates is not a clean-up call.

(3) *Safe harbor.* Although the outstanding principal balance is only one factor to consider, the redemption of a class of regular interests with an outstanding principal balance of no more than 10 percent of its original principal balance is always a clean-up call.

(k) *Startup day.* The term "startup day" means the day on which the REMIC issues all of its regular and residual interests. A sponsor may, however, contribute property to a REMIC in exchange for regular and residual interests over any period of 10 consecutive days and the REMIC may designate any one of those 10 days as its startup day. The day so designated is then the startup day, and all interests are treated as issued on that day.

§ 1.860G-3. Treatment of foreign persons. —

(a) *Transfer of a residual interest with tax avoidance potential* — (1) *In general.* A transfer of a residual interest that has tax avoidance potential is disregarded for all Federal tax purposes if the transferee is a foreign person. Thus, if a residual interest with tax avoidance potential is transferred to a foreign holder at formation of the REMIC, the sponsor is liable for the tax on any excess inclusion that accrues with respect to that residual interest.

(2) *Tax avoidance potential* — (i) *Defined.* A residual interest has tax avoidance potential for purposes of this section unless, at the time of the transfer, the transferor reasonably expects that, for each excess inclusion, the REMIC will distribute to the transferee residual interest holder an amount that will equal at least 30 percent of the excess inclusion, and that each such amount will be distributed at or after the time at which the excess inclusion accrues and not later than the close of the calendar year following the calendar year of accrual.

(ii) *Safe harbor.* For purposes of paragraph (a)(2)(i) of this section, a transferor has a reasonable expectation if the 30-percent test would be satisfied were the REMIC's qualified mortgages to prepay at each rate within a range of rates from 50 percent to 200 percent of the rate assumed under section 1272(a)(6) with respect to the qualified mortgages (or the rate that would have been assumed had the mortgages been issued with original issue discount).

(3) *Effectively connected income.* Paragraph (a)(1) of this section will not apply if the transferee's income from the residual interest is subject to tax under section 871(b) or section 882.

(4) *Transfer by a foreign holder.* If a foreign person transfers a residual interest to a United States person or a foreign holder in whose hands the income from a residual interest would be effectively connected income, and if the transfer has the effect of allowing the transferor to avoid tax on accrued excess inclusions, then the transfer is disregarded and the transferor continues to be treated as the owner of the residual interest for purposes of section 871(a), 881, 1441, or 1442.

(b) [Reserved]

NOTICE 87-41: REAL ESTATE MORTGAGE INVESTMENT CONDUITS

Notice 87-41 provides taxpayers with guidance concerning variable-rate regular interests and manufactured housing and the effective date for the REMIC provisions added by §671 of the Tax Reform Act of 1986.

Real Estate Mortgage Investment Conduits Notice 87-41

This notice provides guidance with respect to certain provisions of the Internal Revenue Code concerning real estate mortgage investment conduits, or REMICs. Taxpayers may rely on this notice until further guidance is issued relating to these provisions. To the extent that future guidance is inconsistent with the guidance provided by this notice, such future guidance will be given prospective effect only.

1. *Variable rate regular interests.*

Section 860G(a)(1) of the Code defines the term "regular interest" to mean, among other things, an interest that "provides that interest payments (or other similar amounts), if any, at or before maturity are payable based on a fixed rate (or to the extent provided in regulations, at a variable rate)." The Internal Revenue Service will issue regulations that permit variable rate regular interests, if those interests would qualify as "variable rate debt instruments" within the meaning of paragraphs (a), (b), and (c) of proposed Treasury regulation section 1.1275-5, as published in the Federal Register for Tuesday, April 8, 1986 (51 FR 12094). The phrase "interest based on current values of an objective interest index" in §1.1275-5(a) of the proposed regulations will be applied, for purposes of section 860G, to permit interest expressed as a fixed multiple of an objective interest index plus or minus a constant number of basis or percentage points to qualify as interest based on an objective interest index. In addition, regulations will provide that an interest in a REMIC shall not fail to qualify as a regular interest because the rate of interest may not exceed a maximum or be less than a minimum rate. Regulations permitting variable rate regular interests will be effective for interests issued on or after June 15, 1987.

2. *Manufactured housing.*

Section 860G(a)(3) defines the term "qualified mortgage" to include, among other things, an obligation which is principally secured, directly or indirectly, by an interest in real property. For purposes of this provision, regulations will provide that manufactured housing or mobile homes that are single family residences under section 25(e)(10) of the Code qualify as real property without regard to state law classifications. The regulations will clarify that recreational vehicles, campers, and similar vehicles do not qualify as real property under this rule.

3. *Effective date of section 671 of the Tax Reform Act of 1986.*

Section 671 of the Tax Reform Act of 1986 (the Act) (1986-3 C.B. (Vol. 1) 225) added sections 860A through 860G to the Code, which govern the taxation of REMICs, and made related technical amendments to other sections of the Code. Section 675(a) of the Act provides, in effect, that these additions and amendments

Appendix B. REMIC Tax Law

to the Code apply generally to taxable years beginning after December 31, 1986. Regulations will clarify that in the case of holders of interests in a REMIC, section 671 of the Act applies with respect to interests in a REMIC issued after December 31, 1986, without regard to the taxable year of the holder.

NOTICE 87-67: REAL ESTATE MORTGAGE INVESTMENT CONDUITS

Notice 87-67 provides taxpayers with guidance concerning payment of interest on a REMIC regular interest at a variable rate based on a weighted average of the interest rates on the qualified mortgages held by the REMIC.

Real Estate Mortgage Investment Conduits Notice 87-67

This notice provides guidance with respect to certain provisions of the Internal Revenue Code concerning real estate mortgage investment conduits, or REMICs. Taxpayers may rely on this notice until regulations are issued relating to these provisions. To the extent that future guidance is inconsistent with the guidance provided by this notice, such future guidance will be given prospective effect only. This notice is intended to supplement Notice 87-41, 1987-1 C.B. 500.

Section 860G(a)(1) of the Code defines the term "regular interest" to mean an interest that, among other things, "provides that interest payments (or other similar amounts), if any, at or before maturity are payable based on a fixed rate (or to the extent provided in regulations, at a variable rate)." In addition to variable rate regular interest that qualify under Notice 87-41, the Internal Revenue Service intends to issue regulations that authorize the payment of interest on a REMIC regular interest at a variable rate based on a weighted average of the interest rates on the qualified mortgages held by the REMIC. This rule will apply only if interest on each qualified mortgage is payable, during each accrual period, at a fixed rate, or at a variable rate based on current values of an objective interest index (within the meaning of paragraphs (a), (b) and (c) of proposed Treasury regulation §1.1275-5, as published in the Federal Register for Tuesday, April 8, 1986 (51 FR 12094)). Thus, for example, a mortgage could have a fixed interest rate for one or more accrual periods and a variable interest rate for other accrual periods.

For this purpose, in determining whether interest on a qualified mortgage held by the REMIC is payable at a variable rate, the phrase "interest based on current values of an objective interest index" in paragraph (a) of proposed Treasury regulation §1.1275-5 will be applied to permit interest on a qualified mortgage to be expressed as a fixed multiple of an objective interest index plus or minus a constant number of basis or percentage points and to permit the interest rate to be subject to a maximum or minimum rate. In addition, for this purpose, the phrase "objective interest index" in paragraph (b) of §1.1275-5 will be applied to include a rate reflecting the average cost of funds of one or more financial institutions.

Regulations permitting variable rate regular interests as described in this notice will be effective for regular interests issued on or after June 15, 1987.

APPENDIX C

Practitioner Planning Aids

GRANTOR TRUST OPINION LETTER

Below is an opinion letter written for the benefit of a customer whereby it is outlined that the customer's operating trust will be treated as a trust under subchapter J of the Code and not as an association taxable as a corporation.

[Letterhead of Law Firm]

June _____, 1995

Re: XYZ Trust

Ladies and Gentlemen:

We have acted as counsel to A Co. in connection with the offering of Certificates of Beneficial Interest ("Certificates") in the XYZ Trust (the "Trust") pursuant to the Offering Memorandum dated June _____, 1995 (the "Offering Memorandum"). The Certificates are to be issued by the Trust pursuant to a Deposit Trust Agreement ("Trust Agreement") among T Co., as trustee ("Trustee"), and D Co., as Depositor. All capitalized terms used herein and not otherwise defined shall have the respective meanings set forth in the Trust Agreement and the Offering Memorandum.

In arriving at the opinion expressed below, we have examined and relied upon originals, or copies certified or otherwise identified to our satisfaction, of the Trust Agreement dated as of June _____, 1995 and the Administrative Agency Agreement, dated as of June _____, 1995, between the Trust and B Co. acting as Agent. For purposes of such examination, we have assumed the genuineness of all signatures, the legal capacity of natural persons, and the authenticity of all documents submitted to us as relevant to this opinion, and we have relied upon the agreements, instruments, certificates and documents referred to above. We have assumed that all parties had the corporate power and authority to enter into and perform all obligations thereunder, and we have also assumed the due authorization by all requisite corporate actions, the due execution and delivery and the validity, binding effect and enforceability of such documents. We have made investigations of such matters of law and fact as we have considered necessary or appropriate for the purpose of this opinion.

On the basis of the foregoing and assuming compliance with the Trust Agreement, we are of the opinion that under existing laws (i) the Trust will be classified as a trust under subpart E, Part I of subchapter J of the Internal Revenue Code of 1986, as amended ("Code"), and not as an association taxable as a corporation, and (ii) pursuant to the grantor trust rules of Code sections 671-679, the Certificateholders will be treated as owners of undivided interests in the assets of the Trust.

This opinion is limited to the treatment of the above-described transaction under the federal income tax laws of the United States as in effect as of the date hereof. This opinion may not be relied upon by any other person or by you in any other context without our prior written consent.

Very truly yours,

REMIC OPINION LETTER

Below is a copy of an opinion letter to a client that a trust fund operating in accordance with a pooling and servicing agreement will be treated as a REMIC for income tax purposes.

[Letterhead of Law Firm]

June _____, 1995

Re: *REMIC Mortgage Pass-Through Certificates, Series A*

Ladies and Gentlemen:

We have acted as counsel for A Co. (the "Seller") in connection with the transactions described in the Underwriting Agreement dated June _____, 1995 (the "Underwriting Agreement"), between the Seller and the Underwriters named in Schedule I thereto (the "Underwriters"), providing for the sale by the Seller to the Underwriters of the above-captioned Mortgage Pass-Through Certificates, Series A (the "Certificates").

This opinion letter is furnished pursuant to Section _____ of the Underwriting Agreement. Capitalized terms not otherwise defined herein are defined as set forth in the Underwriting Agreement.

In arriving at the opinion expressed below, we have examined and relied upon originals, or copies certified or otherwise identified to our satisfaction, of such documents as we have deemed necessary, including the following:

(a)   the Basic Prospectus, dated May _____, 1995 and Prospectus Supplement, dated June _____, 1995, relating to the Certificates; and

(b)   the Pooling and Servicing Agreement, dated as of June _____, 1995, among the Seller, B Co. (the "Servicer") and T Co. (the "Trustee") as trustee.

Based on the foregoing, we are of the opinion that under existing law, assuming compliance with the Pooling and Servicing Agreement, the Trust Fund, as defined in the Pooling and Servicing Agreement, will be treated for federal income tax purposes as a "real estate mortgage investment conduit" ("REMIC") within the meaning of Section 860D of the Internal Revenue Code of 1986, as amended.

We are furnishing this opinion letter to the addressees hereof, solely for the benefit of such addressees. This opinion letter is not to be used, circulated, quoted or otherwise referred to for any other purpose.

Very truly yours,

TRANSFEREE AFFIDAVIT

Below is a transferee affidavit for a proposed transferee of residual interests issued by a mortgage-backed trust pursuant to a pooling and servicing agreement.

STATE OF   )
                :   ss.:
COUNTY   )
The undersigned, being first duly sworn, deposes and says as follows:

1. The undersigned is an officer of _____, a corporation duly organized and existing under the laws of the State of _____, the proposed transferee (the "Transferee") of the Residual Interests from the XYZ Corporation Mortgage-Backed Trust 1995-1, issued pursuant to the Pooling and Servicing Agreement, dated as of _____, 1995 (the "Agreement"), by and among XYZ Corporation, as depositor, ABC Corp., as servicer, and Trust Company, as trustee. Capitalized terms used but not defined herein shall have the meanings ascribed to such terms in the Agreement. The Transferee has authorized the undersigned to make this affidavit on behalf of the Transferee.

2. The Transferee is, as of the date hereof, and will be, as of the date of the Transfer, a Permitted Transferee. The Transferee is acquiring the Residual Interests either (i) for its own account or (ii) as nominee, trustee or agent for another Person and has attached hereto an affidavit from such Person in substantially the same form as this affidavit. The Transferee has no knowledge that any such affidavit is false.

3. The Transferee has been advised and understands that (i) a tax shall be imposed on Transfers of Residual Interests to Persons that are not Permitted Transferees; (ii) such tax is imposed on the transferor, or, if such Transfer is through an agent (which includes a broker, nominee or middleman) for a Person that is not a Permitted Transferee, on the agent; and (iii) the Person otherwise liable for the tax shall be relieved of liability for the tax if the subsequent Transferee furnished to such Person an affidavit that such subsequent Transferee is a Permitted Transferee and, at the time of transfer, such person does not have actual knowledge that the affidavit is false.

4. The Transferee has been advised, and understands that a tax shall be imposed on a "pass-through entity" holding Residual Interests if at any time during the taxable year of the pass-through entity a Person that is not a Permitted Transferee is the record holder of an interest in such entity. The Transferee understands that no tax will be imposed for any period for which the record holder furnishes to the pass-through entity an affidavit stating that the record holder is a Permitted Transferee and the pass-through entity does not have actual knowledge that such affidavit is false. (For this purpose, a "pass-through entity" includes a regulated investment company, a real estate investment trust or common trust fund, a

partnership, trust or estate, and certain cooperatives and, except as may be provided in Treasury Regulations, persons holding interests in pass-through entities as a nominee for another Person.)

5. Transferee has reviewed the provisions of Section _____ of the Agreement (attached hereto as Exhibit 1 and incorporated herein by reference) and understands the legal consequences of the acquisition of the Residual Interests including, without limitations, the restrictions on subsequent Transfers and the provisions regarding voiding the Transfer and mandatory sales. The Transferee expressly agrees to be bound by and to abide by the provisions of Section _____ of the Agreement. The Transferee understands and agrees that any breach of any of the representations included herein shall render the Transfer to the Transferee contemplated hereby null and void.

6. The Transferee agrees to require a Transfer Affidavit from any Person to whom the Transferee attempts to Transfer the Residual Interests and in connection with any Transfer by a Person for whom the Transferee is acting as nominee, trustee or agent, and the Transferee will not Transfer the Residual Interests or cause any Residual Interests to be Transferred to any Person that the Transferee knows is not a Permitted Transferee.

7. The Transferee's taxpayer identification number is _____.

8. The Transferee (i) is not a Non-U.S. Person or (ii) is a Non-U.S. Person that holds the Residual Interest in connection with the conduct of a trade or business in the United States and has furnished the transferor and the Trustee with an effective Internal Revenue Service Form 4224 or successor form at the time and in the manner required by the Code or (iii) is a Non-U.S. Person that has delivered to both the transferor and the Trustee an opinion of a nationally recognized tax counsel to the effect that the transfer of the Residual Interest to it is in accordance with the requirements of the Code and the regulations promulgated thereunder and that such transfer of the Residual Interest will not be disregarded for federal income tax purposes. "Non-U.S. Person" means an individual, corporation, partnership or other person other than a citizen or resident of the United States, a corporation, partnership or other entity created or organized in or under the laws of the United States or any political subdivision thereof, or an estate or trust that is subject to U.S. federal income tax regardless of the source of its income.

9. The Transferee does not have the intention to impede the assessment or collection of any federal, state or local taxes legally required to be paid with respect to such Residual Interest and the Transferee hereby acknowledges that the Residual Interest may generate tax liabilities in excess of the cash flow associated with the Residual Interest and intends to pay such taxes associated with the Residual Interest when they become due.

IN WITNESS WHEREOF, the Transferee has caused this instrument to be executed on its behalf, pursuant to authority of its Board of Directors, by its duly authorized officer and its corporate seal to be hereunto affixed, duly attested, this _____ day of _____, 199__.

[Name of transferee]

By: _____
Name:
Title:

[Corporate Seal]

ATTEST:

_____
[Assistant] Secretary

Personally appeared before me the above-named _____, known or proved to me to be the same person who executed the foregoing instrument and to be the _____ of the Transferee, and acknowledged that he executed the same as his free act and deed and the free act and deed of the Transferee.

Subscribed and sworn before me this _____ day of _____, 199__.

_____
NOTARY PUBLIC

My Commission expires the _____ day of _____, 199__.

CUSTOMARY REASONABLE SERVICING FEE
REPRESENTATION LETTER

Below is a letter representing to a law firm that the compensation payable to a servicer under a pooling and servicing agreement concerning mortgage pass-through certificates is reasonable.

June _____, 1995

[Law Firm]

Re: *Mortgage Pass-Through Certificates, Series A*

Ladies and Gentlemen:

This letter is furnished in connection with the transactions described in the Pooling and Servicing Agreement, dated as of June _____, 1995, among the Seller, A Co. (the "Servicer") and T Co. (the "Trustee"), concerning the above-captioned Mortgage Pass-Through Certificates, Series A (the "Certificates"). In order to permit you to render the opinion set forth in your letter dated the date hereof, regarding the treatment of the Trust Fund as a "real estate mortgage investment conduit" ("REMIC"), the Servicer hereby certifies as follows (capitalized terms not otherwise defined herein are defined as set forth in the Pooling and Servicing Agreement):

The compensation the Servicer will receive pursuant to the Pooling and Servicing Agreement in respect of servicing the Mortgage Loans, including in particular the incentive fee provided under Section _____, represents reasonable arm's length compensation for such services.

Very truly yours,
[SERVICER]

By _____

CUSTOMARY PREPAYMENT PENALTY REPRESENTATION LETTER

Below is a letter wherein advice is rendered to a law firm that a make-whole or yield maintenance premium that is payable under certain circumstances is a prepayment penalty that is commonly found in recently originated commercial mortgage loans that have terms permitting prepayment within 12 months of issuance.

[Letterhead of Underwriter or Servicer]

June ———, 1995

[Law Firm]

Re: *Secured Lease Bonds, Series A*

Ladies and Gentlemen:

The undersigned is acting as [underwriter] [servicer] of the Secured Lease Bonds, Series A (the "Bonds"), which are being issued by A Co. (the "Issuer") pursuant to an indenture (the "Bond Indenture") dated as of the date hereof between the Issuer and T Co., as trustee. The principal assets pledged as security for the Bonds under the Bond Indenture are mortgage notes (the "Notes") issued by Owner Trusts and secured by (i) mortgages (the "Mortgages") on certain commercial real properties (each, a "Property") owned by various Owner Trusts and (ii) the Owner Trusts' rights as lessors of the related Properties under leases to B Co. ("Corporation"). The Issuer will elect to have the Notes treated as a real estate mortgage investment conduit ("REMIC") for federal income tax purposes.

In connection with your delivery of the opinion required by Section ——— of the Underwriting Agreement, dated as of June ———, 1995, between Corporation and the undersigned, the undersigned, based solely upon its experience and participation in recently originated, long term, fixed-interest rate commercial mortgage loans, advises you that a make-whole or yield maintenance premium, such as the Make-Whole Premium on the Notes, that is payable under certain circumstances is a prepayment penalty commonly found in recently originated, long term, fixed-interest rate commercial mortgage loans (other than loans originated by the Resolution Trust Corporation) that have terms providing for the possible prepayment thereof (other than in connection with events of casualty and condemnation) within 12 months of issuance. It should be noted, however, that no such optional prepayment provisions were incorporated in the structure in some recent transactions in that the debt was non-callable.

Appendix C.   Practitioner Planning Aids

[Underwriter] [Servicer]

By: _____
Name:
Title:

REPRESENTATION LETTER — INVESTMENT UNIT PURCHASE PRICE ALLOCATION

Below is a copy of a representation letter that allocates the investment unit purchase price of mortgage pass-through certificates.

[Letterhead of Underwriter]

June _____, 1995

[Issuer's Counsel]

[Address]

    Re: [REMIC Sponsor]

    Mortgage Pass-Through Certificates Series 1995-A

    In connection with your delivery of the opinion required by Section [ ] of the Underwriting Agreement, dated June _____, 1995 (the "Underwriting Agreement"), the undersigned hereby certifies that the first price at which 10 percent of the aggregate principal balance of the Class A-1 Certificates were sold to the public was 100 percent. Assuming the Class A-1 Certificates were sold to the public without any contractual right to payments from the Basis Reserve Fund, the undersigned believes that such certificates would have been sold for a price equal to approximately 99.45 percent.

[Underwriter's Name]

By: _____
Name: [Officer's Name]
Title:

APPENDIX D

Foreign Withholding and Other Reporting

FORM W-8: CERTIFICATE OF FOREIGN STATUS

Form W-8 is used by a foreign person to claim the portfolio debt exemption from the 30 percent withholding tax imposed on interest payments by U.S. persons to foreign persons.

FORM 1099-INT: INTEREST INCOME

Form 1099-INT must be completed annually by the issuer of a REMIC regular interest that paid $10 or more of interest to a holder during the calendar year. If the REMIC regular interest has more than a de minimis amount of OID, the issuer must report interest on Form 1099-OID.

FORM W-9

Form W-9 is used by resident alien taxpayers to report their taxpayer identification number in order not to be subject to the 31 percent backup withholding.

FORM 4224

Form 4224 is used to obtain an exemption from withholding of tax on income effectively connected with the conduct of a trade or business in the United States by nonresident alien individuals and fiduciaries, foreign partnerships, and foreign corporations.

FORM 1001

Form 1001 is used by beneficial owners of certain types of income to report to a withholding agent the ownership of the income and the reduced rate of tax or exemption from tax under tax conventions or treaties. Form 1001 can also be used to claim a release of tax withheld at the source.

FORM 1041: U.S. FIDUCIARY INCOME TAX RETURN; SCHEDULE K-1 — BENEFICIARY'S SHARE OF INCOME, DEDUCTIONS, CREDITS, ETC.

These forms must be completed annually by the trustee of a trust and are used to report the income, deductions, and any gains and losses of a grantor trust.

Appendix D. Foreign Withholding and Other Reporting

Form **W-8** (Rev. November 1992) Department of the Treasury Internal Revenue Service	**Certificate of Foreign Status**	

Please print or type	Name of owner (If joint account, also give joint owner's name.) (See Specific Instructions.)	U.S. taxpayer identification number (if any)
	Permanent address (See Specific Instructions.) (Include apt. or suite no.)	
	City, province or state, postal code, and country	
	Current mailing address, if different from permanent address (Include apt. or suite no., or P.O. box if mail is not delivered to street address.)	
	City, town or post office, state, and ZIP code (If foreign address, enter city, province or state, postal code, and country.)	

List account information here (Optional, see Specific Instructions.)	Account number	Account type	Account number	Account type

Notice of Change in Status.—To notify the payer, mortgage interest recipient, broker, or barter exchange that you no longer qualify for exemption, check here . . . . ▶ ☐
If you check this box, reporting will begin on the account(s) listed.

Please Sign Here

Certification.—(Check applicable box(es)). Under penalties of perjury, I certify that:

☐ For **INTEREST PAYMENTS**, I am not a U.S. citizen or resident (or I am filing for a foreign corporation, partnership, estate, or trust).

☐ For **DIVIDENDS**, I am not a U.S. citizen or resident (or I am filing for a foreign corporation, partnership, estate, or trust).

☐ For **BROKER TRANSACTIONS** or **BARTER EXCHANGES**, I am an exempt foreign person as defined in the instructions below.

▶ Signature _____ Date _____

General Instructions

(Section references are to the Internal Revenue Code unless otherwise noted.)

Purpose

Use Form W-8 or a substitute form containing a substantially similar statement to tell the payer, mortgage interest recipient, middleman, broker, or barter exchange that you are a nonresident alien individual, foreign entity, or exempt foreign person not subject to certain U.S. information return reporting or backup withholding rules.

Caution: *Form W-8 does not exempt the payee from the 30% (or lower treaty) nonresident withholding rates.*

Nonresident Alien Individual

For income tax purposes, "nonresident alien individual" means an individual who is neither a U.S. citizen nor resident. Generally, an alien is considered to be a U.S. resident if:

• The individual was a lawful permanent resident of the United States at any time during the calendar year, that is, the alien held an immigrant visa (a "green card"), or

• The individual was physically present in the United States on:

(1) at least 31 days during the calendar year, and

(2) 183 days or more during the current year and the 2 preceding calendar years (counting all the days of physical presence in the current year, one-third the number of days of presence in the first preceding year, and only one-sixth the number of days of presence in the second preceding year).

See Pub. 519, U.S. Tax Guide for Aliens, for more information on resident and nonresident alien status.

Note: *If you are a nonresident alien individual married to a U.S. citizen or resident and have made an election under section 6013(g) or (h), you are treated as a U.S. resident and may not use Form W-8.*

Exempt Foreign Person

For purposes of this form, you are an "exempt foreign person" for a calendar year in which:

1. You are a nonresident alien individual or a foreign corporation, partnership, estate, or trust,

2. You are an individual who has not been, and plans not to be, present in the United States for a total of 183 days or more during the calendar year, and

3. You are neither engaged, nor plan to be engaged during the year, in a U.S. trade or business that has effectively connected gains from transactions with a broker or barter exchange.

If you do not meet the requirements of **2** or **3** above, you may instead certify on **Form 1001**, Ownership, Exemption, or Reduced Rate Certificate, that your country has a tax treaty with the United States that exempts your transactions from U.S. tax.

Filing Instructions

When To File.—File Form W-8 or substitute form before a payment is made. Otherwise, the payer may have to withhold and send part of the payment to the Internal Revenue Service (see **Backup Withholding** below). This certificate generally remains in effect for three calendar years. However, the payer may require you to file a new certificate each time a payment is made to you.

Where To File.—File this form with the payer of the qualifying income who is the withholding agent (see **Withholding Agent** on page 2). Keep a copy for your own records.

Backup Withholding

A U.S. taxpayer identification number or Form W-8 or substitute form must be given to the payers of certain income. If a taxpayer identification number or Form W-8 or substitute form is not provided or the wrong taxpayer identification number is provided, these payers may have to withhold 20% of each payment or transaction. This is called backup withholding.

Note: *On January 1, 1993, the backup withholding rate increases from 20% to 31%.*

Reportable payments subject to backup withholding rules are:

• Interest payments under section 6049(a).

• Dividend payments under sections 6042(a) and 6044.

• Other payments (i.e., royalties and payments from brokers and barter exchanges) under sections 6041, 6041A(a), 6045, 6050A, and 6050N.

If backup withholding occurs, an exempt foreign person who is a nonresident alien individual may get a refund by filing **Form 1040NR**, U.S. Nonresident Alien Income Tax Return, with the Internal Revenue

(Continued on back.)

Cat. No. 10230M

Form **W-8** (Rev. 11-92)

Service Center, Philadelphia, PA 19255, even if filing the return is not otherwise required.

U.S. Taxpayer Identification Number

The Internal Revenue law requires that certain income be reported to the Internal Revenue Service using a U.S. taxpayer identification number (TIN). This number can be a social security number assigned to individuals by the Social Security Administration or an employer identification number assigned to businesses and other entities by the Internal Revenue Service.

Payments to account holders who are foreign persons (nonresident alien individuals, foreign corporations, partnerships, estates, or trusts) generally are not subject to U.S. reporting requirements. Also, foreign persons are not generally required to have a TIN, nor are they subject to any backup withholding because they do not furnish a TIN to a payer or broker.

However, foreign persons with income effectively connected with a trade or business in the United States (income subject to regular (graduated) income tax), must have a TIN. To apply for a TIN, use **Form SS-4,** Application for Employer Identification Number, available from local Internal Revenue Service offices, or **Form SS-5,** Application for a Social Security Card, available from local Social Security Administration offices.

Special Rules

Mortgage Interest.—For purposes of the reporting rules, mortgage interest is interest paid on a mortgage to a person engaged in a trade or business originating mortgages in the course of that trade or business. A mortgage interest recipient is one who receives interest on a mortgage that was acquired in the course of a trade or business.

Mortgage interest is not subject to backup withholding rules, but is subject to reporting requirements under section 6050H. Generally, however, the reporting requirements do not apply if the payer of record is a nonresident alien individual who pays interest on a mortgage not secured by real property in the United States. Use Form W-8 or substitute form to notify the mortgage interest recipient that the payer is a nonresident alien individual.

Portfolio Interest.—Generally, portfolio interest paid to a nonresident alien individual or foreign partnership, estate, or trust is not subject to backup withholding rules. However, if interest is paid on portfolio investments to a beneficial owner that is neither a financial institution nor a member of a clearing organization, Form W-8 or substitute form is required.

Registered obligations not targeted to foreign markets qualify as portfolio interest not subject to 30% withholding, but require the filing of Form W-8 or substitute form. See **Instructions to Withholding Agents** on this page for reporting rules.

See **Pub. 515,** Withholding of Tax on Nonresident Aliens and Foreign Corporations, for **registered obligations targeted to foreign markets** and when Form W-8 or substitute form is not required on these payments.

Bearer obligations.—The interest from bearer obligations targeted to foreign markets is treated as portfolio interest and is not subject to 30% withholding. Form W-8 or substitute form is not required.

Dividends.—Any distribution or payment of dividends by a U.S. corporation sent to a foreign address is subject to the 30% (or lower treaty) withholding rate, but is not subject to backup withholding. Also, there is no backup withholding on dividend payments made to a foreign person by a foreign corporation. However, the 30% withholding (or lower treaty) rate applies to dividend payments made to a foreign person by a foreign corporation if:

• 25% or more of the foreign corporation's gross income for the three preceding taxable years was effectively connected with a U.S. trade or business, and

• The corporation was not subject to the branch profits tax because of an income tax treaty (see section 884(e)).

If a foreign corporation makes payments to another foreign corporation, the recipient must be a qualified resident of its country of residence to benefit from that country's tax treaty.

Broker or Barter Exchanges.—Income from transactions with a broker or barter exchanges is subject to reporting rules and backup withholding unless Form W-8 or substitute form is filed to notify the broker or barter exchange that you are an exempt foreign person as defined on page 1.

Specific Instructions

Name of Owner.—If Form W-8 is being filed for portfolio interest, enter the name of the beneficial owner.

U.S. Taxpayer Identification Number.—If you have a U.S. taxpayer identification number, enter your number in this space (see the discussion earlier).

Permanent Address.—Enter your complete address in the country where you reside permanently for income tax purposes.

If you are:	Show the address of:
An individual	Your permanent residence
A partnership or corporation	Principal office
An estate or trust	Permanent residence or principal office of any fiduciary

Also show your current mailing address if it differs from your permanent address.

Account Information (optional).—If you have **more than one account** (savings, certificate of deposit, pension, IRA, etc.) with the same payer, list all account numbers and types on one Form W-8 or

substitute form unless your payer requires you to file a separate certificate for each account.

If you have **more than one payer,** file a separate Form W-8 with each payer.

Signature.—If only one foreign person owns the account(s) listed on this form, that foreign person should sign the Form W-8.

If each owner of a joint account is a foreign person, **each** should sign a separate Form W-8.

Notice of Change in Status.—If you become a U.S. citizen or resident after you have filed Form W-8 or substitute form, or you cease to be an exempt foreign person, you must notify the payer in writing within 30 days of your change in status.

To notify the payer, you may check the box in the space provided on this form or use the method prescribed by the payer.

Reporting will then begin on the account(s) listed and backup withholding may also begin unless you certify to the payer that:

(1) The U.S. taxpayer identification number you have given is correct, **and**

(2) The Internal Revenue Service has not notified you that you are subject to backup withholding because you failed to report certain income.

You may use **Form W-9,** Request for Taxpayer Identification Number and Certification, to make these certifications.

If an account is no longer active, you do not have to notify a payer of your change in status unless you also have another account with the same payer that is still active.

False Certificate.—If you file a false certificate when you are not entitled to the exemption from withholding or reporting, you may be subject to fines and/or imprisonment under U.S. perjury laws.

Instructions to Withholding Agents

Withholding Agent.—Generally, the person responsible for payment of the items discussed above to a nonresident alien individual or foreign entity is the withholding agent (see Pub. 515).

Retention of Statement.—Keep Form W-8 or substitute form in your records for at least four years following the end of the last calendar year during which the payment is paid or collected.

Portfolio Interest.—Although registered obligations not targeted to foreign markets are not subject to 30% withholding, you must file **Form 1042S,** Foreign Person's U.S. Source Income Subject to Withholding, to report the interest payment. Both Form 1042S and a copy of Form W-8 or substitute form must be attached to **Form 1042,** Annual Withholding Tax Return for U.S. Source Income of Foreign Persons.

Appendix D. Foreign Withholding and Other Reporting

Form 1099-INT.

Instructions for Recipient

Box 1.—Shows interest paid to you during the calendar year by the payer. This does not include interest shown in box 3.

If you receive a Form 1099-INT for interest paid on a tax-exempt obligation, please see the instructions for your income tax return.

Box 2.—Shows interest or principal forfeited because of early withdrawal of time savings. You may deduct this on your Federal income tax return only on the specific line of Form 1040 under "Adjustments to Income."

Box 3.—Shows interest on U.S. Savings Bonds, Treasury bills, Treasury bonds, and Treasury notes. This may or may not be all taxable. See **Pub. 550,** Investment Income and Expenses. This interest is exempt from state and local income taxes. **This interest is not included in box 1.**

Box 4.—Shows backup withholding. For example, persons not furnishing their taxpayer identification number to the payer become subject to backup withholding at a 31% rate. See **Form W-9,** Request for Taxpayer Identification Number and Certification, for information on backup withholding. **Include this amount on your income tax return as tax withheld.**

Box 5.—Shows foreign tax paid. You may choose to claim this tax as a deduction or a credit on your Federal income tax return. See **Pub. 514,** Foreign Tax Credit for Individuals.

Nominees.—If your Federal identification number is shown on this form and the form includes amounts belonging to another person, you are considered a nominee recipient. You must file Form 1099-INT for each of the other owners showing the amounts allocable to each. You must also furnish a Form 1099-INT to each of the other owners. File Form(s) 1099-INT with **Form 1096,** Annual Summary and Transmittal of U.S. Information Returns, with the Internal Revenue Service Center for your area. On each Form 1099-INT, list yourself as the "payer" and the other owner as the "recipient." On Form 1096, list yourself as the "filer." A husband or wife is not required to file a nominee return to show amounts owned by the other.

Payers, Please Note—

Specific information needed to complete this form and other forms in the 1099 series is given in the **Instructions for Forms 1099, 1098, 5498, and W-2G.** A chart in those instructions gives a quick guide to which form must be filed to report a particular payment. You can order those instructions and additional forms by calling 1-800-TAX-FORM (1-800-829-3676).

Furnish Copy B of this form to the recipient by January 31, 1995.

File Copy A of this form with the IRS by February 28, 1995.

If you received mortgage interest in the course of your trade or business, you may have to report it to the payer of such mortgage interest and to the IRS on **Form 1098,** Mortgage Interest Statement. Do not report mortgage interest to the payer on Form 1099-INT. The main purpose of Form 1098 is to report a mortgage interest **deduction.** The purpose of Form 1099-INT is to report interest **income.** See the Instructions for Forms 1099, 1098, 5498, and W-2G.

9292 ☐ VOID ☐ CORRECTED

PAYER'S name, street address, city, state, and ZIP code	Payer's RTN (optional)	OMB No. 1545-0112
		1994 **Interest Income**

PAYER'S Federal identification number	RECIPIENT'S identification number	1 Interest income not included in box 3 $	**Copy A**
RECIPIENT'S name		2 Early withdrawal penalty $ / 3 Interest on U.S. Savings Bonds and Treas. obligations $	**For Internal Revenue Service Center** File with Form 1096.
Street address (including apt. no.)		4 Federal income tax withheld $	For Paperwork Reduction Act Notice and instructions for
City, state, and ZIP code		5 Foreign tax paid / 6 Foreign country or U.S. possession	completing this form, see Instructions for Forms 1099, 1098,
Account number (optional)	2nd TIN Not. ☐	$	5498, and W-2G.

Form **1099-INT**   Cat. No. 14410K   Department of the Treasury - Internal Revenue Service

Do NOT Cut or Separate Forms on This Page

☐ CORRECTED (if checked)

PAYER'S name, street address, city, state, and ZIP code	Payer's RTN (optional)	OMB No. 1545-0112 **1994**	Interest Income

PAYER'S Federal identification number	RECIPIENT'S identification number	1 Interest income not included in box 3 $		**Copy B**

| RECIPIENT'S name | 2 Early withdrawal penalty $ | 3 Interest on U.S. Savings Bonds and Treas. obligations $ | **For Recipient** |

Street address (including apt. no.)

4 Federal income tax withheld $

City, state, and ZIP code

5 Foreign tax paid $ | 6 Foreign country or U.S. possession

Account number (optional) $

This is important tax information and is being furnished to the Internal Revenue Service. If you are required to file a return, a negligence penalty or other sanction may be imposed on you if this income is taxable and the IRS determines that it has not been reported.

Form **1099-INT**   (Keep for your records.)   Department of the Treasury - Internal Revenue Service

---

☐ VOID   ☐ CORRECTED

PAYER'S name, street address, city, state, and ZIP code	Payer's RTN (optional)	OMB No. 1545-0112 **1994**	Interest Income

| PAYER'S Federal identification number | RECIPIENT'S identification number | 1 Interest income not included in box 3 $ | **Copy C** |

RECIPIENT'S name

2 Early withdrawal penalty $ | 3 Interest on U.S. Savings Bonds and Treas. obligations $

For Payer

Street address (including apt. no.)

4 Federal income tax withheld $

City, state, and ZIP code

5 Foreign tax paid | 6 Foreign country or U.S. possession

Account number (optional) | 2nd TIN Not. ☐ $

For Paperwork Reduction Act Notice and instructions for completing this form, see **Instructions for Forms 1099, 1098, 5498, and W-2G.**

Form **1099-INT**   Department of the Treasury - Internal Revenue Service

Appendix D. Foreign Withholding and Other Reporting

Form **W-9** (Rev. March 1994) Department of the Treasury Internal Revenue Service	**Request for Taxpayer Identification Number and Certification**	**Give form to the requester. Do NOT send to the IRS.**

Please print or type

Name (If joint names, list first and circle the name of the person or entity whose number you enter in Part I below. **See instructions on page 2 if your name has changed.**)

Business name (Sole proprietors see instructions on page 2.)

Please check appropriate box: ☐ Individual/Sole proprietor   ☐ Corporation   ☐ Partnership   ☐ Other ▶ ....

Address (number, street, and apt. or suite no.)

City, state, and ZIP code

Requester's name and address (optional)

Part I Taxpayer Identification Number (TIN)	List account number(s) here (optional)

Enter your TIN in the appropriate box. For individuals, this is your social security number (SSN). For sole proprietors, see the instructions on page 2. For other entities, it is your employer identification number (EIN). If you do not have a number, see **How To Get a TIN** below.

Social security number | | | | | |

OR

Employer identification number | | | | | |

Note: If the account is in more than one name, see the chart on page 2 for guidelines on whose number to enter.

Part II   For Payees Exempt From Backup Withholding (See Part II instructions on page 2)

▶

Part III   Certification

Under penalties of perjury, I certify that:

1. The number shown on this form is my correct taxpayer identification number (or I am waiting for a number to be issued to me), **and**

2. I am not subject to backup withholding because: (a) I am exempt from backup withholding, or (b) I have not been notified by the Internal Revenue Service that I am subject to backup withholding as a result of a failure to report all interest or dividends, or (c) the IRS has notified me that I am no longer subject to backup withholding.

Certification Instructions.—You must cross out item 2 above if you have been notified by the IRS that you are currently subject to backup withholding because of underreporting interest or dividends on your tax return. For real estate transactions, item 2 does not apply. For mortgage interest paid, the acquisition or abandonment of secured property, cancellation of debt, contributions to an individual retirement arrangement (IRA), and generally payments other than interest and dividends, you are not required to sign the Certification, but you must provide your correct TIN. (Also see **Part III Instructions** on page 2.)

Sign Here	Signature ▶	Date ▶

Section references are to the Internal Revenue Code.

Purpose of Form.—A person who is required to file an information return with the IRS must get your correct TIN to report income paid to you, real estate transactions, mortgage interest you paid, the acquisition or abandonment of secured property, cancellation of debt, or contributions you made to an IRA. Use Form W-9 to give your correct TIN to the requester (the person requesting your TIN) and, when applicable, (1) to certify the TIN you are giving is correct (or you are waiting for a number to be issued), (2) to certify you are not subject to backup withholding, or (3) to claim exemption from backup withholding if you are an exempt payee. Giving your correct TIN and making the appropriate certifications will prevent certain payments from being subject to backup withholding.

Note: If a requester gives you a form other than a W-9 to request your TIN, you must use the requester's form if it is substantially similar to this Form W-9.

What is Backup Withholding?—Persons making certain payments to you must withhold and pay to the IRS 31% of such payments under certain conditions. This is called "backup withholding." Payments that could be subject to backup withholding include interest, dividends, broker and barter exchange transactions, rents, royalties, nonemployee pay, and certain payments from fishing boat operators. Real estate transactions are not subject to backup withholding.

If you give the requester your correct TIN, make the proper certifications, and report all your taxable interest and dividends on your tax return, your payments will not be subject to backup withholding. Payments you receive will be subject to backup withholding if:

1. You do not furnish your TIN to the requester, or

2. The IRS tells the requester that you furnished an incorrect TIN, or

3. The IRS tells you that you are subject to backup withholding because you did not report all your interest and dividends on your tax return (for reportable interest and dividends only), or

4. You do not certify to the requester that you are not subject to backup withholding under 3 above (for reportable interest and dividend accounts opened after 1983 only), or

5. You do not certify your TIN. See the Part III instructions for exceptions.

Certain payees and payments are exempt from backup withholding and information reporting. See the Part II instructions and the separate **Instructions for the Requester of Form W-9.**

How To Get a TIN.—If you do not have a TIN, apply for one immediately. To apply, get **Form SS-5,** Application for a Social Security Number Card (for individuals), from your local office of the Social Security Administration, or **Form SS-4,** Application for Employer Identification Number (for businesses and all other entities), from your local IRS office.

If you do not have a TIN, write "Applied For" in the space for the TIN in Part I, sign and date the form, and give it to the requester. Generally, you will then have 60 days to get a TIN and give it to the requester. If the requester does not receive your TIN within 60 days, backup withholding, if applicable, will begin and continue until you furnish your TIN.

Form **W-9** (Rev. 3-94)

Note: *Writing "Applied For" on the form means that you have already applied for a TIN OR that you intend to apply for one soon.*

As soon as you receive your TIN, complete another Form W-9, include your TIN, sign and date the form, and give it to the requester.

Penalties

Failure To Furnish TIN.—If you fail to furnish your correct TIN to a requester, you are subject to a penalty of $50 for each such failure unless your failure is due to reasonable cause and not to willful neglect.

Civil Penalty for False Information With Respect to Withholding.—If you make a false statement with no reasonable basis that results in no backup withholding, you are subject to a $500 penalty.

Criminal Penalty for Falsifying Information.— Willfully falsifying certifications or affirmations may subject you to criminal penalties including fines and/or imprisonment.

Misuse of TINs.—If the requester discloses or uses TINs in violation of Federal law, the requester may be subject to civil and criminal penalties.

Specific Instructions

Name.—If you are an individual, you must generally enter the name shown on your social security card. However, if you have changed your last name, for instance, due to marriage, without informing the Social Security Administration of the name change, please enter your first name, the last name shown on your social security card, and your new last name.

Sole Proprietor.—You must enter your individual name. (Enter either your SSN or EIN in Part I.) You may also enter your business name or "doing business as" name on the business name line. Enter your name as shown on your social security card and business name as it was used to apply for your EIN on Form SS-4.

Part I—Taxpayer Identification Number (TIN)

You must enter your TIN in the appropriate box. If you are a sole proprietor, you may enter your SSN or EIN. Also see the chart on this page for further clarification of name and TIN combinations. If you do not have a TIN, follow the instructions under How To Get a TIN on page 1.

Part II—For Payees Exempt From Backup Withholding

Individuals (including sole proprietors) are not exempt from backup withholding. Corporations are exempt from backup withholding for certain payments, such as interest and dividends. For a complete list of exempt payees, see the separate Instructions for the Requester of Form W-9.

If you are exempt from backup withholding, you should still complete this form to avoid possible erroneous backup withholding. Enter your correct TIN in Part I, write "Exempt" in Part II, and sign and date the form. If you are a nonresident alien or a foreign entity not subject to backup withholding, give the requester a completed Form W-8, Certificate of Foreign Status.

Part III—Certification

For a joint account, only the person whose TIN is shown in Part I should sign.

1. Interest, Dividend, and Barter Exchange Accounts Opened Before 1984 and Broker Accounts Considered Active During 1983. You must give your correct TIN, but you do not have to sign the certification.

2. Interest, Dividend, Broker, and Barter Exchange Accounts Opened After 1983 and Broker Accounts Considered Inactive During 1983. You must sign the certification or backup withholding will apply. If you are subject to backup withholding and you are merely providing your correct TIN to the requester, you must cross out item 2 in the certification before signing the form.

3. Real Estate Transactions. You must sign the certification. You may cross out item 2 of the certification.

4. Other Payments. You must give your correct TIN, but you do not have to sign the certification unless you have been notified of an incorrect TIN. Other payments include payments made in the course of the requester's trade or business for rents, royalties, goods (other than bills for merchandise), medical and health care services, payments to a nonemployee for services (including attorney and accounting fees), and payments to certain fishing boat crew members.

5. Mortgage Interest Paid by You, Acquisition or Abandonment of Secured Property, Cancellation of Debt, or IRA Contributions. You must give your correct TIN, but you do not have to sign the certification.

Privacy Act Notice

Section 6109 requires you to give your correct TIN to persons who must file information returns with the IRS to report interest, dividends, and certain other income paid to you, mortgage interest you paid, the acquisition or abandonment of secured property, cancellation of debt, or contributions you made to an IRA. The IRS uses the numbers for identification purposes and to help verify the accuracy of your tax return. You must provide your TIN whether or not you are required to file a tax return. Payers must generally withhold 31% of taxable interest, dividend, and certain other payments to a payee who does not give a TIN to a payer. Certain penalties may also apply.

What Name and Number To Give the Requester

For this type of account:	Give name and SSN of:
1. Individual	The individual
2. Two or more individuals (joint account)	The actual owner of the account or, if combined funds, the first individual on the account [1]
3. Custodian account of a minor (Uniform Gift to Minors Act)	The minor [2]
4. a. The usual revocable savings trust (grantor is also trustee)	The grantor-trustee [1]
b. So-called trust account that is not a legal or valid trust under state law	The actual owner [1]
5. Sole proprietorship	The owner [3]

For this type of account:	Give name and EIN of:
6. Sole proprietorship	The owner [3]
7. A valid trust, estate, or pension trust	Legal entity [4]
8. Corporate	The corporation
9. Association, club, religious, charitable, educational, or other tax-exempt organization	The organization
10. Partnership	The partnership
11. A broker or registered nominee	The broker or nominee
12. Account with the Department of Agriculture in the name of a public entity (such as a state or local government, school district, or prison) that receives agricultural program payments	The public entity

[1] List first and circle the name of the person whose number you furnish.

[2] Circle the minor's name and furnish the minor's SSN.

[3] You must show your individual name, but you may also enter your business or "doing business as" name. You may use either your SSN or EIN.

[4] List first and circle the name of the legal trust, estate, or pension trust. (Do not furnish the TIN of the personal representative or trustee unless the legal entity itself is not designated in the account title.)

Note: *If no name is circled when more than one name is listed, the number will be considered to be that of the first name listed.*

 **Department of the Treasury**
Internal Revenue Service

Instructions for the Requester of Form W-9

(March 1994)

Request for Taxpayer Identification Number and Certification

Section references are to the Internal Revenue Code, unless otherwise noted.

These instructions supplement the instructions on the Form W-9, for the requester. The payee may also need these instructions.

Substitute Form W-9

You may use a substitute Form W-9 (your own version) as long as it is substantially similar to the official Form W-9 and conforms to Temporary Regulations section 35a.9999-1, Q/A-36. You may not use a substitute form to require the payee, by signing, to agree to provisions unrelated to TIN certification.

TIN Applied For

If the payee returns the Form W-9 with "Applied For" written in Part I, the payee must provide you with a TIN within 60 days. During this 60-day period, you have two options for withholding on reportable interest or dividend payments. For other reportable payments, if you do not receive the payee's TIN within the 60 days you must backup withhold, until the payee furnishes you with his or her TIN.

Option 1.—You must backup withhold on any withdrawals the payee makes from the account after 7 business days after you receive the Form W-9.

Option 2.—You must backup withhold on any reportable interest or dividend payments made to the payee's account, regardless of whether the payee makes any withdrawals. Backup withholding under this option must begin no later than 7 business days after you receive the Form W-9. Under this option, you must refund the amounts withheld if you receive the payee's certified TIN within the 60-day period and the payee was

not otherwise subject to backup withholding during the period.

Payees and Payments Exempt From Backup Withholding

The following is a list of payees exempt from backup withholding and for which no information reporting is required. For interest and dividends, all listed payees are exempt except item (9). For broker transactions, payees listed in items (1) through (13) and a person registered under the Investment Advisers Act of 1940 who regularly acts as a broker are exempt. Payments subject to reporting under sections 6041 and 6041A are generally exempt from backup withholding only if made to payees described in items (1) through (7), except a corporation that provides medical and health care services or bills and collects payments for such services is not exempt from backup withholding or information reporting. Only payees described in items (2) through (6) are exempt from backup withholding for barter exchange transactions, patronage dividends, and payments by certain fishing boat operators.

(1) A corporation.

(2) An organization exempt from tax under section 501(a), or an IRA, or a custodial account under section 403(b)(7).

(3) The United States or any of its agencies or instrumentalities.

(4) A state, the District of Columbia, a possession of the United States, or any of their political subdivisions or instrumentalities.

(5) A foreign government or any of its political subdivisions, agencies, or instrumentalities.

(6) An international organization or any of its agencies or instrumentalities.

(7) A foreign central bank of issue.

(8) A dealer in securities or commodities required to register in the United States or a possession of the United States.

(9) A futures commission merchant registered with the Commodity Futures Trading Commission.

(10) A real estate investment trust.

(11) An entity registered at all times during the tax year under the Investment Company Act of 1940.

(12) A common trust fund operated by a bank under section 584(a).

(13) A financial institution.

(14) A middleman known in the investment community as a nominee or listed in the most recent publication of the American Society of Corporate Secretaries, Inc., Nominee List.

(15) A trust exempt from tax under section 664 or described in section 4947.

Payments of **dividends and patronage dividends** generally not subject to backup withholding include the following:

● Payments to nonresident aliens subject to withholding under section 1441.

● Payments to partnerships not engaged in a trade or business in the United States and that have at least one nonresident partner.

● Payments of patronage dividends not paid in money.

Cat. No. 20479P

• Payments made by certain foreign organizations.

Payments of **interest** generally not subject to backup withholding include the following:

• Payments of interest on obligations issued by individuals.

Note: *The payee may be subject to backup withholding if this interest is $600 or more and is paid in the course of your trade or business and the payee has not provided his or her correct TIN to you.*

• Payments of tax-exempt interest (including exempt-interest dividends under section 852).

• Payments described in section 6049(b)(5) to nonresident aliens.

• Payments on tax-free covenant bonds under section 1451.

• Payments made by certain foreign organizations.

• Mortgage interest paid to you.

Payments that are not subject to information reporting are also not subject to backup withholding. For details, see sections 6041, 6041A(a), 6042, 6044, 6045, 6049, 6050A, and 6050N, and their regulations.

For more information on backup withholding and your requirements, get **Pub. 1679**, A Guide to Backup Withholding, and **Pub. 1281**, Backup Withholding on Missing and Incorrect TINs.

Names and TINs To Use for Information Reporting

Show the full name and address as provided on the Form W-9 on the appropriate information return. If payments have been made to more than one recipient or the account is in more than one name, enter ONLY on the first name line the name of the recipient whose TIN is shown on the information return. Show the names of any other individual recipients in the area below the first name line, if desired.

For sole proprietors, show the individual's name on the first name line. On the second name line, you may enter the business name if provided. You may not enter only the business name. For the TIN, enter either the individual's SSN or the EIN of the business (sole proprietorship).

Notices From the IRS About Your Payees

We will send you a notice if the payee's name and TIN on the information return you filed do not match our records. You may need to send a "B" Notice to the payee to solicit his or her TIN. See Pub. 1679 and Pub. 1281 for copies of the two different "B" Notices.

Page 2

254

Appendix D. Foreign Withholding and Other Reporting

Form **4224** (Rev. March 1993) Department of the Treasury Internal Revenue Service	**Exemption From Withholding of Tax on Income Effectively Connected With the Conduct of a Trade or Business in the United States** ▶ File this form with your withholding agent. (For use by a nonresident alien individual or fiduciary, foreign partnership, or foreign corporation)	OMB No. 1545-0165 Expires 3-31-96

This exemption is applicable for calendar year 19_____ , or other tax year beginning _____ ,19_____ ,and ending _____ ,19_____

Please Type or Print	Owner of income	U.S. identifying number
	Foreign address (number and street) (Include apt. or suite no.)	
	City, province or state, and postal code	Country

Trade or Business in the United States

Name of trade or business	Type of business

Address (number and street) (Include apt. or suite no. or P.O. box if mail is not delivered to street address.)

City, state, and ZIP code

Describe each item of income that is, or is expected to be, effectively connected with the owner's U.S. trade or business: ....

Withholding Agent

Name of withholding agent	Employer identification number

U.S. address (number and street) (Include apt. or suite no. or P.O. box if mail is not delivered to street address.)

City, state, and ZIP code

I certify to the best of my knowledge and belief that the income described above is, or is expected to be, effectively connected with the conduct of the owner's trade or business in the United States and is includible in gross income for the tax year.

Signature of owner, fiduciary, trustee, or agent	Date

If an estate or trust, give name here

Address of fiduciary, trustee, or agent (number and street) (Include apt. or suite no. or P.O. box if mail is not delivered to street address.)

City, state, and ZIP code (If a foreign address, see instructions.)

For Paperwork Reduction Act Notice, see back of form.   Cat. No. 41460A   Form **4224** (Rev. 3-93)

Instructions

(Section references are to the Internal Revenue Code.)

Paperwork Reduction Act Notice

We ask for the information on this form to carry out the Internal Revenue laws of the United States. You are required to give the information. We need it to ensure that you are complying with these laws and to allow us to figure and collect the right amount of tax.

The time needed to complete and file this form will vary depending on individual circumstances. The estimated average time is:

Recordkeeping	7 min.
Learning about the law or the form	11 min.
Preparing the form	14 min.
Copying and sending the form	14 min.

If you have comments concerning the accuracy of these time estimates or suggestions for making this form more simple, we would be happy to hear from you. You can write to both the **Internal Revenue Service,** Washington, DC 20224, Attention: IRS Reports Clearance Officer, T:FP; and the **Office of Management and Budget,** Paperwork Reduction Project (1545-0165), Washington, DC 20503. **DO NOT** send this form to either of these offices. Instead, see Filing Form 4224 on this page.

General Information

Purpose of Form.—This form is used to obtain an exemption from withholding of tax on certain income for nonresident alien individuals and fiduciaries, foreign partnerships, and foreign corporations. See **Pub. 519,** U.S. Tax Guide for Aliens, for details on alien status.

When Exemption Applies.—The exemption from withholding applies only to eligible income paid after the withholding agent receives this form. It applies only for the tax year of the owner (the person entitled to the income) whose name appears on the form. See **Pub. 515,** Withholding of Tax on Nonresident Aliens and Foreign Corporations, for further information.

Income Eligible for Exemption.—In general, to be exempt from withholding, the income must be effectively connected with the conduct of the owner's trade or business in the United States, and must be included in the owner's gross income under section 871(b)(2), 842, or 882(a)(2) for the tax year. If these requirements are met, the following items of income may be exempt from withholding: interest, dividends, rent, royalties, salaries, wages, premiums, annuities, compensation, remuneration, emoluments, and other fixed or determinable annual or periodic gains, profits, and income; gains described in section 631(b) or (c); amounts subject to tax under section 871(a)(1)(C) or 881(a)(3); gains subject to tax under section 871(a)(1)(D) or 881(a)(4); and gains on transfers described in section 1235 made by October 4, 1966.

If a nonresident alien individual or foreign corporation is a member of a domestic partnership, the exemption applies only to the income items included in the distributive share of that partnership's income.

Income Not Eligible for Exemption.—The following are not eligible for exemption from withholding: compensation for personal services by a nonresident alien individual (but see **Form 8233,** Exemption From Withholding on Compensation for Independent Personal Services of a Nonresident Alien Individual), compensation described in section 543(a)(7) received by a foreign corporation that is a personal holding company, and income resulting from a section 897 disposition of an investment in U. S. real property.

Filing Form 4224

Owner of Income.—File this form with your withholding agent to obtain exemption from withholding. (If you do not know the withholding agent's employer identification number, please get it from the withholding agent.) You may want to keep a copy for your records. File Form 4224 before payment of any income to which it applies. When the income to which the form applies is no longer effectively connected with the conduct of a trade or business in the United States, promptly notify your agent by letter.

Withholding Agent.—Keep this form for your records. You are no longer required to attach Form 4224 to **Form 1042,** Annual Withholding Tax Return for U.S. Source Income of Foreign Persons, or to **Form 1042S,** Foreign Person's U.S. Source Income Subject to Withholding.

Address of Fiduciary, Trustee, or Agent.—For a foreign address enter the city, province or state, postal code, and country. Do **not** abbreviate the country name.

Appendix D. Foreign Withholding and Other Reporting

Form **1001** (Rev. November 1992) Department of the Treasury Internal Revenue Service	**Ownership, Exemption, or Reduced Rate Certificate** ▶ File this form with your withholding agent.	OMB No. 1545-0055 Expires 10-31-95

<table>
<tr><td rowspan="3">Please Type or Print</td><td>Name of beneficial owner</td><td>U.S. identifying number, if any</td></tr>
<tr><td>Address (number and street, or P.O. Box number if mail is not delivered to street address)</td><td>Recipient's country of residence for tax purposes</td></tr>
<tr><td>City, province or state, and postal code</td><td>Country</td></tr>
</table>

1 Check type of income for which this certificate applies. *(If you check box a, you do not have to check any other box.):*

a ☐ Income from a trust, estate, or investment account
b ☐ Coupon bond interest (including tax-free covenant bonds)
c ☐ Interest, other than coupon bond interest
d ☐ Rents
e ☐ Natural resource royalties and income from real property

f ☐ Royalties from use of patents, secret processes, etc.
g ☐ Royalties from use of films, television tapes, etc.
h ☐ Annuities
i ☐ Other income (specify)..

If you checked box b, complete items 2a through 2h and, if applicable, line 4 or line 5.
If you checked any box other than b, complete either line 3 or line 4, whichever applies. Also complete line 5 if applicable.
Note: *Before completing line 4 or line 5, see instructions.*

2 Information on coupon bonds
a Name and address of obligor of bonds

b Identification of bond			**c** Date of issue	
d Date interest due	**e** Date interest paid	**f** Gross amount of interest paid	**g** Rate of tax (see instructions)	**h** Amount of tax withheld
		$	%	$

3 Calendar years for which the reduced rate of tax or exemption from tax applies to other than coupon bond interest:

First year	Second year	Third year

4 Withheld tax requested to be released (see instructions) . . . . $

5 Qualified resident status. If you are a corporation claiming treaty benefits for dividends you received from another foreign corporation or interest you received from a U.S. trade or business of another foreign corporation, explain how you meet qualified resident status (see instructions).

I certify that the information entered above is correct; and, if a reduced rate of tax or exemption from tax applies, I further certify that I have complied with all requirements to qualify for the reduced rate of tax or exemption from tax.

Sign Here ▶ _____

(Signature of beneficial owner, fiduciary, trustee, or agent)   (Date)

_____
(If trust or estate, enter name)

_____
(Address of fiduciary, trustee, or agent)

General Instructions

Section references are to the Internal Revenue Code unless otherwise noted.

Paperwork Reduction Act Notice

We ask for the information on this form to carry out the Internal Revenue laws of the United States. You are required to provide the information. It is needed to ensure that you are complying with these laws and to ensure that the correct amount of tax is withheld.

The time needed to complete and file this form will vary depending on individual circumstances. The estimated average time is:

Recordkeeping . . . . 4 hr., 32 min.
Learning about the law or the form . . . . 1 hr.
Preparing and sending the form . . . . 1 hr., 7 min.

If you have comments concerning the accuracy of these time estimates or suggestions for making this form more simple, we would be happy to hear from you. You can write to both the **Internal Revenue Service,** Washington, DC 20224, Attention: IRS Reports Clearance Officer, T:FP; and the **Office of Management and Budget,** Paperwork Reduction Project (1545-0055), Washington, DC 20503.

DO NOT file this form with the IRS. Instead, file it with the withholding agent.

Cat. No. 17110L   Form **1001** (Rev. 11-92)

Purpose of Form

Beneficial owners of certain types of income (or owners' trustees or agents) use this form to report to a withholding agent both the ownership of the income and the reduced rate of tax or exemption from tax on the income under tax conventions or treaties. The form can also be used to claim a release of tax withheld at source.

Instructions for Owners, Trustees, or Agents

Who Must File.—You must file Form 1001 if you are the beneficial owner of income subject to withholding under section 1441, 1442, or 1451 (or you are the trustee or agent of the beneficial owner) and the owner is a nonresident alien individual or fiduciary, a foreign partnership, or a foreign corporation or other foreign entity.

The term "beneficial owner" means the person ultimately entitled to control the income. A nominee or any person acting in a similar capacity is not the beneficial owner.

Who Does Not Have To File.—The following are exceptions to **Who Must File.** You do not have to file this form if you are:

1. A beneficial owner, trustee, or agent who receives only dividends, except as provided below. (The withholding agent may generally rely on an owner's address of record as the basis for allowing the benefit of any income tax treaty to the dividends being paid to the owner.)

However, a foreign corporation that receives dividends from another foreign corporation that are treated as income from sources within the United States under section 861(a)(2)(B) must file Form 1001 unless the dividends are exempt from tax under section 884(e)(3) (relating to earnings and profits subject to the branch profits tax).

2. A beneficial owner, trustee, or agent who receives only income other than coupon bond interest and who does **not** claim the benefit of an income tax treaty.

3. A nonresident alien individual or fiduciary, foreign partnership, or foreign corporation engaged in a trade or business in the United States during the tax year if the income is **(a)** effectively connected with the conduct of a trade or business in the United States by the individual, fiduciary, partnership, or corporation, and **(b)** exempt from withholding under section 1441 or 1442 because of Regulations section 1.1441-4(a). (In this case, file **Form 4224,** Exemption From Withholding of Tax on Income Effectively Connected With the Conduct of a Trade or Business in the United States.)

4. A nonresident alien individual who claims exemption from withholding on compensation for independent personal services based on a U.S. tax treaty or the personal exemption amount. (File **Form 8233,** Exemption From Withholding on Compensation for Independent Personal Services of a Nonresident Alien Individual.)

5. A nonresident alien individual or fiduciary, a foreign corporation, or a foreign partnership made up entirely of nonresident alien individuals and foreign corporations, if the interest is exempt from withholding under section 1441 or 1442 because of section 1441(c)(9) or (10).

6. A foreign partnership or foreign corporation engaged in a trade or business in the United States during the tax year if the income is exempt from withholding under section 1441 or 1442 because of Regulations section 1.1441-4(f).

Where and When To File.—File this form with the withholding agent. When you file depends on the type of income to which Form 1001 applies, as specified in the boxes in item 1:

Box 1b.—For interest on coupon bonds, including tax-free covenant bonds, file the form each time you present a coupon for payment. (Use a separate Form 1001 for each issue of bonds.)

All other item 1 boxes.—For all other types of income, file the form as soon as you can for any successive 3-calendar-year period during which you expect to receive the income. Use a separate Form 1001 for each type of income, except for income received from a trust, estate, or investment account (box 1a). For that type of income, use a separate Form 1001 for each different trust, estate, or investment account.

If after filing a form you become ineligible for the benefits of the tax treaty for the income, notify the withholding agent by letter. If the beneficial ownership of the income changes hands, the new beneficial owner of record may receive the reduced or exempt rate of tax under the treaty only if entitled to it. In addition, the new beneficial owner must properly file Form 1001 with the withholding agent.

Specific Instructions

Address.—Enter your address in the space provided. For an individual, your address is your permanent place of residence. For partnerships or corporations, the address is the principal office or place of business. For estates and trusts, the address is the permanent residence or principal office of the fiduciary.

Note: *To qualify for treaty benefits, a taxpayer must be a resident of a treaty country. (In some cases, a corporate taxpayer must also be a "qualified resident." See the instructions for line 5.) The withholding agent may presume that the beneficial owner of the income is not a resident (or qualified resident) of a treaty country, and is not entitled to treaty benefits, if the owner does not have a resident address in that country. The beneficial owner of the income may nevertheless demonstrate that he or she was a resident (or qualified resident) of the treaty country and was entitled to treaty benefits.*

Line 2g—Rate of tax.—Get **Pub. 901,** U.S. Tax Treaties, for the applicable rate, if any, to enter on line 2g. If the interest is exempt from tax, write "None."

Line 3—If you checked any box on line 1 other than box b, enter the years for which the reduced rate of tax or exemption from tax applies.

Line 4—Withheld tax requested to be released.—If you use this form to claim a release of tax withheld at source, enter the amount claimed on line 4. In the space to the left of the dollar entry space on line 4, identify the income tax treaty and the rate of tax for items 1a and 1c through 1i.

Such release is only available prior to the filing of **Form 1042,** Annual Withholding Tax Return for U.S. Source Income of Foreign Persons, for the calendar year by the withholding agent (Regulations section 1.1461-4).

Line 5—Qualified resident status.— This line applies only to a corporation that claims treaty benefits for dividends paid to it by another foreign corporation or interest paid to it by a U.S. trade or business of another foreign corporation. To obtain treaty benefits for these payments, the recipient corporation must generally be a "qualified resident" of a treaty country or meet the requirements of a limitation on benefits article that entered into force after 1986. (See section 884 and its regulations for the definition of interest paid by a U.S. trade or business, and other applicable rules.) In general, a foreign corporation is a qualified resident of a country if any of the following applies: **(a)** it meets a 50% ownership and base erosion test, **(b)** it is primarily and regularly traded on an established securities market in its country of residence or the United States, **(c)** it carries on an active trade or business in its country of residence, or **(d)** it obtains a ruling from the IRS that it is a qualified resident. See Temporary Regulations section 1.884-5T for the specific requirements that must be met to satisfy each of these tests. Complete this line by indicating which of these tests has been met (if you claim qualified resident status) or that you meet the requirements of a limitation on benefits article that entered into force after 1986.

Instructions for Withholding Agent

As a withholding agent, you are not required to send Form 1001 to the IRS. Instead, use Form 1001 to prepare magnetic tape or paper document **Form 1042S,** Foreign Person's U.S. Source Income Subject to Withholding. Keep Form 1001 for at least 4 years after the end of the last calendar year in which the income to which the form pertains is paid. Prepare a Form 1042S for each separate payment during the calendar year of any item of income (including coupon bond interest). If you receive more than one Form 1001 for an owner during the calendar year, prepare only one Form 1042S to show the total amount of any item paid to the owner for that year.

For withholding rates and other information, get **Pub. 515,** Withholding of Tax on Nonresident Aliens and Foreign Corporations.

Appendix D. Foreign Withholding and Other Reporting

Form 1041 Department of the Treasury—Internal Revenue Service
U.S. Income Tax Return for Estates and Trusts **1994**

For the calendar year 1994 or fiscal year beginning _____, 1994, and ending _____, 19____

A Type of entity:
- ☐ Decedent's estate
- ☐ Simple trust
- ☐ Complex trust
- ☐ Grantor type trust
- ☐ Bankruptcy estate–Ch. 7
- ☐ Bankruptcy estate–Ch. 11
- ☐ Pooled income fund

B Number of Schedules K-1 attached (see instructions) ▪ ►

Name of estate or trust (if a grantor type trust, see page 7 of the instructions)

Name and title of fiduciary

Number, street, and room or suite no. (If a P.O. box, see instructions.)

City or town, state, and ZIP code

C Employer identification number

D Date entity created

E Nonexempt charitable and split-interest trusts, check applicable boxes (see page 8 of the instructions):
- ☐ Described in section 4947(a)(1)
- ☐ Not a private foundation
- ☐ Described in section 4947(a)(2)

F Check applicable boxes:
- ☐ Initial return
- ☐ Final return
- ☐ Amended return
- ☐ Change in fiduciary's name
- ☐ Change in fiduciary's address

G Pooled mortgage account (see instructions):
- ☐ Bought
- ☐ Sold   Date:

Income

1	Interest income	1
2	Dividends	2
3	Business income or (loss) (attach Schedule C or C-EZ (Form 1040))	3
4	Capital gain or (loss) (attach Schedule D (Form 1041))	4
5	Rents, royalties, partnerships, other estates and trusts, etc. (attach Schedule E (Form 1040))	5
6	Farm income or (loss) (attach Schedule F (Form 1040))	6
7	Ordinary gain or (loss) (attach Form 4797)	7
8	Other income. List type and amount	8
9	**Total income.** Combine lines 1 through 8 ►	9

Deductions

10	Interest. Check if Form 4952 is attached ► ☐	10
11	Taxes	11
12	Fiduciary fees	12
13	Charitable deduction (from Schedule A, line 7)	13
14	Attorney, accountant, and return preparer fees	14
15a	Other deductions NOT subject to the 2% floor (attach schedule)	15a
b	Allowable miscellaneous itemized deductions subject to the 2% floor	15b
16	**Total.** Add lines 10 through 15b	16
17	Adjusted total income or (loss). Subtract line 16 from line 9. Enter here and on Schedule B, line 1 ►	17
18	Income distribution deduction (from Schedule B, line 17) (attach Schedules K-1 (Form 1041))	18
19	Estate tax deduction (including certain generation-skipping taxes) (attach computation)	19
20	Exemption	20
21	**Total deductions.** Add lines 18 through 20 ►	21

Tax and Payments

22	Taxable income. Subtract line 21 from line 17. If a loss, see instructions	22
23	**Total tax** (from Schedule G, line 7)	23
24	**Payments: a** 1994 estimated tax payments and amount applied from 1993 return	24a
b	Estimated tax payments allocated to beneficiaries (from Form 1041-T)	24b
c	Subtract line 24b from line 24a	24c
d	Tax paid with extension of time to file: ☐ Form 2758 ☐ Form 8736 ☐ Form 8800	24d
e	Federal income tax withheld. If any is from Form(s) 1099, check ► ☐	24e
	Other payments: f Form 2439 _____; g Form 4136 _____; Total ►	24h
25	**Total payments.** Add lines 24c through 24e, and 24h ►	25
26	Estimated tax penalty (see instructions)	26
27	**Tax due.** If line 25 is smaller than the total of lines 23 and 26, enter amount owed	27
28	**Overpayment.** If line 25 is larger than the total of lines 23 and 26, enter amount overpaid	28
29	Amount of line 28 to be: **a** Credited to 1995 estimated tax ► _____; **b** Refunded ►	29

Please Sign Here

Under penalties of perjury, I declare that I have examined this return, including accompanying schedules and statements, and to the best of my knowledge and belief, it is true, correct, and complete. Declaration of preparer (other than fiduciary) is based on all information of which preparer has any knowledge.

► Signature of fiduciary or officer representing fiduciary   Date   ► EIN of fiduciary if a financial institution (see page 3 of the instructions)

Paid Preparer's Use Only

Preparer's signature ►	Date	Check if self-employed ► ☐	Preparer's social security no.
Firm's name (or yours if self-employed) and address ►		E.I. No. ►	
		ZIP code ►	

For Paperwork Reduction Act Notice, see page 1 of the separate instructions.   Cat. No. 11370H   Form **1041** (1994)

Form 1041 (1994)   Page **2**

Schedule A — Charitable Deduction. Do not complete for a simple trust or a pooled income fund.

1	Amounts paid for charitable purposes from gross income . . . . ⟋ .	**1**	
2	Amounts permanently set aside for charitable purposes from gross income	**2**	
3	Add lines 1 and 2	**3**	
4	Tax-exempt income allocable to charitable contributions (see instructions).	**4**	
5	Subtract line 4 from line 3	**5**	
6	Capital gains for the tax year allocated to corpus and paid or permanently set aside for charitable purposes.	**6**	
7	**Charitable deduction.** Add lines 5 and 6. Enter here and on page 1, line 13.	**7**	

Schedule B — Income Distribution Deduction (see instructions)

1	Adjusted total income (from page 1, line 17) (see instructions).	**1**	
2	Adjusted tax-exempt interest	**2**	
3	Total net gain from Schedule D (Form 1041), line 17, column (a) (see instructions)	**3**	
4	Enter amount from Schedule A, line 6	**4**	
5	Long-term capital gain for the tax year included on Schedule A, line 3	**5**	
6	Short-term capital gain for the tax year included on Schedule A, line 3	**6**	
7	If the amount on page 1, line 4, is a capital loss, enter here as a positive figure	**7**	
8	If the amount on page 1, line 4, is a capital gain, enter here as a negative figure	**8**	
9	**Distributable net income (DNI).** Combine lines 1 through 8	**9**	
10	If a complex trust, enter accounting income for the tax year as determined under the governing instrument and applicable local law ☐ **10**		
11	Income required to be distributed currently	**11**	
12	Other amounts paid, credited, or otherwise required to be distributed	**12**	
13	Total distributions. Add lines 11 and 12. If greater than line 10, see instructions	**13**	
14	Enter the amount of tax-exempt income included on line 13	**14**	
15	Tentative income distribution deduction. Subtract line 14 from line 13	**15**	
16	Tentative income distribution deduction. Subtract line 2 from line 9	**16**	
17	**Income distribution deduction.** Enter the smaller of line 15 or line 16 here and on page 1, line 18	**17**	

Schedule G — Tax Computation (see instructions)

1	**Tax: a** ☐ Tax rate schedule or ☐ Schedule D (Form 1041) . . **1a**		
	b Other taxes **1b**		
	c Total. Add lines 1a and 1b. . . . . ▶	**1c**	
2a	Foreign tax credit (attach Form 1116) **2a**		
b	Check: ☐ Nonconventional source fuel credit ☐ Form 8834 . **2b**		
c	General business credit. Enter here and check which forms are attached: ☐ Form 3800 or ☐ Forms (specify) ▶ **2c**		
d	Credit for prior year minimum tax (attach Form 8801) **2d**		
3	**Total credits.** Add lines 2a through 2d . . . . ▶	**3**	
4	Subtract line 3 from line 1c	**4**	
5	Recapture taxes. Check if from: ☐ Form 4255 ☐ Form 8611.	**5**	
6	Alternative minimum tax (from Schedule H, line 39)	**6**	
7	**Total tax.** Add lines 4 through 6. Enter here and on page 1, line 23 . . . . ▶	**7**	

Other Information (see instructions)

		Yes	No
1	Did the estate or trust receive tax-exempt income? If "Yes," attach a computation of the allocation of expenses. Enter the amount of tax-exempt interest income and exempt-interest dividends ▶ $		
2	Did the estate or trust receive all or any part of the earnings (salary, wages, and other compensation) of any individual by reason of a contract assignment or similar arrangement?		
3	At any time during calendar year 1994, did the estate or trust have an interest in or a signature or other authority over a bank, securities, or other financial account in a foreign country? See the instructions for exceptions and filing requirements for Form TD F 90-22.1. If "Yes," enter the name of the foreign country ▶		
4	Was the estate or trust the grantor of, or transferor to, a foreign trust which existed during the current tax year, whether or not the estate or trust has any beneficial interest in it? If "Yes," you may have to file Form 3520, 3520-A, or 926 .		
5	Did the estate or trust receive, or pay, any seller-financed mortgage interest? If "Yes," see instructions for required attachment		
6	If this is a complex trust making the section 663(b) election, check here . . . . ▶ ☐		
7	To make a section 643(e)(3) election, attach Schedule D (Form 1041), and check here . . . . . ▶ ☐		
8	If the decedent's estate has been open for more than 2 years, check here . . . . ▶ ☐		

Appendix D. Foreign Withholding and Other Reporting

| Schedule H | Alternative Minimum Tax (see instructions) |

Part I—Estate's or Trust's Share of Alternative Minimum Taxable Income

1	Adjusted total income or (loss) (from page 1, line 17)	**1**	
2	Net operating loss deduction. Enter as a positive amount	**2**	
3	Add lines 1 and 2	**3**	
4	**Adjustments and tax preference items:**		
a	Interest	**4a**	
b	Taxes	**4b**	
c	Miscellaneous itemized deductions (from page 1, line 15b)	**4c**	
d	Refund of taxes	**4d** ( )	
e	Depreciation of property placed in service after 1986	**4e**	
f	Circulation and research and experimental expenditures paid or incurred after 1986	**4f**	
g	Mining exploration and development costs paid or incurred after 1986	**4g**	
h	Long-term contracts entered into after February 28, 1986	**4h**	
i	Pollution control facilities placed in service after 1986	**4i**	
j	Installment sales of certain property	**4j**	
k	Adjusted gain or loss (including incentive stock options).	**4k**	
l	Certain loss limitations	**4l**	
m	Tax shelter farm activities	**4m**	
n	Passive activities	**4n**	
o	Beneficiaries of other trusts or decedent's estates	**4o**	
p	Tax-exempt interest from specified private activity bonds	**4p**	
q	Depletion	**4q**	
r	Accelerated depreciation of real property placed in service before 1987	**4r**	
s	Accelerated depreciation of leased personal property placed in service before 1987	**4s**	
t	Intangible drilling costs.	**4t**	
u	Other adjustments	**4u**	
5	Combine lines 4a through 4u.	**5**	
6	Add lines 3 and 5	**6**	
7	Alternative tax net operating loss deduction (see instructions for limitations)	**7**	
8	Adjusted alternative minimum taxable income. Subtract line 7 from line 6. Enter here and on line 13	**8**	
	Note: *Complete Part II before proceeding with line 9.*		
9	Income distribution deduction from line 27	**9**	
10	Estate tax deduction (from page 1, line 19)	**10**	
11	Add lines 9 and 10	**11**	
12	Estate's or trust's share of alternative minimum taxable income. Subtract line 11 from line 8 .	**12**	

Note: *If line 12 is more than $22,500, proceed to Part III. If line 12 is $22,500 or less, stop here and enter -0- on Schedule G, line 6; the estate or trust is not liable for the alternative minimum tax.*

(continued on page 4)

261

Form 1041 (1994)   Page **4**

Part II—Income Distribution Deduction on a Minimum Tax Basis

13	Adjusted alternative minimum taxable income (from line 8)	**13**	
14	Adjusted tax-exempt interest (other than amounts included on line 4p)	**14**	
15	Total net gain from Schedule D (Form 1041), line 17, column (a). If a loss, enter -0-	**15**	
16	Capital gains for the tax year allocated to corpus and paid or permanently set aside for charitable purposes (from Schedule A, line 6)	**16**	
17	Capital gains paid or permanently set aside for charitable purposes from current year's income (see instructions)	**17**	
18	Capital gains computed on a minimum tax basis included on line 8	**18**	( )
19	Capital losses computed on a minimum tax basis included on line 8. Enter as a positive amount	**19**	
20	Distributable net alternative minimum taxable income (DNAMTI). Combine lines 13 through 19 .	**20**	
21	Income required to be distributed currently (from Schedule B, line 11)	**21**	
22	Other amounts paid, credited, or otherwise required to be distributed (from Schedule B, line 12)	**22**	
23	Total distributions. Add lines 21 and 22	**23**	
24	Tax-exempt income included on line 23 (other than amounts included on line 4p)	**24**	
25	Tentative income distribution deduction on a minimum tax basis. Subtract line 24 from line 23 .	**25**	
26	Tentative income distribution deduction on a minimum tax basis. Subtract line 14 from line 20 .	**26**	
27	**Income distribution deduction on a minimum tax basis.** Enter the smaller of line 25 or line 26. Enter here and on line 9	**27**	

Part III—Alternative Minimum Tax

28	Enter the amount from line 12. If line 12 is: • Less than $165,000, go to line 30. • At least $165,000, but not over $175,000, skip lines 29a through 33. • Over $175,000, skip lines 29a through 34.			**28**
29a	Exemption amount	**29a**	$22,500	
b	Phase-out of exemption amount	**29b**	$75,000	
30	Subtract line 29b from line 28. If zero or less, enter -0-			**30**
31	Multiply line 30 by 25% (.25)			**31**
32	Subtract line 31 from line 29a. If zero or less, enter -0-			**32**
33	Subtract line 32 from line 28			**33**
34	If line 28 is: • Less than $165,000, multiply line 33 by 26% (.26). • $165,000 or more, multiply line 28 by 26% (.26). Enter the result here and skip line 35			**34**
35	Multiply line 28 by 28% (.28) and subtract $3,500 from the result			**35**
36	Alternative minimum tax foreign tax credit (see instructions)			**36**
37	Tentative minimum tax. Subtract line 36 from line 34 or 35, whichever applies			**37**
38a	Regular tax before credits (see instructions)	**38a**		
b	Section 644 tax (see instructions)	**38b**		
c	Add lines 38a and 38b			**38c**
39	**Alternative minimum tax.** Subtract line 38c from line 37. If zero or less, enter -0-. Enter here and on Schedule G, line 6			**39**

♻ *Printed on recycled paper*

Appendix D.   Foreign Withholding and Other Reporting

SCHEDULE K-1 (Form 1041) Department of the Treasury Internal Revenue Service	**Beneficiary's Share of Income, Deductions, Credits, etc.** for the calendar year 1994, or fiscal year beginning .... , 1994, ending .... , 19 .... ▶ Complete a separate Schedule K-1 for each beneficiary.	OMB No. 1545-0092 **1994**
Name of trust or decedent's estate		☐ Amended K-1 ☐ Final K-1

Beneficiary's identifying number ▶		Estate's or trust's EIN ▶	
Beneficiary's name, address, and ZIP code		Fiduciary's name, address, and ZIP code	

(a) Allocable share item		(b) Amount	(c) Calendar year 1994 Form 1040 filers enter the amounts in column (b) on:
1 Interest.	1		Schedule B, Part I, line 1
2 Dividends	2		Schedule B, Part II, line 5
3a Net short-term capital gain	3a		Schedule D, line 5, column (g)
b Net long-term capital gain	3b		Schedule D, line 13, column (g)
4a Annuities, royalties, and other nonpassive income before directly apportioned deductions	4a		Schedule E, Part III, column (f)
b Depreciation	4b		Include on the applicable line of the appropriate tax form
c Depletion	4c		
d Amortization	4d		
5a Trade or business, rental real estate, and other rental income before directly apportioned deductions (see instructions) .	5a		Schedule E, Part III
b Depreciation	5b		Include on the applicable line of the appropriate tax form
c Depletion	5c		
d Amortization	5d		
6 Income for minimum tax purposes	6		
7 Income for regular tax purposes (add lines 1 through 3b, 4a, and 5a)	7		
8 Adjustment for minimum tax purposes (subtract line 7 from line 6).	8		Form 6251, line 12
9 Estate tax deduction (including certain generation-skipping transfer taxes)	9		Schedule A, line 28
10 Foreign taxes.	10		Form 1116 or Schedule A (Form 1040), line 8
11 Adjustments and tax preference items (itemize):			
a Accelerated depreciation	11a		Include on the applicable line of Form 6251
b Depletion	11b		
c Amortization	11c		
d Exclusion items	11d		1995 Form 8801
12 Deductions in the final year of trust or decedent's estate:			
a Excess deductions on termination (see instructions)	12a		Schedule A, line 22
b Short-term capital loss carryover	12b		Schedule D, line 5, column (f)
c Long-term capital loss carryover	12c		Schedule D, line 13, column (f)
d Net operating loss (NOL) carryover for regular tax purposes	12d		Form 1040, line 21
e NOL carryover for minimum tax purposes	12e		See the instructions for Form 6251, line 20
f	12f		Include on the applicable line of the appropriate tax form
g	12g		
13 Other (itemize):			
a Payments of estimated taxes credited to you . .	13a		Form 1040, line 55
b Tax-exempt interest	13b		Form 1040, line 8b
c	13c		
d	13d		Include on the applicable line of the appropriate tax form
e	13e		
f	13f		
g	13g		
h	13h		

For Paperwork Reduction Act Notice, see page 1 of the Instructions for Form 1041.   Cat. No. 11380D   **Schedule K-1 (Form 1041) 1994**

Instructions for Beneficiary Filing Form 1040

Note: *The fiduciary's instructions for completing Schedule K-1 are in the Instructions for Form 1041.*

General Instructions

Purpose of Form

The fiduciary of a trust or decedent's estate uses Schedule K-1 to report your share of the trust's or estate's income, credits, deductions, etc. **Keep it for your records. Do not file it with your tax return.** A copy has been filed with the IRS.

Tax Shelters

If you receive a copy of **Form 8271,** Investor Reporting of Tax Shelter Registration Number, see the instructions for Form 8271 to determine your reporting requirements.

Errors

If you think the fiduciary has made an error on your Schedule K-1, notify the fiduciary and ask for an amended or a corrected Schedule K-1. Do not change any items on your copy. Be sure that the fiduciary sends a copy of the amended Schedule K-1 to the IRS.

Beneficiaries of Generation-Skipping Trusts

If you received **Form 706GS(D-1),** Notification of Distribution From a Generation-Skipping Trust, and paid a generation-skipping transfer (GST) tax on **Form 706GS(D),** Generation-Skipping Transfer Tax Return for Distributions, you can deduct the GST tax paid on income distributions on Schedule A (Form 1040), line 8. To figure the deduction, see the instructions for Form 706GS(D).

Specific Instructions

Lines 3a and 3b

If there is an attachment to this Schedule K-1 reporting a disposition of a passive activity, see the instructions for **Form 8582,** Passive Activity Loss Limitations, for information on the treatment of dispositions of interests in a passive activity.

Lines 5b through 5d

The deductions on lines 5b through 5d may be subject to the passive loss limitations of Internal Revenue Code section 469, which generally limits deductions from passive activities to the income from those activities. The rules for applying these limitations to beneficiaries have not yet been issued. For more details, see **Pub. 925,** Passive Activity and At-Risk Rules.

Line 11d

If you pay alternative minimum tax in 1994, the amount on line 11d will help you figure any minimum tax credit for 1995. See the 1994 **Form 8801,** Credit for Prior Year Minimum Tax—Individuals, Estates, and Trusts, for more information.

Line 13a

To figure any underpayment and penalty on **Form 2210,** Underpayment of Estimated Tax by Individuals, Estates, and Trusts, treat the amount entered on line 13a as an estimated tax payment made on January 17, 1995.

Lines 13c through 13h

The amount of gross farming and fishing income is included on line 5a. This income is also separately stated on line 13 to help you determine if you are subject to a penalty for underpayment of estimated tax. Report the amount of gross farming and fishing income on Schedule E (Form 1040), line 41.

1994

Department of the Treasury
Internal Revenue Service

Instructions for Form 1041 and Schedules A, B, D, G, H, J, and K-1

U.S. Income Tax Return for Estates and Trusts

Section references are to the Internal Revenue Code unless otherwise noted.

Paperwork Reduction Act Notice

We ask for the information on this form to carry out the Internal Revenue laws of the United States. You are required to give us the information. We need it to ensure that you are complying with these laws and to allow us to figure and collect the right amount of tax.

The time needed to complete and file this form and related schedules will vary depending on individual circumstances. The estimated average times are:

	Form 1041	Schedule D	Schedule J	Schedule K-1
Recordkeeping	40 hr., 53 min.	16 hr., 1 min.	39 hr., 28 min.	8 hr., 22 min.
Learning about the law or the form	18 hr., 8 min.	1 hr., 41 min.	1 hr., 5 min.	1 hr., 12 min.
Preparing the form	33 hr., 34 min.	2 hr., 2 min.	1 hr., 47 min.	1 hr., 23 min.
Copying, assembling, and sending the form to the IRS	4 hr., 1 min.			

If you have comments concerning the accuracy of these time estimates or suggestions for making these forms simpler, we would be happy to hear from you. You can write to both the **Internal Revenue Service,** Attention: Tax Forms Committee, PC:FP, Washington, DC 20224; and the **Office of Management and Budget,** Paperwork Reduction Project (1545-0092), Washington, DC 20503. **DO NOT** send the tax form to either of these offices. Instead, see **Where To File** on page 3.

Contents

Changes To Note

• If an estate or trust makes a qualified cash contribution to a community development corporation selected by the Secretary of Housing and Urban Development, 5% of the contribution may be claimed as a credit for each tax year during the 10-year period beginning with the year the contribution was made. Get **Form 8847,** Credit for Contributions to Selected Community Development Corporations, for more details.

• Employers may be able to claim a credit of 20% of a limited amount of the wages and health insurance costs paid or incurred for services performed on an Indian reservation by certain enrolled members of an Indian tribe (or their spouses). Services performed in certain gaming activities or buildings housing those activities do not qualify for the credit. Get **Form 8845,** Indian Employment Credit, for details.

• Food and beverage establishments may claim a credit equal to the employer's social security and Medicare tax obligation attributable to tips in excess of those treated as wages for purposes of Federal minimum wage laws. Get **Form 8846,** Credit for Employer Social Security and Medicare Taxes Paid on Certain Employee Tips, for more details.

• Estates and trusts that have employees who lived and worked in an area designated by the Federal government as an "empowerment zone" may be able to claim the credit figured on **Form 8844,** Empowerment Zone Employment Credit.

• For tax years beginning in 1994, the filing requirement for bankruptcy estates is increased to $5,625.

Cat. No. 11372D

Form 1041.

General Instructions

Purpose of Form

The fiduciary of a domestic decedent's estate, trust, or bankruptcy estate uses Form 1041 to report: (a) the income, deductions, gains, losses, etc. of the estate or trust; (b) the income that is either accumulated or held for future distribution or distributed currently to the beneficiaries; and (c) any income tax liability of the estate or trust.

Income Taxation of Trusts and Decedents' Estates

A trust (except a grantor type trust) or a decedent's estate is a separate legal entity for Federal tax purposes. A decedent's estate comes into existence at the time of death of an individual. A trust may be created during an individual's life (inter vivos) or at the time of his or her death under a will (testamentary). If the trust instrument contains certain provisions, then the person creating the trust (the grantor) is treated as the owner of the trust's assets. Such a trust is a grantor type trust.

A trust or decedent's estate figures its gross income in much the same manner as an individual. Most deductions and credits allowed to individuals are also allowed to estates and trusts. However, there is one major distinction. A trust or decedent's estate is allowed an income distribution deduction for distributions to beneficiaries. To figure this deduction, the fiduciary must complete Schedule B. The income distribution deduction determines the amount of the distribution that is taxed to the beneficiaries.

For this reason, a trust or decedent's estate sometimes is referred to as a "pass-through" entity. The beneficiary, and not the trust or decedent's estate, pays income tax on his or her distributive share of income. Schedule K-1 (Form 1041) is used to notify the beneficiaries of the amounts to be included on their income tax returns.

Before preparing Form 1041, the fiduciary must figure the accounting income of the estate or trust under the will or trust instrument to determine the amount, if any, of income that is required to be distributed because the income distribution deduction is based, in part, on that amount.

Definitions

Beneficiary

A beneficiary is an heir, a legatee, or a devisee.

Distributable Net Income (DNI)

The income distribution deduction allowable to estates and trusts for

Page 2

amounts paid, credited, or required to be distributed to beneficiaries is limited to distributable net income (DNI). This amount, which is figured on Schedule B, line 9, is also used to determine how much of an amount paid, credited, or required to be distributed to a beneficiary will be includible in his or her gross income.

Income and Deductions in Respect of a Decedent

When completing Form 1041, you must take into account any items that are income in respect of a decedent (IRD).

In general, income in respect of a decedent is income that a decedent was entitled to receive but that was not properly includible in the decedent's final Form 1040 under the decedent's method of accounting.

IRD includes: (a) all accrued income of a decedent who reported his or her income on a cash method of accounting; (b) income accrued solely because of the decedent's death in the case of a decedent who reported his or her income on the accrual method of accounting; and (c) income to which the decedent had a contingent claim at the time of his or her death.

Some examples of IRD of a decedent who kept his or her books on a cash method are:

- Deferred salary payments that are payable to the decedent's estate.
- Uncollected interest on U.S. savings bonds.
- Proceeds from the completed sale of farm produce.
- The portion of a lump sum distribution to the beneficiary of a decedent's IRA that equals the balance in the IRA at the time of the owner's death. This includes unrealized appreciation and income accrued to that date, less the aggregate amount of the owner's nondeductible contributions to the IRA. Such amounts are included in the beneficiary's gross income in the tax year that the distribution is received.

The IRD has the same character it would have had if the decedent lived and received such amount.

The following deductions and credits, when paid by the decedent's estate, are allowed on Form 1041 even though they were not allowable on the decedent's final Form 1040:

- Business expenses deductible under section 162.
- Interest deductible under section 163.
- Taxes deductible under section 164.
- Investment expenses described in section 212 (in excess of 2% of AGI).
- Percentage depletion allowed under section 611.
- Foreign tax credit.

For more information, see section 691.

Income Required To Be Distributed Currently

Income required to be distributed currently is income that is required to be distributed in the year it is received. The fiduciary must be under a duty to distribute the income currently, even if the actual distribution is not made until after the close of the trust's tax year. See Regulations section 1.651(a)-2.

Fiduciary

A fiduciary is a trustee of a trust; or an executor, executrix, administrator, administratrix, personal representative, or person in possession of property of a decedent's estate.

Note: *Any reference in these instructions to "you" means the fiduciary of the estate or trust.*

Trust

A trust is an arrangement created either by a will or by an inter vivos declaration by which trustees take title to property for the purpose of protecting or conserving it for the beneficiaries under the ordinary rules applied in chancery or probate courts.

Who Must File

Decedent's Estate

The fiduciary (or one of the joint fiduciaries) must file Form 1041 for the estate of a domestic decedent that has:

1. Gross income for the tax year of $600 or more, or

2. A beneficiary who is a nonresident alien.

Trust

The fiduciary (or one of the joint fiduciaries) must file Form 1041 for a domestic trust taxable under section 641 that has:

1. Any taxable income for the tax year, or

2. Gross income of $600 or more (regardless of taxable income), or

3. A beneficiary who is a nonresident alien.

Two or more trusts are treated as one trust if such trusts have substantially the same grantor(s) and substantially the same primary beneficiary(ies), and a principal purpose of such trusts is avoidance of tax. This provision applies only to that portion of the trust that is attributable to contributions to corpus made after March 1, 1984.

If you are a fiduciary of a nonresident alien estate or foreign trust with U.S. source income, file **Form 1040NR, U.S. Nonresident Alien Income Tax Return.**

Bankruptcy Estate

The bankruptcy trustee or debtor-in-possession must file Form

Appendix D.   Foreign Withholding and Other Reporting

Form 1041.

1041 for the estate of an individual involved in bankruptcy proceedings under chapter 7 or 11 of title 11 of the United States Code if the estate has gross income for the tax year of $5,625 or more. See **Of Special Interest To Bankruptcy Trustees and Debtors-in-Possession** on page 5 for other details.

Qualified Settlement Funds

The trustee of a designated or qualified settlement fund should file **Form 1120-SF,** U.S. Income Tax Return for Settlement Funds. See Regulations section 1.468B-5.

Electronic Filing

Qualified tax return filers can file Form 1041 and related schedules via magnetic media (magnetic tapes, floppy diskettes) or electronically. If you file the estate's or trust's return electronically or on magnetic tape, you must also file **Form 8453-F,** U.S. Estate or Trust Income Tax Declaration and Signature for Electronic and Magnetic Media Filing. See **Pub. 1437,** Procedures for Electronic and Magnetic Media Filing of U.S. Income Tax Return for Estates and Trusts, Form 1041, for more information.

You may order Pub. 1437 and an application form to participate in the electronic filing program by calling the Magnetic Media Unit at the Philadelphia Service Center at (215) 516-7533 (not a toll-free number) or by writing to:

Internal Revenue Service
Philadelphia Service Center
ATTN: Magnetic Media Unit–DP 115
11601 Roosevelt Blvd.
Philadelphia, PA 19154

When To File

For calendar year estates and trusts, file Form 1041 and Schedules K-1 on or before April 17, 1995. For fiscal year estates and trusts, file Form 1041 by the 15th day of the 4th month following the close of the tax year. If the due date falls on a Saturday, Sunday, or legal holiday, file on the next business day. For example, an estate that has a tax year that ends on June 30, 1995, must file Form 1041 by October 16, 1995.

Extension of Time To File

Estates.—Use **Form 2758,** Application for Extension of Time To File Certain Excise, Income, Information, and Other Returns, to apply for an extension of time to file.

Trusts.—Use **Form 8736,** Application for Automatic Extension of Time To File U.S. Return for a Partnership, REMIC, or for Certain Trusts, to request an automatic 3-month extension of time to file.

If more time is needed, file **Form 8800,** Application for Additional Extension of Time To File U.S. Return for a Partnership, REMIC, or for Certain

Trusts, for an additional extension of up to 3 months. To obtain this additional extension of time to file, you must show reasonable cause for the additional time you are requesting. Form 8800 must be filed by the extended due date for Form 1041.

Period Covered

File the 1994 return for calendar year 1994 and fiscal years beginning in 1994 and ending in 1995. If the return is for a fiscal year or a short tax year, fill in the tax year space at the top of the form.

The 1994 Form 1041 may also be used for a tax year beginning in 1995 if:

1. The estate or trust has a tax year of less than 12 months that begins and ends in 1995; and

2. The 1995 Form 1041 is not available by the time the estate or trust is required to file its tax return. However, the estate or trust must show its 1995 tax year on the 1994 Form 1041 and incorporate any tax law changes that are effective for tax years beginning after December 31, 1994.

Where To File

For all estates and trusts, except charitable and split-interest trusts and pooled income funds:

If you are located in	Please mail to the following Internal Revenue Service Center
New Jersey, New York (New York City and counties of Nassau, Rockland, Suffolk, and Westchester)	Holtsville, NY 00501
New York (all other counties), Connecticut, Maine, Massachusetts, New Hampshire, Rhode Island, Vermont	Andover, MA 05501
Florida, Georgia, South Carolina	Atlanta, GA 39901
Indiana, Kentucky, Michigan, Ohio, West Virginia	Cincinnati, OH 45999
Kansas, New Mexico, Oklahoma, Texas	Austin, TX 73301
Alaska, Arizona, California (counties of Alpine, Amador, Butte, Calaveras, Colusa, Contra Costa, Del Norte, El Dorado, Glenn, Humboldt, Lake, Lassen, Marin, Mendocino, Modoc, Napa, Nevada, Placer, Plumas, Sacramento, San Joaquin, Shasta, Sierra, Siskiyou, Solano, Sonoma, Sutter, Tehama, Trinity, Yolo, and Yuba), Colorado, Idaho, Montana, Nebraska, Nevada, North Dakota, Oregon, South Dakota, Utah, Washington, Wyoming	Ogden, UT 84201
California (all other counties), Hawaii	Fresno, CA 93888

Illinois, Iowa, Minnesota, Missouri, Wisconsin	Kansas City, MO 64999
Alabama, Arkansas, Louisiana, Mississippi, North Carolina, Tennessee	Memphis, TN 37501
Delaware, District of Columbia, Maryland, Pennsylvania, Virginia, any U.S. possession, or foreign country	Philadelphia, PA 19255

For a charitable or split-interest trust described in section 4947(a) and a pooled income fund defined in section 642(c)(5):

If you are located in	Please mail to the following Internal Revenue Service Center
Alabama, Arkansas, Florida, Georgia, Louisiana, Mississippi, North Carolina, South Carolina, Tennessee	Atlanta, GA 39901
Arizona, Colorado, Kansas, New Mexico, Oklahoma, Texas, Utah, Wyoming	Austin, TX 73301
Indiana, Kentucky, Michigan, Ohio, West Virginia	Cincinnati, OH 45999
Alaska, California, Hawaii, Idaho, Nevada, Oregon, Washington	Fresno, CA 93888
Connecticut, Maine, Massachusetts, New Hampshire, New York, Rhode Island, Vermont	Holtsville, NY 00501
Illinois, Iowa, Minnesota, Missouri, Montana, Nebraska, North Dakota, South Dakota, Wisconsin	Kansas City, MO 64999
Delaware, District of Columbia, Maryland, New Jersey, Pennsylvania, Virginia, any U.S. possession, or foreign country	Philadelphia, PA 19255

Who Must Sign

The fiduciary, or an authorized representative, must sign Form 1041.

A financial institution that submitted estimated tax payments for trusts for which it is the trustee must enter its EIN in the space provided for the EIN of the fiduciary. Do not enter the EIN of the trust. For this purpose, a financial institution is one that maintains a Treasury Tax and Loan account. If you are an attorney or other individual functioning in a fiduciary capacity, leave this space blank. DO NOT enter your individual social security number (SSN).

If you, as fiduciary, fill in Form 1041, leave the Paid Preparer's space blank. If someone prepares this return and does not charge you, that person should not sign the return.

Generally, anyone who is paid to prepare a tax return must sign the return and fill in the other blanks in the Paid Preparer's Use Only area of the return.

Page 3

267

Form 1041.

The person required to sign the return must complete the required preparer information and:

● Sign it in the space provided for the preparer's signature. A facsimile signature is acceptable if certain conditions are met. See Regulations section 1.6695-1(b)(4)(iv) for details.

● Give you a copy of the return in addition to the copy to be filed with the IRS.

Accounting Methods

Figure taxable income using the method of accounting regularly used in keeping the estate's or trust's books and records. Generally, permissible methods include the cash method, the accrual method, or any other method authorized by the Internal Revenue Code. In all cases, the method used must clearly reflect income.

Generally, the estate or trust may change its accounting method (for income as a whole or for any material item) only by getting consent on **Form 3115,** Application for Change in Accounting Method. For more information, get **Pub. 538,** Accounting Periods and Methods.

Accounting Periods

For a decedent's estate, the moment of death determines the end of the decedent's tax year and the beginning of the estate's tax year. As executor or administrator, you choose the estate's tax period when you file its first income tax return. The estate's first tax year may be any period of 12 months or less that ends on the last day of a month. If you select the last day of any month other than December, you are adopting a fiscal tax year.

Generally, a trust must adopt a calendar year. The following trusts are exempt from this requirement:

● A trust that is exempt from tax under section 501(a);

● A charitable trust described in section 4947(a)(1); and

● A trust that is treated as wholly owned by a grantor under the rules of sections 671 through 679.

To change the accounting period of an estate, get **Form 1128,** Application To Adopt, Change, or Retain a Tax Year.

Rounding Off to Whole Dollars

You may show the money items on the return and accompanying schedules as whole-dollar amounts. To do so, drop amounts less than 50 cents and increase any amounts from 50 to 99 cents to the next dollar.

Estimated Tax

Generally, an estate or trust must pay estimated income tax for 1995 if it expects to owe, after subtracting any withholding and credits, at least $500 in tax, and it expects the withholding and credits to be less than the smaller of:

1. 90% of the tax shown on the 1995 tax return, or

2. 100% of the tax shown on the 1994 tax return (110% of that amount if the estate's or trust's adjusted gross income on that return is more than $150,000, and less than ⅔ of gross income for 1994 or 1995 is from farming or fishing).

However, if a return was not filed for 1994 or that return did not cover a full 12 months, item **2** does not apply.

Exceptions

Estimated tax payments are not required from:

1. An estate of a domestic decedent or a domestic trust that had no tax liability for the full 12-month 1994 tax year;

2. A decedent's estate for any tax year ending before the date that is 2 years after the decedent's death; or

3. A trust that was treated as owned by the decedent if the trust will receive the residue of the decedent's estate under the will (or if no will is admitted to probate, the trust primarily responsible for paying debts, taxes, and expenses of administration) for any tax year ending before the date that is 2 years after the decedent's death.

For more information, get **Form 1041-ES,** Estimated Income Tax for Estates and Trusts.

Section 643(g) Election

Fiduciaries of trusts that pay estimated tax may elect under section 643(g) to have any portion of their estimated tax payments allocated to any of the beneficiaries.

The fiduciary of a decedent's estate may make a section 643(g) election only for the final year of the estate.

See the instructions for line 24b for more details.

Interest and Penalties

Interest

Interest is charged on taxes not paid by the due date, even if an extension of time to file is granted.

Interest is also charged on the failure-to-file penalty, the accuracy-related penalty, and the fraud penalty. The interest charge is figured at a rate determined under section 6621.

Late Filing of Return

The law provides a penalty of 5% a month, or part of a month, up to a

maximum of 25%, for each month the return is not filed. The penalty is imposed on the net amount due. If the return is more than 60 days late, the minimum penalty is the smaller of $100 or the tax due. The penalty will not be imposed if you can show that the failure to file on time was due to reasonable cause. If the failure is due to reasonable cause, attach an explanation to the return.

Late Payment of Tax

Generally, the penalty for not paying tax when due is ½ of 1% of the unpaid amount for each month or part of a month it remains unpaid. The maximum penalty is 25% of the unpaid amount. The penalty is imposed on the net amount due. Any penalty is in addition to interest charges on late payments.

Note: If you include interest or either of these penalties with your payment, identify and enter these amounts in the bottom margin of Form 1041, page 1. Do not include the interest or penalty amount in the balance of tax due on line 27.

Failure To Supply Schedule K-1

The fiduciary must provide Schedule K-1 (Form 1041) to each beneficiary who receives a distribution of property or an allocation of an item of the estate. A penalty of $50 (not to exceed $100,000 for any calendar year) will be imposed on the fiduciary for each failure to furnish Schedule K-1 to each beneficiary unless reasonable cause for each failure is established.

Underpaid Estimated Tax

If the fiduciary underpaid estimated tax, get **Form 2210,** Underpayment of Estimated Tax by Individuals, Estates, and Trusts, to figure any penalty. Enter the amount of any penalty on line 26, Form 1041.

Other Penalties

Other penalties can be imposed for negligence, substantial underpayment of tax, and fraud. Get **Pub. 17,** Your Federal Income Tax, for details on these penalties.

Other Forms That May Be Required

Forms W-2 and **W-3,** Wage and Tax Statement; and Transmittal of Income and Tax Statements.

Form 56, Notice Concerning Fiduciary Relationship.

Form 706, United States Estate (and Generation-Skipping Transfer) Tax Return; or **Form 706-NA,** United States Estate (and Generation-Skipping Transfer) Tax Return, Estate of nonresident not a citizen of the United States.

Appendix D.   Foreign Withholding and Other Reporting

Form 1041.

Form 706GS(D), Generation-Skipping Transfer Tax Return For Distributions.

Form 706GS(D-1), Notification of Distribution From a Generation-Skipping Trust.

Form 706GS(T), Generation-Skipping Transfer Tax Return for Terminations.

Form 940 or **Form 940-EZ,** Employer's Annual Federal Unemployment (FUTA) Tax Return. The estate or trust may be liable for FUTA tax and may have to file Form 940 or 940-EZ if it paid wages of $1,500 or more in any calendar quarter during the calendar year (or the preceding calendar year) or one or more employees worked for the estate or trust for some part of a day in any 20 different weeks during the calendar year.

Form 941, Employer's Quarterly Federal Tax Return. Employers must file this form quarterly to report income tax withheld on wages and employer and employee social security and Medicare taxes. Agricultural employers must file **Form 943,** Employer's Annual Tax Return for Agricultural Employees, instead of Form 941, to report income tax withheld and employer and employee social security and Medicare taxes on farmworkers.

Caution: *A trust fund recovery penalty may apply where income, social security, and Medicare taxes that should be withheld are not withheld or are not paid to the IRS. Under this penalty, certain employees of the estate or trust become personally liable for payment of the taxes and may be penalized in an amount equal to the unpaid taxes. Get* **Circular E,** *Employer's Tax Guide (or* **Circular A,** *Agricultural Employer's Tax Guide), for more details.*

Form 945, Annual Return of Withheld Federal Income Tax. Use this form to report income tax withheld from nonpayroll payments, including pensions, annuities, IRAs, gambling winnings, and backup withholding.

Form 1040, U.S. Individual Income Tax Return.

Form 1040NR, U.S. Nonresident Alien Income Tax Return.

Form 1041-A, U.S. Information Return—Trust Accumulation of Charitable Amounts.

Forms 1042 and **1042-S,** Annual Withholding Tax Return for U.S. Source Income of Foreign Persons; and Foreign Person's U.S. Source Income Subject to Withholding. Use these forms to report and transmit withheld tax on payments or distributions made to nonresident alien individuals, foreign partnerships, or foreign corporations to the extent such payments or distributions constitute gross income from sources within the United States that is not effectively connected with a U.S. trade or business. For more information, see sections 1441 and 1442, and **Pub. 515,** Withholding of

Tax on Nonresident Aliens and Foreign Corporations.

Forms 1099-A, B, INT, MISC, OID, R, and **S.**—You may have to file these information returns to report abandonments, acquisitions through foreclosure, proceeds from broker and barter exchange transactions, interest payments, medical and dental health care payments, miscellaneous income, original issue discount, distributions from pensions, annuities, retirement or profit-sharing plans, individual retirement arrangements, insurance contracts, and proceeds from real estate transactions.

Also, use these returns to report amounts received as a nominee on behalf of another person, except amounts reported to beneficiaries on Schedule K-1 (Form 1041).

Form 8275, Disclosure Statement, is used by taxpayers and income tax return preparers to disclose items or positions, except those contrary to a regulation, that are not otherwise adequately disclosed on a tax return. The disclosure is made to avoid parts of the accuracy-related penalty imposed for disregard of rules or substantial understatement of tax. Form 8275 is also used for disclosures relating to preparer penalties for understatements due to unrealistic positions or for willful or reckless conduct.

Form 8275-R, Regulation Disclosure Statement, is used to disclose any item on a tax return for which a position has been taken that is contrary to Treasury regulations.

Forms 8288 and **8288-A,** U.S. Withholding Tax Return for Dispositions by Foreign Persons of U.S. Real Property Interests; and Statement of Withholding on Dispositions by Foreign Persons of U.S. Real Property Interests. Use these forms to report and transmit withheld tax on the sale of U.S. real property by a foreign person. Also, use these forms to report and transmit tax withheld from amounts distributed to a foreign beneficiary from a "U.S. real property interest account" that a domestic estate or trust is required to establish under Regulations section 1.1445-5(c)(1)(iii).

Form 8300, Report of Cash Payments Over $10,000 Received in a Trade or Business. Generally, this form is used to report the receipt of more than $10,000 in cash or foreign currency in one transaction (or a series of related transactions).

Attachments

If you need more space on the forms or schedules, attach separate sheets. Use the same size and format as on the printed forms. **But show the totals on the printed forms.**

Attach these separate sheets after all the schedules and forms. Enter the

estate's or trust's employer identification number on each sheet.

Do not file a copy of the decedent's will or the trust instrument unless the IRS requests it.

Additional Information

The following publications may assist you in preparing Form 1041.

Pub. 448, Federal Estate and Gift Taxes;

Pub. 550, Investment Income and Expenses; and

Pub. 559, Survivors, Executors, and Administrators.

These and other publications may be obtained at most IRS offices. To order publications and forms, call our toll-free number 1-800-TAX-FORM (1-800-829-3676).

Unresolved Tax Problems

The IRS has a Problem Resolution Program for taxpayers who have been unable to resolve their problems with the IRS. If you have a tax problem you have been unable to resolve through normal channels, write to your local IRS District Director, or call your local IRS office and ask for Problem Resolution assistance. Hearing-impaired persons who have access to TDD equipment may call 1-800-829-4059 to ask for help.

The Problem Resolution Office will ensure that your problem receives proper attention. Although the office cannot change the tax law or make technical decisions, it can help you clear up problems that resulted from previous contacts.

Of Special Interest to Bankruptcy Trustees and Debtors-in-Possession

Taxation of Bankruptcy Estates of an Individual

A bankruptcy estate is a separate taxable entity created when an individual debtor files a petition under either chapter 7 or 11 of title 11 of the U.S. Code. The estate is administered by a trustee, or a debtor-in-possession. If the case is later dismissed by the bankruptcy court, the debtor is treated as if the bankruptcy petition had never been filed. This provision does NOT apply to partnerships or corporations.

Who Must File

Every trustee (or debtor-in-possession) for an individual's bankruptcy estate under chapter 7 or 11 of title 11 of the U.S. Code must file a return if the bankruptcy estate has gross income for the tax year beginning in 1994 of $5,625 or more.

Page 5

269

Form 1041.

Failure to do so may result in an estimated Request for Administrative Expenses being filed by the IRS in the bankruptcy proceeding or a motion to compel filing of the return.

Note: *The filing of a tax return for the bankruptcy estate does not relieve the individual debtor of his or her (or their) individual tax obligations.*

Employer Identification Number (EIN)

Every bankruptcy estate of an individual required to file a return must have its own employer identification number. You may apply for one on **Form SS-4,** Application for Employer Identification Number. The social security number (SSN) of the individual debtor cannot be used as the EIN for the bankruptcy estate.

Accounting Period

A bankruptcy estate is allowed to have a fiscal year. The period can be no longer than 12 months.

When To File

File Form 1041 on or before the 15th day of the 4th month following the close of the tax year. Use Form 2758 to apply for an extension of time to file.

Disclosure of Return Information

Under section 6103(e)(5), tax returns of individual debtors who have filed for bankruptcy under chapters 7 or 11 of title 11 are, upon written request, open to inspection by or disclosure to the trustee.

The returns subject to disclosure to the trustee are those for the year the bankruptcy begins and prior years. Use **Form 4506,** Request for Copy or Transcript of Tax Form, to request copies of the individual debtor's tax returns.

If the bankruptcy case was not voluntary, disclosure cannot be made before the bankruptcy court has entered an order for relief, unless the court rules that the disclosure is needed for determining whether relief should be ordered.

Transfer of Tax Attributes From the Individual Debtor to the Bankruptcy Estate

The bankruptcy estate succeeds to the following tax attributes of the individual debtor:

1. Net operating loss (NOL) carryovers;

2. Charitable contributions carryovers;

3. Recovery of tax benefit items;

4. Credit carryovers;

5. Capital loss carryovers;

6. Basis, holding period, and character of assets;

Page 6

7. Method of accounting; and

8. Other tax attributes to the extent provided by regulations.

For bankruptcy cases beginning after November 8, 1992, the bankruptcy estate succeeds to the individual debtor's unused passive activity losses, unused passive activity credits, and unused section 465 losses. For cases beginning before November 9, 1992, the individual debtor and bankruptcy estate may jointly elect to have the estate succeed to these attributes. See Regulations sections 1.1398-1 and 1.1398-2 for more details.

Income, Deductions, and Credits

Under section 1398(c), the taxable income of the bankruptcy estate generally is computed in the same manner as an individual. The gross income of the bankruptcy estate includes any income included in property of the estate as defined in Bankruptcy Code section 541. Also included is gain from the sale of property. To compute gain, the trustee or debtor-in-possession must determine the correct basis of the property.

To determine whether any amount paid or incurred by the bankruptcy estate is allowable as a deduction or credit, or is treated as wages for employment tax purposes, treat the amount as if it were paid or incurred by the individual debtor in the same trade or business or other activity the debtor engaged in before the bankruptcy proceedings began.

Administrative expenses.—The bankruptcy estate is allowed a deduction for any administrative expense allowed under section 503 of title 11 of the U.S. Code, and any fee or charge assessed under chapter 123 of title 28 of the U.S. Code, to the extent not disallowed under an Internal Revenue Code provision (e.g., section 263, 265, or 275).

Administrative expense loss.—When figuring a net operating loss, nonbusiness deductions (including administrative expenses) are limited under section 172(d)(4) to the bankruptcy estate's nonbusiness income. The excess nonbusiness deductions are an administrative expense loss that may be carried back to each of the 3 preceding tax years and forward to each of the 7 succeeding tax years of the bankruptcy estate. The amount of an administrative expense loss that may be carried to any tax year is determined after the net operating loss deductions allowed for that year. An administrative expense loss is allowed only to the bankruptcy estate and cannot be carried to any tax year of the individual debtor.

Carryback of net operating losses and credits.—If the bankruptcy estate itself incurs a net operating loss (apart from

losses carried forward to the estate from the individual debtor), it can carry back its net operating losses not only to previous tax years of the bankruptcy estate, but also to tax years of the individual debtor prior to the year in which the bankruptcy proceedings began. Excess credits, such as the foreign tax credit, also may be carried back to pre-bankruptcy years of the individual debtor.

Exemption.—For tax years beginning in 1994, a bankruptcy estate is allowed a personal exemption of $2,450.

Standard deduction.—For tax years beginning in 1994, a bankruptcy estate that does not itemize deductions is allowed a standard deduction of $3,175.

Discharge of indebtedness.—In a title 11 case, gross income does not include amounts that normally would be included in gross income resulting from the discharge of indebtedness. However, any amounts excluded from gross income must be applied to reduce certain tax attributes in a certain order. Attach **Form 982,** Reduction of Tax Attributes Due to Discharge of Indebtedness, to show the reduction of tax attributes.

Tax Rate Schedule

Figure the tax for the bankruptcy estate using the tax rate schedule shown below. Enter the tax on Form 1040, line 38.

If taxable income is:

Over—	But not over—	The tax is:	Of the amount over—
$0	$19,000	15%	$0
19,000	45,925	$2,850.00 + 28%	19,000
45,925	70,000	10,389.00 + 31%	45,925
70,000	125,000	17,852.25 + 36%	70,000
125,000	- - - - -	37,652.25 + 39.6%	125,000

Prompt Determination of Tax Liability

To request a prompt determination of the tax liability of the bankruptcy estate, the trustee or debtor-in-possession must file a written application for the determination with the IRS District Director for the district in which the bankruptcy case is pending. The application must be submitted in duplicate and executed under the penalties of perjury. The trustee or debtor-in-possession must submit with the application an exact *copy* of the return (or returns) filed by the trustee with the IRS for a completed tax period, and a statement of the name and location of the office where the return was filed. The envelope should be marked, "Personal Attention of the Special Procedures Function (Bankruptcy Section). DO NOT OPEN IN MAILROOM."

The IRS will notify the trustee or debtor-in-possession within 60 days from receipt of the application whether

Appendix D.   Foreign Withholding and Other Reporting

Form 1041.

the return filed by the trustee or debtor-in-possession has been selected for examination or has been accepted as filed. If the return is selected for examination, it will be examined as soon as possible. The IRS will notify the trustee or debtor-in-possession of any tax due within 180 days from receipt of the application or within any additional time permitted by the bankruptcy court.

See Rev. Proc. 81-17, 1981-1 C.B. 688.

Special Filing Instructions for Bankruptcy Estates

Use Form 1041 only as a transmittal for Form 1040. In the top margin of Form 1040 write "Attachment to Form 1041. DO NOT DETACH." Attach Form 1040 to Form 1041. Complete only the identification area at the top of Form 1041. Enter the name of the individual debtor in the following format: "John Q. Public Bankruptcy Estate." Beneath, enter the name of the trustee in the following format: "Avery Snow, Trustee." In item D, enter the date the petition was filed or the date of conversion to a chapter 7 or 11 case. Enter on Form 1041, line 23, any tax due from line 53 of Form 1040. Sign and date Form 1041.

Specific Instructions

Name of Estate or Trust

Copy the exact name of the estate or trust from the **Form SS-4,** Application for Employer Identification Number, that you used to apply for the employer identification number.

If a grantor type trust (discussed below), write the name, identification number, and address of the grantor(s) or other person(s) in parentheses after the name of the trust.

Address

Include the suite, room, or other unit number after the street address.

If the Post Office does not deliver mail to the street address and the fiduciary has a P.O. box, show the box number instead of the street address.

If you change your address after filing Form 1041, use **Form 8822,** Change of Address, to notify the IRS.

A. Type of Entity

Check the appropriate box that describes the entity for which you are filing the return.

Note: *There are special filing requirements for grantor type trusts and bankruptcy estates (discussed below).*

Decedent's Estate

An estate of a deceased person is a taxable entity separate from the decedent. It generally continues to exist until the final distribution of the assets of the estate is made to the heirs and other beneficiaries. The income earned from the property of the estate during the period of administration or settlement must be accounted for and reported by the estate.

Simple Trust

A trust may qualify as a simple trust if:

1. The trust instrument requires that all income must be distributed currently;

2. The trust instrument does not provide that any amounts are to be paid, permanently set aside, or used for charitable purposes; and

3. The trust does not distribute amounts allocated to the corpus of the trust.

Complex Trust

A complex trust is any trust that does not qualify as a simple trust as explained above.

Grantor Type Trust

A grantor type trust is a legal trust under applicable state law that is not recognized as a separate taxable entity for income tax purposes because the grantor or other substantial owners have not relinquished complete dominion and control over the trust.

Generally, for transfers made in trust after March 1, 1986, the grantor is treated as the owner of any portion of a trust in which he or she has a reversionary interest in either the income or corpus therefrom, if, as of the inception of that portion of the trust, the value of that interest is more than 5% of the value of that portion. Further, the grantor is treated as holding any power or interest that was held by either the grantor's spouse at the time that the power or interest was created or who became the grantor's spouse after the creation of that power or interest.

Report on Form 1041 the part of the income that is taxable to the trust. Do not report on Form 1041 the income that is taxable to the grantor or another person. Instead, attach a separate sheet to report the following:

● The income of the trust that is taxable to the grantor or another person under sections 671 through 678;

● The name, identifying number, and address of the person(s) to whom the income is taxable; and

● Any deductions or credits applied to this income.

The income taxable to the grantor or another person under sections 671 through 678 and the deductions and credits applied to the income must be

reported on the income tax return that person files.

Family estate trust.—A family estate trust is also known as a family, family estate, pure, equity, equity pure, prime, or constitutional trust.

In most cases, the grantor transfers property to the trust or assigns to the trust the income for services the grantor performs. The trust instrument usually provides:

● Evidence of ownership, such as certificates of beneficial interest in the trust.

● That the grantor is a trustee and executive officer.

● That the trust pays the living expenses for the grantor and the grantor's family.

● That the corpus and undistributed income are distributed to the owners after the trust is terminated.

Generally, a family estate trust is treated as a grantor type trust. For more information, see Rev. Rul. 75-257, 1975-2 C.B. 251.

Mortgage pools.—The trustee of a mortgage pool, such as the Federal National Mortgage Association, collects principal and interest payments on each mortgage and makes distributions to the certificate holders. Each pool is considered a grantor type trust, and each certificate holder is treated as the owner of an undivided interest in the entire trust under the grantor trust rules. Certificate holders must report their proportionate share of the mortgage interest and other items of income on their individual tax returns.

Pre-need funeral trusts.—The purchasers of pre-need funeral services are the grantors and the owners of pre-need funeral trusts established under state laws. See Rev. Rul. 87-127, 1987-2 C.B. 156.

Nonqualified deferred compensation plans.—Taxpayers may adopt and maintain grantor trusts in connection with nonqualified deferred compensation plans (sometimes referred to as "rabbi trusts"). Rev. Proc. 92-64, 1992-2 C.B. 422, provides a "model grantor trust" for use in rabbi trust arrangements. The procedure also provides guidance for requesting rulings on the plans that use these trusts.

Simplified filing requirement for certain grantor type trusts.—The grantor/trustee for a trust described below that was created in a tax year beginning on or after January 1, 1981, should not file Form 1041 and therefore will not need an EIN for the trust. The grantor/trustee must furnish his or her social security number (SSN) to payers of income and report all items of income, deduction, and credit from the trust on his or her Form 1040.

This special rule applies to certain revocable trusts that are located in the

Form 1041.

United States and have all assets located in the United States if:

- The same individual is both grantor and trustee (or co-trustee) of the trust; and

- The individual is treated as owner of all trust assets under section 676 (power to revoke) for the tax year.

These rules also apply to certain other revocable trusts in which:

- A husband and wife are the sole grantors;

- One spouse is trustee or co-trustee with a third party or both spouses are trustees or co-trustees with a third party;

- One or both spouses are treated as owners of all trust assets under section 676 (power to revoke) for the tax year; and

- The husband and wife file a joint income tax return for the tax year.

Grantor trusts created in tax years beginning before 1981.—The grantor/trustee for a trust described above who has previously filed Form 1041 can take advantage of the simplified reporting requirements in the future by filing a Form 1041 for the current year, writing on it "Pursuant to section 1.671-4(b), this is the final return for this grantor trust," and checking the "Final return" box.

A grantor/trustee who chooses this option must furnish his or her SSN to payers of income for the next year and report the trust income on his or her Form 1040 for the next tax year and for future years. The grantor/trustee must not file Form 1041 for future years.

Backup withholding.—Generally, a grantor trust is considered a payor of reportable payments received by the trust for purposes of backup withholding. If the trust has 10 or fewer grantors, a reportable payment made to the trust is treated as a reportable payment of the same kind made to the grantors on the date the trust received the payment. If the trust has more than 10 grantors, a reportable payment made to the trust is treated as a payment of the same kind made by the trust to each grantor in an amount equal to the distribution made to each grantor on the date the grantor is paid or credited. The trustee is required to withhold 31% of reportable payments made to any grantor who is subject to backup withholding. For more information, see section 3406 and Temporary Regulations section 35a.9999-2, Q&A 20.

Bankruptcy Estate

A chapter 7 or 11 bankruptcy estate is a separate and distinct taxable entity from the individual debtor for Federal income tax purposes. See **Of Special Interest to Bankruptcy Trustees and Debtors-in-Possession** on page 5.

For more information, see section 1398 and **Pub. 908,** Tax Information on Bankruptcy.

Pooled Income Fund

A pooled income fund is a split-interest trust with a remainder interest for a public charity and a life income interest retained by the donor or for another person. The property is held in a pool with other pooled income fund property and does not include any tax-exempt securities. The income for a retained life interest is figured using the yearly rate of return earned by the trust. See section 642(c) and the related regulations for more information.

If you are filing for a pooled income fund, attach a statement to support the following:

- The calculation of the yearly rate of return.

- The computation of the deduction for distributions to the beneficiaries.

- The computation of any charitable deduction.

You do not have to complete Schedules A or B of Form 1041.

If the fund has accumulations of income, file Form 1041-A unless the fund is required to distribute all of its net income to beneficiaries currently.

You must also file **Form 5227,** Split-Interest Trust Information Return, for the pooled income fund.

B. Number of Schedules K-1 Attached

Every trust or decedent's estate claiming an income distribution deduction on page 1, line 18, must enter the number of Schedules K-1 (Form 1041) that are attached to Form 1041.

C. Employer Identification Number (EIN)

Every estate or trust must have an employer identification number (EIN). To apply for one, use Form SS-4. You may get this form from the IRS or the Social Security Administration. See **Pub. 583,** Taxpayers Starting a Business, for more information.

If you are filing a return for a mortgage pool, such as one created under the mortgage-backed security programs administered by the Federal National Mortgage Association ("Fannie Mae") or the Government National Mortgage Association ("Ginnie Mae"), the EIN stays with the pool if that pool is traded from one financial institution to another.

D. Date Entity Created

Enter the date the trust was created, or, if a decedent's estate, the date of the decedent's death.

E. Nonexempt Charitable and Split-Interest Trusts

Section 4947(a)(1) Trust

Check this box if the trust is a nonexempt charitable trust within the meaning of section 4947(a)(1). A nonexempt charitable trust is a trust that is not exempt from tax under section 501(a); all of the unexpired interests are devoted to one or more charitable purposes described in section 170(c)(2)(B); and for which a deduction was allowed under section 170 (for individual taxpayers) or similar Code section for personal holding companies, foreign personal holding companies, or estates or trusts (including a deduction for estate or gift tax purposes).

Not a Private Foundation

Check this box if the charitable trust is not treated as a private foundation under section 509. For more information, see Regulations section 53.4947-1.

If a nonexempt charitable trust is not treated as though it were a private foundation, the fiduciary must file **Form 990 (or Form 990-EZ),** Return of Organization Exempt From Income Tax, and **Schedule A (Form 990),** Organization Exempt Under Section 501(c)(3), in addition to Form 1041 if the trust's gross receipts are normally more than $25,000.

If a nonexempt charitable trust is not treated as though it were a private foundation, and it has no taxable income under Subtitle A, it can file either Form 990 or Form 990-EZ instead of Form 1041 to meet its section 6012 filing requirement.

Section 4947(a)(2) Trust

Check this box if the trust is a split-interest trust described in section 4947(a)(2). A split-interest trust is a trust that is not exempt from tax under section 501(a); has some unexpired interests that are devoted to purposes other than religious, charitable, or similar purposes described in section 170(c)(2)(B); and has amounts transferred in trust after May 26, 1969, for which a deduction was allowed under section 170 (for individual taxpayers) or similar Code section for personal holding companies, foreign personal holding companies, or estates or trusts (including a deduction for estate or gift tax purposes).

The fiduciary of a split-interest trust must also file Form 5227 (for amounts transferred in trust after May 26, 1969); and Form 1041-A if the trust's governing instrument does not require that all of the trust's income be distributed currently.

If a split-interest trust has any unrelated business taxable income,

Page 8

Appendix D. Foreign Withholding and Other Reporting

Form 1041.

however, it must file Form 1041 to report all of its income and to pay any tax due.

Nonexempt Charitable Trust Treated as a Private Foundation

If a nonexempt charitable trust is treated as though it were a private foundation under section 509, then the fiduciary must file **Form 990-PF**, Return of Private Foundation, in addition to Form 1041.

If a nonexempt charitable trust is subject to any of the private foundation excise taxes, then it must also file **Form 4720**, Return of Certain Excise Taxes on Charities and Other Persons Under Chapters 41 and 42 of the Internal Revenue Code. Any private foundation taxes paid by the trust cannot be taken as a deduction on Form 1041.

If a nonexempt charitable trust is treated as though it were a private foundation, and it has no taxable income under Subtitle A, it may file Form 990-PF instead of Form 1041 to meet its section 6012 filing requirement.

F. Initial Return, Amended Return, Final Return; or Change in Fiduciary's Name or Address

Amended Return

If you are filing an amended Form 1041, check the "Amended return" box. Complete the entire return, correct the appropriate line(s) with the new information, and refigure the estate's or trust's tax liability. On an attached sheet explain the reason for the amendment(s) and identify the line(s) and amount(s) being changed on the amended return.

If the amended return results in a change to income, or a change in distribution of any income or other information provided to a beneficiary, an amended Schedule K-1 (Form 1041) must also be filed with the amended Form 1041 and given to each beneficiary. Check the "Amended K-1" box at the top of the amended Schedule K-1.

Final Return

Check this box if this is a final return because the estate or trust has terminated. Also, check the "Final K-1" box at the top of Schedule K-1.

If there is an unused capital loss carryover, net operating loss carryover, or excess deductions on the final return, see the discussion in the Schedule K-1 instructions on page 28. Figure the deductions on an attached sheet.

G. Pooled Mortgage Account

If you bought a pooled mortgage account during the year, and still have that pool at the end of the tax year, check the "Bought" box and enter the date of purchase.

If you sold a pooled mortgage account that was purchased during this, or a previous, tax year, check the "Sold" box and enter the date of sale.

If you neither bought nor sold a pooled mortgage account, skip this item.

Income

Special Rule for Blind Trust

If you are reporting income from a qualified blind trust (under the Ethics in Government Act of 1978), do not identify the payer of any income to the trust but complete the rest of the return as provided in the instructions. Also write "Blind Trust" at the top of page 1.

Line 1—Interest Income

Report the estate's or trust's share of all taxable interest income that was received during the tax year. Examples of taxable interest include interest from:
- Accounts (including certificates of deposit and money market accounts) with banks, credit unions, and thrifts.
- Notes, loans, and mortgages.
- U.S. Treasury bills, notes, and bonds.
- U.S. savings bonds.
- Original issue discount.
- Income received as a regular interest holder of a real estate mortgage investment conduit (REMIC).

For taxable bonds acquired after 1987, amortizable bond premium is treated as an offset to the interest income instead of as a separate interest deduction. See Pub. 550.

For the year of the decedent's death, Forms 1099-INT issued in the decedent's name may include interest income earned after the date of death that should be reported on the income tax return of the decedent's estate. When preparing the decedent's final income tax return, report on line 1 of Schedule B (Form 1040) or Schedule 1 (Form 1040A) the total interest shown on Form 1099-INT. Under the last entry on line 1, subtotal all the interest reported on line 1. Below the subtotal, write "Form 1041" and the name and address shown on Form 1041 for the decedent's estate. Also, show the part of the interest reported on Form 1041 and subtract it from the subtotal.

Line 2—Dividends

Report the estate's or trust's share of all ordinary dividends received during the tax year.

For the year of the decedent's death, Forms 1099-DIV issued in the decedent's name may include dividends earned after the date of death that should be reported on the income tax return of the decedent's estate. When preparing the decedent's final income tax return, report on line 5 of Schedule B (Form 1040) or Schedule 1 (Form 1040A) the total dividends shown on Form 1099-DIV. Under the last entry on line 5, subtotal all the dividends reported on line 5. Below the subtotal, write "Form 1041" and the name and address shown on Form 1041 for the decedent's estate. Also, show the part of the dividends reported on Form 1041 and subtract it from the subtotal.

Note: *Report capital gain distributions on Schedule D (Form 1041), line 10.*

Line 3—Business Income or (Loss)

If the estate or trust operated a business, report the income and expenses on **Schedule C (Form 1040)**, Profit or Loss From Business (or **Schedule C-EZ (Form 1040)**, Net Profit From Business). Enter the net profit or (loss) from Schedule C (or Schedule C-EZ) on line 3.

Line 4—Capital Gain or (Loss)

Enter the gain from Schedule D (Form 1041), Part III, line 17, column (c); or the loss from Part IV, line 18.

Note: *Do not substitute Schedule D (Form 1040) for Schedule D (Form 1041).*

Line 5—Rents, Royalties, Partnerships, Other Estates and Trusts, etc.

Use **Schedule E (Form 1040)**, Supplemental Income and Loss, to report the estate's or trust's share of income or (losses) from rents, royalties, partnerships, S corporations, other estates and trusts, and REMICs. Enter the net profit or (loss) from Schedule E on line 5. See the instructions for Schedule E (Form 1040) for reporting requirements.

If the estate or trust received a Schedule K-1 from a partnership, S corporation, or other flow-through entity, use the corresponding lines on Form 1041 to report the interest, dividends, capital gains, etc., from the flow-through entity.

Line 6—Farm Income or (Loss)

If the estate or trust operated a farm, use **Schedule F (Form 1040)**, Profit or Loss From Farming, to report farm income and expenses. Enter the net profit or (loss) from Schedule F on line 6.

Line 7—Ordinary Gain or (Loss)

Enter from line 20, **Form 4797**, Sales of Business Property, the ordinary gain or loss from the sale or exchange of property other than capital assets and also from involuntary conversions (other than casualty or theft).

Line 8—Other Income

Enter other items of income not included on lines 1 through 7. List the type and amount on an attached schedule if the estate or trust has more than one item.

Page 9

273

Form 1041.

Items to be reported on line 8 include:

• Unpaid compensation received by the decedent's estate that is income in respect of a decedent.

• Any part of a total distribution shown on **Form 1099-R**, Distributions From Pensions, Annuities, Retirement or Profit-Sharing Plans, IRAs, Insurance Contracts, etc., that is treated as ordinary income. For more information, see the separate instructions for **Form 4972**, Tax on Lump-Sum Distributions.

Deductions

Amortization, Depletion, and Depreciation

A trust or decedent's estate is allowed a deduction for amortization, depletion, and depreciation only to the extent the deductions are not apportioned to the beneficiaries.

For a decedent's estate, the depreciation deduction is apportioned between the estate and the heirs, legatees, and devisees on the basis of the estate's income allocable to each.

For a trust, the depreciation deduction is apportioned between the income beneficiaries and the trust on the basis of the trust income allocable to each, unless the governing instrument (or local law) requires or permits the trustee to maintain a depreciation reserve. If the trustee is required to maintain a reserve, the deduction is first allocated to the trust, up to the amount of the reserve. Any excess is allocated among the beneficiaries in the same manner as the trust's accounting income. See Regulations section 1.167(h)-1(b).

For mineral or timber property held by a decedent's estate, the depletion deduction is apportioned between the estate and the heirs, legatees, and devisees on the basis of the estate's income from such property allocable to each.

For mineral or timber property held in trust, the depletion deduction is apportioned between the income beneficiaries and the trust based on the trust income from such property allocable to each, unless the governing instrument (or local law) requires or permits the trustee to maintain a reserve for depletion. If the trustee is required to maintain a reserve, the deduction is first allocated to the trust, up to the amount of the reserve. Any excess is allocated among the beneficiaries in the same manner as the trust's accounting income. See Regulations section 1.611-1(c)(4).

The deduction for amortization is apportioned between an estate or trust and its beneficiaries under the same principles for apportioning the deductions for depreciation and depletion.

An estate or trust is not allowed to make an election under section 179 to expense certain tangible property.

The deduction for the amortization of reforestation expenditures under section 194 is allowed only to an estate.

The estate's or trust's share of amortization, depletion, and depreciation should be reported on the appropriate lines of Schedule C (or C-EZ), E, or F (Form 1040), the net income or loss from which is shown on line 3, 5, or 6 of Form 1041. If the deduction is not related to a specific business or activity, then report it on line 15a.

Allocation of Deductions for Tax-Exempt Income

Generally, no deduction that would otherwise be allowable is allowed for any expense (whether for business or for the production of income) that is allocable to tax-exempt income. Examples of tax-exempt income include:

• Certain death benefits (section 101);

• Interest on state or local bonds (section 103);

• Compensation for injuries or sickness (section 104); and

• Income from discharge of indebtedness in a title 11 case (section 108).

Exception. State income taxes and business expenses that are allocable to tax-exempt interest are deductible.

Expenses that are directly allocable to tax-exempt income are allocated only to tax-exempt income. A reasonable proportion of expenses indirectly allocable to both tax-exempt income and other income must be allocated to each class of income.

Deductions That May Be Allowable for Estate Tax Purposes

Administration expenses and casualty and theft losses deductible on Form 706 may be deducted, to the extent otherwise deductible for income tax purposes, on Form 1041 if the fiduciary files a statement waiving the right to deduct the expenses and losses on Form 706. The statement must be filed before the expiration of the statutory period of limitations for the tax year the deduction is claimed. See Pub. 559 for more information.

Accrued Expenses

Generally, an accrual basis taxpayer can deduct accrued expenses in the tax year that: **(a)** all events have occurred that determine the liability; and **(b)** the amount of the liability can be figured with reasonable accuracy. However, all the events that establish liability are treated as occurring only when economic performance takes place. There are exceptions for recurring items. See section 461(h).

Limitations on Deductions

At-Risk Loss Limitations

Generally, the amount the estate or trust has "at risk" limits the loss it can deduct for any tax year. Use **Form 6198**, At-Risk Limitations, to figure the deductible loss for the year and file it with Form 1041. For more information, get **Pub. 925**, Passive Activity and At-Risk Rules.

Passive Activity Loss and Credit Limitations

Section 469 and the regulations thereunder generally limit losses from passive activities to the amount of income derived from all passive activities. Similarly, credits from passive activities are generally limited to the tax attributable to such activities. These limitations are first applied at the estate or trust level.

Generally, an activity is a passive activity if it involves the conduct of any trade or business, and the taxpayer does not materially participate in the activity. Passive activities do not include working interests in oil and gas properties. See section 469(c)(3).

For a grantor trust, material participation is determined at the grantor level.

Generally, rental activities are passive activities, whether or not the taxpayer materially participates. However, certain taxpayers who materially participate in real property trades or businesses are not subject to the passive activity limitations on losses from rental real estate activities in which they materially participate. For more details, see section 469(c)(7).

Note: *Material participation standards for estates and trusts had not been established by regulations at the time these instructions went to print.*

For tax years of an estate ending less than 2 years after the decedent's date of death, up to $25,000 of deductions and deduction equivalents of credits from rental real estate activities in which the decedent actively participated is allowed. Any excess losses and/or credits are suspended for the year and carried forward.

If the estate or trust distributes an interest in a passive activity, the basis of the property immediately before the distribution is increased by the passive activity losses allocable to the interest; and such losses cannot be deducted. See section 469(j)(12).

Note: *Losses from passive activities are first subject to the at-risk rules. When the losses are deductible under the at-risk rules, the passive activity rules then apply.*

Portfolio income is not treated as income from a passive activity, and passive losses and credits generally may

Appendix D. Foreign Withholding and Other Reporting

Form 1041.

not be applied to offset it. Portfolio income generally includes interest, dividends, royalties, and income from annuities. Portfolio income of an estate or trust must be accounted for separately. See **Form 8582,** Passive Activity Loss Limitations, to figure the amount of losses allowed from passive activities. See **Form 8582-CR,** Passive Activity Credit Limitations, to compute the amount of credit allowed for the current year.

Transactions Between Related Taxpayers

Under section 267, a trust that uses the accrual method of accounting may only deduct business expenses and interest owed to a related party in the year the payment is included in the income of the related party. For this purpose, a related party includes:

1. A grantor and a fiduciary of any trust;

2. A fiduciary of a trust and a fiduciary of another trust, if the same person is a grantor of both trusts;

3. A fiduciary of a trust and a beneficiary of such trust;

4. A fiduciary of a trust and a beneficiary of another trust, if the same person is a grantor of both trusts; and

5. A fiduciary of a trust and a corporation more than 50% in value of the outstanding stock of which is owned, directly or indirectly, by or for the trust or by or for a person who is a grantor of the trust.

Line 10—Interest

Enter the amount of interest (subject to limitations) paid or incurred by the estate or trust on amounts borrowed by the estate or trust, or on debt acquired by the estate or trust (e.g., outstanding obligations from the decedent) that is not claimed elsewhere on the return.

If the proceeds of a loan were used for more than one purpose (e.g., to purchase a portfolio investment and to acquire an interest in a passive activity), the fiduciary must make an interest allocation according to the rules in Temporary Regulations section 1.163-8T.

Do not include interest paid on indebtedness incurred or continued to purchase or carry obligations on which the interest is wholly exempt from income tax.

Personal interest is not deductible. Examples of personal interest include interest paid on:

● Revolving charge accounts.

● Personal notes for money borrowed from a bank, credit union, or other person.

● Installment loans on personal use property.

● Underpayments of Federal, state, or local income taxes.

Interest that is paid or incurred on indebtedness allocable to a trade or business (including a rental activity) should be deducted on the appropriate line of Schedule C (or C-EZ), E, or F (Form 1040), the net income or loss from which is shown on line 3, 5, or 6 of Form 1041.

Types of interest to include on line 10 are:

1. Any investment interest (subject to limitations);

2. Any qualified residence interest; and

3. Any interest payable under section 6601 on any unpaid portion of the estate tax attributable to the value of a reversionary or remainder interest in property, or an interest in a closely held business for the period during which an extension of time for payment of such tax is in effect.

Investment interest.—Generally, investment interest is interest (including amortizable bond premium on taxable bonds acquired after October 22, 1986, but before January 1, 1988) that is paid or incurred on indebtedness that is properly allocable to property held for investment. Investment interest does not include any qualified residence interest, or interest that is taken into account under section 469 in computing income or loss from a passive activity.

Generally, net investment income is the excess of investment income over investment expenses. Investment expenses are those expenses (other than interest) allowable after application of the 2% floor on miscellaneous itemized deductions.

The amount of the investment interest deduction may be limited. Use **Form 4952,** Investment Interest Expense Deduction, to figure the allowable investment interest deduction.

If Form 4952 is required to be completed, check the box on line 10 and attach Form 4952. Then add the deductible investment interest to the other types of deductible interest and enter the total on line 10.

Qualified residence interest.—Interest paid or incurred by an estate or trust on indebtedness secured by a qualified residence of a beneficiary of an estate or trust is treated as qualified residence interest if the residence would be a qualified residence (i.e., the principal residence or the second residence selected by the beneficiary) if owned by the beneficiary. The beneficiary must have a present interest in the estate or trust or an interest in the residuary of the estate or trust. See **Pub. 936,** Home Mortgage Interest Deduction, for an explanation of the general rules for deducting home mortgage interest.

See section 163(h)(3) for a definition of qualified residence interest and for limitations on indebtedness.

Line 11—Taxes

Enter any deductible taxes paid or incurred during the tax year that are not deductible elsewhere on Form 1041.

Deductible taxes include:

● State and local income or real property taxes.

● The generation-skipping transfer (GST) tax imposed on income distributions.

Do not deduct:

● Federal income taxes.

● Estate, inheritance, legacy, succession, and gift taxes.

● Federal duties and excise taxes.

● State and local sales taxes. Instead, treat these taxes as part of the cost of the property.

Line 12—Fiduciary Fees

Enter the deductible fees paid or incurred to the fiduciary for administering the estate or trust during the tax year.

Note: *Fiduciary fees deducted on Form 706 cannot be deducted on Form 1041.*

Line 15a—Other Deductions NOT Subject to the 2% Floor

Attach your own schedule, listing by type and amount, all allowable deductions that are not deductible elsewhere on Form 1041.

Do not include any losses on worthless bonds and similar obligations and nonbusiness bad debts. Report these losses on Schedule D (Form 1041).

Do not deduct medical or funeral expenses on Form 1041. Medical expenses of the decedent paid by the estate may be deductible on the decedent's income tax return for the year incurred. See section 213(c). Funeral expenses are deductible ONLY on Form 706.

The following are examples of deductions that are reported on line 15a.

Bond premium(s).—For taxable bonds acquired before October 23, 1986, if the fiduciary elected to amortize the premium, report the amortization on this line. For tax-exempt bonds, the amortization cannot be deducted. In all cases where the fiduciary has made an election to amortize the premium, the basis must be reduced by the amount of amortization.

For more information, see section 171 and Pub. 550.

If you claim a bond premium deduction for the estate or trust, figure the deduction on a separate sheet and attach it to Form 1041.

Casualty and theft losses.—Use **Form 4684,** Casualties and Thefts, to figure any deductible casualty and theft losses.

Deduction for clean-fuel vehicles.—Section 179A allows a deduction for part

Page 11

275

Form 1041.

of the cost of qualified clean-fuel vehicle property. Get **Pub. 535,** Business Expenses, for more details.

Net operating loss deduction (NOLD).—An estate or trust is allowed the net operating loss deduction (NOLD) under section 172.

If you claim an NOLD for the estate or trust, figure the deduction on a separate sheet and attach it to this return.

Estate's or trust's share of amortization, depreciation, and depletion not claimed elsewhere.—If you cannot deduct the amortization, depreciation, and depletion as rent or royalty expenses on Schedule E (Form 1040), or as business or farm expenses on Schedule C, C-EZ, or F (Form 1040), itemize the fiduciary's share of the deductions on an attached sheet. Then include them on line 15a. Itemize each beneficiary's share of the deductions and report them on the appropriate line of Schedule K-1 (Form 1041).

Line 15b—Allowable Miscellaneous Itemized Deductions Subject to the 2% Floor

Miscellaneous itemized deductions are deductible only to the extent that the aggregate amount of such deductions exceeds 2% of adjusted gross income (AGI).

Miscellaneous itemized deductions do not include deductions for:

- Interest under section 163.
- Taxes under section 164.
- The amortization of bond premium under section 171.
- Estate taxes attributable to income in respect of a decedent under section 691(c).

For other exceptions, see section 67(b).

For estates and trusts, the AGI is computed by subtracting the following from total income on line 9 of page 1:

1. The administration costs of the estate or trust (the total of lines 12, 14, and 15a to the extent they are costs incurred in the administration of the estate or trust) that would not have been incurred if the property were NOT held by the estate or trust;

2. The income distribution deduction (line 18);

3. The amount of the exemption (line 20);

4. The deduction for clean-fuel vehicles claimed on line 15a; and

5. The net operating loss deduction claimed on line 15a.

For those estates and trusts whose income distribution deduction is limited to the actual distribution, and NOT the DNI (i.e., the income distribution is less than the DNI), when computing the AGI,

use the amount of the actual distribution.

For those estates and trusts whose income distribution deduction is limited to the DNI (i.e., the actual distribution exceeds the DNI), the DNI must be figured taking into account the allowable miscellaneous itemized deductions (AMID) after application of the 2% floor. In this situation there are two unknown amounts: **(a)** the AMID; and **(b)** the DNI.

The following example illustrates how an algebraic equation can be used to solve for these unknown amounts:

The Malcolm Smith Trust, a complex trust, earned $20,000 of dividend income, $20,000 of capital gains, and a fully deductible $5,000 loss from XYZ partnership (chargeable to corpus) in 1994. The trust instrument provides that capital gains are added to corpus. 50% of the fiduciary fees are allocated to income and 50% to corpus. The trust claimed a $2,000 deduction on line 12 of Form 1041. The trust incurred $1,500 of miscellaneous itemized deductions (chargeable to income), which are subject to the 2% floor. There are no other deductions. The trustee made a discretionary distribution of the accounting income of $17,500 to the trust's sole beneficiary.

Because the actual distribution can reasonably be expected to exceed the DNI, the trust must compute the DNI, taking into account the allowable miscellaneous itemized deductions, to determine the amount to enter on line 15b.

The trust also claims an exemption of $100 on line 20.

To compute line 15b, use the equation below:

AMID = total miscellaneous itemized deductions − (.02(AGI))

In the above example:

AMID = 1,500 − (.02(AGI))

In all situations, use the following equation to compute the AGI:

AGI = (line 9) − (the total of lines 12, 14, and 15a to the extent they are costs incurred in the administration of the estate or trust that would not have been incurred if the property were NOT held by the estate or trust) − (line 18) − (line 20) Note: *There are no other deductions claimed by the trust on line 15a that are deductible in arriving at AGI.*

In the above example:

AGI = 35,000 − 2,000 − DNI − 100

Since the value of line 18 is not known because it is limited to the DNI, you are left with the following:

AGI = 32,900 − DNI

Substitute the value of AGI in the equation:

AMID = 1,500 − (.02(32,900 − DNI))

The equation cannot be solved until the value of DNI is known. The DNI can

be expressed in terms of the AMID. To do this, compute the DNI using the known values. In this example, the DNI is equal to the total income of the trust (less any capital gains allocated to corpus; or plus any capital loss from line 4); less total deductions from line 16 (excluding any miscellaneous itemized deductions); less the AMID.

Thus, DNI = (line 9) − (line 17, column (b) of Schedule D (Form 1041)) − (line 16) − (AMID)

Substitute the known values:

DNI = 35,000 − 20,000 − 2,000 − AMID

DNI = 13,000 − AMID

Substitute the value of DNI in the equation to solve for AMID:

AMID = 1,500 − (.02(32,900 − (13,000 − AMID)))

AMID = 1,500 − (.02(32,900 − 13,000 + AMID))

AMID = 1,500 − (658 − 260 + .02 AMID)

AMID = 1,102 − .02AMID

1.02AMID = 1,102

AMID = 1,080

DNI = 11,920 (i.e., 13,000 − 1,080)

AGI = 20,980 (i.e., 32,900 − 11,920)

Note: *The income distribution deduction is equal to the smaller of the distribution ($17,500) or the DNI ($11,920).*

Enter the value of AMID on line 15b (the DNI should equal line 9 of Schedule B) and complete the rest of Form 1041 according to the instructions.

If the 2% floor is more than the deductions subject to the 2% floor, no deductions are allowed.

Line 18—Income Distribution Deduction

If the estate or trust was required to distribute income currently or if it paid, credited, or was required to distribute any other amounts to beneficiaries during the tax year, complete Schedule B to determine the estate's or trust's income distribution deduction. However, if you are filing for a pooled income fund, do not complete Schedule B. Instead, attach a statement to support the computation of the income distribution deduction. If the estate or trust claims an income distribution deduction, complete and attach:

- Parts I and II of Schedule H to refigure the deduction on a minimum tax basis; AND

- Schedule K-1 (Form 1041) for each beneficiary to which a distribution was made or required to be made.

Cemetery perpetual care fund.—On line 18, deduct the amount, not more than $5 per gravesite, paid for maintenance of cemetery property. To the right of the entry space for line 18, enter the number of gravesites. Also write "Section 642(i) trust" in

Page 12

Appendix D.   Foreign Withholding and Other Reporting

Form 1041.

parentheses after the trust's name at the top of Form 1041. You do not have to complete Schedules B of Form 1041 and K-1 (Form 1041).

Line 19—Estate Tax Deduction (Including Certain Generation-Skipping Transfer Taxes)

If the estate or trust includes income in respect of a decedent (IRD) in its gross income, and such amount was included in the decedent's gross estate for estate tax purposes, the estate or trust is allowed to deduct in the same tax year that portion of the estate tax imposed on the decedent's estate that is attributable to the inclusion of the IRD in the decedent's estate. For an example of the computation, see Regulations section 1.691(c)-1 and Pub. 559.

If any amount properly paid, credited, or required to be distributed by an estate or trust to a beneficiary consists of IRD received by the estate or trust, do not include such amounts in determining the estate tax deduction for the estate or trust. Figure the deduction on a separate sheet. Attach the sheet to your return. Also, a deduction is allowed for the GST tax imposed as a result of a taxable termination, or a direct skip occurring as a result of the death of the transferor. See section 691(c)(3). Enter the estate's or trust's share of these deductions on line 19.

Line 20—Exemption

Decedent's estates.—A decedent's estate is allowed a $600 exemption.

Trusts.—A trust whose governing instrument requires that all income be distributed currently is allowed a $300 exemption, even if it distributed amounts other than income during the tax year. All other trusts are allowed a $100 exemption. See Regulations section 1.642(b)-1.

Tax and Payments

Line 22—Taxable Income

Net operating loss.—If line 22 is a loss, the estate or trust may have a net operating loss (NOL). Do not include the deductions claimed on lines 13, 18, and 20 when figuring the amount of the NOL. An NOL generally may be carried back to the 3 prior tax years and forward to the following 15 tax years. Complete Schedule A of **Form 1045,** Application for Tentative Refund, to figure the amount of the NOL that is available for carryback or carryover. Use Form 1045 or file an amended return to apply for a refund based on an NOL carryback. For more information, get **Pub. 536,** Net Operating Losses. On the termination of the estate or trust, any unused NOL carryover that would be allowable to the estate or trust in a later tax year, but for the termination, is allowed to the beneficiaries succeeding

to the property of the estate or trust. See the instructions for Schedule K-1, lines 12d and 12e.

Excess deductions on termination.—If the estate or trust has for its final year deductions (excluding the charitable deduction and exemption) in excess of its gross income, the excess is allowed as an itemized deduction to the beneficiaries succeeding to the property of the estate or trust. However, an unused NOL carryover that is allowed to beneficiaries (as explained in the above paragraph) cannot also be treated as an excess deduction. If the final year of the estate or trust is also the last year of the NOL carryover period, the NOL carryover not absorbed in that tax year by the estate or trust is included as an excess deduction. See the instructions for Schedule K-1, line 12a.

Line 24a—1994 Estimated Tax Payments and Amount Applied From 1993 Return

Enter the amount of any estimated tax payment you made with Form 1041-ES for 1994 plus the amount of any overpayment from the 1993 return that was applied to the 1994 estimated tax.

If the estate or trust is the beneficiary of another trust, and received a payment of estimated tax that was credited to the trust (as reflected on the Schedule K-1 issued to the trust), then report this amount separately with the notation "section 643(g)" in the space next to line 24a.

Note: *Do not include on Form 1041 estimated tax paid by an individual before death. Instead, include the payments on the decedent's final Form 1040.*

Line 24b—Estimated Tax Payments Allocated to Beneficiaries

The trustee (or executor, for the final year of the estate) may elect under section 643(g) to have any portion of its estimated tax treated as a payment of estimated tax made by a beneficiary or beneficiaries. The election is made on **Form 1041-T,** Allocation of Estimated Tax Payments to Beneficiaries, which must be filed by the 65th day after the close of the trust's tax year. Form 1041-T shows the amounts to be allocated to each beneficiary. This amount is reported on the beneficiary's Schedule K-1, line 13a.

Failure to file Form 1041-T by the due date (March 6, 1995, for calendar year estates and trusts) will result in an invalid election. An invalid election will require the filing of amended Schedules K-1 for each beneficiary who was allocated a payment of estimated tax. Be sure to attach Form 1041-T to your return ONLY if you have not yet filed it. If

you have already filed Form 1041-T, do not attach a copy to your return.

Line 24d—Tax Paid With Extension of Time To File

If you filed either Form 2758 (for estates only), Form 8736, or Form 8800 to request an extension of time to file Form 1041, enter the amount that you paid with the extension request and check the appropriate box(es).

Line 24e—Federal Income Tax Withheld

Use line 24e to claim a credit for any Federal income tax withheld (and not repaid) by: **(a)** an employer on wages and salaries of a decedent received by the decedent's estate; **(b)** a payer of certain gambling winnings (e.g., state lottery winnings); or **(c)** a payer of distributions from pensions, annuities, retirement or profit-sharing plans, IRAs, insurance contracts, etc., received by a decedent's estate or trust. Attach a copy of **Form W-2, Form W-2G,** or **Form 1099-R.**

Backup withholding.—If the estate or trust received a 1994 Form 1099 showing Federal income tax withheld (i.e., backup withholding) on interest income, dividends, or other income, check the box and include the amount withheld on income retained by the estate or trust in the total for line 24e.

Report on Schedule K-1 (Form 1041), line 13, any credit for backup withholding on income distributed to the beneficiary.

Line 24f—Credit From Regulated Investment Companies

Attach copy B of **Form 2439,** Notice to Shareholder of Undistributed Long-Term Capital Gains.

Line 24g—Credit for Federal Tax on Fuels

Include any credit for Federal excise taxes paid on fuels that are ultimately used for nontaxable purposes (e.g., an off-highway business use) and any credit for the purchase of a diesel-powered car, van, or light truck. Attach **Form 4136,** Credit for Federal Tax Paid on Fuels. Get **Pub. 378,** Fuel Tax Credits and Refunds, for more information.

Line 26—Underpayment of Estimated Tax

If line 27 is at least $500 and more than 10% of the tax shown on Form 1041, or the estate or trust underpaid its 1994 estimated tax liability for any payment period, it may owe a penalty. See Form 2210 to determine whether the estate or trust owes a penalty, and to figure the amount of the penalty.

Note: *The penalty may be waived under certain conditions. Get Pub. 505, Tax*

Page 13

277

Form 1041.

Withholding and Estimated Tax, for details.

Line 27—Tax Due

You must pay the tax in full when the return is filed. Make the check or money order payable to "Internal Revenue Service." Write the EIN and "1994 Form 1041" on the payment. Enclose, but do not attach, the payment with Form 1041.

Line 29a—Credit to 1995 Estimated Tax

Enter the amount from line 28 that you want applied to the estate's or trust's 1995 estimated tax.

Schedule A—Charitable Deduction

General Instructions

Generally, any part of the gross income of an estate or trust (other than a simple trust) that, under the terms of the will or governing instrument, is paid (or treated as paid) during the tax year for a charitable purpose specified in section 170(c) is allowed as a deduction to the estate or trust. It is not necessary that the charitable organization be created or organized in the United States.

Trusts that claim a charitable deduction must also file Form 1041-A. See Form 1041-A for exceptions.

A pooled income fund, nonexempt private foundation, or trust with unrelated business income should attach a separate sheet to Form 1041 instead of using Schedule A of Form 1041 to figure the charitable deduction.

Election to treat contributions as paid in the prior tax year.—The fiduciary of an estate or trust may elect to treat as paid during the tax year any amount of gross income received during that tax year or any prior tax year that was paid in the next tax year for a charitable purpose.

To make the election, the fiduciary must file a statement with Form 1041 for the tax year in which the contribution is treated as paid. This statement must include:

1. The name and address of the fiduciary;

2. The name of the estate or trust;

3. An indication that the fiduciary is making an election under section 642(c)(1) for contributions treated as paid during such tax year;

4. The name and address of each organization to which any such contribution is paid; and

5. The amount of each contribution and date of actual payment or, if applicable, the total amount of contributions paid to each organization

during the next tax year, to be treated as paid in the prior tax year.

The election must be filed by the due date (including extensions) for Form 1041 for the next tax year.

For more information about the charitable deduction, see section 642(c) and related regulations.

Specific Instructions

Line 1—Amounts Paid for Charitable Purposes From Gross Income

Enter amounts that were paid for a charitable purpose out of the estate's or trust's gross income, including any capital gains that are attributable to income under the governing instrument or local law. Include amounts paid during the tax year from gross income received in a prior tax year, but only if no deduction was allowed for any prior tax year for these amounts. Do not include any capital gains for the tax year allocated to corpus and paid or permanently set aside for charitable purposes. Instead, enter these amounts on line 6.

Line 2—Amounts Permanently Set Aside for Charitable Purposes From Gross Income

Estates, and certain trusts, may claim a deduction for amounts permanently set aside for a charitable purpose from gross income. Such amounts must be permanently set aside during the tax year or be used exclusively for religious, charitable, scientific, literary, or educational purposes, or for the prevention of cruelty to children or animals, or for the establishment, acquisition, maintenance, or operation of a public cemetery not operated for profit.

For a trust to qualify, the trust may not be a simple trust, and the set aside amounts must be required by the terms of a trust instrument that was created on or before October 9, 1969.

Further, the trust instrument must provide for an irrevocable remainder interest to be transferred to or for the use of an organization described in section 170(c); OR the trust must have been created by a grantor who was at all times after October 9, 1969, under a mental disability to change the terms of the trust.

Also, certain testamentary trusts that were established by a will that was executed on or before October 9, 1969, may qualify. See Regulations section 1.642(c)-2(b).

Do not include any capital gains for the tax year allocated to corpus and paid or permanently set aside for charitable purposes. Instead, enter these amounts on line 6.

Line 4—Tax-Exempt Income Allocable to Charitable Contributions

Any estate or trust that pays or sets aside any part of its income for a charitable purpose must reduce the deduction by the portion allocable to any tax-exempt income. If the governing instrument specifically provides as to the source from which amounts are paid, permanently set aside, or to be used for charitable purposes, the specific provisions control. In all other cases, determine the amount of tax-exempt income allocable to charitable contributions by multiplying line 3 by a fraction, the numerator of which is the total tax-exempt income of the estate or trust; and the denominator of which is the gross income of the estate or trust. Do not include in the denominator any losses allocated to corpus.

Line 6—Capital Gains for the Tax Year Allocated to Corpus and Paid or Permanently Set Aside for Charitable Purposes

Enter the total of all capital gains for the tax year that are:

● Allocated to corpus; and

● Paid or permanently set aside for charitable purposes.

Schedule B—Income Distribution Deduction

General Instructions

If the estate or trust was required to distribute income currently or if it paid, credited, or was required to distribute any other amounts to beneficiaries during the tax year, complete Schedule B to determine the estate's or trust's income distribution deduction. However, if you are filing for a pooled income fund, do not complete Schedule B. Instead, attach a statement to support the computation of the income distribution deduction.

Note: *Use Schedule H to compute the DNI and income distribution deduction on a minimum tax basis.*

Separate share rule.—If a single trust has more than one beneficiary, and if different beneficiaries have substantially separate and independent shares, their shares are treated as separate trusts for the sole purpose of determining the DNI allocable to the respective beneficiaries. If the separate share rule applies, figure the DNI allocable to each beneficiary on a separate sheet and attach the sheet to this return. Any deduction or loss that is applicable solely to one separate share of the trust is not available to any other share of the same trust. For more information, see section 663(c) and related regulations.

Appendix D. Foreign Withholding and Other Reporting

Form 1041.

Specific Instructions

Line 1—Adjusted Total Income

If the amount on line 17 of page 1 is a loss that is attributable wholly or in part to the capital loss limitation rules under section 1211(b) (line 4), then enter as a negative amount on line 1, Schedule B, the smaller of the loss from line 17 on page 1, or the loss from line 4 on page 1. If the line 17 loss is not attributable to the capital loss on line 4, enter zero.

If you are filing for a simple trust, subtract from adjusted total income any extraordinary dividends or taxable stock dividends included on page 1, line 2, and determined under the governing instrument and applicable local law to be allocable to corpus.

Line 2—Adjusted Tax-Exempt Interest

To figure the adjusted tax-exempt interest:

Step 1. Add tax-exempt interest income on line 4 of Schedule A, any expenses allowable under section 212 allocable to tax-exempt interest, and any interest expense allocable to tax-exempt interest.

Step 2. Subtract the Step 1 total from the amount of tax-exempt interest (including exempt-interest dividends) received.

Section 212 expenses that are directly allocable to tax-exempt interest are allocated only to tax-exempt interest. A reasonable proportion of section 212 expenses that are indirectly allocable to both tax-exempt interest and other income must be allocated to each class of income.

Figure the interest expense allocable to tax-exempt interest according to the guidelines in Rev. Proc. 72-18, 1972-1 C.B. 740.

See Regulations sections 1.643(a)-5 and 1.265-1 for more information.

Line 3

Include all capital gains, whether or not they are distributed, that are attributable to income under the governing instrument or local law. For example, if the trustee distributed 50% of the current year's capital gains to the income beneficiaries (and reflects this amount in column (a), line 17 of Schedule D (Form 1041)), but under the governing instrument all capital gains are attributable to income, then include 100% of the capital gains on line 3. If the amount on Schedule D (Form 1041), line 17, column (a) is a net loss, enter zero.

Line 5

In figuring the amount of long-term capital gain for the tax year included on Schedule A, line 3, the specific provisions of the governing instrument control if the instrument specifically provides as to the source from which amounts are paid, permanently set aside, or to be used for charitable purposes. In all other cases, determine the amount to enter by multiplying line 3 of Schedule A by a fraction, the numerator of which is the amount of long-term capital gains that are included in the accounting income of the estate or trust (i.e., not allocated to corpus) AND are distributed to charities, and the denominator of which is all items of income (including the amount of such long-term capital gains) included in the DNI.

Line 6

Figure line 6 in a similar manner as line 5.

Line 10—Accounting Income

If you are filing for a decedent's estate or a simple trust, skip this line. If you are filing for a complex trust, enter the income for the tax year determined under the terms of the governing instrument and applicable local law. Do not include extraordinary dividends or taxable stock dividends determined under the governing instrument and applicable local law to be allocable to corpus.

Lines 11 and 12

Do not include any:

• Amounts deducted on prior year's return that were required to be distributed in the prior year.

• Amount that is properly paid or credited as a gift or bequest of a specific amount of money or specific property. (To qualify as a gift or bequest, the amount must be paid in three or fewer installments.) An amount that can be paid or credited only from income is not considered a gift or bequest.

• Amount paid or permanently set aside for charitable purposes or otherwise qualifying for the charitable deduction.

Line 11—Income Required To Be Distributed Currently

Line 11 is to be completed by all simple trusts as well as complex trusts, and decedent's estates, that are required to distribute income currently, whether it is distributed or not. The determination of whether trust income is required to be distributed currently depends upon the terms of the governing instrument and the applicable local law.

The line 11 distributions are referred to as first tier distributions and are deductible by the estate or trust to the extent of the DNI. The beneficiary includes such amounts in his or her income to the extent of his or her proportionate share of the DNI.

Line 12—Other Amounts Paid, Credited, or Otherwise Required To Be Distributed

Line 12 is to be completed ONLY by a decedent's estate or complex trust. These distributions consist of any other amounts paid, credited, or required to be distributed and are referred to as second tier distributions. Such amounts include annuities to the extent not paid out of income, discretionary distributions of corpus, and distributions of property in kind.

If Form 1041-T was filed to elect to treat estimated tax payments as made by a beneficiary, the payments are treated as paid or credited to the beneficiary on the last day of the tax year and must be included on line 12.

Unless a section 643(e)(3) election is made, the value of all noncash property actually paid, credited, or required to be distributed to any beneficiaries is the smaller of:

1. The estate's or trust's adjusted basis in the property immediately before distribution, plus minus any loss recognized by the estate or trust on the distribution (basis of beneficiary), or

2. The fair market value (FMV) of such property.

If a section 643(e)(3) election is made by the fiduciary, then the amount entered on line 12 will be the FMV of the property.

A fiduciary of a complex trust may elect to treat any amount paid or credited to a beneficiary within 65 days following the close of the tax year as being paid or credited on the last day of that tax year. To make this election, see the instructions for Question 6 on page 17.

The beneficiary includes the amounts on line 12 in his or her income only to the extent of his or her proportionate share of the DNI.

Complex trusts.—If the second tier distributions exceed the DNI allocable to the second tier, the trust may have an accumulation distribution. See the line 13 instructions below.

Line 13—Total Distributions

If line 13 is more than line 10 and you are filing for a complex trust, complete **Schedule J (Form 1041)** and file it with Form 1041 unless the trust has no previously accumulated income.

Line 14—Adjustment for Tax-Exempt Income

In computing the income distribution deduction, the estate or trust is not allowed a deduction for any item of the DNI that is not included in the gross income of the estate or trust. Thus, for purposes of computing the allowable income distribution deduction, the DNI (line 9) is computed without regard to any tax-exempt interest.

Page 15

Form 1041.

If tax-exempt interest is the only tax-exempt income included in the total distributions (line 13), and the DNI (line 9) is less than or equal to line 13, then enter on line 14 the amount from line 2.

If tax-exempt interest is the only tax-exempt income included in the total distributions (line 13), and the DNI is more than line 13 (i.e., the estate or trust made a distribution that is less than the DNI), then compute the adjustment by multiplying line 2 by a fraction, the numerator of which is the total distributions (line 13), and the denominator of which is the DNI (line 9). Enter the result on line 14.

If line 13 includes tax-exempt income other than tax-exempt interest, figure line 14 by subtracting the total of the following from tax-exempt income included in line 13:

1. The charitable contribution deduction allocable to such tax-exempt income, and

2. Expenses allocable to tax-exempt income.

Expenses that are directly allocable to tax-exempt income are allocated only to tax-exempt income. A reasonable proportion of expenses indirectly allocable to both tax-exempt income and other income must be allocated to each class of income.

Line 17—Income Distribution Deduction

The income distribution deduction determines the amount of income that will be taxed to the beneficiaries. The total amount of income for regular tax purposes that is reflected on line 7 of the individual beneficiaries' Schedules K-1 should equal the amount claimed on line 17.

Schedule G—Tax Computation

Line 1a

Tax rate schedule.—For tax years beginning in 1994, figure the tax using the Tax Rate Schedule below. Enter the tax on line 1a and check the "Tax Rate Schedule" box.

1994 Tax Rate Schedule

If the amount on
line 22, page 1, is:

Over—	But not over—	Enter on line 1a:	Of the amount over—
$0	$1,500	15%	$0
1,500	3,600	$225 + 28%	1,500
3,600	5,500	813 + 31%	3,600
5,500	7,500	1,402 + 36%	5,500
7,500	- - - - -	2,122 + 39.6%	7,500

Schedule D.—If the estate or trust had a net capital gain and taxable income of more than $3,600, complete Part VI of

Schedule D (Form 1041), enter the tax from line 45 of Schedule D, and check the "Schedule D" box.

Line 1b

Other taxes.—Include any additional tax from the following:

● **Form 4970,** Tax on Accumulation Distribution of Trusts.

● **Form 4972,** Tax on Lump-Sum Distributions.

● Section 644 tax on trusts.

Section 644 tax.—If the trust sells or exchanges property at a gain within 2 years after receiving it from a transferor, a section 644 tax may be due. The tax may be due if both **1** and **2** below apply:

1. There is an includible gain (defined below) recognized by the trust; and

2. At the time the trust received the property, the property had an FMV higher than its adjusted basis.

The trustee is authorized by section 6103(e)(1)(A)(ii) to inspect the transferor's income tax return to the extent necessary to figure the section 644 tax if the transferor refuses to make a disclosure to the trustee.

Includible gain is the smaller of **1** or **2** below:

1. The gain recognized by the trust on the sale or exchange of the property; or

2. The amount by which the FMV of the property at the time of the initial transfer to the trust exceeds the adjusted basis of the property immediately after the transfer.

Figure the tax on the includible gain by subtracting the transferor's actual tax for the tax year of the sale or exchange from the transferor's tax for the year of the sale or exchange refigured to include the includible gain minus any deductions allocable to the gain.

See section 644 for additional information, including character rules, special rules, exceptions, installment sale rules, and the interest due on the tax if the transferor and the trust have different tax years.

If the section 644 tax is the only tax due on line 1b, enter the amount of the tax on line 1b and write "Section 644 tax" to the left of the amount column on line 1b. If there is more than one tax, include the amount of the section 644 tax in the total tax entered on line 1b.

Attach the section 644 tax computation to the return. When figuring the trust's taxable income, exclude the amount of any includible gain minus any deductions allocable to the gain.

Line 2a—Foreign Tax Credit

Attach **Form 1116,** Foreign Tax Credit (Individual, Estate, Trust, or Nonresident Alien Individual), if you elect to claim credit for income or profits taxes paid or accrued to a foreign country or a U.S. possession. The estate or trust may

claim credit for that part of the foreign taxes not allocable to the beneficiaries (including charitable beneficiaries). Enter the estate's or trust's share of the credit on line 2a. See **Pub. 514,** Foreign Tax Credit for Individuals, for details.

Line 2b—Nonconventional Source Fuel Credit

If the estate or trust can claim any section 29 credit for producing fuel from a nonconventional source, figure the credit on a separate sheet and attach it to the return. Include the credit on line 2b.

Qualified Electric Vehicle Credit

Use **Form 8834,** Qualified Electric Vehicle Credit, if the estate or trust can claim a credit for the purchase of a new qualified electric vehicle. Include the credit on line 2b.

Line 2c—General Business Credit

Complete this line if the estate or trust is claiming any of the credits listed below. Use the appropriate credit form to figure the credit. If the estate or trust is claiming only one credit, enter the form number and the amount of the credit in the space provided.

If the estate or trust is claiming more than one credit (not including the empowerment zone employment credit), a credit from a passive activity (other than the low-income housing credit or the empowerment zone employment credit), or a credit carryforward, also complete **Form 3800,** General Business Credit, to figure the total credit and enter the amount from Form 3800 on line 2c. Also, be sure to check the box for Form 3800.

Do not include any amounts that are allocated to a beneficiary. Credits that are allocated between the estate or trust and the beneficiaries are listed in the instructions for Schedule K-1, line 13, on page 28. Generally, these credits are apportioned on the basis of the income allocable to the estate or trust and the beneficiaries.

● Investment credit (Form 3468).

● Jobs credit (Form 5884).

● Credit for alcohol used as fuel (Form 6478).

● Credit for increasing research activities and orphan drug credit (Form 6765).

● Low-income housing credit (Form 8586).

● Disabled access credit (Form 8826).

● Enhanced oil recovery credit (Form 8830).

● Renewable electricity production credit (Form 8835).

● Empowerment zone employment credit (Form 8844).

● Indian employment credit (Form 8845).

Page 16

Appendix D. Foreign Withholding and Other Reporting

Form 1041.

- Credit for employer social security and Medicare taxes paid on certain employee tips (Form 8846).
- Credit for contributions to selected community development corporations (Form 8847).

Line 2d—Credit for Prior Year Minimum Tax

An estate or trust that paid alternative minimum tax in a previous year, may be eligible for a minimum tax credit in 1994. See **Form 8801**, Credit for Prior Year Minimum Tax—Individuals, Estates, and Trusts.

Line 5—Recapture Taxes

Recapture of investment credit.—If the estate or trust disposed of investment credit property or changed its use before the end of its useful life or recovery period, get **Form 4255**, Recapture of Investment Credit, to figure the recapture tax allocable to the estate or trust.

Recapture of low-income housing credit.—If the estate or trust disposed of property (or there was a reduction in the qualified basis of the property) on which the low-income housing credit was claimed, get **Form 8611**, Recapture of Low-Income Housing Credit, to figure any recapture tax allocable to the estate or trust.

Recapture of qualified electric vehicle credit.—If the estate or trust claimed the qualified electric vehicle credit in a prior tax year for a vehicle that ceased to qualify for the credit, part or all of the credit may have to be recaptured. See Pub. 535 for details. If the estate or trust owes any recapture tax, include it on line 5 and write "QEV" on the dotted line to the left of the entry space.

Line 7—Total Tax

Interest on tax deferred under the installment method for certain nondealer real property installment obligations.—If an obligation arising from the disposition of real property to which section 453A applies is outstanding at the close of the year, the estate or trust must include the interest due under section 453A(c) in the amount to be entered on line 7 of Schedule G, Form 1041, with the notation "Section 453A(c) interest." Attach a schedule showing the computation.

Form 8697, Interest Computation Under the Look-Back Method for Completed Long-Term Contracts.—Include the interest due under the look-back method of section 460(b)(2). To the left of the entry space, write "From Form 8697" and the amount of interest due.

Form 5329, Additional Taxes Attributable to Qualified Retirement Plans (Including IRAs), Annuities, and Modified Endowment Contracts.—If the estate or trust fails to receive the minimum distribution under section 4974, use Form 5329 to pay the excise tax. To the left of the entry space, write "From Form 5329" and the amount of the tax.

Other Information

Question 1

If the estate or trust received tax-exempt income, figure the allocation of expenses between tax-exempt and taxable income on a separate sheet and attach it to the return. Enter only the deductible amounts on the return. Do not figure the allocation on the return itself. For more information, see the instructions for **Allocation of Deductions for Tax-Exempt Income** on page 10.

Report the amount of tax-exempt interest income received or accrued in the space provided below Question 1.

Also, include any exempt-interest dividends the estate or trust received as a shareholder in a mutual fund or other regulated investment company.

Question 2

All salaries, wages, and other compensation for personal services must be included on the return of the person who earned the income, even if the income was irrevocably assigned to a trust by a contract assignment or similar arrangement.

The grantor or person creating the trust is considered the owner if he or she keeps "beneficial enjoyment" of or substantial control over the trust property. The trust's income, deductions, and credits are allocable to the owner.

If you checked "Yes" for Question 2, see the **Grantor Type Trust** instructions on page 7.

Question 3

Check the "Yes" box and enter the name of the foreign country if either 1 or 2 below applies.

1. At any time during the year the estate or trust had an interest in or signature or other authority over a bank, securities, or other financial account in a foreign country.

Exception. Check "No" if either of the following applies to the estate or trust:

- The combined value of the accounts was $10,000 or less during the whole year; OR
- The accounts were with a U.S. military banking facility operated by a U.S. financial institution.

2. The estate or trust owns more than 50% of the stock in any corporation that owns one or more foreign bank accounts.

Get **Form TD F 90-22.1**, Report of Foreign Bank and Financial Accounts, to see if the estate or trust is considered to have an interest in or signature or other authority over a bank, securities, or other financial account in a foreign country.

If you checked "Yes" for Question 3, file Form TD F 90-22.1 by June 30, 1995, with the Department of the Treasury at the address shown on the form. Form TD F 90-22.1 is not a tax return, so do not file it with Form 1041.

You may order Form TD F 90-22.1 by calling our toll-free number, 1-800-829-3676.

Question 4

An estate or trust that transferred property to a foreign corporation, foreign estate or trust, or foreign partnership must file **Form 926**, Return by a U.S. Transferor of Property to a Foreign Corporation, Foreign Estate or Trust, or Foreign Partnership, even if the transfer is nontaxable. Form 926 is also used to pay any excise tax due under section 1491.

Form 3520, Creation of or Transfers to Certain Foreign Trusts, is used by the grantor of an inter vivos trust, the fiduciary of a testamentary trust, or the transferor, to meet the reporting requirements under section 6048 with respect to transfers of money or property to a foreign trust, or the creation of a foreign trust.

Form 3520-A, Annual Return of Foreign Trust With U.S. Beneficiaries, must be filed under section 6048(c) by any U.S. person who directly or indirectly transfers property to a foreign trust (with certain exceptions) that has one or more U.S. beneficiaries.

Question 5

An estate or trust claiming an interest deduction for qualified residence interest (as defined in section 163(h)(3)) on seller-provided financing, must include on an attachment to the 1994 Form 1041 the name, address, and taxpayer identifying number of the person to whom the interest was paid or accrued (i.e., the seller).

If the estate or trust received or accrued such interest, it must provide identical information on the person liable for such interest (i.e., the buyer). This information does not need to be reported if it duplicates information already reported on Form 1098.

Question 6

To make the section 663(b) election for a complex trust to treat any amount paid or credited to a beneficiary within 65 days following the close of the tax year as being paid or credited on the last day of that tax year, check the box. For the election to be valid, you must file Form 1041 by the due date (including

Form 1041.

extensions). Once made, the election is irrevocable.

Question 7

To make the section 643(e)(3) election to recognize gain on property distributed in kind, check the box and see the Instructions for Schedule D (Form 1041).

Question 8

If the decedent's estate has been open for more than 2 years, check the box and attach an explanation for the delay in closing the estate.

Schedule H—Alternative Minimum Tax

Changes To Note

● For tax years beginning after 1993, any reference to the adjusted gross income (AGI) of the estate or trust for purposes of figuring alternative minimum taxable income is treated as a reference to AGI as figured for regular tax purposes.

● The limit on the benefit of the exclusion of the preference for intangible drilling costs has been increased from 30% to 40% of alternative minimum taxable income with certain adjustments. See the instructions for line 4t.

● Distributions the estate or trust received from a cooperative may be includible in income. Unless the distributions are nontaxable, the estate or trust must include on line 4u the total AMT patronage dividend and per-unit retain allocation adjustment reported by the cooperative.

General Instructions

Use Schedule H to compute:

1. The estate's or trust's alternative minimum taxable income;

2. The income distribution deduction on a minimum tax basis; and

3. The estate's or trust's alternative minimum tax (AMT).

Who Must Complete

● Complete Schedule H, Parts I and II, if the decedent's estate or trust is required to complete Schedule B.

● Complete Schedule H, Parts I and III, if the decedent's estate's or trust's share of alternative minimum taxable income (Part I, line 12) exceeds $22,500.

Recordkeeping

Schedule H contains adjustments and tax preference items that are treated differently for regular tax and AMT purposes. If you, as fiduciary for the estate or trust, completed a form to figure an item for regular tax purposes, you may have to complete it a second time for AMT purposes. Generally, the

Page 18

difference between the amounts on the two forms is the AMT adjustment or tax preference item to enter on Schedule H. Except for Form 1116, any additional form completed for AMT purposes does not have to be filed with Form 1041.

For regular tax purposes, some deductions and credits may result in carrybacks or carryforwards to other tax years. Examples are: investment interest expense; a net operating loss deduction; a capital loss; and the foreign tax credit. Because these items may be refigured for the AMT, the carryback or carryforward amount may be different for regular and AMT purposes. Therefore, you should keep records of these different carryforward and carryback amounts for the AMT and regular tax. The AMT carryforward will be important in completing Schedule H for 1995.

Credit for Prior Year Minimum Tax

Estates and trusts that paid alternative minimum tax in 1993, or had a minimum tax credit carryforward, may be eligible for a minimum tax credit in 1994. See Form 8801.

Partners, Shareholders, etc.

An estate or trust that is a partner in a partnership or a shareholder in an S corporation must take into account its share of items of income and deductions that enter into the computation of its adjustments and tax preference items.

Allocation of Deductions to Beneficiaries

The distributable net alternative minimum taxable income (DNAMTI) of the estate or trust does not include amounts of depreciation, depletion, and amortization that are allocated to the beneficiaries, just as the distributable net income (DNI) of the estate or trust does not include these items for regular tax purposes.

Report separately on line 11 of Schedule K-1 (Form 1041) any adjustments or tax preference items attributable to depreciation, depletion, and amortization that were allocated to the beneficiaries.

Optional Write-Off Period Under Section 59(e)

The estate or trust may elect under section 59(e) to use an optional 10-year (60-month for intangible drilling and development expenditures and 3-year for circulation expenditures) write-off period for certain adjustments and tax preference items. If this election is made, the optional write-off period is used for regular tax purposes and there is no AMT adjustment. This election can be made for the following items:

● Circulation expenditures (section 173).

● Research and experimental expenditures (section 174).

● Intangible drilling and development expenditures (section 263(c)).

● Development expenditures for mines and natural deposits (section 616).

● Mining exploration expenditures (section 617(a)).

The election must be made in the year the expenditure was made and may be revoked only with IRS consent. See section 59(e) for more details.

Specific Instructions

Part I—Estate's or Trust's Share of Alternative Minimum Taxable Income

Line 1—Adjusted Total Income or (Loss)

Enter the amount from line 17 of page 1. If the adjusted total income includes the amount of the alcohol fuel credit as required under section 87, reduce the adjusted total income by the credit included in income.

Line 2—Net Operating Loss Deduction

Enter any net operating loss deduction (NOLD) from line 15a of page 1 as a positive amount.

Line 4a—Interest

In determining the alternative minimum taxable income, qualified residence interest (other than qualified housing interest defined in section 56(e)) is not allowed.

If you completed Form 4952 for regular tax purposes, you may have an adjustment on this line. Refigure your investment interest expense on another Form 4952 as follows:

Step 1. On line 1 of Form 4952, add any interest expense allocable to specified private activity bonds issued after August 7, 1986, to the other interest expense. For a definition of "specified private activity bonds," see the instructions for line 4p.

Step 2. On line 2, enter the AMT disallowed investment interest expense from 1993.

Step 3. When completing Part II of Form 4952, refigure gross income from property held for investment, any net gain from the disposition of property held for investment, and any investment expenses, taking into account all AMT adjustments and tax preference items that apply. Include any interest income and investment expenses from private activity bonds issued after August 7, 1986.

To figure the adjustment for line 4a, subtract the total interest allowable for AMT purposes from the interest deduction claimed on line 10 of page 1. If the total interest expense allowed for AMT purposes is more than that allowed for regular tax purposes, enter the

Form 1041.

difference as a negative amount on line 4a.

Line 4b—Taxes

Enter any state, local, or foreign real property taxes; state or local personal property taxes; and state, local, or foreign income taxes that were included on line 11 of page 1.

Line 4d—Refund of Taxes

Enter any refunds received in 1994 of taxes described for line 4b above that were deducted in a tax year after 1986.

Line 4e—Depreciation of Property Placed in Service After 1986

Caution: *Do not include on this line any depreciation adjustment from:* **(a)** an activity for which you are not at risk; **(b)** a partnership or an S corporation if the basis limitations under section 704(d) or 1366(d) apply; **(c)** a tax shelter farm activity; or **(d)** a passive activity. Instead, take these depreciation adjustments into account when figuring the adjustments on line 4l, 4m, or 4n, whichever applies.

For AMT purposes, the depreciation deduction for tangible property placed in service after 1986 (or after July 31, 1986, if an election was made) must be refigured under the alternative depreciation system (ADS) described in section 168(g).

For property, other than residential rental and nonresidential real property, use the 150% declining balance method (switching to the straight line method in the first tax year when that method gives a better result). However, use the straight line method if that method was used for regular tax purposes. Generally, ADS depreciation is computed over the class life of the property. For tangible personal property not assigned a class life, use 12 years. See **Pub. 534,** Depreciation, for a discussion of class lives.

For residential rental and nonresidential real property, use the straight line method over 40 years.

Use the same convention that was used for regular tax purposes.

See Rev. Proc. 87-57, 1987-2 C.B. 687, or Pub. 534 for the optional tables for the alternative minimum tax, using the 150% declining balance method.

Do not make an adjustment for motion picture films, videotapes, sound recordings, or property depreciated under the unit-of-production method or any other method not expressed in a term of years. (See section 168(f)(1), (2), (3), or (4).)

When refiguring the depreciation deduction, be sure to report any adjustment from depreciation that was allocated to the beneficiary for regular tax purposes separately on line 11 of Schedule K-1 (Form 1041).

To figure the adjustment, subtract the depreciation for AMT purposes from the depreciation for regular tax purposes.

If the depreciation figured for AMT purposes exceeds the depreciation allowed for regular tax purposes, enter the adjustment as a negative amount.

Line 4f—Circulation and Research and Experimental Expenditures Paid or Incurred After 1986

Caution: *Do not make this adjustment for expenditures for which you elected the optional 3-year write-off period (10-year for research and experimental expenditures) under section 59(e) for regular tax purposes.*

Circulation expenditures.—Circulation expenditures deducted under section 173(a) for regular tax purposes must be amortized for AMT purposes over 3 years beginning with the year the expenditures were paid or incurred.

Research and experimental expenditures.—Research and experimental expenditures deducted under section 174(a) for regular tax purposes generally must be amortized for AMT purposes over 10 years beginning with the year the expenditures were paid or incurred. However, do not make an adjustment for expenditures paid or incurred in connection with an activity in which the estate or trust materially participated under the passive activity rules.

Enter the difference between the amount allowed for AMT purposes and the amount allowed for regular tax purposes. If the amount for AMT purposes exceeds the amount allowed for regular tax purposes, enter the difference as a negative amount.

See section 56(b)(2)(B) for a discussion of the rules for losses on properties for which a deduction was allowed under section 173(a) or 174(a).

Line 4g—Mining Exploration and Development Costs Paid or Incurred After 1986

Caution: *Do not make this adjustment for costs for which you elected the optional 10-year write-off period under section 59(e) for regular tax purposes.*

Expenditures for the development or exploration of a mine or certain other mineral deposits (other than an oil, gas, or geothermal well) deducted under sections 616(a) and 617(a) for regular tax purposes must be amortized for AMT purposes over 10 years beginning with the year the expenditures were paid or incurred.

Enter the difference between the amount allowed for AMT purposes and the amount allowed for regular tax purposes. If the amount allowed for AMT purposes exceeds the amount deducted for regular tax purposes, enter the difference as a negative amount.

See section 56(a)(2)(B) for a discussion of the rules for losses sustained on properties for which a deduction was allowed under section 616(a) or 617(a).

Line 4h—Long-Term Contracts Entered Into After February 28, 1986

For AMT purposes, the percentage of completion method of accounting described in section 460(b) generally must be used. This rule generally does not apply to home construction contracts (as defined in section 460(e)(6)).

Note: *Contracts described in section 460(e)(1) are subject to the simplified method of cost allocation of section 460(b)(4).*

Enter the difference between the amount reported for regular tax purposes and the AMT amount. If the AMT amount is less than the amount figured for regular tax purposes, enter the difference as a negative amount.

Line 4i—Pollution Control Facilities Placed in Service After 1986

For any certified pollution control facility placed in service after 1986, the deduction under section 169 is not allowed for AMT purposes. Instead, the deduction is determined under the ADS described in section 168(g) using the Asset Depreciation Range class life for the facility under the straight line method.

To figure the adjustment, subtract the amortization deduction taken for regular tax purposes, from the depreciation deduction determined under the ADS.

If the deduction allowed for AMT purposes is more than the amount allowed for regular tax purposes, enter the difference as a negative amount.

Line 4j—Installment Sales of Certain Property

For either of the following kinds of dispositions in which the estate or trust used the installment method for regular tax purposes, refigure the income for AMT purposes without regard to the installment method:

1. Any disposition after March 1, 1986, of property used or produced in a farming business that was held primarily for sale to customers.

2. Any nondealer disposition of property that occurred after August 16, 1986, but before the first day of your tax year that began in 1987, if an obligation that arose from the disposition was an installment obligation to which the proportionate disallowance rule applied.

Enter the difference between the income that was reported for regular tax purposes and the income for AMT purposes. If the AMT amount is less than that reported for the regular tax, enter the difference as a negative amount.

Page 19

283

Form 1041.

Line 4k—Adjusted Gain or Loss (Including Incentive Stock Options)

Adjusted gain or loss.—If the estate or trust sold or exchanged property during the year, or had a casualty gain or loss to business or income-producing property, it may have an adjustment. The gain or loss on the disposition of certain assets is refigured for AMT purposes. Use this line if the estate or trust reported a gain or loss on Form 4797, Schedule D (Form 1041), or Form 4684 (Section B). When figuring the adjusted basis for those forms, take into account any AMT adjustments made this year, or in previous years, for items related to lines 4e, 4f, 4g, and 4i of Schedule H. For example, to figure the adjusted basis for AMT purposes, reduce the cost of an asset only by the depreciation allowed for AMT purposes.

Enter the difference between the gain or loss reported for regular tax purposes, and that figured for AMT purposes. If the AMT gain is less than the gain reported for regular tax purposes, enter the adjustment as a negative amount. If the AMT loss is more than the loss allowed for regular tax purposes, enter the adjustment as a negative amount.

Incentive stock options (ISOs).—For regular tax purposes, no income is recognized when an incentive stock option (as defined in section 422(b)) is granted or exercised. However, this rule does not apply for AMT purposes. Instead, the estate or trust must generally include the excess, if any, of:

1. The fair market value of the option (determined without regard to any lapse restriction) at the first time its rights in the option become transferable or when these rights are no longer subject to a substantial risk of forfeiture, over

2. The amount paid for the option.

Increase the AMT basis of any stock acquired through the exercise of an incentive stock option by the amount of the adjustment.

If the estate or trust acquired stock by exercising an incentive stock option and disposed of that stock in the same year, the tax treatment for regular and AMT purposes is the same.

See section 83 for more details.

Line 4l—Certain Loss Limitations

Caution: *If the loss is from a passive activity, use line 4n instead. If the loss is from a tax shelter farm activity (that is not passive), use line 4m.*

Refigure your allowable losses for AMT purposes from activities for which you are not at risk and basis limitations applicable to interests in partnerships and stock in S corporations, by taking into account your AMT adjustments and tax preference items. See sections 59(h), 465, 704(d), and 1366(d).

Enter the difference between the loss reported for regular tax purposes and the AMT loss. If the AMT loss is more than the loss reported for regular tax purposes, enter the adjustment as a negative amount.

Line 4m—Tax Shelter Farm Activities

Note: *Use this line only if the tax shelter farm activity is not a passive activity. Otherwise, use line 4n.*

For AMT purposes, no loss is allowed from any tax shelter farm activity as defined in section 58(a)(2).

An excess farm loss from one farm activity cannot be netted against income from another farm activity. Any disallowed loss (for AMT purposes) is carried forward until offset by income from the same activity or when the entire activity is sold.

Include any other adjustment or tax preference item and your prior year AMT unallowed loss when refiguring the farm loss. For example, if depreciation must be refigured for AMT purposes, include the adjustment on this line. DO NOT include it again on line 4e, 4r, or 4s.

Determine your tax shelter farm activity gain or loss for AMT purposes using the same rules you used for regular tax purposes except that any AMT loss is allowed only to the extent that a taxpayer is insolvent (see section 58(c)(1)). Any AMT loss may not be used in the current tax year to offset gains from other tax shelter farm activities. Instead, it must be suspended and carried forward indefinitely until either you have a gain in a subsequent tax year from that same tax shelter farm activity or the activity is disposed of.

Line 4n—Passive Activities

For AMT purposes, the rules described in section 469 apply, except that in applying the limitations, minimum tax rules apply.

Refigure passive activity gains and losses on an AMT basis. Refigure a passive activity gain or loss by taking into account all AMT adjustments or tax preference items that pertain to that activity.

You may complete a second Form 8582 to determine the passive activity losses allowed for AMT purposes, but do not send this AMT Form 8582 to the IRS.

Note: *The amount of any passive activity loss that is not deductible (and is therefore carried forward) for AMT purposes is likely to differ from the amount (if any) that is carried forward for regular tax purposes. Therefore, it is essential that you retain adequate records for both AMT and regular tax purposes.*

Enter the difference between the loss reported on page 1, and the AMT loss, if any.

Caution: *Do not account for any AMT adjustment or tax preference item twice. Any AMT adjustment or tax preference item included on this line is not to be entered again elsewhere on this schedule.*

Publicly traded partnerships (PTPs).— If the estate or trust had a loss from a PTP, refigure the loss using any AMT adjustments and tax preference items.

Line 4o—Beneficiaries of Other Trusts or Decedent's Estates

If the estate or trust is the beneficiary of another estate or trust, enter the adjustment for minimum tax purposes from line 8, Schedule K-1 (Form 1041).

Line 4p—Tax-Exempt Interest From Specified Private Activity Bonds

Enter the interest earned from specified private activity bonds reduced (but not below zero) by any deduction that would have been allowable if the interest were includible in gross income for regular tax purposes. Specified private activity bonds are any qualified bonds (as defined in section 141) issued after August 7, 1986. See section 57(a)(5) for more information.

Exempt-interest dividends paid by a regulated investment company are treated as interest from a specified private activity bond to the extent the company received interest on the bond.

Line 4q—Depletion

Refigure the depletion deduction for AMT purposes by using only the income and deductions allowed for the AMT when refiguring the limit based on taxable income from the property under section 613(a) and the limit based on taxable income, with certain adjustments, under section 613A(d)(1). Also, the depletion deduction for mines, wells, and other natural deposits under section 611 is limited to the property's adjusted basis at the end of the year, as refigured for the AMT, unless the estate or trust is an independent producer or royalty owner claiming percentage depletion for oil and gas wells. Figure this limit separately for each property. When refiguring the property's adjusted basis, take into account any AMT adjustments made this year or in previous years that affect basis (other than the current year's depletion).

Enter on line 4q the difference between the regular tax and AMT deduction. If the AMT deduction is more than the regular tax deduction, enter the difference as a negative amount.

Line 4r—Accelerated Depreciation of Real Property Placed in Service Before 1987

For AMT purposes, use the straight line method to figure depreciation. Use a recovery period of 19 years for 19-year real property and 15 years for

Form 1041.

low-income housing. Enter the excess of depreciation claimed for regular tax purposes over depreciation refigured using the straight line method. Figure this amount separately for each property and include on line 4r only positive amounts.

Line 4s—Accelerated Depreciation of Leased Personal Property Placed in Service Before 1987

For leased 10-year recovery property and leased 15-year public utility property, enter the amount by which the depreciation deduction determined for regular tax purposes is more than the deduction allowable using the straight line method with a half-year convention, no salvage value, and the following recovery period:

10-year property . . . . . 15 years
15-year public utility
property . . . . 22 years

Figure this amount separately for each property and include on line 4s only positive amounts.

Line 4t—Intangible Drilling Costs

Caution: *Do not make this adjustment for costs for which you elected the optional 60-month write-off under section 59(e) for regular tax purposes.*

Except as provided below, intangible drilling costs (IDCs) from oil, gas, and geothermal wells are a tax preference item to the extent that the excess IDCs exceed 65% of the net income from the wells. Figure the tax preference item for all geothermal properties separately from the preference for all oil and gas properties.

Excess IDCs are computed by taking the amount of your IDCs allowed for regular tax purposes under section 263(c) (not including any section 263(c) deduction for nonproductive wells) minus the amount that would have been allowed if that amount had been amortized over a 120-month period starting with the month the well was placed in production.

Note: *Cost depletion can be substituted for the amount allowed using amortization over 120 months.*

Net income is determined by taking the gross income from all oil, gas, and geothermal wells reduced by the deductions allocable to those properties (determined without regard to excess IDCs). When figuring net income, use only income and deductions allowed for the AMT.

Exception. The preference for IDCs from oil and gas wells does not apply to taxpayers who are independent producers (i.e., not integrated oil companies as defined in section 291(b)(4)). However, this benefit may be limited. First, figure the IDC preference as if this exception did not apply. Then, for purposes of this exception, complete

Schedule H through line 6, including the IDC preference. If the amount of the IDC preference exceeds 40% of the amount figured for line 6, enter the excess on line 4t (the benefit of this exception is limited). If the amount of the IDC preference is equal to or less than 40% of the amount figured for line 6, do not enter an amount on line 4t (the benefit of this exception is not limited).

Line 4u—Other Adjustments

Include on this line:

● **Patron's adjustment.**—Distributions the estate or trust received from a cooperative may be includible in income. Unless the distributions are nontaxable, include on line 4u the total AMT patronage dividend and per-unit retain allocation adjustment reported to the estate or trust from the cooperative.

● **Related adjustments.**—AMT adjustments and tax preference items may affect deductions that are based on an income limit other than AGI or modified AGI (e.g., farm conservation expenses). Refigure these deductions using the income limit as modified for the AMT. Include the difference between the regular tax and AMT deduction on line 4u. If the AMT deduction is more than the regular tax deduction, include the difference as a negative amount.

Note: *Do not make an adjustment on line 4u for an item you refigured on another line of Schedule H (e.g., line 4q).*

Line 7—Alternative Tax Net Operating Loss Deduction (ATNOLD)

For tax years beginning after 1986, the net operating loss (NOL) under section 172(c) is modified for alternative tax purposes by (a) adding the adjustments made under sections 56 and 58 (subtracting if the adjustments are negative); and (b) reducing the NOL by any item of tax preference under section 57 (except the appreciated charitable contribution preference item).

When figuring an NOL from a loss year prior to 1987, the rules in effect before enactment of the Tax Reform Act (TRA) of 1986 apply. The NOL under section 172(c) is reduced by the amount of the tax preference items that were taken into account in computing the NOL. In addition, the NOL is figured by taking into account only itemized deductions that were alternative tax itemized deductions for the tax year and that were a modification to the NOL under section 172(d). See sections 55(d) and 172 as in effect before the TRA of 1986.

If this estate or trust is the beneficiary of another estate or trust that terminated in 1994, include any AMT NOL carryover that was reported on line 12e of Schedule K-1 (Form 1041).

The ATNOLD may be limited. To figure the ATNOLD limitation, first figure AMTI without regard to the ATNOLD. For this

purpose, figure a tentative amount for line 4q of Schedule H by treating line 7 as if it were zero. Then, figure a tentative amount for line 6 of Schedule H. The ATNOLD limitation is 90% of the tentative line 6 amount. Enter on line 7 the smaller of the ATNOLD or the ATNOLD limitation. Any alternative tax NOL not used because of the ATNOLD limitation can be carried back or forward. See section 172(b) for details. The treatment of alternative tax NOLs does not affect your regular tax NOL.

Note: *If you elected under section 172(b)(3) to forego the carryback period for regular tax purposes, the election will also apply for the AMT.*

Part II—Income Distribution Deduction on a Minimum Tax Basis

Line 13—Adjusted Alternative Minimum Taxable Income

If the amount on line 8 of Schedule H is less than zero, and the negative number is attributable wholly or in part to the capital loss limitation rules under section 1211(b), then enter as a negative number the smaller of (a) the loss from line 8; or (b) the loss from line 4 on page 1.

Line 14—Adjusted Tax-Exempt Interest

To figure the adjusted tax-exempt interest (including exempt-interest dividends received as a shareholder in a mutual fund or other regulated investment company), subtract the total of (a) any tax-exempt interest from line 4 of Schedule A of Form 1041 computed for AMT purposes; and (b) any section 212 expenses allowable for AMT purposes allocable to tax-exempt interest from the amount of tax-exempt interest received. DO NOT subtract any deductions reported on lines 4a through 4c. Section 212 expenses that are directly allocable to tax-exempt interest are allocated only to tax-exempt interest. A reasonable proportion of section 212 expenses that are indirectly allocable to both tax-exempt interest and other income must be allocated to each class of income.

Line 17

Enter any capital gains that were paid or permanently set aside for charitable purposes from the current year's income included on line 3 of Schedule A.

Lines 18 and 19

Capital gains and losses must take into account any basis adjustments from line 4k, Part I.

Line 24—Adjustment for Tax-Exempt Income

In computing the income distribution deduction on a minimum tax basis, the

Page 21

285

Form 1041.

estate or trust is not allowed a deduction for any item of DNAMTI (line 20) that is not included in the gross income of the estate or trust computed on an AMT basis. Thus, for purposes of computing the allowable income distribution deduction on a minimum tax basis, the DNAMTI is computed without regard to any tax-exempt interest (except for amounts from line 4p).

If tax-exempt interest is the only tax-exempt income included in the total distributions (line 23), and the DNAMTI (line 20) is less than or equal to line 23, then enter on line 24 the amount from line 14.

If tax-exempt interest is the only tax-exempt income included in the total distributions (line 23), and the DNAMTI is more than line 23 (i.e., the estate or trust made a distribution that is less than the DNAMTI), then compute the adjustment by multiplying line 14 by a fraction, the numerator of which is the total distributions (line 23), and the denominator of which is the DNAMTI (line 20). Enter the result on line 24.

If line 23 includes tax-exempt income other than tax-exempt interest (except for amounts from line 4p), figure line 24 by subtracting the total expenses allocable to tax-exempt income that are allowable for AMT purposes from tax-exempt income included on line 23.

Expenses that are directly allocable to tax-exempt income are allocated only to tax-exempt income. A reasonable proportion of expenses indirectly allocable to both tax-exempt income and other income must be allocated to each class of income.

Line 27—Income Distribution Deduction on a Minimum Tax Basis

Allocate the income distribution deduction figured on a minimum tax basis among the beneficiaries in the same manner as income was allocated for regular tax purposes. Report each beneficiary's share on line 6 of Schedule K-1 (Form 1041).

Part III—Alternative Minimum Tax Computation

Line 36—Alternative Minimum Tax Foreign Tax Credit

To figure the AMT foreign tax credit:

1. Complete and attach Form 1116, with the notation at the top, "Alt Min Tax" for each type of income specified at the top of Form 1116.

2. Complete Part I, entering income, deductions, etc., attributable to sources outside the United States computed on a minimum tax basis.

3. Complete Part III. On line 9, do not enter any taxes taken into account in a tax year beginning after 1986 that are treated under section 904(c) as paid or accrued in a tax year beginning before

1987. On line 10 of Form 1116, enter the alternative minimum tax foreign tax credit carryover, and on line 17 of Form 1116, enter the alternative minimum taxable income from line 12 of Schedule H. On line 19 of Form 1116, enter the amount from line 34 or 35 of Schedule H.

Complete Part IV. The foreign tax credit from line 32 of the AMT Form 1116 is limited to the tax on line 34 or 35 of Schedule H, less 10% of what would have been the tax on line 34 or 35 of Schedule H, if line 7 of Schedule H had been zero and the exception for intangible drilling costs does not apply (see the instructions for line 4t on page 21). If Schedule H, line 7, is zero or blank, and the estate or trust has no intangible drilling costs (or the exception does not apply), enter on Schedule H, line 36, the smaller of Form 1116, line 32; or 90% of Schedule H, line 34 or 35. If line 7 has an entry (other than zero), or the exception for intangible drilling costs applies, for purposes of this line refigure what the tax would have been on Schedule H, line 34 or 35, if line 7 were zero and the exception did not apply. Multiply that amount by 10% and subtract the result from line 34 or 35, whichever applies. Enter on Schedule H, line 36, the smaller of that amount or the amount from Form 1116, line 32.

If the AMT foreign tax credit is limited, any unused amount can be carried back or forward in accordance with section 904(c).

Note: *The election to forego the carryback period for regular tax purposes also applies for the AMT.*

Line 38a—Regular Tax Before Credits

Enter the tax from line 1a of Schedule G plus any section 667(b) tax from Form 4970 entered on line 1b of Schedule G. From that amount subtract any foreign tax credit entered on line 2a of Schedule G. DO NOT deduct any foreign tax credit that was allocated to the beneficiaries.

Line 38b—Section 644 Tax

Enter any section 644 tax included on line 1b of Schedule G.

Schedule D (Form 1041)—Capital Gains and Losses

General Instructions

Use Schedule D (Form 1041) to report gains and losses from the sale or exchange of capital assets by an estate or trust.

To report sales or exchanges of property other than capital assets, including the sale or exchange of property used in a trade or business and involuntary conversions (other than

casualties and thefts), see Form 4797 and related instructions.

If property is involuntarily converted because of a casualty or theft, use Form 4684.

Capital Asset

Each item of property held by the estate or trust (whether or not connected with its trade or business) is a capital asset except:

● Inventoriable assets or property held primarily for sale to customers;

● Depreciable or real property used in a trade or business;

● Certain copyrights, literary, musical, or artistic compositions, letters or memoranda, or similar property;

● Accounts or notes receivable acquired in the ordinary course of a trade or business for services rendered or from the sale of inventoriable assets or property held primarily for sale to customers; and

● Certain U.S. Government publications not purchased at the public sale price.

You may find additional helpful information in the following publications that are available from the IRS:

● **Pub. 544,** Sales and Other Dispositions of Assets; and

● **Pub. 551,** Basis of Assets.

Short-Term or Long-Term

Separate the capital gains and losses according to how long the estate or trust held or owned the property. The holding period for short-term capital gains and losses is 1 year or less. The holding period for long-term capital gains and losses is more than 1 year. Property acquired by a decedent's estate from the decedent is considered as held for more than 1 year.

When you figure the length of the period the estate or trust held property, begin counting on the day after the estate or trust acquired the property and include the day the estate or trust disposed of it. Use the trade dates for the date of acquisition and sale of stocks and bonds traded on an exchange or over-the-counter market.

Section 643(e)(3) Election

For noncash property distributions a fiduciary may elect to have the estate or trust recognize gain or loss in the same manner as if the distributed property had been sold to the beneficiary at its fair market value (FMV). The distribution deduction is the property's FMV. This election applies to all distributions made by the estate or trust during the tax year and, once made, may be revoked only with the consent of the IRS.

Note that section 267 does not allow a deduction for any loss from the sale of property on which a trust makes a section 643(e)(3) election. In addition,

Appendix D. Foreign Withholding and Other Reporting

Form 1041.

when a trust distributes depreciable property, section 1239 applies to deny capital gains treatment on the gain to the trust if the trust makes a section 643(e)(3) election.

Section 644 Tax on Trusts

If a trust sells or exchanges property at a gain within 2 years after receiving it from a transferor, a special tax may be due. **Do not report includible gains under section 644 on Schedule D.** The tax on these gains is reported separately on Form 1041. For more information, see the instructions for Schedule G, line 1b.

Related Persons

A trust cannot deduct a loss from the sale or exchange of property directly or indirectly between any of the following:

● A grantor and a fiduciary of a trust;

● A fiduciary and a fiduciary or beneficiary of another trust created by the same grantor;

● A fiduciary and a beneficiary of the same trust; or

● A trust fiduciary and a corporation of which more than 50% in value of the outstanding stock is owned directly or indirectly by or for the trust or by or for the grantor of the trust.

Items for Special Treatment

The following items may require special treatment:

● Exchange of "like-kind" property.

● Wash sales of stock or securities (including contracts or options to acquire or sell stock or securities) (section 1091).

● Gain or loss on options to buy or sell (section 1234).

● Certain real estate subdivided for sale that may be considered a capital asset (section 1237).

● Gain on disposition of stock in an Interest Charge Domestic International Sales Corporation (section 995(c)).

● Gain on the sale or exchange of stock in certain foreign corporations (section 1248).

● Sales of stock received under a qualified public utility dividend reinvestment plan. See Pub. 550 for details.

● Transfer of appreciated property to a political organization (section 84).

● Distributions received from an employee pension, profit sharing, or stock bonus plan. See Form 4972.

● Disposition of market discount bonds (section 1276).

● Section 1256 contracts and straddles are reported on **Form 6781,** Gains and Losses From Section 1256 Contracts and Straddles.

Specific Instructions

Lines 1 and 7

Short-term and long-term capital gains and losses.—Enter all sales of stocks, bonds, etc.

Redemption of stock to pay death taxes.—If stock is redeemed under the provisions of section 303, list and identify it on line 7 and give the name of the decedent and the IRS office where the estate tax or generation-skipping transfer tax return was filed.

If you are reporting capital gain from a lump-sum distribution, see the instructions for Form 4972 for information about the death benefit exclusion and the Federal estate tax.

Column (d)—Sales Price

Enter either the gross sales price or the net sales price from the sale. On sales of stocks and bonds, report the gross amount as reported to the estate or trust on Form 1099-B or similar statement. However, if the estate or trust was advised that gross proceeds less commissions and option premiums were reported to the IRS, enter that net amount in column (d).

Column (e)—Cost or Other Basis

Basis of trust property.—Generally, the basis of property acquired by gift is the same as the basis in the hands of the donor. If the FMV of the property at the time it was transferred to the trust is less than the transferor's basis, then the FMV is used for determining any loss on disposition.

If the property was transferred to the trust after 1976, and a gift tax was paid under Chapter 12, then increase the donor's basis as follows:

Multiply the amount of the gift tax paid by a fraction, the numerator of which is the net appreciation in value of the gift (discussed below), and the denominator of which is the amount of the gift. For this purpose, the **net appreciation in value of the gift** is the amount by which the FMV of the gift exceeds the donor's adjusted basis.

Basis of decedent's estate property.—Generally, the basis of property acquired by a decedent's estate is the FMV of the property at the date of the decedent's death, or the alternate valuation date if the executor elected to use an alternate valuation under section 2032.

See Pub. 551 for a discussion of the valuation of qualified real property under section 2032A.

Basis of property for bankruptcy estates.—Generally, the basis of property held by the bankruptcy estate is the same as the basis in the hands of the individual debtor.

Adjustments to basis.—Before figuring any gain or loss on the sale, exchange, or other disposition of property owned by the estate or trust, adjustments to the property's basis may be required.

Some items that may increase the basis include:

1. Broker's fees and commissions.

2. Reinvested dividends that were previously reported as income.

3. Reinvested capital gains that were previously reported as income.

4. Costs that were capitalized.

5. Original issue discount that has been previously included in income.

Some items that may decrease the basis include:

1. Nontaxable distributions that consist of return of capital.

2. Deductions previously allowed or allowable for depreciation.

3. Casualty or theft loss deductions.

See Pub. 551 for additional information.

See section 852(f) for treatment of load charges incurred in acquiring stock in a regulated investment company.

Carryover basis.—Carryover basis determined under repealed section 1023 applies to property acquired from a decedent who died after December 31, 1976, and before November 7, 1978, only if the executor elected it on a **Form 5970-A,** Election of Carryover Basis, that was filed on time.

Lines 2 and 8

Installment sales.—If the estate or trust sold property at a gain during the tax year, and will receive a payment in a later tax year, report the sale on the installment method and file **Form 6252,** Installment Sale Income, unless you elect not to do so.

Also, use Form 6252 to report any payment received in 1994 from a sale made in an earlier tax year that was reported on the installment method.

To elect out of the installment method, report the full amount of the gain on a timely filed return (including extensions).

Exchange of "like-kind" property.—Generally, no gain or loss is recognized when property held for productive use in a trade or business or for investment is exchanged solely for property of a like-kind to be held either for productive use in a trade or business or for investment. However, if a trust exchanges like-kind property with a related person (see **Related Persons** above), and before 2 years after the date of the last transfer that was part of the exchange the related person disposes of the property, or the trust disposes of the property received in exchange from the related person, then the original exchange will not qualify for nonrecognition. See section 1031(f) for exceptions.

Page 23

287

Form 1041.

Complete and attach **Form 8824**, Like-Kind Exchanges, to Form 1041 for each exchange.

Line 10—Capital Gain Distributions

Enter on line 10 capital gain distributions paid during the year as a long-term capital gain, regardless of how long the estate or trust held its investment. Also enter any amounts shown on Form 2439 that represent the estate's or trust's share of the undistributed capital gains of a regulated investment company. Include on Form 1041, line 24f, the tax paid by the company as shown on Form 2439. Add to the basis of the stock, the excess of the amount included in income over the credit if the amount is not distributed.

Line 15, column (a)—Beneficiaries' Net Short-Term Capital Gain or Loss

Enter the amount of net short-term capital gain or loss allocable to the beneficiary or beneficiaries. Except in the final year, include only those short-term capital losses that are taken into account in determining the amount of gain from the sale or exchange of capital assets that is paid, credited, or required to be distributed to any beneficiary during the tax year. See Regulations section 1.643(a)-3 for more information about allocation of capital gains and losses.

Except in the final year, if the losses from the sale or exchange of capital assets are more than the gains, all of the losses are allocated to the estate or trust and none are allocated to the beneficiaries.

Line 15, column (b)—Estate's or Trust's Net Short-Term Capital Gain or Loss

Enter the amount of the net short-term capital gain or loss allocable to the estate or trust. Include any capital gain paid or permanently set aside for a charitable purpose specified in section 642(c).

Line 15, column (c)—Total

Enter the total of the amounts entered in columns (a) and (b). The amount in column (c) should be the same as the amount on line 6.

Line 16—Net Long-Term Capital Gain or Loss

Allocate the net long-term capital gain or loss on line 16 in the same manner as the net short-term capital gain or loss on line 15.

Part IV—Capital Loss Limitation

If the sum of all the capital losses is more than the sum of all the capital gains, then these capital losses are allowed as a deduction only to the extent of the smaller of the net loss or $3,000.

Page 24

Part V—Capital Loss Carryovers From 1994 to 1995

For any year (including the final year) in which capital losses exceed capital gains, complete Part V to figure the capital loss carryover. A capital loss carryover may be carried forward indefinitely. Capital losses keep their character as either short-term or long-term when carried over to the following year.

Part VI—Tax Computation Using Maximum Capital Gains Rate

Line 37c

If the estate or trust received capital gains that were derived from income in respect of a decedent, and a section 691(c)(4) deduction was claimed, then line 37c must be reduced by the portion of the section 691(c)(4) deduction claimed on Form 1041, page 1, line 19.

Line 44

To compute the regular tax, use the 1994 Tax Rate Schedule on page 16.

Line 45

If the tax, using the maximum capital gains rate (line 43), is less than the regular tax (line 44), then enter the amount from line 45 on line 1a of Schedule G, Form 1041, and check the "Schedule D" box.

Schedule J (Form 1041)— Accumulation Distribution for a Complex Trust

General Instructions

Use Schedule J (Form 1041) to report an accumulation distribution for a complex trust. An accumulation distribution is the excess of amounts properly paid, credited, or required to be distributed (other than income required to be distributed currently) over the DNI of the trust reduced by income required to be distributed currently. To have an accumulation distribution, the distribution must exceed the accounting income of the trust.

Specific Instructions

Part I—Accumulation Distribution in 1994

Line 1—Distribution Under Section 661(a)(2)

Enter the amount from Schedule B of Form 1041, line 12, for 1994. This is the amount properly paid, credited, or required to be distributed other than the amount of income for the current tax year required to be distributed currently.

Line 2—Distributable Net Income

Enter the amount from Schedule B of Form 1041, line 9, for 1994. This is the amount of distributable net income (DNI) for the current tax year determined under section 643(a).

Line 3—Distribution Under Section 661(a)(1)

Enter the amount from Schedule B of Form 1041, line 11, for 1994. This is the amount of income for the current tax year required to be distributed currently.

Line 5—Accumulation Distribution

If line 13, Schedule B of Form 1041 is more than line 10, Schedule B of Form 1041, complete the rest of Schedule J and file it with Form 1041, unless the trust has no previously accumulated income.

Generally, amounts accumulated before a beneficiary reaches age 21 may be excluded by the beneficiary. See sections 665 and 667(c) for exceptions relating to multiple trusts. The trustee reports to the IRS the total amount of the accumulation distribution before any reduction for income accumulated before the beneficiary reaches age 21. If the multiple trusts rules do not apply, the beneficiary claims the exclusion when filing **Form 4970**, Tax on Accumulation Distribution of Trusts, as you may not be aware that the beneficiary may be a beneficiary of other trusts with other trustees.

For examples of accumulation distributions that include payments from one trust to another trust, and amounts distributed for a dependent's support, see Regulations section 1.665(b)-1A(b).

Part II—Ordinary Income Accumulation Distribution

Line 6—Distributable Net Income for Earlier Years

Enter the applicable amounts as follows:

Throwback year(s)	Amount from line
1969–1977	Schedule C, Form 1041, line 5
1978–1979	Form 1041, line 61
1980	Form 1041, line 60
1981–1982	Form 1041, line 58
1983–1993	Schedule B, Form 1041, line 9

For information about throwback years, see the instructions for line 13. For purposes of line 6, in figuring the DNI of the trust for a throwback year, subtract any estate tax deduction for income in respect of a decedent if the income is includible in figuring the DNI of the trust for that year.

Form 1041.

Line 7—Distributions Made During Earlier Years

Enter the applicable amounts as follows:

Throwback year(s)	Amount from line
1969–1977	Schedule C, Form 1041, line 8
1978	Form 1041, line 64
1979	Form 1041, line 65
1980	Form 1041, line 64
1981–1982	Form 1041, line 62
1983–1993	Schedule B, Form 1041, line 13

Line 11—Prior Accumulation Distribution Thrown Back to any Throwback Year

Enter the amount of prior accumulation distributions thrown back to the throwback years. Do not enter distributions excluded under section 663(a)(1) for gifts, bequests, etc.

Line 13—Throwback Years

Allocate the amount on line 5 that is an accumulation distribution to the earliest applicable year first, but do not allocate more than the amount on line 12 for any throwback year. An accumulation distribution is thrown back first to the earliest preceding tax year in which there is undistributed net income (UNI). Then it is thrown back beginning with the next earliest year to any remaining preceding tax years of the trust. The portion of the accumulation distribution allocated to the earliest preceding tax year is the amount of the UNI for that year. The portion of the accumulation distribution allocated to any remaining preceding tax year is the amount by which the accumulation distribution is larger than the total of the UNI for all earlier preceding tax years. A tax year of a trust during which the trust was a simple trust for the entire year is not a preceding tax year unless (a) during that year the trust received outside income or (b) the trustee did not distribute all of the trust's income that was required to be distributed currently for that year. In this case, UNI for that year must not be more than the greater of the outside income or income not distributed during that year.

The term "outside income" means amounts that are included in the DNI of the trust for that year but that are not "income" of the trust as defined in Regulations section 1.643(b)-1. Some examples of outside income are (a) income taxable to the trust under section 691; (b) unrealized accounts receivable that were assigned to the trust; and (c) distributions from another trust that include the DNI or UNI of the other trust. Enter the applicable year at the top of each column for each throwback year.

Line 16—Tax-Exempt Interest Included on Line 13

For each throwback year, divide line 15 by line 6 and multiply the result by the following:

Throwback year(s)	Amount from line
1969–1977	Schedule C, Form 1041, line 2(a)
1978–1979	Form 1041, line 58(a)
1980	Form 1041, line 57(a)
1981–1982	Form 1041, line 55(a)
1983–1993	Schedule B, Form 1041, line 2

Part III—Taxes Imposed on Undistributed Net Income

For the regular tax computation, if there is a capital gain, complete lines 18 through 25 for each throwback year. If the trustee elected the alternative tax on capital gains, complete lines 26 through 31 instead of lines 18 through 25 for each applicable year. If there is no capital gain for any year, or there is a capital loss for every year, enter on line 9 the amount of the tax for each year identified in the instruction for line 18 and do not complete Part III. If the trust received an accumulation distribution from another trust, see Regulations section 1.665(b)-1A.

Note: *The alternative tax on capital gains was repealed for tax years beginning after December 31, 1978. Neither the 1981, 1987, nor maximum rate on net capital gains for 1991, 1992, or 1993 is an alternative tax for this purpose.*

Line 18—Regular Tax

Enter the applicable amounts as follows:

Throwback year(s)	Amount from line
1969–1976	Form 1041, page 1, line 24
1977	Form 1041, page 1, line 26
1978–1979	Form 1041, line 27
1980–1984	Form 1041, line 26c
1985–1986	Form 1041, line 25c
1987	Form 1041, line 22c
1988–1993	Schedule G, Form 1041, line 1a

Line 19—Trust's Share of Net Short-Term Gain

For each throwback year, enter the smaller of the capital gain from the two lines indicated. If there is a capital loss or a zero on either or both of the two lines indicated, enter zero on line 19.

Throwback year(s)	Amount from line
1969–1970	Schedule D, line 10, column 2, or Schedule D, line 12, column 2.
1971–1978	Schedule D, line 14, column 2, or Schedule D, line 16, column 2.
1979	Schedule D, line 18, column (b), or Schedule D, line 20, column (b).
1980–1981	Schedule D, line 14, column (b), or Schedule D, line 16, column (b).
1982	Schedule D, line 16, column (b), or Schedule D, line 18, column (b).
1983–1993	Schedule D, line 15, column (b), or Schedule D, line 17, column (b).

Line 20—Trust's Share of Net Long-Term Gain

Enter the applicable amounts as follows:

Throwback year(s)	Amount from line
1969–1970	50% of Schedule D, line 13(e)
1971–1977	50% of Schedule D, line 17(e)
1978	Schedule D, line 17(e) or line 31, whichever is applicable, less Form 1041, line 23.
1979	Schedule D, line 25 or line 27, whichever is applicable, less Form 1041, line 23.
1980–1981	Schedule D, line 21, less Schedule D, line 22.
1982	Schedule D, line 23, less Schedule D, line 24.
1983–1986	Schedule D, line 22, less Schedule D, line 23.
1987–1993	Schedule D, the smaller of any gain on line 16 or 17, column (b).

Line 22—Taxable Income

Enter the applicable amounts as follows:

Throwback year(s)	Amount from line
1969–1976	Form 1041, page 1, line 23
1977	Form 1041, page 1, line 25
1978–1979	Form 1041, line 26
1980–1984	Form 1041, line 25
1985–1986	Form 1041, line 24
1987	Form 1041, line 21
1988–1993	Form 1041, line 22

Line 26—Tax on Income Other Than Long-Term Capital Gain

Enter the applicable amounts as follows:

Throwback year(s)	Amount from line
1969	Schedule D, line 20
1970	Schedule D, line 19
1971	Schedule D, line 50
1972–1975	Schedule D, line 48
1976–1978	Schedule D, line 27

Line 27—Trust's Share of Net Short-Term Gain

If there is a loss on any of the following lines, enter zero on line 27 for the applicable throwback year. Otherwise, enter the applicable amounts as follows:

Throwback year(s)	Amount from line
1969–1970	Schedule D, line 10, column 2
1971–1978	Schedule D, line 14, column 2

Line 28—Trust's Share of Taxable Income Less Section 1202 Deduction

Enter the applicable amounts as follows:

Throwback year(s)	Amount from line
1969	Schedule D, line 19
1970	Schedule D, line 18
1971	Schedule D, line 38
1972–1975	Schedule D, line 39
1976–1978	Schedule D, line 21

Form 1041.

Part IV—Allocation to Beneficiary

Complete Part IV for each beneficiary. If the accumulation distribution is allocated to more than one beneficiary, attach an additional copy of Schedule J with Part IV completed for each additional beneficiary. Give each beneficiary a copy of his or her respective Part IV information. If more than 5 throwback years are involved, use another Schedule J, completing Parts II and III for each additional throwback year.

If the beneficiary is a nonresident alien individual or a foreign corporation, see section 667(e) about retaining the character of the amounts distributed to determine the amount of the U.S. withholding tax.

The beneficiary uses Form 4970 to compute the tax on the distribution. The beneficiary also uses Form 4970 for the section 667(b)(6) tax adjustment if an accumulation distribution is subject to estate or generation-skipping transfer tax. This is because the trustee may not be the estate or generation-skipping transfer tax return filer.

Schedule K-1 (Form 1041)—Beneficiary's Share of Income, Deductions, Credits, etc.

General Instructions

Use Schedule K-1 (Form 1041) to report the beneficiary's share of income, deductions, and credits from a trust or a decedent's estate.

Who Must File

The fiduciary (or one of the joint fiduciaries) must file Schedule K-1. A copy of each beneficiary's Schedule K-1 is attached to the Form 1041 filed with the IRS and each beneficiary is given a copy of his or her respective Schedule K-1. One copy of each Schedule K-1 must be retained for the fiduciary's records.

Beneficiary's Identifying Number

As a payer of income, you are required under section 6109 to request and provide a proper identifying number for each recipient of income. Enter the beneficiary's number on the respective Schedules K-1 when you file Form 1041. Individuals and business recipients are responsible for giving you their taxpayer identification numbers upon request. You may use Form W-9, Request for Taxpayer Identification Number and Certification, to request the beneficiary's identifying number.

Penalty.—Under section 6723, the payer is charged a $50 penalty for each failure to provide a required taxpayer identification number, unless reasonable

cause is established for not providing it. Explain any reasonable cause in a signed affidavit and attach it to this return.

Tax Shelter's Identification Number

If the estate or trust is a tax shelter, is involved in a tax shelter, or is considered to be the organizer of a tax shelter, there are reporting requirements under section 6111 for both the fiduciaries and the beneficiaries.

See **Form 8264,** Application for Registration of a Tax Shelter, and **Form 8271,** Investor Reporting of Tax Shelter Registration Number, and their related instructions for information regarding the fiduciary's reporting requirements.

Substitute Forms

You do not need prior IRS approval for a substitute Schedule K-1 (Form 1041) that follows the specifications for filing substitute Schedules K-1 in **Pub. 1167,** Substitute Printed, Computer-Prepared, and Computer-Generated Tax Forms and Schedules, or is an exact copy of an IRS Schedule K-1. You must request IRS approval to use other substitute Schedules K-1. To request approval, write to: Internal Revenue Service, Attention: Substitute Forms Program Coordinator, PC:FP:FS, 1111 Constitution Avenue, N.W., Washington, DC 20224.

Inclusion of Amounts in Beneficiaries' Income

Simple trust.—The beneficiary of a simple trust must include in his or her gross income the amount of the income required to be distributed currently, whether or not distributed, or if the income required to be distributed currently to all beneficiaries exceeds the distributable net income (DNI), his or her proportionate share of the DNI. The determination of whether trust income is required to be distributed currently depends upon the terms of the trust instrument and applicable local law. See Regulations section 1.652(c)-4 for a comprehensive example.

Estates and complex trusts.—The beneficiary of a decedent's estate or complex trust must include in his or her gross income the sum of:

1. The amount of the income required to be distributed currently, or if the income required to be distributed currently to all beneficiaries exceeds the DNI (figured without taking into account the charitable deduction), his or her proportionate share of the DNI (as so figured); and

2. All other amounts properly paid, credited, or required to be distributed, or if the sum of the income required to be distributed currently and other amounts properly paid, credited, or required to be distributed to all beneficiaries exceeds

the DNI, his or her proportionate share of the excess of DNI over the income required to be distributed currently.

See Regulations section 1.662(c)-4 for a comprehensive example.

For estates and complex trusts that have more than one beneficiary, and if different beneficiaries have substantially separate and independent shares, their shares are treated as a single trust for the sole purpose of determining the amount of DNI allocable to the respective beneficiaries. For examples of the application of the separate share rule, see the regulations under section 663(c).

Character of income.—The beneficiary's income is considered to have the same proportion of each class of items entering into the computation of DNI that the total of each class has to the DNI (e.g., half dividends and half interest if the income of the estate or trust is half dividends and half interest).

Allocation of deductions.—Generally, items of deduction that enter into the computation of DNI are allocated among the items of income to the extent such allocation is not inconsistent with the rules set out in section 469 and its regulations, relating to passive activity loss limitations, in the following order.

First, all deductions directly attributable to a specific class of income are deducted from that income. For example, rental expenses, to the extent allowable, are deducted from rental income.

Second, deductions that are not directly attributable to a specific class of income generally may be allocated to any class of income, as long as a reasonable portion is allocated to any tax-exempt income. Deductions considered not directly attributable to a specific class of income under this rule include fiduciary fees, safe deposit box rental charges, and state income and personal property taxes. The charitable deduction, however, must be ratably apportioned among each class of income included in DNI.

Finally, any excess deductions that are directly attributable to a class of income may be allocated to another class of income. In no case can excess deductions from a passive activity be allocated to income from a nonpassive activity, or to portfolio income earned by the estate or trust. Excess deductions attributable to tax-exempt income cannot offset any other class of income.

In no case can deductions be allocated to an item of income that is not included in the computation of DNI, or attributable to corpus.

Except for the final year, and for depreciation or depletion allocations in excess of income (see Rev. Rul. 74-530, 1974-2 C.B. 188), you may not show any negative amounts for any class of

290

Appendix D.   Foreign Withholding and Other Reporting

Form 1041.

income because the beneficiary generally may not claim losses or deductions from the estate or trust.

Gifts and bequests.—Do not include in the beneficiary's income any gifts or bequests of a specific sum of money or of specific property under the terms of the governing instrument that are paid or credited in three installments or less.

Amounts that can be paid or credited only from income of the estate or trust do not qualify as a gift or bequest of a specific sum of money.

Past years.—Do not include in the beneficiary's income any amounts deducted on Form 1041 for an earlier year that were credited or required to be distributed in that earlier year.

Beneficiary's Tax Year

The beneficiary's income from the estate or trust must be included in the beneficiary's tax year during which the tax year of the estate or trust ends. See Pub. 559 for more information, including the effect of the death of a beneficiary during the tax year of the estate or trust.

Specific Instructions

Line 1—Interest

Enter the beneficiary's share of the taxable interest income minus allocable deductions.

Line 2—Dividends

Enter the beneficiary's share of dividend income minus allocable deductions.

Line 3a—Net Short-Term Capital Gain

Enter the beneficiary's share of the net short-term capital gain from line 15, column (a), Schedule D (Form 1041), minus allocable deductions. Do not enter a loss on line 3a. If, for the final year of the estate or trust, there is a capital loss carryover, enter on line 12b the beneficiary's share of short-term capital loss carryover as a loss in parentheses. However, if the beneficiary is a corporation, enter on line 12b the beneficiary's share of all short- and long-term capital loss carryovers as a single item in parentheses. See section 642(h) and related regulations for more information.

Line 3b—Net Long-Term Capital Gain

Enter the beneficiary's share of the net long-term capital gain from line 16, column (a), Schedule D (Form 1041), minus allocable deductions. Do not enter a loss on line 3b. If, for the final year of the estate or trust, there is a capital loss carryover, enter on line 12c the beneficiary's share of the long-term capital loss carryover as a loss in parentheses. (If the beneficiary is a corporation, see the instructions for line 3a.) See section 642(h) and related regulations for more information.

Gains, or losses, from the complete, or partial, disposition of a rental, rental real estate, or trade or business activity that is a passive activity, must be shown on an attachment to Schedule K-1.

Line 4a—Annuities, Royalties, and Other Nonpassive Income

Enter the beneficiary's share of annuities, royalties, or any other income, minus allocable deductions (other than directly apportionable deductions), that is NOT subject to any passive activity loss limitation rules at the beneficiary level. Use line 5a to report income items subject to the passive activity rules at the beneficiary's level.

Lines 4b and 5b—Depreciation

Enter the beneficiary's share of the depreciation deductions attributable to each activity reported on lines 4a and 5a. See the instructions on page 9 for a discussion of how the depreciation deduction is apportioned between the beneficiaries and the estate or trust. Report any AMT adjustment or tax preference item attributable to depreciation separately on line 11a.

Note: *An estate or trust cannot make an election under section 179 to expense certain tangible property.*

Lines 4c and 5c—Depletion

Enter the beneficiary's share of the depletion deduction under section 611 attributable to each activity reported on lines 4a and 5a. See the instructions on page 9 for a discussion of how the depletion deduction is apportioned between the beneficiaries and the estate or trust. Report any tax preference item attributable to depletion separately on line 11b.

Lines 4d and 5d—Amortization

Itemize the beneficiary's share of the amortization deductions attributable to each activity reported on lines 4a and 5a. Apportion the amortization deductions between the estate or trust and the beneficiaries in the same way that the depreciation and depletion deductions are divided. Report any AMT adjustment attributable to amortization separately on line 11c.

Line 5a—Trade or Business, Rental Real Estate, and Other Rental Income

Enter the beneficiary's share of trade or business, rental real estate, and other rental income, minus allocable deductions (other than directly apportionable deductions). To assist the beneficiary in figuring any applicable passive activity loss limitations, also attach a separate schedule showing the beneficiary's share of income derived from each trade or business, rental real estate, and other rental activity.

Lines 5b through 5d

Caution: *The limitations on passive activity losses and credits under section 469 apply to estates and trusts. Estates and trusts that distribute income to beneficiaries are allowed to apportion depreciation, depletion, and amortization deductions to the beneficiaries. These deductions are referred to as "directly apportionable deductions."*

Rules for treating a beneficiary's income and directly apportionable deductions from an estate or trust and other rules for applying the passive loss and credit limitations to beneficiaries of estates and trusts have not yet been issued.

Any directly apportionable deduction, such as depreciation, is treated by the beneficiary as having been incurred in the same activity as incurred by the estate or trust. However, the character of such deduction may be determined as if the beneficiary incurred the deduction directly.

To assist the beneficiary in computing any applicable passive activity loss limitations, also attach a separate schedule showing the beneficiary's share of directly apportionable deductions derived from each trade or business, rental real estate, and other rental activity.

Line 6—Income for Minimum Tax Purposes

Enter the beneficiary's share of the income distribution deduction computed on a minimum tax basis from line 27 of Schedule H.

Line 7—Income for Regular Tax Purposes

Enter the beneficiary's share of the income distribution deduction computed on line 17 of Schedule B. This amount should equal the sum of lines 1 through 3b, 4a, and 5a.

Line 9—Estate Tax Deduction (Including Generation-Skipping Transfer Taxes)

If the distribution deduction consists of any income in respect of a decedent, and the estate or trust was allowed a deduction under section 691(c) for the estate tax paid attributable to such income (see the line 19 instructions on page 13), then the beneficiary is allowed an estate tax deduction in proportion to his or her share of the distribution that consists of such income. For an example of the computation, see Regulations section 1.691(c)-2. Figure the computation on a separate sheet and attach it to the return.

Line 10—Foreign Taxes

List on a separate sheet the beneficiary's share of the applicable foreign taxes paid or accrued and the various foreign source figures needed to

Page 27

Form 1041.

compute the beneficiary's foreign tax credit. See Pub. 514, and section 901(b)(5) for special rules about foreign taxes.

Lines 11a through 11c

Enter any adjustments or tax preference items attributable to depreciation, depletion, or amortization that were allocated to the beneficiary. For property placed in service before 1987, report separately the accelerated depreciation of real and leased personal property.

Line 11d—Exclusion Items

Enter the beneficiary's share of the adjustment for minimum tax purposes from Schedule K-1, line 8, that is attributable to exclusion items (Schedule H, lines 4a through 4d, 4p, and 4q).

Line 12a—Excess Deductions on Termination

If this is the final return and there are excess deductions on termination (see the instructions for line 22 on page 13), enter the beneficiary's share of the excess deductions on line 12a. Figure the deductions on a separate sheet and attach it to the return.

Excess deductions on termination occur only during the last tax year of the trust or decedent's estate when the total deductions (excluding the charitable deduction and exemption) are greater than the gross income during that tax year. Generally, a deduction based upon an NOL carryover is not available to a beneficiary as an excess deduction. However, if the last tax year of the estate or trust is also the last year in which an NOL carryover may be taken (see section 172(b)), then the NOL carryover is considered an excess deduction on the termination of the estate or trust to the extent it is not absorbed by the estate or trust during its final tax year. For more information, see Regulations section 1.642(h)-4 for a discussion of the allocation of the carryover among the beneficiaries.

Only the beneficiary of an estate or trust that succeeds to its property is allowed to deduct that entity's excess deductions on termination. A beneficiary who does not have enough income in that year to absorb the entire deduction may not carry the balance over to any succeeding year. An individual beneficiary must be able to itemize deductions in order to claim the excess deductions in determining taxable income.

Lines 12b and 12c—Unused Capital Loss Carryover

Upon termination of the trust or decedent's estate, the beneficiary succeeding to the property is allowed as a deduction any unused capital loss carryover under section 1212. If the estate or trust incurs capital losses in the final year, use Part V of Schedule D (Form 1041) to figure the amount of capital loss carryover to be allocated to the beneficiary.

Lines 12d and 12e—Net Operating Loss (NOL) Carryover

Upon termination of a trust or decedent's estate, a beneficiary succeeding to its property is allowed to deduct any unused NOL (and any AMT NOL) carryover for regular and AMT purposes if the carryover would be allowable to the estate or trust in a later tax year but for the termination. Enter on lines 12d and 12e the unused carryover amounts.

Line 13—Other

Itemize on line 13, or on a separate sheet if more space is needed, the beneficiary's tax information not entered elsewhere on Schedule K-1. This includes the allocable share, if any, of:

● Payment of estimated tax to be credited to the beneficiary (section 643(g));

● Tax-exempt interest income received or accrued by the trust (including exempt-interest dividends from a mutual fund or other regulated investment company);

● Investment income (section 163(d));

● Gross farming and fishing income;

● Credit for backup withholding (section 3406);

● Low-income housing credit;

● The jobs credit;

● The alcohol fuel credit;

● The credit for increasing research activities;

● The renewable electricity production credit;

● The Indian employment credit;

● The empowerment zone employment credit;

● The information a beneficiary will need to figure any investment credit; and

● The information a beneficiary will need to figure any recapture taxes.

Note: *Upon termination of an estate or trust, any suspended passive activity losses (PALs) relating to an interest in a passive activity cannot be allocated to the beneficiary. Instead, the basis in such activity is increased by the amount of any PALs allocable to the interest, and no losses are allowed as a deduction on the estate's or trust's final Form 1041.*

Page 28

292

Table of Cases

Table of Internal Revenue Code Sections

860E(e)(6)	308.4	1272(a)(2)	107.2.1
860E(e)(7)	308.5	1272(a)(6)	107.2.1, 107.2.3,
860F	307.1.8		107.2.4, 308.3, 309.1,
860F(a)(1)	310.1, 312.1		313.2.8, 315.3, 316, 503, 504
860F(a)(2)	307.2, 312.1	1272(a)(7)	107.2.1
860F(a)(3)	312.1	1273	310.1.1
860F(a)(5)	312.1	1273(a)(1)	107.2.1
860F(b)(1)	310.1, 310.1.1, 310.1.2	1273(a)(3)	107.2.1, 107.2.2
860F(b)(2)	310.1.5	1275	107.2.1, 107.2.2
860F(c)(1)	311	1275(c)(1)	504.1
860F(e)	315.1	1276 through 1278	107.2.4
860G(a)(1)	201.1, 305.1, 305.1.3,	1276	107.2.4
	305.1.8, 305.2.3	1276(a)(1)	107.1, 107.2.4
860G(a)(3)	109, 204, 307.1.1,	1276(a)(3)	107.2.4
	307.1.2, 307.1.6,	1276(b)	310.1.1
	307.1.8, 314.2	1276(b)(3)	107.2.4
860G(a)(4)	307.1.6	1276(e)	107.2.4
860G(a)(5)	307.1.9	1277	107.2.4
860G(a)(6)	307.2	1278	107.2.2
860G(a)(7)	307.2.1	1278(a)(1)	107.2.4
860G(a)(8)	307.2.3	1278(a)(2)	107.2.4
860G(a)(9)	307	1278(a)(4)	107.2.4
860G(b)	313.2	1278(b)	107.2.4
860G(c)	307.2.3	1286	106, 107.1.1, 107.2.2, 109,
860G(d)	307.1.8, 312.2		305.1.8
860G(d)(2)	313.2.3	1286(a)	107.2.1, 107.2.2, 107.2.4
864(c)(2)	108	1286(b)	107.1, 107.1.1
871(a)(1)	108	1286(b)(1)	107.2.2
871(h)	108	1286(e)(1)	106
871(h)(2)	108	1286(e)(2)	106
871(h)(3)	108	1286(e)(3)	106
881(a)(1)	108	1286(e)(5)	106
881(c)(2)	108	1361(b)(1)	306
881(c)(3)	108	1361(c)(4)	306
957	108	1441	108
1001	107.1, 307.1.4	1442	108
1032	310.1.5	1501	105.1
1221	107.1	3406	312.3
1221(1)	307.2.3	6049	110, 505.1
1223(1)	310.1.4	6049(b)(2)	110
1231	310.1.4	6050H	110
1232	502, 502.1, 502.2	6050J	110
1232(a)	502.2	6662	407
1232(a)(2)	502.2	6706(a)	505.1
1232A	502, 502.1.1	6706(b)	505.2
1271 through 1273	107.2.1	7701(a)(19)	109, 204, 307.1.3, 313.1.3,
1271 through 1275	305.1.3		314.2
1271(a)	107.2.4	7701(a)(30)	108
1271(a)(1)	107.2.1	7701(i)	401
1271(b)	107.2.4	7701(i)(1)	402
1271(b)(1)	107.2.1	7701(i)(2)	403
1272	107.2.4	7701(i)(3)	404
1272(a)(1)	107.2.1		

Table of Treasury Regulations

PROPOSED REGULATIONS

Table of Treasury Rulings

References are to sections.

Bibliography

Certain Federal Income Tax Consequences in the Prospectus Supplement dated June 9, 1987 for the Imperial Savings Association Mortgage Pass-Through Certificates, Class A, Series 1987-3.

Edson & Jacobs, Secondary Mortgage Market Guide, Mathew Bender & Co., §4.01[3], at 4-4 (1987).

Fannie Mae Investor/Analyst Report, Third Quarter 1987.
Fannie Mae Investor/Analyst Report, First Quarter 1993.

Ginnie Mae Investment Facts, U.S. Department of Housing and Urban Development (July 1992).

IRS Publication 938, Real Estate Mortgage Investment Conduits (REMICs) Reporting Information (Including Other Issuers of Collateralized Debt Obligations).

Mortgage-Backed Securities Letter, Vol. II, No. 1 (Jan. 5, 1987).

Offering Circular dated September 22, 1977 for the Bank of American National Trust and Savings Assoc. Mortgage-Backed Certificates, Series A.
Offering Circular dated June 7, 1983 for the Federal Home Loan Mortgage Corporation Collateralized Mortgage Obligations, Series 1983-A.

Peaslee & Nirenberg, Federal Income Taxation of Mortgage-Backed Securities (1994).
Prospectus Supplement dated October 23, 1986 for the Fannie Mae Stripped Mortgage-Backed Securities, SMBS Series F, G, H, and I, Fixed Rate GPM Residential Mortgage Loans.
Prospectus Supplement dated December 23, 1986 for the Standard Mortgage Pass-Through Certificates, Series 1986-H, Series Mortgage Securities Corporation.
Prospectus Supplement dated June 9, 1987 for the Collateralized Mortgage Obligation Trust 32, Collateralized Mortgage Obligations.
Prospectus Supplement dated December 15, 1987 for the Countrywide Funding Corporation Mortgage Pass-Through Certificates, Series 1987-2, Class A.
Prospectus Supplement dated January 25, 1988 for the Conduit Senior Mortgage Pass-Through Certificates, Series 1988-S1.

Reporting by Transferors for Transfers of Receivables with Recourse, Statement of Financial Accounting Standards No. 77.

Simon, Selected Federal Income Tax Aspects of Securitizing Debt Obligations, 66 Taxes—The Tax Magazine 897 (December 1988).

Index

References are to sections.

CMO. *See* Collateralized mortgage obligations (CMO)
Collateralized mortgage obligations (CMO)
  generally, 202
  call features, 203.4
  equity
    definition, 203.3
    necessity of, 203.2
  "fast-pay, slow-pay" structure, 202, 202.1
  guaranteed investment contracts, purchase of, 203.4
  income tax issues
    generally, 203, 203.1
    call features, 203.4
    equity, 203.2, 203.3
    mismatching of cash flows, 203.4
    partnership status of owner trust, 205
    qualifying assets, treatment as, 204
  interest in underlying mortgage, status as, 204
  mismatching of cash flows, 203.4
  mortgage pass-through compared, 203.1
  OID rules. *See* Original issue discount (OID)
  owner trusts
    generally, 202, 205
    partnership status, 205
    trust agreement provisions, 205
  qualifying assets, treatment as, 204
  REIT compared, 201.2
  structure, 202
  transactions, 201-201.2, 202
  use of, reasons for
    generally, 201
    inability to make REMIC transaction, 201.1
    undesirable effects associated with REMIC, 201.2

GIC. *See* Guaranteed investment contracts (GIC)
Guaranteed investment contracts (GIC)
  CMO and, 203.4

mortgage pass-throughs and, 104.1.1

Mortgage pass-throughs
  advantages of, 101
  certificate holders, taxation of
    generally, 107.2
    foreign holders, 108
    "look-through" rules, 109
    market discount rules, 107.2.2, 107.2.4
    methods of accounting, 107.2
    OID, 107.2.1-107.2.4
    premium, 107.2.4
    stripped mortgage loans, 107.2.2, 109
    super-premium certificate, 107.2.3
  CMO compared, 203.1
  double taxation, 103
  "fast-pay, slow-pay" structure, 104.2
  foreign certificate holders, 108
  grantor trust classification, 103, 104.1
  guaranteed investment contracts, purchase of, 104.1.1
  income tax issues
    generally, 104
    certificate holders, taxation of, 107.2-107.2.4, 108, 109
    double taxation, 103
    foreign certificate holders, 108
    investment, powers to vary, 104.1-104.1.3
    multiple-class trusts, prohibition against, 104.2
    qualifying assets, treatment as, 109
    REIT, treatment of, 109
    reporting requirements, 110
    seller, taxation of, 107.1-107.1.3
    senior-subordinated trusts, 105-105.2.2
    stripped certificates, 106.1, 107.1.1, 107.2.2, 109
  investment of certificate holders, powers to vary
    generally, 104.1
    limited powers, 104.1.1, 104.1.2
    power defined, 104.1

Index